THE STATE IN BURMA

ROBERT H. TAYLOR

The State in Burma

University of Hawaii Press
Honolulu

© Robert H. Taylor, 1987
All Rights Reserved

Published in North America by
University of Hawaii Press
2840 Kolowalu Street
Honolulu, Hawaii 96822

First published in the United Kingdom by
C. Hurst & Co. (Publishers) Ltd.
38 King Street, London WC2E 8JT

Printed in England on long-life paper

Library of Congress Cataloging-in-Publication Data

Taylor, Robert H., 1943–
    The state in Burma.

    Bibliography: p.
    Includes index.
    1. Burma—Politics and government. I. Title.
JQ442.T39 1987   320.9591   87–16200
ISBN 0–8248–1141–0 (alk. paper)

PREFACE AND ACKNOWLEDGEMENTS

In 1982 I wrote a short monograph reviewing the development of the study of modern Burma's politics.[1] In it I argued that students of the subject had failed to pursue a line of inquiry first pointed out by John S. Furnivall in his long article 'The Fashioning of Leviathan', published in 1939 in the now defunct *Journal of the Burma Research Society*.[2] Furnivall drew attention explicitly to the development of the British colonial state by tracing its origins back to the first British administration in Tenasserim. In his classic work *Colonial Policy and Practice*,[3] Furnivall demonstrated the consequences of the policies of the colonial state upon Burmese society. This volume, which was written at the request of the British publisher Christopher Hurst, is an attempt to follow Furnivall's notion through a study of the development of the state and its relationship with civil society from the time of the first early modern monarchic state through the colonial period — which he had traced — to the post-colonial period — at the start of which he was working as a government advisor. In so doing, I seek to explain the contemporary state in Burma by comparing it with previous ones, and to suggest the social and economic consequences of different state formations.

Each of the five substantive chapters which follow looks at the nature of the state and its politics in different periods, attempting to draw out the most important parallels and contrasts of different state forms. Each has had to rely on different sources, and I have been dependent upon the scholarship of others in large sections of the book. In Chapter I, I am indebted to the work of Victor B. Lieberman and Michael Aung Thwin: I owe special thanks to Lieberman for reading the draft of the manuscript and making significant improvements in it. The second chapter is in inspiration and argument derived from Furnivall's *Colonial Policy and Practice*. Parts of Chapter II and most of Chapter III are based largely upon my own unpublished Ph.D. dissertation. Chapter IV owes a great

1. Robert H. Taylor, *An Undeveloped State: The Study of Modern Burma's Politics* Melbourne: Monash University Centre of Southeast Asian Studies Working Paper no. 28, 1983.
2. John S. Furnivall; 'The Fashioning of Leviathan', *Journal of the Burma Research Society*, Rangoon, vol. XXIX, no. 3 (1939), pp. 1–138.
3. John S. Furnivall, *Colonial Policy and Practice* (Cambridge University Press, 1948; New York University Press, 1956).

deal to the numerous secondary sources cited in the notes. The 1950s saw a boom in Burma studies, especially in the United States, and I have profited from the work done then. However, it is almost certain that the scholars of that generation will disagree with many of my judgements. The final chapter is based upon secondary accounts as well as government documents. I was fortunate to have been able to live and study in Burma in 1978 and in 1982, and the experiences of those extended stays are reflected in my judgements.

In many ways, this book is premature. Too little is firmly known about important aspects of the state in Burma, both historically and contemporaneously, to make hard-and-fast judgements about what is being discussed. Therefore I am at one with Michael Faraday, holding my theories on the tips of my fingers in order to allow them to be blown away by the first puff of fact. Perhaps the suggestions made in these pages will encourage others to unearth these facts.

Acknowledgements

In addition to Victor Lieberman, I have received help, directly and indirectly, from many people during the preparation of this volume. My appreciation of Burma's history and politics stems from my undergraduate studies at Ohio University with John F. Cady, one of the best teachers one could hope for. At Cornell University I had the privilege of studying Burma's history with D.G.E. Hall. I thus had the benefit of hearing explanations of Burma's past from leading American and British historians of their generation. Subsequently, I have studied Burma from a variety of other perspectives, and have profited from lengthy discussions with scholars in Burma, especially at the Department of History and the Institute of Economics at Rangoon University. Many others have unwittingly taught me about the administrative and political system of Burma.

In conducting the research that has made this book possible, I have received a great deal of assistance. In 1978 I was an Australian exchange student under the Colombo Plan scheme, and benefited from the help of the Foreign Economic Relations Department of the Ministry of Planning and Finance of the government of Burma, and the Burmese Department at Rangoon University. In 1982, I received a British Academy Leverhulme South East Asian Studies Fellowship which allowed me to work in the Department of History and the Universities' Central Library in Rangoon. At that time, the Ministry of Education kindly arranged for me to tour much of Burma for several weeks and to visit various economic development projects. Friends in various parts of Burma, including those on state farms and in factories, as well as universities and research centres, were very helpful in explaining to me the nature and purpose of their work. Thanks to a grant from the Nuffield Foundation, I was able to spend several weeks in Rangoon in 1984 learning more about the workings of the court system and of local government. Other trips to Burma since 1975 have been made possible through financial assistance from the University of Sydney, the Australian Academy of Social Science and the Research Committee of the School of Oriental and African Studies, London.

It would be invidious to single out individuals in Burma for thanks, but they, I believe, know of my gratitude. Overworked as the staff of the universities and libraries are, they were always unfailingly cooperative. My colleagues in the Department of Economic and Political Studies at the School of Oriental and African Studies allowed me to test some of my preliminary thoughts upon them. I am especially grateful to David Taylor and Richard Boyd for their comments on my tentative and less than fully formed ideas. Students in my South East Asian politics seminar in 1985–6 were sufficiently tolerant to let me talk through the book with them. Michael Dwyer of C. Hurst Co. has been a most helpful and careful editor. As always, my wife Joan has been of immeasurable assistance in the writing of this book.

London R.H.T.
April 1987

CONTENTS

Preface and Acknowledgements	*page* v
Glossary	xii
Abbreviations	xv

Introduction	1

Chapters
1. The Precolonial State	13
The Evolution of the Precolonial State	13
The Territorial Organization of the Precolonial State	20
Authority Relations in the Precolonial State	25
Financing the Precolonial State	37
The Agencies of the Precolonial State	46
The Legitimacy of the Precolonial State	54
Politics under the Precolonial State	60
2. The Rationalization of the State, 1825–1942	66
Introduction	66
Transforming the Structures of the State	67
The Territorial Organization of the State	79
The Rationalization of Authority Relations	82
Financing the Rationalized State	88
The Shan States under the British	91
Rationalizing and Expanding the Functions of the State	98
State Security and Public Order	99
Courts and the Law	102
State and Economy	106
The Development of New State Functions	111
Education	112
State 'Legitimacy' and Constitutional Policy	115
New Class and Ethnic Formations	123
The New Middle Class	134
Workers and Peasants	145

Contents

3. Politics under the Rationalized State, 1886–1942 — 148
   - Introduction — 148
   - Early Responses to the Colonial State — 153
   - The Emergence of the Middle Class Political Elite — 162
   - The Emergence of Burmese Political Parties — 174
   - Peasants and Politics under the Colonial State — 188
   - Youth and Students in late Colonial Politics — 202

4. The Displacement of the State, 1942–1962 — 217
   - War, Revolution and the State — 217
   - The Reorganization of the State — 222
   - The Contestants for State Power — 229
     - The Army — 232
     - The Communists — 237
     - Non-Communist Movements and Political Parties — 243
   - Old and New Functions of the State — 249
     - Law and Order — 250
     - Economic and Financial — 253
     - External Relations — 260
   - The Rise of Alternative Authorities — 264
   - Economic and Social Change — 270
     - The Peasantry — 272
     - Urban Classes — 279
   - The Search for Legitimacy — 283

5. Reasserting the State, 1962–1987 — 291
   - The Consequences of the March 2nd Coup — 291
   - Territorial Reorganization — 300
   - Changing Relations with State Authority — 304
     - Security and Administration Committees (SACs) — 313
     - Organizing the State/Party and Mass/Class Organizations — 315
     - Participation in State Management — 326
   - The Functions of the State — 333
     - State Security and Public Order — 333
     - Courts and the Law — 338
     - Economic and Financial — 341
     - External Relations — 353
   - Legitimacy and the State — 356
   - Politics under the Socialist State — 364

Bibliography	373
Index	387

MAPS

Burma and the Kingdom of Pagan	21
Major Administrative Units of Burma	306

TABLES

2.1.	Population of Burma by Ethnicity, 1931	128
2.2.	Labour Force Participants by Ethnicity and Occupation, 1931	130
2.3	Ethnicity and Income/Supertax Payment in Rangoon, 1931–2	131
2.4.	Earners and Working Dependents by Ethnicity in Middle Class Positions, 1931	139
4.1.	Distribution of Gross Domestic Product	259
5.1.	Data on the Territorial Organization of the State/Division	305
5.2.	Growth in Full-Time Central State Employment, 1962–1973	311
5.3.	Growth in Total Expenditure of Central Ministries, 1961–1973	312
5.4.	BSPP Membership Figures	317
5.5.	Gross Domestic Product (GDP) at Constant 1969/70 Prices, Rate of GDP Growth, Investment at Constant 1969/70 Prices, and Rate of Growth of Investment, 1961/2–1985/6	342
5.6.	Origins of Gross Domestic Product, 1961/2 and 1985/6	343
5.7.	Distribution of Labour Force, 1931 and 1984/5	344

GLOSSARY

Ahkin wun	Centrally appointed revenue supervisors under the precolonial state.
Ahmu-dan	Persons living on royal lands and owing immediate obligation to the crown; crown service men.
Asiayon	Organization, association, body.
Athi	Persons living at a distance from the court and owing the state primarily tax obligations.
Atwin-wun	An interior minister or member of the *bye-daik*.
Baho	Central (as in central government).
Bayin	Autonomous provincial governors before the Toungoo reforms.
Bo	An officer; name given to local strongmen and political bosses during the 1950s.
Bodhissatta	Emergent Buddha; occasional claim about kings.
Bu athin	Village peasant organizations in the 1920s and 1930s which opposed the paying of taxes and rents.
Bye-daik	The king's privy council.
Cakkavatti	Aspect of kingship; universal monarch or world conqueror.
Chettiars	Caste of moneylenders from Madras.
Dhamma	Law
Dhammakatika	Buddhist monks who toured villages and organized peasants in the 1920s.
Dhammaraja	Aspect of kingship; lord of the law
Do Bama Asiayon	'Our Burma' or 'We Burmese' Association; political organization of the *thakins* in the 1930s.
First Anglo-Burmese War	1824–1826; led to the loss of Arakan and Tenasserim by the king to the British as well as ending Burma's efforts to gain control of Assam and other eastern parts of what is now India.
Gaung	Subordinate to headmen during the colonial period who served as a police officer and assisted with tax collection.
Hluttaw	The council of ministers in the precolonial court.
Hpayalaung	Burmese for *bodhissatta*.
Hpon	Innate power or glory; as in *pongyi*, 'great power', the title of Buddhist monks.
Hsinyeitha	Poor man or proletarian; name of Dr Ba Maw's political party in the 1930s.

Glossary

Kamma	Burmese for *karma*.
Karma	Buddhist notion of fate as determined by deeds in previous existences.
Kin-wun	Minister responsible for crown service men or *ahmudan* population.
Ko Min Ko Chin	One's Own King — One's Own Kind; name of the political party formed by the *Thakins* for the 1936 election.
Kutho	Merit as earned by a Buddhist devotee.
Kyedangyi	A subordinate to a village headman with responsibilities for taxation.
Let-yon	Force; military power.
Maha Bama	Greater Burma; Second World War period political organization.
Maistry	Labour recruiters from India who brought workmen to Burma.
Min	King or monarch.
Myei-daing	Assistant to *thu-gyi* with special responsibilities for property and taxation.
Myo	Township or town in precolonial administration.
Myochit	Patriot or lover of one's country; name of political party founded by U Saw in the 1930s.
Myo-ok	Township officer appointed under the British.
Myo-sa	Appenage holder.
Myo-thu-gi	Village headman.
Myo-wun	Provincial governors appointed by the Toungoo and Konbaung kings.
Naingngan (naingngantaaw)	Current usage for the state; previously implied area conquered by the state. *Taw* is a suffix implying religious or state power and sanctity.
Nat	The animistic beings thought to people a good part of the conceptual world of many villagers.
Pongyi	A Buddhist monk.
Pongyi kyaung	Monastery; centre of education in the monastic order.
Pyithu Hluttaw	People's Assembly.
Sangha	Collective term for the Buddhist monkhood.
Sasana	The Buddhist monkhood and its institutions.
Sawbwa	Normally hereditary ruler of a large or medium-size area in what are now referred to as the Shan and Kayah states.
Sayadaw	Senior monk or head of a monastery.

Second Anglo-Burmese War	1852; led to the monarchical state losing Pegu, also known as the Burma Delta (which the British called Lower Burma).
Sibwayei athin	Economy organization; village organizations in the 1920s and 1930s similar to the *wunthanu athin*.
Sit-ke	Military officers assigned by the monarchical court to supervise local administrations (especially in the Shan areas) and to direct military and police arrangements.
Taik	Township in the precolonial period; the term implies a less settled community than a *myo*.
Thakin	Literally master; used as equivalent to *sahib* by the British and taken as their own title by Burmese nationalists in the 1930s.
Thathameda	Head tax.
Thathanabaing	The head of the Buddhist monkhood appointed by the king.
Third Anglo-Burmese War	1885; led to the destruction of the indigeneous monarchy and the annexation of all of Burma to British India.
Thu-gyi	Headmen of villages or townships.
Thuriya	Sun; name of first Rangoon nationalist newspaper.
Vinaya	The rules of obligation of a Buddhist monk.
Wun-gyi	A monarchical minister or member of the *hluttaw*.
Wunthanu athin	Village nationalist organizations widespread in the 1920s and early 1930s.
Yazawut	King's business; eventually criminal law.
Ywa	Village.

ABBREVIATIONS

ABPO	All Burma Peasants' Organization.
ABSU	All Burma Students' Union.
AFPFL	Anti-Fascist People's Freedom League.
AFO	Anti-Fascist Organization.
BCP	Burma Communist Party; White Flag.
BIA	Burma Independence Army.
BNA	Burma National Army.
BPF	Burma Patriotic Forces.
BSPP	Burma Socialist Programme Party.
CAS(B)	Civil Affairs Service (Burma); British military administration after the Second World War.
CP(B)	Communist Party (Burma); Red Flag.
DSI	Defence Services Institute.
GCBA	General Council of Burmese Associations.
GCSS	General Council of Sangha Sammeggi; parallel organization to the GBCA for monks.
KCO	Karen Central Organization.
KMT	Chinese Nationalist Party; Kuomintang.
KNDO	Karen National Defence Organization.
KNLA	Karen National Liberation Army.
KNU	Karen National Union.
NUF	National United Front.
PVO	People's Volunteer Organization.
SAB	State Agricultural Bank.
SAC	Security and Administration Committee.
SAMB	State Agricultural Marketing Board.
TUC-B	Trades Union Congress — Burma.
YMBA	Young Men's Buddhist Association.

'. . . ultimately, Leviathan had to learn that enduring empires are not built on common sense. When Leviathan endeavours to organise society for production he forgets that man cannot live by bread alone. But in this he is fighting against human nature and in the long run, for all his tale of martyrs, Leviathan himself must fail unless he can adapt himself to human nature. Fashioned by Art, he must be born again by grace beyond the reach of art.'

J.S. Furnivall, 'The Fashioning of Leviathan', in *Journal of the Burma Research Society*, vol. XXIX, no. 3, Rangoon, 1939, p. 137

INTRODUCTION

This book is an essay on the kinds of politics which have appeared in Burma during the past few hundred years and the reasons for their development. The principal issue which it addresses centres on the relationship between the state and society within the country. Burma's political history since the late sixteenth century can be conveniently divided into three or four obvious periods, distinguishable by the prevailing style of state-society relationship: the time of the kings, between the founding of the Restored Toungoo dynasty in 1597 to the deposition of King Thibaw in 1885; the period of British colonial rule, cut off by the Japanese invasion of 1942 but not terminating until Burma's attainment of sovereignty and membership of the comity of nations in 1948; and independent government and politics to the present day. The latter period can be divided, at 1962, between the predominantly civilian government which preceded that date and subsequent military dominance. It is the nature of the state and its personnel which provides meaning to these historical periods, for it is the state which has been the dominant institution in shaping economic, social and other opportunities for the population. In turn, the way in which the state has created and maintained order in society, and the way in which it has directed economic activities and permitted or denied the existence of rival institutions, has been a function of the conditions in which it has existed, as well as the manner in which the state's leading personnel have interpreted the opportunities these conditions have provided for the state's perpetuation.

The current official name for the institution known to the English-speaking world as the state of Burma is *Pyihtaungsu Hsoshelit Thammata Myanma Naingngantaw*, or the Socialist Republic of the Union of Burma. The word 'state' does not appear in the official English translation of the title. But in the Burmese version, the final word, *Naingngantaw*, is the current term used to describe the institution which is recognized as the state. *Naingngantaw* is apparently derived from the verb *naing*, which carries the meanings of 'to prevail, conquer, overcome' and 'to be competent to perform, or to be prevalent', combined with the verb *ngan*, meaning 'to be enough' or 'sufficient'. The suffix *taw* connotes the notion of royalty or of religious sanctity and lends the term a degree of dignity. *Naingngan* was used over a thousand years ago to denote the periphery of the kingdom of Pagan. In the nineteenth century, the term was accepted as meaning a kingdom or a country under one jurisdiction or government; or an authority or power; or figuratively, as a domain. In the mid-twentieth century, *naingngan* came to mean 'nation', and thus in contemporary Burma state and nation have been linked conceptually.

Prior to that time, the state was referred to by other terms, indicating both its nature and the ideas its controllers had about its relationship with society. During the British colonial period the ruling institution was referred to as the *asoya*, which was translated, in the style of the nineteenth and early twentieth century, as 'the Government'. *Aso* comes from the verb *so*, 'to rule over', and with *ya*, which is a verb affix implying necessity, *asoya* has the meaning of 'to have authority over'. Before colonialization and the destruction of the monarchy — which made it necessary to develop neologisms for sovereign authority — what is thought of as the state was referred to by reference to the monarch, for whom there were a variety of titles: *ngado ashin*, our lord; *bawa shin*, lord of life; *yei-myei thahkin*, master of water and earth; or *maha dama yaza*, lord of the law. The basic and most simple words for the king were *buyin* or *min*.[1]

The development during the past two hundred years of new terms to nominate the state suggests that there is possibly little or no continuity between the state in Burma in the latter half of the twentieth century and the state in the seventeenth or nineteenth centuries. However, such a possibility is belied by several factors, including the state's very title. The contemporary state, despite its modern guise, which includes the use of the neologism *pyihtaungsu* (group of countries gathered together) to mean union, and the transliterated English term *hsoshelit* (socialist) in its title, also uses the term *thammata* ('elect' or 'chosen') to convey the notion of a republic. This stems from Buddhist philosophy, in which the first king chosen to protect man from his own base nature was elected by the people, and was also elect inasmuch as this superior man could be trusted to curb his own nature in the interests of others. The first king was the *thammata*. The title also includes the term *Myanma*, denoting the idea of the Burmese people as a group of persons distinct from all the rest of humanity who live under this state.

Thus the adjectives which modify *naingngantaw* bring together both ancient and modern notions. It represents the classical myth of the need

---

1. Hla Pe, *Burma: Literature, Historiography, Scholarship, Language, Life and Buddhism* (Singapore: Institute of Southeast Asian Studies, 1985), p. 119.

for control, for his own benefit, over man's behaviour in society. It represents several nineteenth-century myths that were introduced to Southeast Asia with colonial rule. One of these was that Burma is composed of many 'races', and that these must be brought together in a federation like that of England, Scotland and Wales (or Yugoslavia), under the mythical sovereign power of a recognized institution which has uniform authority throughout a territory depicted on a map. It also represents the dominant organizational notion of the globe for the past one hundred years, namely that groups of people defined as nations should be separately identified in a community of such nations and recognized by distinctive ethnic labels. Furthermore, it conveys the idea that this institution has an obligation not only to control the behaviour of the people who live within this demarcated territory, but that it should assist them in improving their condition by organizing production and distribution so as to benefit the entire population.

This accretion of modifiers to the word for state suggests the manner in which the state has evolved in the past two hundred or so years. In this process the state has accumulated new roles and responsibilities, but none of its leading personnel, be they Burmese kings, British civil servants, or Burmese politicians or army officers, have ever sought to deny the lineage of the institution they controlled and which most of the population has accepted as the putative ruling authority in their lives. Equally, other institutions in society have recognized the salience of the state and its leading personnel as possessing the ability, and usually the right, to determine the parameters of their own existence. Through its various guises there has been a continuity to the state, but the personnel and context of the state have changed and this has forced the state to alter society in ways which have created new or rival personnel and established new contexts.

The analytical problem involved in the study of the state in Burma centres primarily upon describing the characteristics of the state and analyzing its relationships with other institutions in society. In that way it is possible to see how it has changed over time and what the consequences of these changes have been for society. What we are attempting to understand is the state which is given a capital 's' when it is considered to be more than just a human institution, but has a life and spirit of its own, separate, if not superior to the individuals who compose it. As Anderson has written:

> the state has to be understood as an *institution*, of the same species as the Church, the university, and the modern corporation. Like them, it ingests and excretes

personnel in a continuous, steady process, often over long periods of time. It is characteristic of such institutions that 'they' have precise rules for entry — at least age, often sex, education, etc., and, no less important, for exit. . . . the state not only has its own memory but harbors self-preserving and self-aggrandizing impulses, which at any given moment are 'expressed' through its living members, but which cannot be reduced to their passing personal ambitions.[2]

There is an alternative analytical approach which suggests that it is more appropriate to examine the relationship between regimes or governments with counter-institutions such as evolving property relations or developing ideological constructions. Clearly, what Perlin refers to as 'non-official aspects of the economy and society' — and which, he suggests, need a broader analytical discussion in order to treat appropriately — cannot be ignored.[3] However, in the approach taken in this volume it is the interaction of the official state and non-official institutions which is being examined, and it is argued that the evidence suggests that in this relationship, most of the time, it is the state which is expected to be — and which is — the determining partner in such relationships.

In this sense, the state, through its 'continuous administrative, legal, bureaucratic and coercive systems' shapes the relationship between itself and civil society, but also shapes the structure of 'many crucial relationships within civil society as well'.[4] The state is thus normally able to determine what is a viable and appropriate political issue and what is not capable of political solution, as it limits the growth of institutions which can express official and private political options.[5]

In those rare historical periods when the state is not the dominant institution in society, but must compete with a variety of other groups which are mobilizing significant competition to it, individuals or corporate groups whose careers are linked directly to the state will soon take

---

2. Benedict R. O'G. Anderson, 'Old State, New Society: Indonesia's New Order in Comparative Historical Perspective', *Journal of Asian Studies*, XLII, 3 (May 1983), p. 478.
3. Frank Perlin, 'State Formation Reconsidered', *Modern Asian Studies*, 19, 3 (July 1985), pp. 451–2.
4. Alfred Stephan, *The State and Society: Peru in Comparative Perspective* (Princeton University Press, 1978), p. xii, quoted in Theda Skocpol, 'Bringing the State Back In: Current Research', in Peter B. Evans, Dietrich Rueschemeyer and Theda Skocpol (eds), *Bringing the State Back In* (Cambridge University Press, 1985), p. 7.
5. *Ibid.*, p. 21.

action in order to attempt to reassert the position of the state, even if the primary means they have to achieve this initially weakens the state. This allows an élite group, such as the officer corps of the Burma army in 1962, free from obligations to other institutions in society, to launch an act of destruction and simultaneous reconstruction in order to adopt a new pattern for the development of the state and its relationship with society.

This conclusion is based upon the assumption that the contemporary state in Burma cannot be understood other than through an appreciation of the nature of the early modern precolonial state. Both the colonial state and the contemporary state developed and functioned in the same geographical and ecological conditions as the precolonial state, and there are significant cultural continuities between the periods of the state's existence. In these periods, the leading personnel of the state reshaped it and ruled through altered structures and with different ideas of the proper relationship of the state to the individual and society.

The nature of the postcolonial state has made obvious the linkage between the contemporary state and its colonial predecessor throughout Southeast Asia; its bureaucratic and military organizations are readily apparent as descendents of the colonial state. This linkage, which results from the fact that many contemporary states such as Indonesia, the Philippines or Malaysia, were creations of foreign imperialists, should not obscure the fact that for the mainland states of Southeast Asia the core of the contemporary state predates European imperialism. In terms of the state's basic functions to maintain social order, control economic distribution and ensure state and élite perpetuation, the modern state in Burma, like those in Vietnam and Thailand, has a historical lineage that goes back 600 to 1,000 years.

The period before colonization saw the emergence of most of the major factors which have shaped the context of the formation of the contemporary state in Burma. Before the arrival of the British, as a result of monarchical, political and administrative reforms from the beginning of the seventeenth century, the power of the state relative to society increased because of more effective taxation and greater military strength; increased and centralized military strength was also a consequence of advances in technology, together with an altered external political and economic environment, the result of increasingly rapid changes occuring in Europe and in neighbouring areas. These factors led those who controlled the state in Burma and those who challenged that control — for reasons of political opportunity and survival — to develop patterns of control, authority and resistance not unlike those found later under the colonial state and, later still, after independence. But the environment of the contemporary state is obviously different in some regards from that of the precolonial state. The relationship between the state and the world economic and political system is much closer now than it was two hundred years ago. The globalization of the nineteenth-century European state system significantly altered the external environment of the Southeast Asian state, but not its essential functions and purpose.

There are now available many alternative models of the state and of the means by which it can achieve its aims. It is now also assumed that the state has many more obligations to society than merely the maintenance of order. Contemporary state-managers tend to think in terms of the utility of borrowing from experiences different from their own, and they assume that the state must conduct industrial, research, planning and other economic functions that either did not exist or were carried out by other institutions in the past.

Analyzing the contemporary Southeast Asian state solely in terms of its colonial predecessors has cut off comparative study from the literature on the development and perpetuation of the state in Europe. But comparable experiences in the formation and perpetuation of the state in mainland Southeast Asia and Europe are apparent. For example, it has been argued by Charles Tilly that 'the most general conditions' of state-formation and survival in European experience were:

(1) the availability of extractable resources; (2) a relatively protected position in time and space; (3) a continous supply of political entrepreneurs; (4) success in war; (5) homogeneity (and homogenization) of subject populations; (6) strong coalitions of the central power with major segments of the landed élite. A high standing on one of these factors can make up for a low standing on another.[6]

These general conditions for state-making and survival existed in Burma from the late sixteenth century onwards, and the success of Burma's state-makers since then has depended upon their ability to control them. The external forces which created the colonial state briefly altered these conditions by increasing the physical force of the state *vis-à-vis* civil society through greater organizational coherence at the core, demarcated borders on the periphery, and in particular the use of

6. Charles Tilly, 'Reflections on the History of European State-Making', in Charles Tilly (ed.), *The Formation of National States in Western Europe* (Princeton University Press, 1975), p. 40.

externally-derived sources of coercion. The increased coercive capacity of the colonial state was necessary for its maintenance because of its diminished legitimacy in the eyes of the populace.

From the Pagan dynasty (c.849–1287) onwards, the twin resource bases of the state have primarily been its expropriation of the economic surplus that was produced in the rice growing heartland of the central Irrawaddy valley, and its control of foreign trade. The tax-base of the colonial state was founded on this same resource, as are the financial resources of the contemporary state. The size of this surplus and the methods of expropriation have changed over time in response to the capacity of the state to assist or control agricultural production. With sparsely populated mountains on three sides and the sea on the fourth, Burma's relative isolation provided both time and space with which to develop a state before new, industrially-based forms of travel, communications and warfare made for easier penetration of these natural barriers.

Warfare has been a feature of the state's activities from Pagan times and so have been the state's efforts — through the Buddhist religion, and later, education and ideology — to create a homogeneous population from ecologically and culturally variable human settlements. It could be argued that success in warfare, more continuous from the early seventeenth century to the early nineteenth century than before, was greater than success at the homogenization of the population, for it was the expansion of the domain of the state in the late eighteenth and early nineteenth centuries and the consequent incorporation of non-homogeneous populations and rival power centres on its peripheries which led to the first military defeat at the hands of the British-Indian empire in 1826. Nonetheless, from the seventeenth to the nineteenth centuries, the homogenization of population was a key feature of Burmese history.

Domestically, the power of precolonial central state rulers was a function of their ability to form alliances of interest and loyalty with the local gentry through patron-client ties. After colonization, such a system began to re-emerge, though too feebly to form a basis for the state's perpetuation. There is in Burma a clear divergence from the European experience where economic differentiation was allowed to develop and the rulers permitted the expansion of interests not tied to the state. Land surpluses, manpower shortages and particular traditions of land usufruct and sumptuary laws have led to different but no less crucial questions for the architects and maintainers of the state in precolonial and postcolonial Burma.

From the time of the Pagan kings and their competition with the Buddhist monkhood for the control of agricultural land and labour, we can see in Burma a struggle between the state and potential rival institutional interests over economic rights. This factor in the development of the state manifested itself in different forms in later periods. The rulers of the Restored Toungoo (1597–1752) and Konbaung (1752–1885) dynasties were, during the seventeenth and eighteenth centuries, continually attempting to limit the power of the local gentry and provincial governors in order to strengthen the power of the central state. Throughout the precolonial period, the state was determined to ensure that there was no economic or social mobilization outside its control.

In contrast to the era of monarchical rule, during the colonial period the externally buttressed state was sufficiently strong to delegate some of its authority to landlords and moneylenders, though they remained dependent upon the state's legal system for their positions. This was made possible by the vastly increased surplus created by new economic conditions and policies at the expense of the precolonial gentry, and, eventually, of the peasantry. In a sense, the colonial state destroyed the self-perpetuating and integrated social networks created by the monarchical state and replaced them with the bureaucratized networks of 'a business concern'.[7] The contemporary state, by the resumption of all landownership and a monopolistic claim to all surpluses, has attempted to re-establish the dominance of the state and in so doing gain the support of the peasantry at the expense of the landowners, moneylenders, and urban and/or foreign-oriented commercial interests which arose during the colonial period. A similar situation has developed in the relationship between the central power and the political authorities and economic élites in the more peripheral areas of the state's domain. At all times the interests of the state, of course, have been held by its controllers to be paramount, for its interests are their interests.

In Burma, as in Europe, there has been a close relationship between state domination and perpetuation and the expansion of armed forces, rises in taxation and consequent popular rebellions. This relationship is not just a colonial and postcolonial phenomenon however; the outward

---

7. The imagery comes from J.S. Furnivall, 'South Asia and the World Today', in Phillips Talbot (ed.), *South Asia in the World Today* (University of Chicago Press, 1950), p. 7.

manifestations of these activities until the colonial period were often different from the European experience. The political dynamics underlying these activities were, and still are, the same. So too are the basic issues which face the state. But even with differences in style, the analytical generalizations that Tilly draws for Europe are points which can be seen in Burma, and perhaps in much of the rest of mainland Southeast Asia:

> The state-makers only imposed their wills on the populace through centuries of ruthless efforts. The effect took many forms: creating distinct staffs dependent on the crown and loyal to it; making those staffs (armies and bureaucrats alike) reliable, effective instruments of policy; blending coercion, co-optation, and legitimization as means of guaranteeing the acquiescence of different segments of the population; acquiring sound information about the country, its people and its resources; promoting economic activities which would free or create resources for the use of the state. In all these efforts and more, the state-makers frequently found the traditional authorities allied with the people against them. Thus it became a game of shifting coalitions; kings rallying popular support by offering guarantees against cruel and arbitrary local magnates or by challenging their claims to goods, money or services, but not hesitating to crush rebellion when the people were divided or sufficient military force was at hand; magnates parading as defending local liberties against royal oppression, not hesitating to bargain with the crown when it appeared advantageous. Ultimately, the people paid.[8]

What kind of an institution is the state? What sets it apart from other institutions which claim to regulate aspects of social life? Tilly suggests that 'an organization which controls the population occupying a defined territory is a state *in so far as* (1) it is differentiated from other organizations operating in the same territory; (2) it is autonomous; (3) it is centralized; and (4) its divisions are formally coordinated with one another.'[9] Furthermore, it is necessary to add to this definition of the state the fact that it is the only institution which is expected to determine its relationship with other bodies and to determine for other institutions in civil society their relationships with each other. Some would argue that this is to claim too much for the domination of the state in pre-colonial Burma. But essentially it is differences in degree that are seen between the early modern state in Burma and the European state, especially in their early modern forms.

8. Tilly, 'Reflections on the History of European State-Making', p. 24.
9. *Ibid.*, p. 70, emphasis in the original.

For example, precolonial mainland Southeast Asian states did not have a 'population occupying a defined territory' in the sense of a territory demarcated by externally as well as internally recognized and reasonably precise borders. In such circumstances, the concept of 'foreign affairs' would not have the same sense as in Europe. The differences between the European and the mainland Southeast Asian state should not be overstated though. European borders were imprecise and much contested until relatively recent times, and Southeast Asian rulers knew what territory they were able to control and tax, and their subjects knew to whom they owed taxes and service, if not always allegiance. However, crude borders did exist in mainland Southeast Asia before the arrival of European concepts of statecraft.

Another significant comparison between Europe and Southeast Asia is in respect to nationalism. In Burma, as in Europe, mass nationalism is a phenomenon which developed subsequent to the formation of the modern state. In terms of historical evolution, élite or intellectual nationalism in Europe was a force from the early eighteenth century onwards, but its impact on the political élite in Burma only occurred towards the beginning of the twentieth century, after the dissolution of the monarchical state. Nonetheless, proto-nationalism in the form of attachment to the crown and the Buddhist faith pre-dates the modern state.

However, when considered as a mass political phenomenon, the emergence of nationalism as a significant political force — one able to shake not only the foundations of the state, but the stability of the state's external environment — occurred in Burma within twenty years of its near universal impact in Europe. The First World War led to the spread of nationalism to the broad body of the populace of Asia and Europe. The political consequences of this war included the stimulation of a common belief among the broad mass of the European people and many of the colonized peoples of Asia that mass action, interpreted as national action, could change the leadership and behaviour, if not the ultimate nature, of the state. In Burma, as in other Asian countries, nationalist sentiment was constructed upon the institutions of the precolonial state and society, particularly the old governing class and religion.

The development of mass nationalism and its corollary, the belief that the state should belong to the people, presents one of the potential differences in the nature of the state in the premodern and modern periods. Though embedded in society and highly dependent upon it, the precolonial state in Burma was largely autonomous. There was no notion that the king was 'responsible' to the people in any other than a general moral sense for their well-being, and even less of an idea that the state's officials 'represented' the people. However, the growth of the democratic idea and the increasing competitiveness of other institutions threatened to limit the autonomy of the state. This often develops as a consequence of the growth in the power and autonomy of rival institutions, making the state an arena of conflict rather than an arbiter of conflict and allocator of resources.[10] In the case of Burma it was the collapse of the state after 1942 and the simultaneous and nearly spontaneous growth of mass mobilization movements, especially those of peasants and others deprived influence under the colonial state, which overwhelmed the state and severely limited its autonomy. However these mobilization movements were not themselves highly institutionalized and the collapse of the state resulted in a power vacuum in society which no rival could fill.

The reassertion of the predominant position of the state after 1948 was attempted initially by recreating the pattern of the colonial state and increasing its representative quality. The weakness of the state in these circumstances made it difficult for it to penetrate society and regain control over rival institutions. In reality, few states, including authoritarian ones, are able to penetrate society directly to such a degree as to determine all of these relationships. But dominant states are able to structure social relations so as to ensure that no threats to their stability and perpetuation can develop, as the state is the ultimate arbiter of societal conflicts. The establishment of state hegemony and the state's consequent ability to set the limits of acceptable political, economic and social behaviour is only possible when the state is accepted as legitimate and no other institution can effectively deny its dictates.

For state managers in Burma in 1962 such a condition was far removed from existing circumstances. During the previous twenty years the state had been displaced from the apex of society to a position where it was merely the most important competitor for public support and obedience. To those who felt a primary obligation to the perpetuation of the state and whose personal careers were directly linked to its prospects, the state seemed unable to defend itself against other institutions and the classes or groups which led them.

10. Dietrich Rueschemeyer and Peter B. Evans, 'The State and Economic Transformation: Toward an Analysis of the Conditions Underlying Effective Intervention', in P.B. Evans *et al.* (eds), *Bringing the State Back In*, p. 49.

Theoretically, in the post-independence period of most states in Asia and Africa, individuals wishing to resurrect the dominance of a state have two options before them. One is to open the society to external institutions and forces such as the world economy and military alliances with more powerful states. In that way the state, as the institution through which other states and foreign capital must operate in order to penetrate the society and economy, is able to use outside resources to establish its position within the country. But this is at the cost of abandoning a degree of state autonomy (i.e., sovereignty) to other states and institutions whose interests cannot be identical with those of the state itself.

The alternative is to force the state upon the remainder of society with the few weapons at its disposal. Given its lack of positive inducements because of its impecunious nature, this means eliminating its rivals through the power of the law while ensuring that the institutions permitted to exist are dependent upon the state, either through their personnel or their finances, and are therefore unable to organize effective opposition to it. Such an attempt is extremely difficult, and in the end many compromises have to be made between the ideal of state autonomy and dominance and the political, economic and social conditions within which the state and its leading personnel must function. In Burma, the second strategy was chosen by the leaders of the 1962 military coup. This was only to be expected given their own corporate experiences since before independence as well as the relatively unimportant strategic position of Burma in world politics and economics in the 1950s and 1960s.

It is tempting but facile to conclude that the state in Burma by 1987 had returned in character and nature to that of the precolonial state and to thus see the colonial period as a brief and ultimately unimportant episode in the history of the country. Such a return to the past is impossible because too many conditions surrounding the state have changed. Moreover, the managers of the state and the people they govern, as well as the rest of the world, expect a great deal more of the state now than was the case two hundred years ago.

CHAPTER 1
THE PRECOLONIAL STATE

The Evolution of the Precolonial State

The first millennium of the state in Burma, between the founding of the kingdom of Pagan around AD 849 and the fall of the last Konbaung king in 1885, is conveniently divided between the classical Pagan period ending in 1287, a 300-year interregnum with several rival state centres, and the founding of the early modern state of the Restored Toungoo (1587–1752) and Konbaung (1752–1885) dynasties. The reason for ending this period in 1885 is obvious. No event in the history of Burma other than the loss to the British-Indian empire of the monarchical state and the Buddhist order it upheld was as complete and as traumatic to Burma's civilization. But this political and cultural watershed should not obscure the fact that the precolonial period itself was not, in terms of the structure and nature of the state, one long, uninterrupted, unchanging seamless pattern.

Two significant forces caused the nature of the precolonial state to change. One was the force of internally and externally sanctioned economic and technological change. This recast the environment in which the state functioned, especially from the start of the early modern period at the beginning of the seventeenth century. The other force was the evolution of the scale of the state as a consequence of its territorial expansion, some modest population growth,[1] and the accumulated experience of the ruling strata. Throughout the precolonial period, the nature and behaviour of the state in its relationship with important socio-economic institutions in society was far from stagnant, and the evolving relationship of the state with society during the last two dynasties shaped the capabilities the ruling élites possessed to cope with internal and external challenges to their power and authority.

However, there were significant aspects of continuity between classical Pagan and the early modern periods. Clearly the fulcrum of the

---

1. By the middle of the eighteenth century, the best estimates suggest that the state in Burma controlled a population of between 2 and 2.5 million persons. William J. Koenig, 'The Early Kon-baung Polity, 1752–1819: A Study of Politics, Administration and Social Organization in Burma' (unpubl. Ph.D. diss., University of London, 1978), pp. 97–8.

state throughout the precolonial period was the monarch. Strong, charismatic kings, usually the founders or early monarchs of new dynasties, put their personal stamp on their reigns. To the popular mind the monarchy, and often the monarch himself, was seen as the state. Notions of kingship and statecraft derived from classical Indian Buddhist thought persisted throughout the period. Territorial control was seen as the consequence of the king's possession of a full treasury and a strong army, and it was the exercise of that territorial control that made possible the taxation of labour and agriculture which filled the treasury and fed the army.[2]

Throughout the era of the precolonial state, and in the present day, parallel to the state stood the institutional form of the Buddhist faith, the *sangha* or monkhood, usually in a subordinate relationship, but when the state was weak, in a challenging one. Being closer to the people and in a less obviously exploitative or coercive posture, the monkhood survived dynastic changes to provide society in central Burma with a cultural unity that was little questioned and more rarely tested until the rise of the colonial state and mass nationalism during the late nineteenth and early twentieth centuries. The outward manifestations of the institutions of the Buddhist faith, which were remarkably uniform from the fifteenth century onwards, provided the only important, albeit narrow, avenue of social mobility for those who were young and ambitious until the colonial period, and gave the populace a shared experience and social expectations that both explained and justified the vicissitudes of life and the state.

Complementing the order which Buddhist institutions gave to society were 'the hereditary local chieftains', as Furnivall labelled the village (*ywa*) and township (*myo* or *taik*) authorities who regulated the day-to-day lives of most of the population and were the main administrative link between the central state and its subjects. These authorities who constituted the gentry class, together with the monkhood, survived 'through intervals of anarchy' when the power of the state was being contested 'and it was from them that society grew up anew, but on old lines, when order was restored'.[3] Furnivall should not mislead us though, for while it is true that at the base of society

---

2. S.J. Tambiah, *World Conqueror and World Renouncer* (Cambridge University Press, 1976), pp. 52–3, describes the analogous Thai state during the same period.
3. J.S. Furnivall, *Colonial Policy and Practice: A Comparative Study of Burma and Netherlands India* (New York University Press, 1956), p. 17.

the re-establishment of central authority by the state made possible the recreation of order and stability, allowing the annual agricultural and cultural cycles of most of the population to continue essentially unaltered, from the early 1600s onward the state gradually expanded and adapted in response to its changing environment. The precolonial state rested upon a society which had a fundamental stability grounded in agriculture and religion which it was little able, or willing, to alter. The problem for the controllers of the state was how to direct and use these societal institutions for their own purposes, while rivals in the *sangha*, and especially the local gentry, championed the institutional power of religion and the rights of the village and town in the name of ideals and interests which were sometimes at odds with those of the king and the central state.

In the terminology of comparative Weberian sociology, the precolonial state is best described as 'patrimonial'.[4] It contained within it strong centrifugal forces constantly tugging at the authority of the monarch and his central institutions which, in turn, rested on the shifting ties of patron-client diadic relationships. These patron-client ties ran from the royal and court-appointed central officials down to the township and village gentry class. Princes, ministers, provincial officials and village and township headmen, as well as rival power centres on the periphery of the state's domain, were continually seeking opportunities to organize sufficient power to keep wealth and authority in their own hands. The central state had to struggle constantly to regroup and control the resources provided by agriculture and trade, and the king's influence over the institutions of the Buddhist religion made easier the aggrandizement of the state by clothing it with a mantle of legitimacy.

The nature of the administrative and political controls at the king's disposal made for a constant battle between the centre and the extremities of the state. Michael Adas has referred to this form of state structure as a 'contest state', noting that,

central to this form of political organization is the rule by a king or emperor who claims a monopoly of power and authority in a given society but whose effective control is in reality severely restricted by rival power centres among the élite, by weaknesses in administrative organization and institutional commitment on the part of state officials, by poor communications, and by a low

---

4. Max Weber, *Economy and Society* (edited by Guenther Roth and Claus Wittich) (New York: Bedminster Press, 1968), vol. III, pp. 1010–38.

population-to-land ratio, that places a premium on manpower retention and regulation.[5]

Adas draws attention to the significant gap between the theory of the all-powerful and all-knowing monarch, and the practice of the precolonial state in regard to the lives of the peasantry and other non-official sectors of society. Nonetheless, the state's presence was always felt, if not the insecurity caused by its absence, and because of its singular ability to amass power and other resources of rule the wielders of the state's authority were generally in a commanding position.

The widely held assumption by an earlier generation of scholars that the controllers of the state in Burma learned nothing from the failures of their precursors suggested that until the coming of colonial rule the state rose and fell in an inevitable and futile cycle. This is the perception of the state and Burma's rulers conveyed in the first works on the history of the country by foreigners.[6] We know, however, that rulers elsewhere, like their political opponents and rivals, learned from their predecessors' failures. The history of the state in Burma between 1597 and 1885 also reveals a process of accumulation of political and administrative skills. The defeat of the controllers of the state in the face of the British challenge demonstrates that the wielders of state power were unable to create sufficient strength quickly enough to cope with all the new external forces they faced, while continuing to deal with ceaseless domestic political forces. That the reforms and diplomacy of the penultimate king, Mindon, proved to be too little and were introduced too late does not alter the fact that he was well aware of the need for adaptation, as were many of his ministers and advisers who continued in office after him.[7] His Restored Toungoo predecessors, facing less radical external challenges, had had more success in adjusting to internal challenges by using externally derived resources.

With the formation of the Toungoo dynasty, the post-Pagan political order of Burma was destroyed and a unity was created in the central core that has not been broken since, except for the years between 1826 and

5. Michael Adas, 'From Avoidance to Confrontation: Peasant Protest in Precolonial and Colonial Southeast Asia', *Comparative Studies in Society and History*, vol. 23, no. 2 (April 1981), p. 218.
6. A tradition of interpretation best exemplified by G.E. Harvey, *History of Burma* (London: Frank Cass, 1925, repr. 1967).
7. John F. Cady, *A History of Modern Burma* (Ithaca and London: Cornell University Press, 1958), pp. 99–116.

1885 when the British governed Arakan and Tenasserim and, subsequently, southern Burma, separately from the king at Ava or Mandalay. As Lieberman has argued, before the early 1600s only the Pagan empire was able to create this political unity (though within a more limited area).[8] The Pagan state system fell — as Aung Thwin has shown[9] — not only for reasons of the central state's inability to control the wealth of the monkhood and its institutions, but also because of external factors threatening central Burma. These included pressure from the Tai-speaking peoples and the Mongols as well as the growth of Chinese and Indian Ocean trade, which encouraged the formation of a rival kingdom situated on the southern coast away from Pagan.[10] For both internal and external reasons, from the early seventeenth century onwards the state in Burma changed its nature and structural relationships, as well as its bases of stability and power, so that the last two dynasties were 'more stable and militarily more powerful than their Pagan or Avan predecessors'.[11] New commercial patterns, the use of European firearms and mercenaries, the growth of domestic agriculture and population, and the state's greater ability in controlling the internal wealth of its domains made this possible. In turn, the growing power of the state led to longer periods of internal peace and expanded productivity which further strengthened the central state.

But, if this is true, why did the penultimate dynasty, the Restored Toungoo, fall in 1752, to be replaced by the Konbaung dynasty? Lieberman's analysis of the political dynamics of the Restored Toungoo period

8. Victor B. Lieberman, 'Continuity and Change in Burmese History: Some Preliminary Observations', unpubl. paper, p. 12.
9. Michael Aung Thwin, 'The Role of *Sasana* Reform in Burmese History: Economic Dimensions of a Religious Purification', *Journal of Asian Studies*, XXXVIII, 4 (Aug. 1979), p. 673; see also the same author's 'Divinity, Spirit, and Human: Conceptions of Classical Burmese Kingship', in Lorraine Gesick (ed.), *Centers, Symbols, and Hierarchies: Essays on the Classical State of Southeast Asia* (New Haven: Yale University Southeast Asian Studies Series no. 26, 1983), p. 46; and 'Jampudipa: Classical Burma's Camelot', in *Contributions to Asian Studies*, vol. 16, 'Essays on Burma', edited by John P. Ferguson (Leiden: E.J. Brill, 1981), pp. 38–41; and *Pagan: The Origins of Modern Burma* (Honolulu: University of Hawaii Press, 1985).
10. Victor B. Lieberman, 'The Political Significance of Religious Wealth in Burmese History: Some Further Thoughts', *Journal of Asian Studies*, XXXIX (4 Aug. 1980), p. 756.
11. *Ibid.*, p. 766.

in his *Burmese Administrative Cycles* shows why.[12] The continual interaction of three factors — élite autonomy, popular evasions of state authority and requirements, and royal demands — similar to those which tested the control of the early modern European state, brought an end to the Toungoo dynastic line when its rivals managed to construct a coalition of gentry and peasants against it. The state itself, however, was not dissolved with the end of the old dynasty as had occurred in pre-Toungoo times; rather, the new rulers reinvigorated the existing state structures. But the political rivalries and administrative weaknesses which had brought down the final Toungoo ruler did not cease with the decline of his dynasty. Rather, Alaungpaya, the first Konbaung king, having successfully exploited the laxity of the regime to rise to power himself, had in turn to quell his extra-state allies with the power of the state he captured. He understood the weaknesses of the political and administrative policies of his predecessor and thus knew what to do to ensure that no one wrested power from him. As the state continued as an ongoing institution, he and his successors by and large followed Toungoo 'political organization with only minor modifications until the mid-nineteenth century'.[13] Then, organizational and technological devices borrowed from abroad were introduced at the centre, allowing for a further extension and regularization of central supervision over peripheral political authorities.

The final failure of the Konbaung dynasty would seem to contradict the argument that the state had strengthened itself as a consequence of the changes introduced after 1597. During the final 133 years of the precolonial state, the kings attempted to control élite automony, but the urge for power on the part of rivals continued to provide an incentive for the gentry class to devise new means of avoiding central controls. The centre attempted to reduce popular evasions of state demands for manpower and taxes, but to do so usually required the formation of an alliance with a set of local power-holders or incipient élites, which in turn led to increasing dissatisfaction among other groups, especially the peasantry. The peasants sought to evade state demands, but giving way to popular protests or evasive actions would have weakened the state at

12. Victor B. Lieberman, *Burmese Administrative Cycles: Anarchy and Conquest, c. 1580–1760* (Princeton University Press, 1984).
13. Frank N. Trager and William J. Koenig (eds), *Burmese Sit-tans 1764–1826, Records of Rural Life and Administration* (Tucson: University of Arizona Press, for the Association for Asian Studies, 1979), p. 19.

the expense of greater power accruing to its temporary gentry allies and subordinate state officials. The coming of the British-Indian empire to challenge the king's control of the state and its resources proved too great a burden for the central institutions. Nonetheless, that the idea of the precolonial state proved attractive as a nationalist symbol fifty years after the demise of the last monarch demonstrates the strong image that it had created for itself in the minds of the people, perhaps in part because the weaknesses of the precolonial state had provided a means for local interests to defend themselves against the central rulers, while still maintaining overall political and social order.

Underlying the stability and greater coherence of the state in Burma from the early 1600s onwards were many crucial factors, one of the most important of which was that the most astute kings sought and found alternative sources of power such as foreign trade and technology to help them control internal political rivalries. Thus they were not solely dependent on internal expropriation of the surpluses of the gentry and peasantry which led to the spread of popular evasions, political tensions and weakened central control. 'Rulers from Nyaungyan Min (r. 1587–1606) through Alaungpaya (r. 1752–60) [as well as Mindon Min (r. 1853–78)] showed an appreciation of the military and political value of maritime contacts, and frequently sought to widen these channels.'[14] Perhaps because the last two dynasties were increasingly able to concentrate power in the central state, political rivalries and conflicts in the king's court escalated, making the Konbaung dynasty particularly prone to factionalism. But throughout this period of some 280 years the kingdom as a whole enjoyed a remarkable degree of internal order and stability, except at the very end of the Restored Toungoo period. As in Siam during the same period, there was 'a long-term trend toward centralization',[15] giving this period a unique place as a 'coherent unit in the institutional and administrative history' of Burma.[16]

---

14. Lieberman, *Burmese Administrative Cycles*, p. 277.
15. *Ibid.*, p. 14.
16. Lieberman, 'Continuity and Change', pp. 20–2.

The Territorial Organization of the Precolonial State

In the behaviour as well as in the study of the state theory and practice have to be distinguished. In theory the king was a universal monarch who allowed others the use of his land; they received the benevolence of his tolerance and thus enjoyed the order he bestowed on society and its institutions, especially the Buddhist religion. In reality, the monarch was caught in a web of internal rivalries and external threats to the security of his throne, to the wealth of his treasury, and to the power of his state. In theory the kingdom 'was minutely regulated. The whole kingdom ... was governed by the pen,'[17] and indeed there was a plethora of official regulations limiting the mobility of the population and the consumption or investment of wealth. Because of this, then as now, a great deal of the people's time and ingenuity was devoted to avoiding the bureaucratic strictures and requirements of the state; nullifying theory in practice.

In territorial terms, the structure of the precolonial state evolved from the form established by the founders of the Pagan state to that developed by the Restored Toungoo and Konbaung dynasties. Neither the Pagan nor later administrative systems during the Avan interregnum were stagnant, but rather changed gradually, as indicated by the coinage of a new administrative terminology. Pagan consisted of four different territorial categories: 1. the nucleus, 2. secondary settlements, 3. strategic stockades, and 4. conquered 'foreign' areas. The nucleus was the core of the state's territory from which, by controlling its irrigation system, it derived the bulk of its manpower and revenue and had the greatest control over its subjects' occupations. The secondary settlements on the state's western frontier were probably of little economic value, although some trade may have been conducted there. The relatively undefended nature of the secondary settlements zone suggests that the rulers perceived the area as posing little threat. Threats were perceived to come from the north and east, where the state created a string of forty-six stockades under the control of the king's army. Indicative of the restricted area of the Pagan state in comparison with its seventeenth and eighteenth-century successor, the so-called conquered territories (*naigngan*) lay mainly to the south of the nucleus zone in what became the heart of the state's domain in the last period of the precolonial state. Depending upon the power of the centre in any given period, this

---

17. Furnivall, *Colonial Policy and Practice*, p. 15.

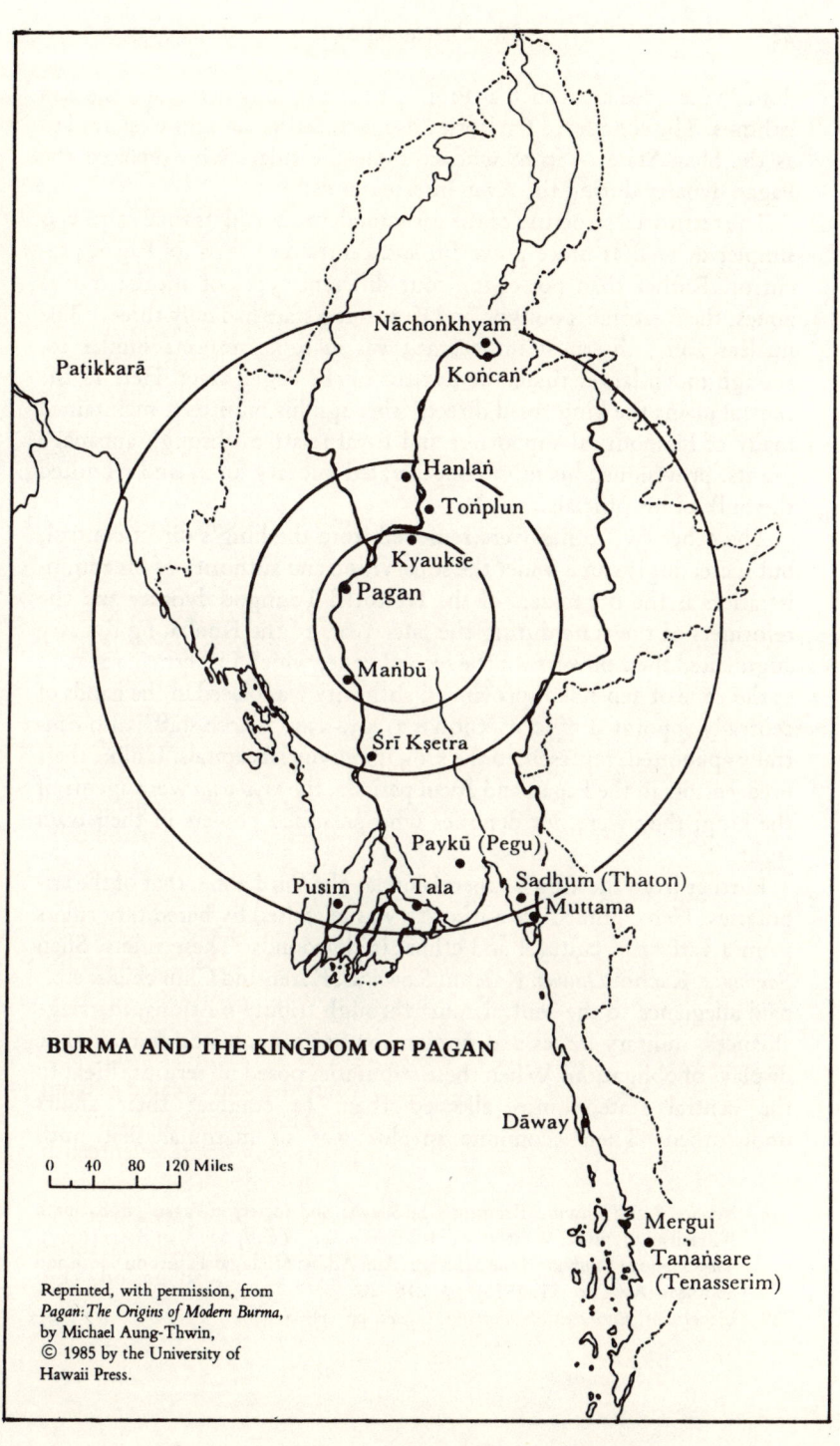

BURMA AND THE KINGDOM OF PAGAN

Reprinted, with permission, from
Pagan: The Origins of Modern Burma,
by Michael Aung-Thwin,
© 1985 by the University of
Hawaii Press.

domain included areas such as Prome, the Irrawaddy delta, and the Kra isthmus. The conquered territories also included what is now referred to as the Shan State — from whence came the rulers who replaced the Pagan dynasty during the Avan interregnum.[18]

The territorial structure of the early modern state in its final form was simpler as well as more powerful and centralized than its Pagan precursor. Rather than possessing four different types of administrative zones, the Restored Toungoo and Konbaung state had only three.[19] The nuclear zone, the most important, was in some respects similar to, though much larger than, the nucleus of the Pagan state. Here in the central plains the king ruled directly through his ministers, maintained many of his political supporters and royal relatives through appanage grants, provisioned his most concentrated military forces and recruited the bulk of his officials.

The other two zones were removed from the king's direct control, but increasingly came under the supervision and authority of his administration as the organizers of the Restored Toungoo dynasty and the reformers of the state during the later years of the Konbaung dynasty augmented their powers. In the second zone, which Lieberman refers to as the zone of dependent provinces, authority was placed in the hands of centrally appointed officials known as *myo-wun*, whose staffs, also centrally appointed, represented the king in provincial capitals. Unlike their predecessors in the Pagan and Avan periods, the *myo-wun* were agents of the king, they were not deputies who possessed powers in their own right.

Further from the king's supervision lay the third zone, that of the tributaries. Here, immediate authority was exercised by hereditary rulers from a variety of cultural and ethnic backgrounds. These rulers, Shan *Sawbwas*, Kachin *Duwas*, Karenni *Sawbwas*, Karen and Chin chiefs, etc., paid allegiance to the central court through tribute missions, marriage alliances, military forces and similar non-permanent, non-bureaucratic displays of obligation. When these tributaries posed no serious threat to the central state, kings allowed them to conduct their affairs undisturbed. Their economic surplus was so marginal that until

18. Michael Aung Thwin, 'Kingship, the *Sangha*, and Society in Pagan', in Kenneth R. Hall and John K. Whitmore (eds), *Explorations in Early Southeast Asian History: The Origins of Southeast Asian Statecraft* (Ann Arbor: Michigan Papers on South and Southeast Asia, no. 11, 1976), pp. 218–20.
19. Lieberman, *Burmese Administrative Cycles*, pp. 54–5.

their minerals and timber became valuable in the nineteenth century security was the king's only concern. Their rulers were permitted to maintain the symbols of office and legitimacy in their own courts as if they were lesser versions of the central state. However, from the middle of the nineteenth century onwards the central state imposed greater control through the stationing of military officers at the larger local courts and through the requisition of regular payments to the central treasury.[20]

Various means were used to achieve greater centralization, particularly in the zone of dependent provinces, during the final 280 years of the precolonial state. The first Restored Toungoo kings began the process of removing the 'aura of independent sovereignty outlying centers had once enjoyed' by taking away the local authorities' symbols of office, replacing the independent *bayin* (provincial governors) with *myowun*, and requiring princes holding distant appanages to reside at the capital.

On a more practical level, Ava [the Restored Toungoo capital] expanded its control over subordinate officials within each lowland province: official spies, military commissioners, treasurers, and so on were now selected by the capital, whereas in earlier periods deputies had usually been appointed by the local governor.[21]

Furthermore, the court concentrated professional soldiers more in the capital area, removing from local princes, other appanage holders and officials, forces with which to challenge the centre, while monopolizing the import and distribution of firearms. All in all, the central state 'trimmed the self-sufficiency of provincial governors' in the most important zones from what had been the practice during the Pagan and Avan period.[22]

Nonetheless, the provinces south of the capital did apparently possess a greater degree of administrative independence than did the provinces

---

20. After 1868, when the *thathameda* tax — a village lump-sum assessment used in central Burma — began to be extended into the Shan States during the reign of King Mindon, continuing the process of regularizing state institutions between the two areas, the 'chief activity of the Burmese political agents was to collect the Thathameda tax for the treasury at Mandalay'. Saimong Mangrai, *The Shan States and the British Annexation* (Ithaca: Cornell University Southeast Asia Program Data Paper no. 57, 1965), pp. 58 and 103.
21. Lieberman, 'Continuity and Change', pp. 15–16.

lying immediately adjacent to the court. If for no other reason, the slow means of communication of this period ensured a degree of provincial administrative autonomy, but the frequent rotation of key officials by the king's ministers indicates a significant degree of central supervision. The state's dependence upon the agricultural and demographic resources of the southern areas, as well as the ports through which cash revenues and firearms flowed to the centre, made these provinces immensely important in maintaining the resources of the central authority, and the reforms and policies of the Restored Toungoo monarchs reflected their awareness of this.[23] In comparison with the Pagan and Avan kingdoms, from the early seventeenth century onwards the state controlled a larger territory under firmer administrative restraint. As a consequence, 'lowland provincial rebellions' led by princely challengers of the type which had plagued the monarchs in the period between the Pagan and the Restored Toungoo dynasties 'were short-lived and infrequent'.[24]

The gradual transformation of the residents' ethnic affinities in the expanded nuclear zone indicates both the greater power of the state as well as its greater ability to affect the identity of its subjects. The permanency and power of the state, and its identity with monarchs who were considered to be ethnically and culturally Burman, led communities and individuals to accept the state's definition of their cultural orientation. As in Europe at the same time, the process of homogenization of personal identity with the state was taking place. The distinctive identity of being a Mon which had marked the south in earlier eras was disappearing,[25] and a proto-national cultural and ethnic formation was being created throughout the Irrawaddy river valley.

The central state's control of the tributary zones also increased during this time as strategic or economic reasons for undertaking political and administrative reforms became more salient. Initially, the Restored

22. Lieberman, *Burmese Administrative Cycles*, p. 64.
23. *Ibid.*, p. 130. The southern area least under the control of the central state lay in the trans-Sittang river littoral and the central lowlands below Pakangyi and Yamethin (areas which have been the most difficult for the contemporary state to control since 1948). Here, from the Restored Toungoo kings until 1885, the administration of the area resembled that of the nuclear and dependent zones. 'However, . . . distance, economic regionalism, and traditions of local sovereignty combined to pose challenges to central authority that were quite unknown in the nuclear zone proper.' *Ibid.*, p. 113.
24. Lieberman, 'Continuity and Change', p. 21.
25. *Ibid.*, p. 36.

Toungoo kings had seen the highlands primarily as military recruitment grounds and the source of highly prized luxury goods (in addition to serving as the trade route to Yunnan).[26] Those tributaries nearest the capital, especially in the western Shan or Tai areas and the southern Kachin zone where minor Shan *Sawbwa*ships were recognized, were most carefully superintended by the king's military officers. Not until the nineteenth century was systematic reform undertaken which began to transform the Shan tributaries into dependent provinces.[27] In these areas, however, the process of the homogenization of ethnic and cultural identities had not advanced as rapidly, and economic exchange with the plains remained infrequent and largely unintegrated with the state's central economy.

Authority Relations in the Precolonial State

The pattern of authority relations in the precolonial state, like its territorial organization, was hierarchical, with the king at the centre/top and the most distant hill-peoples and their tributary rulers at the periphery/bottom. The dominant religious and cosmological ideas of the precolonial world provided a justification for these relations;[28] and the political and economic reality of the precolonial state and the administrative devices at its disposal made such relations possible and perhaps inevitable. According to Aung Thwin, throughout the history of the classical state the 'essence of social and administrative organization' was its structuring along patron-client lines through a form of 'cellular' organization.[29] The king stood at the apex of a society in which the bulk of the population were attached to specific organic communities, tied to him through a network of interlocking relationships which provided the warp and woof of state and society. In practice, the king's ability to control the behaviour of his subjects was limited, as his authority was

---

26. Lieberman, *Burmese Administrative Cycles*, p. 131.
27. Robert H. Taylor, 'British Policy and the Shan States, 1886–1942', in Ronald D. Renard (ed.), *Changes in Northern Thailand and the Shan States, 1886–1940* (Singapore: Southeast Asian Studies Program, Institute of Southeast Asian Studies, forthcoming).
28. The classic statement of the cosmological underpinning of the precolonial state is Robert Heine-Geldern, 'Conceptions of State and Kingship in Southeast Asia,' *The Far Eastern Quarterly* (2 Nov. 1942), pp. 15–30.
29. Aung Thwin, 'Divinity, Spirit, and Human,' p. 46.

mediated through a chain of subordinate authorities of varying kinds. The king's clients had their own interests to pursue and their own sources of extra-state personal authority as well as state-sanctioned power. As the monarch made little differentiation between his property and that of the state, so his subordinates made scant distinction between their official responsibilities and their private interests. And when they did so, private interest often took primary place in their calculus of duty. 'The fact that despite the Restored Toungoo reforms, the imperial administration was loosely integrated both vertically and horizontally, and power was diffuse',[30] meant that central commands and requirements were still of limited effectiveness in the early modern period.

In the lower levels of the administrative and political hierarchy, prestige diminished as did access to direct royal authority. The further from the centre the more difficult it was for officials to convince their subordinates of the state's sanction for their demands. Though in traditional society the prestige gained from the high status of government service provided a good deal of personal authority for the incumbent, the threat of coercion was often necessary when making demands for payments in kind, labour or coin. Tax collectors and other such appointees, including military officers — especially when they exceeded accepted norms of required contributions — were the cause of much of the political discontent and conflict within the precolonial social and political order.

Below the king in the hierarchy stood the princes of the blood, often rivals of the incumbent who became co-rivals on his demise. There were principles of succession, but these were often challenged by the sons, uncles and brothers of the king. From the perspective of the incumbent the princes were a threat to his security, but if carefully supervised were also an asset, for more than any other group in society they saw their personal interests directly linked with the perpetuation of the state upon which their livelihoods and status depended. Furthermore, their élite education in the royal court and monasteries gave them administrative skills and a level of literacy found only among the most privileged, leisured groups. Thus, before the Restored Toungoo reforms, the princes proved very useful as administrators and provincial governors; the king providing for the support of their incomes through the assignment of appanages.

The holder of an appanage was known as a *myo-sa*, literally the eater of

---

30. Lieberman, *Burmese Administrative Cycles*, p. 137.

the town. In order to expropriate their share of the revenues of their fiefs, the *myo-sa* assigned agents to collect on their behalf. Even after the replacement of princely *bayin* with *myo-wun* following the Restored Toungoo reforms, the monarchs continued to assign appanages to royalty in order to ensure their political support. Except for its expansion under the first Konbaung kings, no changes in this system were made until well into the nineteenth century.[31] The appanage system was not allowed to develop into a feudal system, for no proprietary rights were assigned with the grant, no military service was necessarily required, and no grant was made in perpetuity.[32] Herein lay not only one of the fundamental differences between the early modern European state and its counterpart in Burma, but also a key source of the centralizing and dominating power of the early modern Burmese state. The kings developed a system intended to assure that no permanent independent bases of provincial power could arise to challenge their dominant position.

Below the royal princes in the political and social hierarchy stood the state's appointed officials. During the Restored Toungoo and Konbaung dynasties this group grew in size relative to the princely coterie, as the king appointed an increasing number of provincial officials directly dependent upon him while requiring the princes to reside at the capital where they could be watched and prevented from raising provincial revolts. These court-appointed officials became the crucial intermediaries between the court and the hereditary village and town headmen who had direct control over the manpower and resources of the kingdom.

The king, at the centre of the state, was in theory and often in practice involved in the details of the state's administration. All edicts were promulgated in the monarch's name, and while he probably had little involvement in their drafting he had a clear supervisory role. 'Policymaking' in the contemporary sense was not a major activity, as the kings were concerned with the achievement of established goals rather than with the formulation of new ones.[33] Thus, active monarchs were personally involved in what in policy-oriented bureaucracies might seem trivial matters of administration and organization, including the appointment of officials. However, in the precolonial state, personnel

---

31. Koenig, 'Early Kon-baung Polity', p. 249.
32. Lieberman, 'Political Significance of Religious Wealth', p. 758.
33. Koenig, 'Early Kon-baung Polity', p. 218.

appointments were far from trivial and the image of an active, knowledgeable monarch who had not only the power but the ability to check on any of his subordinates was a key to the effective use of authority. Through the network of administrators, princes and spies, information about the affairs of state was conveyed to the king, though doubtless distorted in the process by the interests and perceptions of its sources.[34] The early monarchs of a new dynasty or outsiders within the princely group were probably better equipped to judge the value of information than those who had spent their formative years cosseted in the royal palace. The inability of the last Restored Toungoo monarchs as well as the last Konbaung king, Thibaw, to adequately assess their informants' reports may have been a contributory factor in their downfall.

Despite the king's theoretically all-powerful position, the officials who surrounded him, as well as his cultural and political milieu, placed other limitations on the effectiveness of his authority. Growing bureaucratic tendencies in the administration 'restrained him from having a free hand'. There are documented cases of the most powerful Konbaung kings, Bodawpaya, Bagyidaw and Mindon, bowing to the requirements of their administrative advisors, and it would be safe to assume that if records were available similar examples from the Restored Toungoo period could be found.[35]

The augmentation of central power made the capital and central administration the focus of politics in the early modern state in Burma. As noted above, the Restored Toungoo and Konbaung monarchs increased their control over the administration by requiring the royal appanage holders to reside at the court. They supervised their rivals' daily activities and hindered the development of power bases outside the capital. As a consequence, the princes were in closer contact with the centrally appointed court functionaries and state administrators who carried out the king's bidding, and as administrators became attached to princes, rivalry among individuals in these groups sometimes developed.[36]

In theory, all royal princes and court officials were committed to support the monarch. In practice, the linchpin in the system of monar-

---

34. Lieberman, *Burmese Administrative Cycles*, p. 74.
35. Khin Maung Kyi and Tin Tin, *Administrative Patterns in Historical Burma* (Singapore: Institute of Southeast Asian Studies, Southeast Asian Perspectives, no. 1, 1973), p. 56.
36. Trager and Koenig, *Burmese Sit-tans*, p. 19.

chical controls of the administrators stemmed from the king's position as chief patron of the court. It was he who had the final word over the dispersal of appanage grants, rewards and punishments, promotions and demotions. In the day-to-day operations of the court, even the most ambitious princes were aware of their dependency upon the monarch. It would have been a brave or foolhardy man who would challenge a powerful king unless he was certain of the support of many other princes and officials. The king's ability to control his subordinates was further strengthened by 'an elaborate duplication and fragmentation of authority' which allowed him to keep a firm hand through what would now be called 'checks and balances'. The effect may have resulted in less efficient administrative procedures than a more rationalized bureaucratic system would have produced, but it gave the monarch a greater degree of information and leverage on his subordinates and therefore enhanced his political control.[37]

As Lieberman writes, at the beginning of a dynasty the central and the regional élites 'were tied to the throne by a sense of personal obligation for royal patronage, by fear of offending successful warriors, by the desire to associate themselves with kings of obvious religious merit, and by a practical recognition of the benefits that strong government conferred'.[38] While subsequent monarchs often did not possess the charismatic and dominating qualities of the founders of the final two dynasties, these factors continued to operate to ensure the loyalty to the throne of the majority of officials most of the time. The fact that no appointments were permanent (they could be recalled by the monarch) made jockeying for position among administrators a constant factor of central government.

The non-royal officials in the administration had the least secure positions and therefore were of the greatest use to the king. Being ambitious men without the prestige that came with royal birth, they sought to advance by gaining the king's or another patron's favour. All 'were selected on a personal basis' but 'qualification and efficiency were given due consideration.' Appointees to high office in the capital were men who had become skilled in administration and had worked their way up. Entrance into the administrative corps of the precolonial state remained informal and non-rationalized until the mid-nineteenth century, when King Mindon introduced monastic *pahtamabyan* examina-

37. Lieberman, *Burmese Administrative Cycles*, pp. 85–6.
38. Ibid., p. 11.

tions — intended for testing the skills of members of the *sangha* — as a means of indicating candidates' suitability for admission to government service.[39] Until then nothing had been done to alter the patron-client basis of gaining appointment to the royal service.

The monarchs of the Restored Toungoo and Konbaung dynasties divided the affairs of the central state into two different administrative units, though here, as elsewhere in the system, there was some overlap of duties and functions designed to ensure political reliability. Public affairs of state were primarily the responsibility of the Council of Ministers or *hluttaw*, while the Privy Council, or *bye-daik*, saw to the affairs of the king's court and to private matters. This division of responsibilities persisted unchanged throughout the last two dynasties and its continuity is indicative of the reliability of the system from the political perspective of the crown.[40] Like most administrative agencies, the *hluttaw* and *bye-daik* with their respective subordinate staffs were expected to be the instruments of whoever held power. They also provided continuity to the state when the monarch died, even though in theory there was no legal continuity and occasionally in practice there were significant personnel changes, especially at times of crisis in the regime.

The activities of the *bye-daik* were the focus of the court's administration, as it had ready access to the monarch and was in a superior position to the Council of Ministers. All written communications to the monarch went through its machinery, supervised by the four interior ministers, or *atwin-wun*. Not only were the *atwin-wun* able to censor much of the official information which reached the monarch, but they also had access to the workings of the Council of Ministers which the *hluttaw* members did not have in regard to the Privy Council.[41]

Despite its inferior position in terms of access to the monarch, the Council of Ministers was higher in ceremonial rank than the Privy Council, suggesting that symbolically, the affairs of state were more important than the affairs of the king. Normally composed of four chief ministers, or *wun-gyi*, the *hluttaw*, like the *bye-daik*, operated its decision-making process on a collegial basis. This had the effect of limiting the ability of ambitious individuals to rise in authority over their equals, as did the practice of plural appointments to office.[42]

39. Khin Maung Kyi and Tin Tin, *Administrative Patterns*, pp. 50–1.
40. Lieberman, *Burmese Administrative Cycles*, pp. 86–7.
41. *Ibid.*, p. 89.
42. *Ibid.*, p. 87.

The Council of Ministers, like the Privy Council, posed little political threat to the monarch, and although it did occasionally have a hand in the selection of a new king when princely factionalism made a purely dynastic decision impossible, or dominated the throne toward the end of a dynastic line, the officials never attempted to take the throne themselves. There are various reasons for this. One reason was their non-royal antecedents; another was the fact that ministers lacked a clear corporate identity. Being of equal rank, they were generally unwilling to concede the advancement of one of their number over themselves. The competition between the officials in the Privy Council and the Council of Ministers meant that the monarch had the opportunity to play one group of officials off against another, as well as one individual off against another, especially given the absence of clearly-defined responsibilities. The monarch's access to information, or at least gossip, was thus greatly enhanced.

Within the central administrative service, younger officials keen for promotion often conspired with members of the royal family to unseat an incumbent and thus solidify their utility to a prospective king. Royal intrigues led to administrative duplicity but also to political control of ministers and other officials by the royalty as a ruling group.[43] One consequence of the limitations on the administrative power of princes brought about by the Restored Toungoo reforms was an increase in the autonomous power of the king's ministers. In certain regards, the kings became dependent upon the ministers because of their superior knowledge of the affairs of state.[44] While the central administration of the precolonial state did not approximate the Weberian rational-bureaucratic, ideal-typical, modern state,[45] it would be wrong to conclude that many European states at this time were significantly different at the level of court politics. Indeed, an interesting comparison can be drawn from the fact that at the beginning of the development of the modern state in both Europe and Burma there occurred the rise of powerful ministers as key advisers to the monarch in the place of princes and other hereditary figures.

Beneath the *hluttaw* in the central organization, administrative functions were divided between two types of departments. Territorial

43. Ibid., pp. 140–1.
44. Victor B. Lieberman, 'Provincial Reforms in Taung-ngu Burma', *Bulletin of the School of Oriental and African Studies*, XLIII, 3 (1980), p. 566.
45. See Reinhard Bendix, *Max Weber* (Garden City, New York: Anchor Books, 1960), pp. 423–30.

agencies supervised and organized the activities of the geographical zone under their authority regardless of the social categories resident therein. Departmental agencies, on the other hand, were concerned with the administration of the affairs of particular population groups regardless of their place of residence.[46] This overlapping system provided another check from the centre on the activities of officials and limited their ability to control affairs to the monarch's disadvantage.

The population of the nuclear zone and the zone of dependent provinces which were obligated to serve the state was divided into two different categories under the territorial and geographical agencies of the *hluttaw*. Another population category, slaves or debt bondsmen, did not come directly under the authority of the state, as their labour was the resource of their lay or monastic masters. Those men in the service of the crown (*ahmu-dan*), and the free servicemen (*athi*), were the state's greatest resource, and it was in their control that the state's greatest efforts lay. These manpower categories stood in a hierarchical relationship with each other and with the state.

The higher *ahmu-dan* group 'provided the crown with labour on a fixed, rotational basis'.[47] They tended to live nearest the capital and received grants of land and village sites directly from the central state. *Athi* stood in a more independent posture *vis-à-vis* the capital. They were less likely to reside in the irrigated areas of the centre but were found on the periphery of the nuclear zone and the more distant provinces. In contrast to the *ahmu-dan* communities' dependence on the state-maintained irrigation and distribution systems, the villages and fields of the *athi* were primarily the result of their own efforts to develop new agricultural zones.[48] Exempted from regular military service which the *ahmu-dan* were required to provide, the *athi* were subject to a higher level of taxation but received fewer benefits from the state. Both groups were required to provide corvée labour as demanded by the king's officials. Though the *ahmu-dan* were the permanent core of the state's armed forces, in times of need the *athi* would also be required to serve the state as military auxiliaries.[49] *Ahmu-dan* were generally administered by the departmental and *athi* by the territorial agencies.

From this it can be seen that the *ahmu-dan* villages were the most

46. Lieberman, *Burmese Administrative Cycles*, pp. 87–8.
47. *Ibid.*, p. 97.
48. *Ibid.*, p. 105.
49. *Ibid.*, pp. 106–7.

important cellular groups for the power and stability of the throne, and were consequently under the supervision of the *hluttaw* through the service gentry and the departmental officers. In theory their headmen had less autonomy than those of the *athi* communities. The court attempted to control the hereditary taxpayers and servicemen through a system of quotas and censuses. This highly complex system was actually too elaborate for the meagre administrative resources of the monarchical state to maintain, and over time these groups tended to become lost to the court as individuals drifted into slavery, debt-bondage, vagabondage or dacoity.[50] This would necessitate a particular effort to regroup these persons back under central control, and therefore the *hluttaw* was continually seeking to strengthen its control over these groups.[51]

In practice, the officials appointed directly by the king were usually too few in number to maintain effective control over these manpower resources, and the state had to rely on the cooperation of the gentry who were in direct contact with the local communities. As these members of the gentry were not mainly appointed by the court, but were hereditary officials, the court had limited powers of supervision and dismissal over the state's lowest level agents.[52] The officials in charge of territorial administrations, because of the multifaceted aspects of their posts, were in a position to expand their wealth and power by squeezing taxes and manpower resources from their residents without passing the proceeds on to the central state. This not only weakened the power of the centre in an immediate way, but also tended to create long-term economic and political problems for the state as people migrated or otherwise developed techniques for avoiding the exactions of their rulers.[53]

To obviate these problems, the Restored Toungoo monarchs instituted additional reforms intended to increase central control over manpower and other resources. By raising the proportion of hereditary serviceman in the capital zone from roughly 20 to 45 per cent, the centre had a distinct advantage over other zones which were unable to muster the same level of well-equipped military forces. To the south of the

---

50. Normally these persons were not a serious drain on state resources, but at times of crisis they more easily escaped the state's authority and were thus lost to the crown's power-base when most needed. Koenig, 'Early Kon-baung Polity', pp. 128–32.
51. Lieberman, *Burmese Administrative Cycles*, p. 12.
52. *Ibid.*, p. 112.
53. *Ibid.*, p. 91.

nuclear zone the Restored Toungoo monarchs expanded control over subordinate officials and removed some of their intermediary functions in relation to village headmen. 'The principal significance of these reforms which remained in place after the fall of the Toungoo Dynasty (1752) well into the nineteenth century was that they permitted a more efficient integration of dry zone and coastal resources than at any previous time in Burmese history.'[54]

Under the Restored Toungoo and Konbaung kings, the key centrally-appointed provincial administrators were the *myo-wun*. A *myo-wun* was assisted by a clerk who often served as his deputy. In addition, most districts had assigned by the king's ministers a *sit-ke*, who oversaw military and police matters, and a revenue officer or *ahkin wun*, together with a monarchical representative or spy. These officials, especially the *myo-wun*, worked with the township or village headmen and other local hereditary officials, the chiefs of the crown service units and any local agent of the appanage holder in carrying out the state's wishes.[55] Several of these officers, in particular a *sit-ke* and an *ahkin wun*, were assigned to the major Shan *Sawbwa*s' administrations in the eighteenth and nineteenth centuries. The interesting point about such an administrative system at the local level is that while the state did not have the bureaucratic machinery of the colonial state, the early modern state's reformulators had thought through the problems of political and economic control over resources and the maintenance of order. They had done this in such a way as to elaborate a complex system of checks over local powerholders in order to limit their ability to evade central demands, and to make it extraordinarily difficult for them to create any institutionalized power which countervailed that of the state. Such a system obviously made for less than efficient administration, with many opportunities for lines of authority to become crossed and connivance at misdemeanours to take place. It did mean though that by the judicious rotation of officials, the centre could keep extant reliable sources of intelligence on local political activities and problems. This was at the cost, however, of condoning a large measure of what would now be referred to as peculation or corruption.

Given the relative inefficiency of the provincial administration in such

---

54. Lieberman, 'Continuity and Change', pp. 15–16. The exception were the Karen communities around Kaya, the Sittang valley and the Irrawaddy delta. See Koenig, 'Early Kon-baung Polity', pp. 106–8.
55. Trager and Koenig, *Burmese Sit-tans*, p. 38.

a system, the enduring strength of the economic and social order rested on the local hereditary officials (the gentry) who manned the lowest level of the governmental system.[56] The hereditary headmen were essentially of two types: heads of townships (*myo* or *taik*), and heads of villages (*ywa*). During the Restored Toungoo period, in the core of the state there were more than fifty townships, each containing 12 to 145 villages.[57] The heads of townships were normally titled *myo-* (or *taik-*); *thu-gyi* and their subordinate village heads were called *ywa-thu-gyi*, although there was some variation in the titles used. *Thu-gyi* were often assisted by another official known as a *myei-daing*, who 'in his narrowest definition was responsible for arranging and recording the sale of all immovable property in his jurisdiction and took a commission on the sale price'.[58] Most probably, however, the *myei-daing* served as an assistant to the *thu-gyi*, as he had access to many of the important records of the village and thus was able to assist in levying taxation.

The *myo-thu-gyi* and *thu-gyi* were the pillars of the precolonial state's administration. It was they who gathered the revenue and manpower from the villagers. They were 'the pivotal intermediaries between the state and the mass of the peasantry'[59] and, because of their hereditary status, had both personal power and authority derived from their positions as patrons which was denied the transient appointees of the king who supervised their activities.

The *myo-thu-gyi* and *thu-gyi* were probably the descendants of the headmen of occupational groups in the pre-Pagan period. A headman controlled the social unit 'by the power of the personality and the personal loyalty given him by his followers'.[60] However, unlike the headmen of the Pagan and Avan eras, the *thu-gyi* of the *athi* villages in the early modern period all owed their appointment to the crown rather than to the provincial appanage holder or the *myo-wun*. Nonetheless, as membership in the gentry was mainly inherited their authority towards the residents in their communities was derived from their recognized status in society. This contradiction is suggestive of the nature of the political and administrative problems the late early modern state faced in implementing centralizing reforms. The gap between theory and

56. Lieberman, *Burmese Administrative Cycles*, pp. 92–3; Trager and Koenig, *Burmese Sit-tans*, p. 38.
57. Lieberman, *Burmese Administrative Cycles*, p. 93.
58. Trager and Koenig, *Burmese Sit-tans*, p. 40.
59. Adas, 'From Avoidance to Confrontation', p. 22.
60. Aung Thwin, 'Kingship, the *Sangha*', p. 111.

practice, between ideal political authority and the need to work with historically developed customs, meant that old practices often lived on in new guises.

Myo-thu-gyi and *thu-gyi* incomes came primarily from taking a percentage of tax collections, most of which they were obliged to pass on to the king's provincial administrators and any appanage holder. Their incomes were augmented by gifts given in exchange for protection and by favours such as reduced tax and labour demands. These men, who took a long-term perspective on their positions, were loath to invoke extortionate demands on the population, and thus stood in a protective stance *vis-à-vis* their transient superiors who sometimes tried to quickly amass a personal fortune.[61] Thus, quite unexpectedly, the interests of the king and the central state at the top and the headmen at the bottom coincided. Both sought to increase the manpower and resources at their disposal so as to maintain ongoing personal, familial and institutional interests. In contrast, the layer of ambitious court-appointed provincial officials and royal appanage holders sought to rapidly maximize their earnings. The lack of fixed salaries for state officials made such a situation inevitable, and provided one of the key weaknesses of the administrative system of the precolonial state, all the while creating peasant antagonism toward intermediate state authorities.

In addition to levying taxation, the *myo-thu-gyi* and *thu-gyi* were responsible for the supervision of the allocation of corvée labour demands, military service requirements and the maintenance of law and order. They were also responsible for maintaining detailed census records of all their jurisdiction's inhabitants, including name, age, date of birth and service affiliation, if applicable. The *myo-thu-gyi* were in charge of local judicial administration and personally adjudicated petty civil and criminal cases. Given the manifold nature of their duties and their access to the wealth of the entire township or village, the headmen were substantially better off than the average peasant cultivator.[62] Their wealth, allied with their hereditary and state-sanctioned status, allowed them to publicly display their importance and authority. Their housing and mode of transport set them clearly apart from the rest of local society and outwardly connected them with the power of the state.

The authority relationship of the state to the people living on the periphery of the nuclear and dependent province zones was different from

61. Lieberman, *Burmese Administrative Cycles*, p. 93.
62. Trager and Koenig, *Burmese Sit-tans*, p. 39.

that of the central core, and varied from place to place depending on the nature of settlement under various ecological conditions. The relationship of most concern to the centre was with the rulers of the Tai population groups in the Shan plateau. The relationship of the monarch to these people was analogous to that of the *athi* population in terms of corvée labour, military service and taxation obligations. Politically, the rulers of the Tai communities, the *Sawbwas*, had a different relationship with the central state, somewhere between that of the village headman in the nuclear or dependent province zones and that of the semi-independent appanage holders and officials in the lowlands (before the administrative reforms of the Restored Toungoo dynasty). As Lieberman writes, the Tai tributaries' 'prestige in many cases equalled that of Burman princes, [but] in terms of association with the throne and political autonomy, they were analogous to lowland headmen.'[63]

In regard to control over the more sparsely populated, swidden agricultural areas of the surrounding hills, the power of the centre was mainly derived from military, not administrative, strength. These areas had only a small economic surplus for expropriation by the state because of their meagre populations and difficult agricultural conditions. In addition, the administrative weaknesses of the state, as well as poor communications, made control difficult. Nevertheless, the military threat posed by these peripheral areas required that they be kept under central suzerainty.[64] Because administrative reform outside the nuclear and dependent province zones was put off until so late in the Konbaung period, the administrative and political system of the precolonial state persisted there to a large extent into the twentieth century.

Financing the Precolonial State

The state treasury of the precolonial period rested upon an economy which was not, in comparison with either the late European feudal economy or the colonial economy of Burma, a highly dynamic one. The agricultural technology of the period as well as the relatively modest population base of the state made economic expansion difficult. In order to increase the production of agricultural and other products, monarchs sought to increase their populations through the expansion of their

63. Lieberman, *Burmese Administrative Cycles*, p. 137.
64. *Ibid.*, p. 199.

domains and the capture of skilled artisans in war. The administrative system also limited the state's ability to tap fully the local production surplus.

That the precolonial economy can be characterized as essentially a subsistence economy should not, however, obscure the fact that it did provide a sufficient surplus to support an expensive state structure which demonstrated its power through conspicuous consumption, a sizeable standing army relative to the size of the population, heavy expenditures on religious edifices, and the support of a proportionately large Buddhist *sangha*. During the period of the Restored Toungoo and Konbaung monarchs, as part of its efforts to strengthen administrative controls over provincial political and economic power, the state relied increasingly on revenues gained from trade through the southern seaports. Moreover, the relatively long era of stability during the final two dynasties meant that there was a slow but steady increase in domestic production which tended to benefit the state coffers. The spiral of reinforcing factors during this period indicates a strengthening financial base for the state prior to colonization.

Why then, did the state not undertake a fuller rationalization of its revenue and tax system in order to increase the proportion of the economic surplus going to its treasury by introducing institutions similar to those of a modern bureaucratic state? The reason was essentially political. The experience of the monarchical system in Burma was such as to convince kings that they would be unable to control the private power which would probably have resulted from economic expansion and rationalization, even if this would have increased the overall resource base of society and ultimately the state. Besides, full-scale rationalization was then beyond the technical capacity of the state and, given the delicate balance of interests in the political system, the method of indirect revenue collection, coupled with direct taxation upon trade, provided a system that was easy to operate and lucrative in the short term, as well as being a source of political stability. Reform of the existing system, as the events of the final years of the Konbaung dynasty eventually demonstrated, would have resulted in an unmanageable degree of political opposition.

The subsistence aspects of the economy were, moreover, advantageous to the state's controllers inasmuch as these tended to limit the economic aspirations of the bulk of the population; demands by the society on the state for economic improvements were rare. Avoidance of the state, not appeal to it, was the norm. Aware as they were of how small an individual surplus they actually produced and knowing of their governor's conspicuous consumption patterns, the peasantry attempted to evade tax payments. The religious and cosmological justifications for giving financial support to the state were too ephemeral to induce voluntary contributions. Thus, a variety of means of evading state demands were developed, and the inability of the central state's administrative system to penetrate the village beyond the *thu-gyi* made this all the easier. The decentralized nature of the state's accounting and revenue assessment ensured that the central authorities' knowledge of the real resource base of the state was only as great as the honesty of village officials — who felt a certain but limited sense of personal obligation to the provincial administrators but little administrative obligation to the central state. Inasmuch as the provincial administrators and tax collectors were dependent on the reporting of the *myo-thu-gyi* and *thu-gyi* of each township and village for an assessment of taxable resources, these men were in a key position to limit the state's revenues while protecting their populations and increasing the proportion of wealth that could be retained within their areas for their own and their communities' benefit.[65]

The fact that the economy lacked any standard coinage until the reign of King Mindon in the mid-nineteenth century[66] made any system of standard accounting impossible, as well as preventing any significant rationalization of the taxation system. Nonetheless, there was an apparent tendency for greater reliance on coin and commercial taxes in the early modern period, though taxes in kind or as corvée labour remained the norm until near the time of the formation of the colonial state. Herein lay one of the major differences between the precolonial state in Burma and the early modern European state. The greater strength of the European state at the end of the feudal period rested upon its development of an effective, centralized tax system. The absence of such a system in Burma was the consequence not only of various administrative problems but also of the political and ideological principles of the precolonial state.

The wealth of administrators and the local gentry gave them distinct advantages in the economy. This was because their access to surpluses

65. See Koenig, 'Early Kon-baung Polity', for an excellent description of the Konbaung fiscal system.
66. Trager and Koenig, *Burmese Sit-tans*, p. 50; M. Robinson and L.A. Shaw, *The Coins and Banknotes of Burma* (Manchester: published by the authors, 1980), pp. 82–102.

through the power of the state enabled them to be among the few (as noted above) to have more than a subsistence income. As a consequence of an expansion in agricultural production moneylending became an important aspect of the agrarian economy in the nuclear zone, and the most important lenders to the peasantry were state officials, including both administrators and army commanders together with members of the gentry.[67]

The primary basis of the state's finance was taxation of produce. In regard to land tax, by tradition the king could lay claim to one-tenth of all production which 'was . . . viewed as a return for tenancy',[68] thus making no distinction between land rent and land tax. Scholarly authorities differ in their interpretations as to the legal and actual relationship of the peasant to the land he tilled. Examining the legal theory, Koenig and Trager conclude that though the monarch was the 'owner of all land', land could nevertheless 'be owned privately, alienated, mortgaged and inherited'.[69] This view is supported by Hla Aung.[70] Khin Maung Kyi and Tin Tin contend, however, that usufruct did not give peasants the legal right of title suggested in theory. Rather, because land 'revenue formed an important basis of the king's finances, various orders and edicts were issued to confine the cultivator to his land.' Especially for the lowest segments of society, the traditional Burmese social order had some characteristics of a caste system with little social mobility; an individual was sometimes 'permanently shackled to his order'.[71] Rather than the peasant controlling the use of his land, the state used the land to control the peasant.

Theory and practice differ here, and in reality the system described by Khin Maung Kyi and Tin Tin probably predominated in central areas. Such a system was not maintained because of its economic desirability in terms of increasing production, but because of its political utility in controlling manpower. Given the shortage of labour, the absence of technological innovations and the surplus of land, manpower mobility and land

67. Lieberman, *Burmese Administrative Cycles*, pp. 161–3; Ono Toru, 'Konbaung Hkit Kyeitow Ywa Ngweihkyei Sanit' (The village money lending system of the Konbaung era), *Myawati*, March 1976, pp. 37–42.
68. Trager and Koenig, *Burmese Sit-tans*, p. 45.
69. *Ibid*.
70. Hla Aung, 'The Effect of Anglo-Indian Legislation on Burmese Customary Law', in David C. Buxbaum (ed.), *Family Law and Customary Law in Asia: a Contemporary Legal Perspective* (The Hague: Martinus Nijhoff, 1968), p. 78.
71. Khin Maung Kyi and Tin Tin, *Administrative Patterns*, p. 38.

trading were regulated in order to avoid the destruction of customary social relations upon which the king's power and the state's perpetuation depended.[72] The observations of the first British administrator to govern a part of Burma sheds some light on this problem in southern areas. Colonel Maingy, the Commissioner of Tenasserim, wrote in October, 1825:

> Land Tenures. Land is of no value in the Province of Mergui: it was allowed to be cleared indiscriminately by anyone, and held by no title deeds of any kind, nor could I discover that any of the lands so cleared were ever registered or account kept of them, yet they constitute a clear and distinct private property, some of them ancient, and were never interfered with unless owing to those arbitrary measures under the late absolute and despotic Government. Every landholder is allowed to dispose of his property either by sale or gift, and it regularly descends to his family. It sometimes happens but very rarely, that in the transfer of some lands, bills of sale were drawn out but being written on black tablets in general use among the Burmese might be defaced or altered at pleasure.
>
> Any person quitting his land for a season and leaving no one in charge of it could not on his return to claim it, or turn off the actual possessor, without an order from one of the Members of Government, and this could alone be affected by bribery.[73]

Maingy's account provides a clue to the situation in regard to land ownership and its legal status, although the fact that the area he describes was on the periphery of the state doubtless affects the nature of his account, particularly in regard to land clearance. Nearer the capital, and in particular on *ahmu-dan* lands, the state was much more careful in its regulation of land usage.

In general terms, land usufruct was of three kinds. The first, government land, was cultivated by the *ahmu-dan* population on behalf on the state. Private land, the second kind, belonging ancestrally to a family, clan or village, was rarely taxed by the state until the late nineteenth century when a head tax or *thathameda* became the normal method of taxing the *athi* population. Religious lands, which had been donated by individuals and the monarch for the support of the Buddhist *sangha*, were semi-permanent endowments. This third type was worked by pagoda slaves and others for the benefit of the religious institutions

72. *Ibid.*, p. 27.
73. A.D. Maingy, 12 Oct. 1825, in *Selected Correspondence of Letters from and Received in the Office of the Commissioner Tenasserim Division from the years 1825–26 to 1842–43* (Rangoon: Government Printing and Stationery, Burma, 1929), p. 9.

and was not taxed. During the Restored Toungoo and Konbaung dynasties, the alienation of state land to monastic control was relatively unimportant because of the state's firmer control over the monastic order as well as the generally greater wealth available to the state by then.[74]

In essence, the system of government land use seems to have been this: land was in theory owned solely by the king, and therefore his officials had the right, in his name, to determine use and settlement patterns if their authority was appealed to in cases of disputed usufruct. However, in practice, the overwhelming bulk of land was regulated by customary understandings among the villagers under the supervisory authority of the *thu-gyi*. The commonly accepted understandings of the village on land use gave little leverage for the state to interfere in the community and thus helped fend off the intrusion of the state in local affairs. The state was forced to tolerate such a disjuncture between theory and practice in land ownership and usage because it lacked the political power, administrative means or economic necessity to change it; moreover there was no incentive for the development of state-sanctioned legal concepts of property rights as developed in European feudalism.[75]

Unable to administer land in practice, the precolonial state attempted to regulate the people who cultivated the fields and allowed them to determine usage. However, the authority of the state always lay behind the customary arrangements, and when these were disputed by a segment of the community the king's fictive ownership gave his officials the right to intervene. Politically this arrangement proved beneficial to the maintenance of the monarch's monopoly of power by limiting the growth of independent centres of wealth. Any potential for appanage holders or other wealthy individuals to amass large tracts of private land was blocked and therefore the possible development of a decentralized state was obviated. The price the kings of Burma paid for their centralized power was the opportunity for the emergence of a more dynamic and production-oriented internal economy based upon private property, contract, and the security of investment and trade.

In addition to taxes on land and population, taxes on commerce and trade were increasingly important sources of revenue. The equivalent of customs posts were established to control internal and external trade on

74. Lieberman, *Burmese Administrative Cycles*, pp. 278–9.
75. See Douglass C. North and Robert Paul Thomas, *The Rise of the Western World, A New Economic History* (Cambridge University Press, 1973), pp. 19–24.

the reasonably well developed network of cart and high roads and the rivers which connected the major towns,[76] as well as to perform certain police functions involving the movement of population. These posts were manned by crown service men from the *ahmu-dan* population and were supervised by a minister known as the *kin-wun*. During the Konbaung period there were approximately thirty such posts in the nuclear and dependent province zones and another seventeen or so in the Tai-populated areas east and north of the capital area.[77] The revenue raised by these customs posts was increased by the fact that goods travelling from one region to another as well as those leaving or entering as 'foreign' trade were liable to taxation.

Though trade grew in importance for the finances of the central state, land tax or rent as well as non-sanctioned forms of emolument remained the basis of most of the income of the state's intermediate officials as well as the hereditary gentry. As a slight proportion of land tax revenue was actually passed on to the central court, state projects of a military or economic nature depended greatly on the ability of the king's officials to control manpower. Here, corvée or compulsory labour was a key to the state's capacity to carry out its functions.

Men of all classes, even village . . . headmen, were called upon to afford their labour towards the execution of any public work, and towards the defence of the territory. . . . These compulsory labourers received no remuneration from the Government excepting sometimes, although rarely, a small proportion of grain.[78]

The most important use of corvée labour was in building and maintaining the irrigation systems of the central dry zone which formed the original core of the state. The economic vitality of this zone, with its elaborate expenditures on pagodas and state buildings, was crucial to the state's ability to maintain and provision its élite military forces as well as the central court and administrative officials. Thus it can be seen 'that the aim of the Burmese revenue system was to extract agricultural surplus value to maintain the growing administrative system which was a result of the irrigation system.'[79] The irrigation system itself, however,

76. Koenig, 'Early Kon-baung Polity', p. 134.
77. Trager and Koenig, *Burmese Sit-tans*, p. 49.
78. A.D. Maingy, 1 May 1827, in *Correspondence for the Years 1825–26 to 1842–43 in the Office of the Commissioner Tenasserim Division* (Rangoon: Office of the Superintendent, Government Printing, Burma, 1929), p. 62.
79. Khin Maung Kyi and Tin Tin, *Administrative Patterns*, p. 39.

was apparently not managed by the central state's officers but by local authorities.

As noted above, the system of customs posts served both resource gathering and economic and social control functions. Khin Maung Kyi and Tin Tin stress the secondary purpose of this system (control) over the first, for it was intended, they argue, 'to inhibit any spontaneous growth of commerce'.[80] According to their view, the state attempted consciously to preserve the original agrarian basis of society, and the economic relations therein, from the competition which would have evolved from the growth of free trade and private capital formation and the classes which these would have spawned. While the customs revenue system, like the land revenue system and sumptuary laws, doubtless had this effect, it is arguable as to whether the king and his ministers perceived this as their purpose. Aware of their immediate problems of revenue and political control, and perhaps unaware of the inhibiting effect of their policies on the economic potential of the country, they used the land and customs systems as ways of gaining revenue and of ensuring the state's perpetuation. Customs checks provided a means of monitoring centrally the flow of manpower and other resources in a way no other institution could in such a diffuse administrative system.

It is difficult to estimate what proportion of the economy's surplus reached the state's coffers. The nominally prescribed and religiously sanctioned rate of 10 per cent *ad valorem* taxation was avoided by practices established to reduce the officially recorded value of goods. Misrepresentations and false reporting, as well as the deduction of commissions by headmen, tax collectors and appanage holders, meant that probably only about one-third of tax revenue actually got through the system to the central state institutions.[81] The level of actual taxation must have varied depending upon the rapacity of the local collectors as well as the demands of the state. According to a British account of 1825, the previous court-appointed *myo-wun* in Tenasserim had set the rates quite arbitrarily — though at reasonably low levels.[82] The rate probably went up at times of war or other regime crises and this, rather than the weakness of the state *per se*, speeded the decline of dynasties as they were

80. *Ibid.*, p. 38.
81. Oliver B. Pollack, *Empires in Collision: Anglo-Burmese Relations in the Mid-Nineteenth Century* (Westport, Conn.: Greenwood Press, 1979), p. 117.
82. A.D. Maingy, 12 Oct. 1825, *Selected Correspondence* p. 12.

forced to exact more and more revenue from a shrinking resource base.⁸³

Given the patron-client nature of most authority relationships in the precolonial state, heavy taxation almost inevitably led to a declining tax base. This was because individuals sought to transfer their residence and/or clientage to an area with headmen, appanage holders and officials who were less demanding, or to abandon settled occupations for vagabondage or dacoity. As the size of the state's institutions grew after the founding of the Restored Toungoo dynasty, and as its demands for revenue consequently increased due to its enlarged political patronage as well as continuing religious patronage obligations, so the court attempted to tap more of the resources of those most immediately under its control.

Burma's increasing involvement in Indian Ocean trade from the late sixteenth century onwards undermined the traditional reliance of the state on agrarian-based sources of revenue and provided the financial means for implementing provincial reforms. It also assisted in the amendment and consolidation of the appanage system under the central court.⁸⁴ Lieberman points out three important ways in which this economic change assisted in state consolidation:

> It assisted economic integration and thus helped indirectly to erode regional loyalties that, by definition, were inimical to central authority; it provided Ava with a major source of cash income needed for political patronage and military expeditions; and it furnished the crown with firearms, which afforded a reliable advantage over more traditionally equipped rebels.⁸⁵

The importance of trade with the Indian Ocean and the taxes derived from there can be seen from the fact that by the late eighteenth century, cash income from trade through the port of Rangoon was greater than cash revenues from the traditional Kyaukse irrigated agricultural zone of central Burma.⁸⁶ The total wealth of the economy grew as a result of this trade. The increased strength of the state which followed led in turn to longer periods of tranquility under the Restored Toungoo and Konbaung kings, permitting some modest expansion of agricultural production and internal trade.⁸⁷ Even if the early modern state did not

83. Thus also increasing transaction costs and causing greater financial losses to the state. North and Thomas, *Rise of the Western World*, p. 87.
84. Lieberman, *Burmese Administrative Cycles*, p. 124.
85. *Ibid.*, p. 117.
86. Koenig, 'Early Kon-baung Polity', pp. 240–2.
87. Lieberman, 'Continuity and Change,' p. 18.

develop the capacity to mobilize resources for the state's benefit to the same degree as the colonial and postcolonial state, increased economic productivity resulting from the state's enhanced power laid the basis, by the seventeenth century, for the growth of a more centralized administrative system. The economic reforms, including the initial countrywide monetization introduced by Mindon in the nineteenth century, were the forerunners of the production and trade-oriented state of the late nineteenth and early twentieth centuries.[88]

The Agencies of the Precolonial State

The hierarchical territorial organization and authority relations which provided the order of the precolonial state were designed to enable the rulers to carry out their primary duties of control, security and resource accumulation. This élite identified the interests of the state with their own interests. Therefore, the perpetuation of the state was not merely a matter of abstract problems of government, but of the actual continuity of the traditional ruling strata of royalty, officialdom and gentry. The leaders used military, economic, religious and legal instruments to perpetuate themselves and the state.

During the precolonial period the activities of the central state would have seemed less obvious and obtrusive to the populace than would be the case today, for far more of the regulatory aspects of people's lives were controlled by the patron-client system in the cellular organization of traditional society. Members of different population categories, *ahmudan*, *athi*, slave, Tai, or swidden agriculturalists, knew what the state expected of them and their patron's tasks were normally carried out without the need to invoke the structures of the state or the use of physical coercion. In any event, the weakness of the state's coercive instruments limited the latter option, and this allowed the people to have some degree of self-protection in their relationship with officialdom.

As the areas of settled agriculture and concentrated population slowly grew or shifted, the kings sought to increase the power domain of the state. In order to ensure an adequate economic surplus to maintain the state, new land settlements, the expansion of settled agricultural lands and the development of irrigation systems in the dry zone of central Burma were initiated. In particular, the kings sought to increase the pro-

---

88. See Pollack, *Empires in Collision*, pp. 113–36.

portion of the population classified as *ahmu-dan*, as it was these who owed the most direct royal service and were the most reliable taxpayers. The obverse side of this effort was to ensure that as few persons as possible became classified as slaves to monastic or lay masters and thus lost to the resources of the state. It was the responsibility of the king's officials, both appointed and hereditary, to ensure that these manpower controls were maintained to the state's benefit, and when, instead, the officials used their centrally authorized power for their personal benefit, it was the monarch's task to reimpose control over them. Given the diffuse nature of power in the precolonial state, the maintenance of central control was extremely difficult, and organization and force alone were insufficient. Of great importance to the state was the charisma of the monarch and the ratification of the state's legitimacy created by customary religious beliefs and practices.

Nevertheless, the coercive and defensive power provided by the king's army was the key to the maintenance of the precolonial state's control. This was the force with which the court defended itself against external enemies and maintained its dominance over internal rivals. Any decline in the military capacity of the centre, as at the end of the Restored Toungoo dynasty, made possible the raising of a provincial rebellion and the toppling of the incumbent monarch. The standing army of the classical state was based upon the obligation of the *ahmu-dan* population to provide military service on a rotational basis. *Athi* could be called upon at times of war to assist the state's standing army and recruits to the king's service were sought through the capture of prisoners in battle and from the peoples residing among the tributary groups in the hills.

What distinguished the Restored Toungoo and Konbaung dynasties from their predecessors in this regard, giving the early modern period one of its unique aspects, was the apparent fact that the standing army was both more concentrated and larger than that which had existed in previous periods. By 1862 the standing army was estimated to number about 56,130 men, perhaps slightly more than 1 per cent of the population,[89] compared to about 0.5 per cent of the population today. The enhanced military power of the centre had a consequent deterrent effect, limiting the need for the state to use the army for suppressing frequent internal revolts and forestalling external assaults on its domains. This allowed time for the development of a more effective administrative system to control the population. Unlike the First Toungoo dynasty

---

89. *Ibid.*, p. 119.

which, had 'no internal administrative structure per se.' and therefore relied on punitive expeditions as 'the principal means of maintaining order',[90] the Restored Toungoo and Konbaung dynasties used primarily administrative mechanisms to maintain order, security and population control.

In comparison with the organization of the modern army, the military force of the precolonial state was not rationally organized with clear-cut command structures from the political centre downward. Rather, the army reflected the pattern of political relations which existed in society. It was hierarchical, but the effectiveness of command rested not upon the impersonal authority of rank but upon patron-client relationships. Commanders of platoons were more in the way of patrons than commanding officers as understood today. They were open to persuasion through gifts, and sought to maintain the strength of their units by offering material inducements such as greater status or reduced taxes to men to serve under them. The link between the platoon commanders and their superiors in the court and *hluttaw* was also based upon patron-client ties.[91]

The army of the precolonial state in its later periods was in some ways comparable to the military organization of the early modern European state where military commanders operated much more in the sense of private entrepreneurs rather than as state officials. European kings used indentured companies, then foreign mercenaries and finally *corps entretenus* to form the backbone of their fighting forces. 'The common assumption was that the king would commission a gentleman to raise, equip, officer and lead a given force of men: the king paid him, he for his part did the rest, and if any money stuck to his fingers, this was after all his livelihood.'[92] (As indeed it was for the commanders of the king of Burma's platoons who were members of the gentry class or court officials.) One sought to rise into élite military units, for it was upon these that the king disposed his largess most generously. Some of the king's forces may have actually been spared the drudgery of growing their own food on land assigned to them by the court as they were paid cash salaries instead.[93] It is not possible to determine to what degree the

90. Lieberman, 'Political Significance of Religious Wealth', p. 763.
91. Lieberman, *Burmese Administrative Cycles*, pp. 102–5.
92. Samuel E. Finer, 'State- and Nation-Building in Europe: The Role of the Military', in Charles Tilly (ed.), *Formation of National States in Europe* (Princeton University Press, 1975), pp. 100–1.
93. Lieberman, *Burmese Administrative Cycles*, p. 102.

kings of Burma encroached upon the powers and independence of the platoon commanders during the final years of the precolonial state as they sought to increase their direct control over the state's army, although it is known that the army became fully salaried in 1872.[94] By then, of course, the kings had the model of the European army from which to borrow and adapt institutional practices.

That cash payments had begun to be important in the organization and maintenance of the Burma army during the late classical period suggests that the power of the centre to regulate the armed forces was increasing. The reforms introduced by the Restored Toungoo dynasty, and the hiring of foreign military advisers in the nineteenth century also demonstrates that the rationalization of the armed forces commenced before colonization. It is often forgotten that European armies of the twentieth-century First and Second World War type are distinctly the product of this century. In Europe, 'wholly native armies were a product of the nineteenth century',[95] but this was never the case among the military forces of the European empires in Asia, even in the twentieth century. Native armies are the consequence of nationalism, a political force which was not to touch upon military organization in Burma or most of the old world until this century.

The increasing rationalization of the king's army toward the end of the early modern period was a factor behind the growing reliance of the state upon cash and taxes on internal commerce, as well as foreign trade. This same pattern had developed in Europe as well, and the experience of other mainland Southeast Asian states was probably the same. Until more research is concluded on the political role and nature of the army in the precolonial state and its relationship with the economy and local authority, little more can be confidently said.

The state's perception of the threats to its power from secular economic forces, provincial officials and local gentry has been outlined above. The problem of religious power in the history of Burma during the precolonial period is a much documented feature of the political order and shows most clearly how the state used certain nominally extrastate agencies for its perpetuation. Here, of course, the monarchs were in part over-reacting, for the rival power of the institutions of the Buddhist religion was dependent upon the state and cyclical in nature; it waxed and waned, and could always be brought to heel under the dominance of

---

94. Pollack, *Empires in Collision*, p. 119.
95. Finer, 'State- and Nation-Building', p. 101.

the state, whereas bureaucratic or feudal power, as European monarchs learned, tended to grow unilinerally and therefore required the increasing growth of centralized power in order to keep control of the autonomous centres that private trade makes possible. For the kings of Burma, the growth of autonomous religious power posed a similar continual political concern, though one of a smaller magnitude.

Because 'the relationship between secular and religious pressures was probably reciprocal rather than lineal and sequential' in Burma's precolonial political system,[96] as the power of the religious institutions grew the state was proportionately weakened, and therefore not only did the ruler's ability to control religious institutions decline, but so also did his ability to control secular society. Private and personal wealth then tended to increase, further weakening the state in a process which, if not halted, would have made the king and his state merely *primus inter pares* among the institutions of society. The state's ability to control the political and economic system would then have declined and Burma would have once more been broken up into a number of petty principalities, as in the Avan interregnum. Had the state, as a consequence of the Restored Toungoo reforms, not been able to centralize political power in the Irrawaddy valley, then perhaps a form of feudalism would have emerged, but this was precluded by the powerful central monarchs.

From the perspective of the monarch, the state had to intervene in the affairs of the Buddhist *sangha* to curb religious institutional autonomy. In the process, the state also curbed secular independent wealth by stopping the drift of religious wealth into secular hands. This action, furthermore, re-sacralized the monarch, and thus regained both the faith's political support and a secular and religious economic surplus for the central state. Aung Thwin's description of *sangha* reform in the classical period aptly describes this:

Burmese kings initiated *sasana* reform, or purification of the *sangha*, to regain some of this wealth in a legal and socially acceptable manner. A rich *sangha* meant of course, that the monks were no longer living according to the rules of the *Vinaya*: therefore, reform was ideologically justifiable. *Sasana* reform had the material effect of reducing the size of the *sangha* (and so the tax-free sector), and the ideological effect of purifying it. The reform also enabled the state to regain both cultivable land and labour resources subject to its corvée, and to impose per capita taxes on previously exempt categories. Purifying the Order eliminated sanctuaries for rebel leaders, pretenders to the throne, and other

96. Lieberman, 'Political Significance of Religious Wealth', p. 756.

political opponents to the rulers. The entire process returned usable resources and political security to the state, giving it a new 'lease on life'. Once the *sangha* was purified, however, it began to attract greater public patronage, for the quality of individual merit was contingent on the purity of the monks one supported. The *sangha* also began once more to incur royal favor, since doctrine held the king to be protector and perpetuator of the Religion. Public and royal patronage culminating in monastic landlordism eventually recurred — and once more the state had to intervene to reform the *sangha* — the cycle continued.[97]

It was the inability of the last Pagan dynasty kings to implement *sasana* reform effectively that apparently led to its 'internal decay and fall' in 1287[98] and created major problems for the First Toungoo dynasty as late as the 1590s.[99]

The situation was more complex in the time of the Restored Toungoo dynasty. The phenomenon of *sasana* reform indicates not the autonomous power of the *sangha* even when at its most powerful, if corrupt, but rather its ultimately dependent relationship with the state. In the longer term institutional interest of the religion its purification and control by the state was necessary, and the senior leaders of the monkhood, including the chief abbot or *thathanabaing* who was appointed by the king, were doubtless aware of this. The dependence of the monkhood on the state was solidified by reforms carried out in the time of the Restored Toungoo dynasty. The disintegration of the religion during the Avan period gave the newly centralized state the power to require that monastic lands be cultivated by crown servicemen and taxpayers, rather than pagoda slaves, and therefore their economic surplus beyond the subsistence needs of the tilling peasants and the income requirements of the local monastery were now taxable by the state.[100]

Some scholars have gone so far as to argue that state encouragement of the Theravada form of Buddhism with its requirement for 'the *sangha* to ignore all worldly gains, money and economics,' was a direct consequence of the early kings' desire to maintain control of the country's wealth; and that consequently later kings ensured that Buddhism was the only recognized and encouraged religious form in the country.[101] Whatever the case, the control of the *sangha* was to the

97. Aung Thwin, 'Role of *Sasana* Reform', pp. 672–3.
98. Aung Thwin, 'Kingship, the *Sangha*', p. 206.
99. Lieberman, *Burmese Administrative Cycles*, pp. 109–10.
100. Lieberman, 'Continuity and Change', p. 19.
101. Khin Maung Kyi and Tin Tin, *Administrative Patterns*, p. 45.

advantage of the state and the purity the state could impose upon the *sangha* was to the advantage of the religion. The king always had the final say as to whether monastic practices were legitimate, and he maintained this power through his ability to grant 'tax-exempt status or royal endorsement and approval' through patronage of those institutions and practices which were legitimate *'as interpreted by the king'*.[102]

The relationship of the state to religion in precolonial Burma was similar in some broad respects to that which existed between the monarch and the clerical orders in early modern Europe. Like the kings of Burma, European kings involved in the formation of the early modern state 'had little autonomous coercive power at their disposal' and therefore 'clerics were useful partners' in both an administrative and a legitimizing sense. Religious organization in Europe's Christian orders and the Theravada Buddhist *sangha* were dissimilar, especially in regard to the fact that the pre-national Christian churches had in Rome a suprastate authority to which to appeal. But from the perspective of the state they both had the advantage of having on the one hand, large, wealthy and respected organizations, but on the other, a disadvantage, unlike soldiers, landlords and the gentry class, in converting 'state resources under their control into transmissable private property. They were also less apt to build their own rival dynasties.'[103] The celibacy of the monkhood made it easier for the state to remain the dominant partner in their reciprocal relationship, while its kingdom-wide institutions provided a useful means of communications when the secular administrative order failed to respond to central edicts.

One of the most important indicators of the differences between the precolonial state in Burma in comparison with the early modern state in Europe is the absence of an articulated, country-wide and centrally-administered legal and court system. Herein lay a political strength for the monarch and the perpetuation of the state's monopoly of power, but an administrative weakness and a hindrance to the development of a more integrated political system. The kings of the Restored Toungoo and Konbaung dynasties, until late in the nineteenth century, made few if any attempts to modify the system of the administration of justice which they inherited from the Pagan kingdom. In the main, the state's judicial system rested on the principle that most cases could be settled at the local level by arbitration supervised by village, township and provin-

102. Aung Thwin, 'Role of *Sasana* Reform', p. 681, emphasis in the original.
103. Charles Tilly, 'Reflections on the History of European State-Making', in Tilly (ed.), *Formation of National States in Western Europe*, p. 63.

cial officials. Law and custom were little distinguished and legal codes were intended more as guides to moral conduct than as principles of decision and right. The general concept of law was radically different from that in the modern European state. Viewed like the laws of nature, they were 'a statement of cause and effect', and decisions were to be based upon 'reasonableness' more than 'legality' as found in codified law.[104] The most important law codes, based upon the Indian-derived Code of Manu, were intended to provide 'a compilation in easy-to-read Burmese that judges could understand'.[105]

There was a formal appeals procedure from the lower courts to the *hluttaw* with ultimate appeals on its decisions to the king himself, and more formal judge's courts were established in the capital and major towns.[106] However, there was little effort made to distinguish between the state's executive officers and its judicial officers or functions, and the judicial system was marked by a high degree of personalized behaviour, with little procedure other than prevailing notions of status and etiquette. Indeed, until reforms were introduced during the reign of King Thibaw, most courts were conducted in the private residences of officials.[107] The inability of the central state to provide more than a mere guide to the law meant that there was a distinct absence of uniform decisions throughout the kingdom and local customs generally provided individuals with notions of their rights and obligations.

A more rationalized judicial system would have speeded the centralization of the state and the homogenization of the population. However, such a system would have been dependent upon codes of law which would have established more clearly not only the rights of individuals in civil law *vis-à-vis* one another, but also the subject's rights in relationship to the state. The question of the legal protection of private property would have arisen and the state's ability to monopolize wealth would probably have diminished. Obscure, moralistic codes allowed for the continuity of local customs and ideas of ownership and usufruct, but also provided no bar for the state to intervene in the distribution and use of secular or religious land, labour and other economic resources. The codes also created no notions of legal equality of

104. Hla Aung, 'Effect of Anglo-Indian Legislation', p. 75.
105. Lieberman, *Burmese Administrative Cycles*, p. 263.
106. Alan Gledhill, 'Burma', in John Gilissen (ed.), *Bibliographical Introduction to Legal History and Ethnology*, vol. E, no. 7 (Brussels: Editions de l'Institut de Sociologie, Université Libre de Bruxelles, 1970), p. 10.
107. Khin Maung Kyi and Tin Tin, *Administrative Patterns*, p. 53.

individuals in the eyes of the state, and thus helped preserve the hierarchical, patron-client structures of society. Informal law meant that informal bonds of protection were necessary for the weak. In the precolonial state, law, like the army, the administrative system, the economic order and the religious institutions, was used for the maintenance of royal authority upon which the monarchs depended for the perpetuation of their state.

The Legitimacy of the Precolonial State

Throughout the precolonial period, doubtless the strongest basis for the perpetuation of the state was its clear and unchallenged claims to legitimacy. In the intellectual climate of traditional society, a subject which has yet to be studied fully,[108] it appears that the idea of progress and cumulative linear change coupled with a notion of the separation of society from the state did not exist, and it was thus natural to accept the inevitability of the existing political order. That order was buttressed by both religious doctrine and customary beliefs, and was rarely brought into question until the arrival of rival religions and ideologies from Europe in the early modern period. The king, as the centre of the state, was the focus of the state's legitimizing ideology. The king's claim to be the lord of all life and resources within his kingdom was the basis of the power of his officers, from the *hluttaw* to the *thu-gyi*, to demand taxes, labour and military service from his subjects. In so doing, the king accepted a reciprocal obligation to his subjects to maintain social order for both their economic and physical security and their religious salvation. This in turn justified the economic system of the state as well as the state's intimate involvement in the supervision and management of the institutions of the Buddhist *sangha*.

The apparent continuity of the legitimizing ideology of the classical state has its partial parallel in the development of the modern European state. Even though, as mentioned earlier, the actual functioning of the administrative and political system of the state in Burma was altered during the final two dynasties, there was no obvious change in its justifying ideology. Just as some state-makers in modern Europe justified

---

108. See Koenig, 'Early Kon-baung Polity', ch. 3, 'The State I. — Kingship and Political Thought', pp. 158–217, for the best available guide. See also Donald Eugene Smith, *Religion and Politics in Burma* (Princeton University Press, 1965), pp. 12–37.

The Legitimacy of the Precolonial State 55

their actions on the basis of the tradition of Roman law stretching back for more than 700 years through European tradition,[109] so also did the kings of Burma rely on the doctrines of the Pagan kingdom to justify their rule. The crucial difference between Europe and Burma was in the nature of the classical tradition. In Europe this was a set of legal codes and practices guaranteeing the protection of property and profit from the monopolist desires of the state, whereas in Burma tradition upheld the state's claim to all wealth and power.

The ultimate basis in the belief structure of classical Burma for the legitimacy of the state stemmed from the monarch's descent from the first king of the earthly world, Mahasmmat (*thammata*). He had been 'elected' by the people in exchange for a share of their resources so as to create order out of the natural anarchy of man's condition. Man was inherently greedy and lustful, and these human failings caused him to seek to gain advantage over his fellows which, while to the short-term material advantage of the individual, was to the long-term spiritual disadvantage. The king was 'elect' in two senses. First, he was chosen by the people; secondly, and more importantly, he was morally superior to them, and therefore it was safe and wise to entrust all power in him. In this conception of the social contract, man abandoned all his rights to the state in exchange for total protection. There was no notion of society (man in relationship with his fellows) having any collective rights *vis-à-vis* the state.[110] The consequent unequal division of rights between the king and the populace provided the justification for the social status system, including the 'distinction between the common man and the royal *ahmudan*; and within this *ahmudan* class, the rights and privileges of the people were divided according to their office'.[111]

The ideology of classical kingship was composed of many elements. All were interrelated and sanctioned by the teachings of Theravada Buddhism or by folk beliefs about local and regional gods known as *nats*. Individuals throughout society were taught these doctrines through the life cycle of the Buddhist institutions and through village drama which shaped the views of the population. The ideology also found support in the political history of the precolonial state, for the historical memory of

109. Tilly, 'Reflections on the History of European State-Making', p. 25.
110. Lieberman, *Burmese Administrative Cycles*, p. 65; Aung Thwin, 'Divinity, Spirit, and Human', p. 52; Tambiah, *World Conqueror and World Renouncer*, pp. 13–14; a modern Burmese version is found in Aung Hsan, 'Naingnganyei Amyomyo', *Dagun Maggazin* ('Kinds of Politics', *Dagon Magazine*), no. 234, pp. 61–70.
111. Khin Maung Kyi and Tin Tin, *Administrative Patterns*, pp. 46–7.

the social disorder and personal insecurity which occurred when there was no powerful king to impose order remained strong. While the state could be an evil force in the life of man, demanding, perhaps unfairly, wealth and labour, and even life itself, it, like other evils of existence such as fire and flood, was also necessary and had to be borne for the benefits it granted.

The classical Burmese concept of kingship contained within it several notions of the nature of the monarch himself. He was first of all a human, a man; albeit a superior one. The ruler was obliged to create order primarily by his moral example and the powers of persuasion that his moral superiority provided him. When these failed he was able to use force to gain his ends, although the ultimate purpose of his actions had to be for the good of the religion. Thus he had justification for violating the Buddhist doctrines about the evil of war and killing.[112] On this basis was developed the system of criminal law, *yazawut*, or king's business, which made murder, theft, arson and rebellion crimes against him and the state. His role as *dhammaraja* or lord of the law also made him responsible for the physical well-being of his subjects and this provided the ideological justification for the state's economic system.[113] There existed a dialectic in this notion of kingship that posed severe problems for the legitimacy of the monarch. His power was justified by his ability to maintain order and welfare and to uphold the *dhamma* (law), but if he failed to do so his legitimacy was doubted and therefore rebellion against him became justified.[114] Hence his need to resort to force to maintain order; but an excessive reliance upon coercion rather than example would begin to create doubts in people's minds about his moral superiority.

It was his role as *dhammaraja* which gave the king his power to purify the Buddhist monkhood. Law, understood by the term *dhamma*, was the norm of correct behaviour as comprehended in Buddhist thought. In practice, in relationship to the monkhood, the law is explained in the rules of monastic conduct knows as the *vinaya*. The *vinaya* enjoins members of the *sangha* to abstain from sexual acts or other lustful behaviour, from the possession and enjoyment of wealth and property, and from involvement in the mundane pleasures and entertainments of lay society. Though normally self-regulating, when monks violated these norms and the *sangha* was unable to expell lax members or reform its institu-

112. Aung Thwin, 'Divinity, Spirit, and Human', pp. 52-3.
113. *Ibid.*, p. 54.
114. Lieberman, *Burmese Administrative Cycles*, pp. 67-8.

tional practices, it was the right, even the duty, of the king to intervene and purify the membership and practices of the religious order.[115] Indeed, a king who successfully carried out a purification of the monkhood enhanced his own legitimacy by demonstrating to both lay and religious subjects the strength of his commitment to the upholding of the *dhamma*. While himself subject to the requirements of the law he was also the law's protector, and his unquestionable power, if used righteously, could not only not be questioned but had to be honoured.

'Technically separate from but conceptually related' to the idea of the *dhammaraja* is the notion of the king as being a *cakkavatti*, a universal monarch or world conqueror.[116] As a *cakkavatti*, the king laid claim to being the supreme ruler on earth and from this claim stemmed the obligation of all humans to obey him. It was, in a sense, the source of his and the state's claim to sovereignty but in a form quite different from the idea of sovereignty which developed in European monarchical traditions. This difference resulted in a significant divergence in the development of the state's notions of political order in Europe and Burma, and was one of the ideological hindrances to political unity in the classical and precolonial states in Burma and elsewhere in Southeast Asia. As a universal monarch, not just one of several equally sovereign monarchs within separate territories, the Burmese king was obliged to ensure that within his domain other, lesser monarchs, be allowed to exist.[117] As long as these minor monarchs possessed neither the wealth nor the power to challenge his supremacy, and their domains possessed no important sources of wealth that his state could easily tap, he had no justification for their elimination or the incorporation of their subjects under his direct authority. There was thus an ideological justification for the maintenance of the notion of political and perhaps even ethnic pluralism under the single supreme monarch. It was for this reason that the tributary states of the Shan plateau and states further from the nuclear and dependent province zones were not absorbed more rapidly into the administrative system of the state. The king had to demonstrate his universal conquering powers by a continual display of military victory, but he was constrained from pushing his conquests to their administrative conclusion by destroying local authorities on the edge of the kingdom.

The strength of the king's earthly claims to legitimacy was

115. Aung Thwin, 'Divinity, Spirit, and Human', p. 54.
116. *Ibid.*, p. 55.
117. Tambiah, *World Conqueror and World Renouncer*, pp. 46–7.

reinforced by the power of his image as a semi-divine figure. The king was popularly thought of and often self-described as an emergent Buddha or *bodhissatta* (*hpayalaung* in Burmese). As Aung Thwin writes,

> Although Therevada Buddhist doctrine teaches that each person is ultimately responsible for his or her salvation, in a living community where reciprocity and redistribution were expressions of social concern, and in which those having more merit [as demonstrated by their superior position] shared with those having less, salvation was in practice, the responsibility of the economically endowed. When kings shared their abundant store of merit with their subjects, the latter's chances for salvation by a better rebirth were significantly enhanced. In effect then, the king was like a personal saviour, resembling the compassionate Mahayanist *bodhistva*, filling the void left by the Theravadan *pacceka buddha* who sought salvation only for himself.[118]

In other words, the king, through his display of wealth and solace for the less well off, filled a psychological void in the practice of ascetic Buddhist salvation techniques. The theoretical remoteness and selfishness of the monk who sought his personal salvation with the support of society was countered by the supreme monarch who, though himself capable of gaining Buddhist enlightenment, *nirvana*, and of leaving the toil and travail of the mundane world, held back in order to help in the salvation of those less endowed with merit than himself. The king sacrificed himself for the benefit of man and of religion by his protection of the religion and by the maintenance of order.

This religious aspect of the legitimacy of the king should not, however, be over-emphasized, for kings and the government in Burma, like elsewhere, were seen by most people, most of the time, not as deities on earth but as human rulers.[119] The ideological complex that provided the legitimacy of the Buddhist state in the classical period was much more complex than these Buddhist-derived theories would indicate. Important in this complex of ideas was the monarch's incorporation of various forms of religious and customary beliefs in Burma, most especially the propitiation and support of the cult of the thirty-seven *nats*. This cult was particularly important for its unifying aspect, binding together distinct parts of the country in a commonly-accepted belief about the unity of the kingdom by integrating provincial and local gods into a kingdom-wide pantheon. It also tied the present with the past through ceremonies which contained significant aspects of ancestor

---

118. Aung Thwin, 'Divinity, Spirit, and Human', pp. 56–7.
119. *Ibid.*, pp. 59, 71–2.

worship linking the present king to the first king of Burma and to his ancestors.[120]

However individuals in different periods interpreted the reasons for the legitimacy of the monarch, the ultimate basis of the monarchy stemmed from the notion of *karma*. In Burmese Buddhist thought, as Lieberman nicely puts it, 'The Burmese never asked, "Why is there no necessary correlation between reward and virtue?," for in the Burmese view the correlation was perfect.'[121] To a Burmese Buddhist, the doctrine of *karma* explains one's present status and existence as being the result of the merit (*kutho*) that one has earned through virtuous behaviour in previous incarnations. High or low status, power or slavery, are not the consequence of current behaviour and labour. These are the consequences of previous action and there is nothing one can do to alter one's situation. One can only live virtuously in the expectation that one's position will improve in the next life. Therefore, if one was born or became king, it was because his *karma* was the best of any in the land. Merit causes glory in the logic of Theravada Buddhism.[122]

In contemporary parlance, a king's *hpon* (charismatic glory, innate power), *let-yon* (force, especially military force) and *a-na* (domination, authority) were proportional to the maturity of his Perfections and to his accumulation of good *karma*. These in turn were the keys of Omniscience.[123]

If legitimacy stems from the monarch's *karma*, then illegitimacy and the justification for rebellion against the monarch had to stem from the bad *karma* of the incumbent. Despite the conservative nature of much Buddhist thought as applied to politics, it was not a doctrine which made rebellion impossible. When an unjust or ineffective king was overthrown, he had the act of his demise interpreted in terms of the fact that his *karma* was insufficient to maintain the throne. In fact, the very act of his removal from office was proof not only of this but also of the fact that his successor, the leader of the revolt against him, possessed superior *karma* and therefore rightly deserved the throne.[124] The

---

120. *Ibid*, p. 64; Lieberman, 'Continuity and Change', pp. 7–8.
121. Lieberman, *Burmese Administrative Cycles*, p. 71; Aung Thwin, 'Divinity, Spirit, and Human', p. 69.
122. Aung Thwin, 'Divinity, Spirit, and Human', p. 40; Melford E. Spiro, *Buddhism and Society: A Great Tradition and Its Burmese Vicissitudes* (New York: Harper and Row, 1972), pp. 442–4.
123. Lieberman, *Burmese Administrative Cycles*, p. 72.
124. *Ibid.*, p. 75.

fundamental conservatism of the legitimacy principles of the classical state, justified by the Buddhist theory of the nature of man, however, is revealed in this, for it was not contemplated that a different form of government other than a monarchy could ever replace an unjust king, or that a new monarch had to do more than rule justly in order to demonstrate his *karma*.

Politics under the Precolonial State

The usual image of politics in the precolonial period of Burma's history is that of dynastic politics. The rise and fall of dynastic lines as a consequence of the inability of kings to create self-perpetuating ruling institutions separate from their own person has been uncritically accepted by several generations of students of Burma. There is a degree of truth in this image, but as has been suggested in the work of Lieberman, and reiterated in this Chapter, politics (at least during the last two dynasties) was more institutionalized, centralized and complex than previously allowed. Going further than Lieberman, it has been argued here that in fact the seeds of the contemporary state are to be found in the reforms instituted by the Restored Toungoo and Konbaung monarchs as they came to grips with the opportunities and challenges that changing economic and social conditions provided them with.

A more probing examination of politics and society during the early modern period requires a study not only of court politics, but also of the relationship of provincial officials and the local gentry with the central state and each other, as well as the ways in which the peasantry, the bulk of the population, responded politically to the requirements of their distant and immediate superiors. In examining the relationship of the court, the officialdom and gentry, and the peasants, to the state, one has to remember that the aims of the state were perceived differently by these elements of the polity. To the royalty, the state was the means to the perpetuation of their privileged places in society. To the officialdom and gentry, it was a set of mechanisms which allowed them to perpetuate their difficult hereditary or appointed positions in the state's intermediary administrative structure. In many ways, theirs were the most difficult political roles to play, but the financial and personal benefits were sufficiently greater than those which could be derived from tilling the soil, and no one gave up a position easily. To the peasantry, the state was probably more of a burden than a blessing most of the time, but there were few long-term choices available given the tyranny of chaos that would emerge without the order that the state provided. Exploitative as the state was, it provided a modest degree of security to most of its subjects most of the time, while safeguarding the maintenance of the religion which provided the individual solace necessary the rest of the time.

This review of politics during the precolonial period has also shown a general gap between theory and practice in the nature of the state and its relationship with society. The 'lord of life' monarch, in fact, had only tenuous control over his subjects through a set of institutions which often operated more for the benefit of the state's intermediary functionaries than for the king. As the kings of Burma eventually learned to their disadvantage, however, this was a phenomenon not unique to their form of political and military organization.[125] The divorce between theory and practice made monarchs aware of the political problems they faced, and the strongest of them, or rather those faced with the greatest challenges, undertook various reforms to reintegrate practice with theory in order to strengthen the state, and when that proved impossible, to amend theory where ideologically possible in order to justify new practices.

The final Konbaung dynasty's efforts in this regard are suggestive of the political problems involved. Alaungpaya, who founded the dynasty in 1752, carried out reforms in keeping with the maintenance and perpetuation of the state in an internal and external environment little changed from that which the founder of the Restored Toungoo dynasty faced:

He halted the 'wastage' of manpower to private service and debt-slavery; enlarged the royal service and *athi* populations that in the late Toungoo era had suffered serious attrition; reasserted control over the refactory gentry class; and created a unified system of ministerial patronage whose strength derived from the intense personal attachment of leading officials to the king. Private power centers were restricted, and the formal structure again approximated the actual distribution of authority between the king and his chief ministers.[126]

His successors strove constantly to ensure that his reforms were maintained in order to keep alive the strength of the central state institutions. Succeeding kings 'issued reams of edicts and conducted kingdom-wide cadastral, revenue and population surveys in 1765, 1783 and 1802 in the teeth of local opposition' as part of this effort.[127]

125. Pollack, *Empires in Collision*, p. 95.
126. Lieberman, *Burmese Administrative Cycles*, p. 270.
127. Trager and Koenig, *Burmese Sit-tans*, p. 28.

Local opposition to the centre, however, stemmed not from any desire to abolish the state or monarchy, but rather to weaken its ability to remove from the hands of local communities and intermediary officials the wealth that they were able to amass from agricultural labour or the taxation of other people's labour. Indeed, there was on their part 'an ardent desire to improve their standing within the sociopolitical hierarchy of which the king was apex and guarantor'.[128] The nature of precolonial society worked against the development of ideas of class consciousness, and when peasants rebelled it was

> not to effect fundamental changes in a sociopolitical order, which they accepted as legitimate and divinely ordained, but to back a lord or faction against rivals, to express displeasure with excessive demands of a particular lord or, in times of dynastic collapse, to influence the outcome of contests that would determine which family and factions of the nobility would control the throne.[129]

Consequently, 'despite its long-term centralizing trend, the Burmese monarchy to the end remained less bureaucratic than patrimonial.'[130]

Nonetheless, at this point, it would be to underestimate the significance of the centralization of the early modern state to discontinue an analysis of its potential for further reform and rationalization. A brief examination of how the Konbaung dynasty responded to the final threat posed to it by the British-Indian empire in the nineteenth century will suggest at least the possibility of the precolonial state system's ability to have adopted further centralization and rationalization measures in order to defend itself.[131] However, the nature of the British-Indian challenge was of such a fundamentally different quality than any that previous monarchs had faced that it proved impossible for them to be successful. Their ultimate failure needs to be assessed within the context not only of examining the nature of the external challenge posed by the British, but also in terms of the internal political system which militated against sufficiently rapid reforms.[132]

At the time of the defeat of the Burmese army following the 1824–6 Anglo-Burmese war, the state was little prepared to defend itself against

128. Lieberman, *Burmese Administrative Cycles*, p. 112.
129. Adas, 'From Avoidance to Confrontation', p. 228.
130. Lieberman, 'Continuity and Change', p. 27.
131. See the discussion in Pollack, *Empires in Collision*, ch. 6, 'Burmese Modernization: Administration and Economy (1853–1866)', pp. 113–36.
132. As Pollack, *Empires in Collision*, emphasizes, although in a more balanced manner than earlier standard sources such as Cady, *History of Modern Burma*.

the superior military technology and manpower of the British East India Company. The king not only underemphasized the power of the British but also was over-confident of his own resources. It has been estimated that by 1820 the crown had lost the service to independent secular authorities of perhaps 25 per cent of its *ahmu-dan* and *athi* population compared to 1783.[133] The defeat in 1852 stemmed not only from the inferior power of the state, but also from faulty intelligence, which misunderstood the belligerent nature of the British-Indian commanders, in contrast to the seemingly pacific desires of the civilian governments in London and Calcutta.[134] The defeat of the Burmese troops in the second Anglo-Burmese war of 1852 led to more significant political and administrative changes than did the first defeat, for unlike the earlier war, the results of the second directly weakened the economic resources of the state and suggested the possible collapse of the monarchy.

The removal from the throne of the king at the time of the second war, Pagan Min, was the result of several economic and political factors which factions at the court were able to use in order to replace him with their favourite, Mindon Min. In particular, the loss of the rice surplus produced in southern Burma as a result of the British blockade drove up rice prices at a time when many members of the *ahmu-dan* population were involved in the military campaigns to the south.[135] Also, the loss of revenues from trade through the southern ports weakened the state's financial base. The link between the vitality of the state and its control of the entirety of Burma's agricultural and trade revenues could not be more clearly demonstrated.

Mindon Min launched a series of reforms by centralizing political decision-making designed to strengthen the state and ensure the loyalty of the population. It was deemed necessary to bolster central control over provincial officials; for the conclusion was drawn at the capital that one of the main causes of the second Anglo-Burmese war was that Pagan Min's ministers at Rangoon had been more uncooperative with the British than central policy had intended. Mindon also 'attempted to centralize judicial functions, to group provinces into larger units, to expand the use of cash taxes in both lowlands and hills, to develop a variety of commercial monopolies, and to rationalize military affairs and communications along Western lines.'[136]

133. Lieberman, 'Political Significance of Religious Wealth', pp. 764–5.
134. Pollack, *Empires in Collision*, p. 95.
135. *Ibid.*, p. 103.
136. Lieberman, 'Continuity and Change', p. 23.

Facing a crisis which threatened the perpetuation of the state, Mindon became a policy-oriented ruler. One of his first policies was to try to bring down the price of rice following the southern blockade. The political significance of the high rice price cannot be overemphasized, for with the price at the capital being three times the price at Prome near the frontier with British held territory, there was a significant incentive for people to move out of the king's domains to areas of cheaper food and greater opportunities. In response to this, Mindon both imported rice from British Burma and purchased all the available rice within his kingdom. This was in turn sold at subsidized prices, but as there was insufficient to supply demand, a black market quickly developed and prices went back up.[137] Doubtless those closely connected with the court or who had liquid assets found it easier to purchase the state-priced rice and resell it at a profit. The longer term solution to the food crisis the state faced was to be found in increased production in the remaining domains, and Mindon's officers devoted a great deal of time and money to repairing and expanding the dry zone irrigation systems.

The rationalization measures implemented by the king were designed not only to increase administrative control over provincial officials, but also to increase state revenues. The costs of providing food subsidies, public works and administrative and political reforms were very heavy in comparison to the work the state had previously undertaken, and had to be carried out with declining resources. The effect of the reforms, including the introduction of salaries for officials, was to increase the tax revenues available, but not sufficiently to pay for the additional patronage the king had to dispense in order to keep his political supporters behind him. The reforms did, however, greatly strengthen central control, and 'local officials, now more than ever, were agents for the centre rather than autonomous commanders.'[138] The same is true of the leadership of the *sangha*.[139] The need for extra income to finance these operations though finally spelled the end of the precolonial state.

The dilemma facing the controllers of the early modern state in its final years can be summarized as follows. First, they needed to rationalize the state's administrative and political structures in order to

---

137. Pollack, *Empires in Collision*, pp. 123–4.
138. *Ibid.*, p. 118.
139. E. Michael Mendelson, *Sangha and State in Burma. A Study of Monastic Sectarianism and Leadership* (edited by John P. Ferguson, Ithaca and London: Cornell University Press, 1975), pp. 113–4.

increase revenues. But rationalization meant increasing political patronage in order to buy off political discontent from officials who were losing their independent sources of income. The loss of trade revenues to the south meant that alternative revenues also had to be found through other forms of trade, and here the easiest course to take was to grant timber concessions to foreign, mainly British, firms. This in turn created greater pressures, politically and economically, on the centre, for the foreign concessionaries were always seeking reduced rates, and political opponents of the ruling ministers could always accuse them of selling out the interests of the country to the foreigners. The political intrigues that surrounded Mindon's demise and the placement upon the throne of Thibaw were the product of these political and economic dilemmas.

While involved in these immediate, and in the end most crucial problems, the state still had to contend with the basic political problems that all rulers of Burma have had to face: the need to expropriate as much revenue as possible from an agrarian population which sought to avoid losing control of its product; to control the wealth and influence of the Buddhist *sangha* and other, secular, centres of power and influence, and the need to ensure the security of the state from the loss of control of areas on its periphery. This was enough to tax the most firmly-established of states and rulers.

CHAPTER 2
THE RATIONALIZATION OF THE STATE, 1825–1942

Introduction

How rulers perceive their roles in the manifold forces which shape the societies they govern is an important indicator of the nature of the state they wish to create and perpetuate. Their concepts of the state's duties provide them with the reasons for administering the institutions of social control and economic production in the particular manner which they choose. For the kings and ministers of the precolonial state in Burma, the maintenance of order and security required them to be involved intimately in the symbolic, spiritual, and customary life of society and the regulation of economic affairs. Any distinction between the public and private spheres of life was alien to their conception of the relationship of the state to society.

The colonial rulers, however, viewed their roles and obligations very differently. They were detached from society not merely because they were foreigners but because their ideas of rule presumed a distinction between the public and private aspects of life. The rationality of the modern state was a force separate from the liberty of personal choice, even though it was its guarantor. The ideological justifications of nineteenth-century European liberalism provided them not only with a moral justification for colonialism, but also allowed them to interpret the political and social consequences of the policies they implemented and the institutions they created to carry these out as an integral and necessary consequence of the evolution of the modern world.

From the arrival of the first British officials to govern Arakan and Tenasserim in 1825 until the last of them walked out of the country before the advancing Japanese imperial army in 1942, they believed that the colonial state was 'a benevolent but impartial umpire'[1] which freed the economy of Burma from the precolonial state's restrictions on trade and commerce, and thus liberated the individual from the fetters of custom and the extortion of an exploitative ruling class. By the

---

1. J.S. Furnivall, *Colonial Policy and Practice: A Comparative Study of Burma and Netherlands India* (New York University Press, 1956), p. 64.

twentieth century the élite of the bureaucracy, the officers of the Indian Civil Service (ICS), saw themselves as 'holding the ring' for the political and economic life of Burma in order that the people who resided there, indigenous and foreign, might conduct their political and economic affairs in a safe and peaceful manner.

As the ultimate arbiters and guides of Burma, the British civil servants saw no contradiction between their powers to rule an alien land and their preachments about creating self-government in that country. Recognizing no form of self-government in existence upon their arrival, but only an outdated form of oriental despotism, they saw themselves as the midwives of the modern world in backward Asia. If there was any contradiction between the freedom and prosperity of Burma, which they governed, and that of Britain, for whom they governed, it could and would be resolved by their own abilities to see the 'true' interests of all sides and to govern in the name of fairness, efficiency, and the long-term welfare of all concerned. If the people they governed did not view the state they created and the policies they pursued in this way, this was because they did not as yet understand the intricacies of statecraft in the modern world.[2] In that sense the British who managed the colonial state were like their indigenous predecessors who also believed that their methods of rule were the most appropriate for the maintenance of society, even if occasionally resisted by those they governed.

Transforming the Structures of the State

What distinguishes the early modern state from the colonial state is neither the political problems with which it had to contend nor even the basic functions it had to perform to ensure its perpetuation. Despite its different outward purposes, the *raison d'être* of the state remained the maintenance of order, thus allowing its persistence and ensuring the smooth functioning of the society which provided the state with its resources. What most distinguished the colonial state from its predecessor was that it was self-consciously imposed by a powerful foreign empire which operated under radically different notions about the relationship of the state to society, to the economy, and to the individual

---

2. Robert H. Taylor, 'The Relationship Between Burmese Social Classes and British-Indian Policy on the Behaviour of the Burmese Political Elite, 1937–1942' (unpubl. Ph.D. thesis, Cornell University, 1974), pp. 21–30.

than those behind the political and administrative instruments of the Burmese monarchs. In the early years of British rule the state did little to alter the terminology and basic local institutions of the precolonial state, but, nonetheless, as was occurring in India at the same time, fundamental alterations were taking place in both the nature of the state and society in Burma.[3]

The colonial state was an instrument intended to create and free wealth as efficiently as possible, in the context of a larger set of external imperial, economic, political and strategic interests. The domestic political and social consequences of such a purpose, which no indigenous government could have ignored, were little considered by the British state until this century. Thus, the colonial state had an artificial quality which a genuinely independent state would never have. This major difference existed between the colonial state and that which preceded it, as well as between the colonial and the contemporary state.

In its outward form, what has been the most obvious contrast between the precolonial state and the colonial state is the degree of formal centralization. The colonial state was able to intervene in and direct more effectively the institutions of local government and the lives of the people than the early modern state was able to do. There is a strange paradox in this. The increasing centralization of power meant a greater *decentralization* of the state's means of access into the society, in particular allowing institutions and agencies only partially and indirectly instruments of the state to carry out a number of state functions. The 'central instruments of rule and exploitation' perfected by the colonial state, 'measurement and calculation, involvement in the various occasions of survey and in the distribution of tax burdens within villages . . .', led to the full flowering of a capitalist economy, with dramatic effects on the distribution of power and wealth in Burmese society. While the growth of the use of money allowed for greater state intervention in society, it also created new social and economic skills 'and the means of participation among the population at large', thus increasing the rate of social mobility to levels unknown in the precolonial period. For those able to take advantage of these new opportunities, the colonial state created greater personal autonomy and economic advantages.[4] But

---

3. Frank Perlin, 'State Formation Reconsidered', *Modern Asian Studies*, 19, 3 (July 1985), p. 475. See also Burton Stein's stimulating essay 'State Formation and Economy Reconsidered', pp. 387–414, in the same issue of *Modern Asian Studies*.
4. Perlin, 'State Formation Reconsidered', p. 476.

the distribution of these opportunities was not uniform throughout society and the minority most tied to the colonial state, or who already possessed the necessary skills to take advantage of the new conditions, benefited to a greater extent than others. As will be made clear by the end of this chapter, the majority of the Burmese population were not the main beneficiaries of the changes effected by the colonial state.

The primary reason for this was that from its inception in 1825 until eleven years before independence in 1948, Burma was in the eyes of the imperial government merely a distant provincial appendage of the Indian empire. Even after separation from India on April 1, 1937, the major parameters of economic and security policies in Burma were shaped in the interest of governments in London and New Delhi, and even Tokyo and Washington, as much as the state's own capital, Rangoon. Although as early as 1923 the colonial rulers were impelled to create formal mechanisms for the encouragement of the development of self-governing but truncated national institutions (including political parties, elections and a legislature), the colonial state, because of its external resources, especially the British-Indian army, remained so powerful that it could easily suppress major expressions of discontent. The colonial state was much more remote from the political and economic currents of the country at least until the 1920s than the precolonial state had even been, and this was the basis of its initial strength and ability to rationalize the political, administrative and economic orders. But its remoteness was also the cause of its ultimate collapse, for it could not survive without external support.

Within Burma what made the colonial state seem so different from its predecessor was initially not the fact that it was managed by foreigners, nor even the way in which it functioned, including its reliance upon a Western-derived concept of law and impersonal, bureaucratic authority relationships. Rather, it was the new rulers' concern with the growth of trade which set it apart from the government of the kings. This was the core feature of its own internal rationality, reflecting the nature of its parent, the British East India Company. The precolonial state grew and expanded organically in response to internal political ideas, pressures and challenges until near its demise. The colonial state was not only imposed by the world's then greatest trading empire, but sought to remake the country in its own image and thus had the will to reshape internal social and economic structures to suit its own interests. In consequence, the colonial state in time became more efficient and comprehensive than the precolonial state in the eyes of foreign observers, the British-Indian civil servants who constructed it, and, ultimately, the Burmese political élite who inherited it.

When the British first began to construct their state in the southern peripheries of the Burmese king's domains they found little in the way of the systematic order which they had been taught to recognise as the early modern state, at least in its Indian guise. The Burmese administrative structure was to them 'so lacking in uniformity that they experienced great difficulty in understanding it'.[5] That the existing system had a logic of its own, and was perhaps even preferable to their own schemes for many of their Burmese subjects, they little knew nor cared. For the British officials, the crucial task was to develop as quickly as possible the means to pay for the more elaborate administrative institutions that were the prerequisites for the expansion of trade and production.[6] In this way the state took on new roles while creating additional resources with which to rule. As a consequence, the social structure of Burma as well as the nature of the domestic economy was altered, giving rise to new class and ethnic structures, new ideologies, and more organized and systematic forms of anti-state political action in the twentieth century.

Retrospectively, this transformation seems to have taken place rapidly and to a pre-designed plan. In fact, of course, from the perspective of its participants and subjects the process was gradual and piecemeal. In many ways, the pervasive impact of the rationalization of the state during the colonial period was not reached until well into this century, by which time the basis of its destruction at the hands of rising political forces had already begun. In terms of the lives of most of the population of Burma, the impact of the British-induced changes came only after 1886, when the colonial government removed the last Burmese monarch, demobilized the indigenous military forces, ignored indigenous social and status distinctions, and abandoned constraints on economic growth as well as denigrating the social role of Buddhism. In the place of these core

5. F.S.V. Donnison, *Public Administration in Burma: A Study of Development During the British Connexion* (London: Royal Institute of International Affairs, 1953), p. 13.
6. While their political masters at the centre of the empire may, for political and strategic reasons, have seen advantages in the growth of British power, the administrators who actually had to manage the empire were much less keen. Thus, the Chief Commissioner of British Burma opposed the final annexation of Burma in 1885 because the administrative and military costs would outweigh the increase in revenues. Ni Ni Myint, *Burma's Struggle Against British Imperialism (1885-1895)* (Rangoon: Universities Press, 1983), p. 29.

agencies of the precolonial state, the British built a state based upon a bureaucratic administration backed by a foreign army and justified by Western capitalist conceptions of justice, law and economic rationality. The abandonment of the golden palaces of the kings at Mandalay as the centre of the state for the great utilitarian pile of Victorian brick in Rangoon known as the Secretariat provides a symbol of this transformation.

It has been argued by students of the classical period's history and of the colonial period's political economy that the imposition of the colonial state resulted in the *only* fundamental change in Burmese society from the creation of the Pagan kingdom until the regaining of independence.[7] Their argument is based upon a set of linked contentions concerning the degree of change wrought by the British in regard to the political and administrative structures of the state, the nature of the domestic economy, and the concepts of law and justice that prevailed in both politics and economics. There is a good deal of truth in these contentions, although, as developed in Chapter I, whether the precolonial period was as stagnant as often argued or whether the transformations of the nineteenth century were the result solely of the imposition of British rule is doubtful. The problem needs to be examined from both ends of the historical spectrum. Trends evident well before 1886 suggest that the development of some of these phenomena under monarchical auspices was already taking place and the consequences of these changes are not always as clear or unilinear as often assumed. It should not be forgotten that the British ruled Burma in its entirety for less than 65 years, and the impact of the period on basic societal values and political concepts was less than on institutions and economic structures.

The soul of the precolonial state was the king, who was obliged to guard the customary legal concepts of the Buddhist law of cause and effect. The mind of the colonial state was the civil servant, who was constrained by British legal concepts of precise bounds of authority, rigid rules of procedure and the protection of life and property. The king in the precolonial state was not above the law, he was the fount of law, and from this stemmed both his personal strength and the administrative

---

7. As explicitly argued by Michael Aung Thwin, 'Divinity, Spirit and Human: Conceptions of Classical Burmese Kingship', in Lorraine Gesick (ed.), *Centers, Symbols and Hierarchies: Essays on the Classical States of Southeast Asia* (New Haven: Yale University Southeast Asian Studies Series no. 26, 1983), pp. 45–86, esp. p. 47; and implicitly by Furnivall, *Colonial Policy and Practice*, pp. 23–30.

weaknesses of his state. But, as Furnivall wrote, the colonial state, the new Leviathan, was different:

> Leviathan is a creature of the Law; it is by the law he lives, and laws and regulations are both the substance of his being and the basis of his power. The strong man, like some Burman rulers of the past, can build up an empire, but unless the framework be fashioned out of law his empire will last no longer than his strength. It is not sufficient for him to enforce the law; he must also submit to it, offer himself a willing sacrifice to Leviathan.[8]

The centralizing and perpetuating power of the precolonial state stemmed from the king's ability to shape the law in order to control the economic resources of his kingdom and thus prevent the rise of rival centres of wealth and power. The economic and administrative rationality of the colonial state stemmed from its normal obligation to bend to the law and thus maintain a distinction between public power and private wealth.

But Furnivall claims too much for the law-bound nature of the colonial state. It was legal in the Weberian sense of concepts of state supremacy and it was legalistic in its careful attention to rules of procedure and the protection of life and property. However, when political forces threatened its monopoly of control, it was able to find laws to ensure its perpetuation in the hands of its creators or their designated successors. And when economic power became sufficiently great to create forces to undermine social stability, it was able to use the law to control that force too. The colonial Leviathan was a servant of the law, as Furnivall wrote, but it was also the custodian and author of that same law. Where one finds the most radical difference in the nature of the law in the precolonial state and the colonial state is in the assumption in the colonial law of the legal equality of all subjects, including officialdom. The abolition of the customary status distinctions of the precolonial state was a key aspect of the revolution that the colonial state forced upon Burma.

The implications of the principle of legal equality would not have been in the forefront of the minds of the founders of the colonial state. They had a job to do in difficult and largely unknown circumstances, and had to fashion a state out of the ideas and materials at their disposal as inexpensively as possible. Perhaps no clearer statement of the initial intentions of the colonial state can be found than in the first pronouncement of the Commissioner of Tenasserim, Mr Maingy, to his new adult male subjects on September 30, 1825:

8. J.S. Furnivall, 'The Fashioning of Leviathan', *The Journal of the Burma Research Society*, XXIX, 3 (1939), p. 18.

Proclamation to the Inhabitants of Mergui:
Rest assured that your wives and children shall be defended against all foreign and domestic enemies. That life and property shall enjoy every liberty and protection, and that your religions shall be respected and your Priests and religious edifices secured from every insult and injury. Proper measures shall be immediately adopted for administering justice for you, according to your own established laws as far as they do not militate against the principles of humanity and natural equity. In respect of revenue and all other subjects your own customs and local usages shall be taken into consideration; but the most free and unrestricted internal and external commerce will be established and promoted.

All that is required from you is to aid me towards giving you peace, order and happiness by each inhabitant returning to his usual occupation, by your respecting and cheerfully obeying all such as may be placed in authority over you, and by your discountenancing and pointing out wherever necessary, the seditious and evil disposed enemies of the British Government.

Lastly, I wish it to be clearly understood, that access at all hours and at all places will be afforded by me to any, even the poorest inhabitants, who may desire to see me upon business.⁹

Doubtless to Maingy this proclamation seemed an innocuous statement which would reassure the inhabitants of the new British territory that their rulers would do nothing to harm the customs and practices held most dear by them, but would ensure the creation of a better, more equitable, and egalitarian society. Little did he realize that the two aims of maintaining tradition and establishing an egalitarian, commercially-oriented society would prove, even in the short run, impossible. The liberal ideology which was the root of his assumptions ran counter to the ideological basis of Burmese tradition. The practices of an economy geared to free trade and the free flow of capital and labour made erosion of customary practices inevitable, and the promise of open and equitable government proved impossible to maintain in the face of the demands placed upon it. The liberal umpire could not be unbiased toward the traditional practices which stood in the way of economic and administrative efficiency; and an authoritarian bureaucracy was installed in the name of progress.

There are a variety of criteria by which one can divide the stages of development of the colonial state in Burma. Viewed in terms of the

---

9. In *Selected Correspondence of Letters Issued from and Received in the Office of the Commissioner Tenasserim Division for the Years 1825–26 to 1842–43* (Rangoon: Government Printing and Stationery, Burma, 1928), p. 16.

degree and nature of the authority of the highest executive and legislative officials of the state, the period can be divided into five segments.[10] From the first Anglo-Burmese war until 1834, Tenasserim was governed from Penang, and Arakan was made a part of the Presidency of Bengal. From 1834 to 1862, both were extensions of the Bengal administration located in Calcutta, as was Pegu province, also called Lower Burma after its annexation in 1852. This period ended with the creation of a Chief Commissioner for British Burma in 1862 when the country became a province in its own right, directly under the Governor-General of India. It was during this second period of 35 years which ended in 1897 that the major structures of the colonial bureaucracy, the framework of the central administrative organizations in Rangoon and the local government institutions, were completed. During both these periods the government in Burma possessed no legislative powers and the rules and regulations it followed were those drawn up by and for the government of India.

However, during the third period, from 1897 to 1923, there was established in Rangoon an appointed Legislative Council to advise the Lieutenant-Governor in drafting local legislation. This advisory body grew from nine to thirty members, the majority representing commercial interests, mainly foreign. This development 'tended to increase the preponderance of capitalist interests in the direction of affairs, and reflected their growing importance in the economic life of Burma.'[11] The head of the government was referred to as the Governor from 1923 onwards, when a partially elected assembly was created under the so-called dyarchy constitution (which placed some authority in the hands of non-officials, including two elected indigenous ministers responsible for education, local government, public health, agriculture and forests). This period, the fourth, ended with the separation of Burma from India in 1937 and the establishment at that time of a constitutional order which contained provisions for a significant degree of self-government through a cabinet responsible to a fully elected legislature under the supervision and ultimate veto of the governor, who remained responsible for defence, foreign relations, finance, and the peripheral regions of the state, now called the frontier areas.

One can also conceptualize the periods of British rule from the per-

---

10. Donnison, *Public Administration*, p. 2.
11. Furnivall, *Colonial Policy and Practice*, p. 72.

spective of the nature of the policies the imperial authorities pursued.[12] Here, three periods can be distinguished. From the formation of the initial colonial authority in 1825 until 1879, *laissez-faire* predominated. The state, responsible mainly for maintaining order through the police and courts and collecting taxes to pay for these, made little effort to guide economic forces in the semi-frontier conditions of the southern regions. After 1880, until 1923, the state slowly became more concerned with enhancing the economic efficiency of the society and began to devote resources to the development of communications, schools and rudimentary health and agricultural services in order to support the more rapid development of the country's resources, both human and material. During this period there was a marked improvement in rail and water-borne communications throughout the country, especially after 1886 when the north became integrated into the expanding colonial economy of the export-oriented south.[13]

After the establishment of state policies directed toward progress and welfare, the locus of government policy then turned to the development of liberal democratic political institutions, in particular participatory bodies through which the state could gain legitimacy. This was primarily in response to changing political conditions in India and only subsequently to political demands in Burma.[14] It was during this period that organized Burmese political nationalism developed rapidly in opposition to colonial rule.

For the purposes of this book, it is appropriate to divide the colonial era into just two periods, pre- and post-First World War. The choice of the First World War as a dividing point is not made because the war had many major direct effects upon Burma, but because it was from about this time that the political nature of the state and the popular response to it changed most dramatically. Before then, most of the forms of political action found in the country would have been easily recognizable to anyone who had been familiar with the precolonial state. Land was still relatively plentiful and cheap, labour was still scarce and, by Indian standards, well paid, and people's expectations of the government were few. The political impact of the state was most strongly felt in the

12. The basic and classic source is Furnivall's *Colonial Policy and Practice*, chs. II–VI.
13. Shein, *Burma's Transport and Foreign Trade (1885–1914)* (Rangoon: Department of Economics, University of Rangoon, 1964), chs. II–III.
14. Taylor, 'Relationship Between Burmese Social Classes and British Indian Policy', ch. 2.

newly-developed cities, especially Rangoon, Bassein, Akyab (Sittwe), and Moulmein, located on the edge of rural society. These were essentially foreign trading enclaves with increasing numbers of migrant labourers and entrepreneurs serving to expedite the growing export of rice and other commodities and the importation of manufactured goods. After the First World War, however, the economic and political interests of the cities, and the external economic interests they served, tended increasingly to directly affect the lives and livelihoods of the peasantry in more obvious ways, especially in the delta areas of southern Burma. Parallel with the development of the modern political state grew political interests and expectations that mobilized demands on the state and new political élites to found and control institutions articulating these demands.

The development of the colonial state involved a rationalization of the procedures of the state as it attempted to maintain itself in the face of the political and other conditions that it inherited from its predecessor. However, in the process of achieving its larger imperial functions as an appendage of the British-Indian empire, as it evolved the colonial state also created new social structures and interests in Burma. The promise of the first Commissioner to the people of Mergui in 1825 (see above, p. 73) was partially fulfilled. 'The most free and unrestricted internal and external commerce' was largely established and not only did agricultural production dramatically increase, leading to the export of a large surplus of rice as well as timber and eventually rubber and minerals, it also allowed for the importation of large quantities of foreign-made consumer goods and even food. Further, in order to make up the labour shortage that existed in the country, the immigration of foreign labour, primarily Indian, but also Chinese, was encouraged. Foreign capital, mainly British and Indian, flowed in as investments and flowed out as profits and central Indian government revenues; Burma became firmly linked to the world economy. In effect, the colonial government willed the abandonment of the economic and social stability that the pre-colonial state had maintained as the basis of its political power for the more dynamic but unstable fluctuations of world trade and social change.

In the early years of this development, conditions were such that there was sufficient land, employment and profits for everyone; so that while there was rapid economic growth, there was little social mobilization. Unlike the experience of the early modern European societies where the state maintained stricter controls over economic development and social change, the colonial state was sufficiently powerful that it felt it could ignore the political consequences of change until the 1920s. In Burma, mainly Indian migrant labour filled the new employment roles in the urban and commercial sectors of the economy, while indigenous labour remained wedded to the agricultural sector. Those in the minority who benefited most significantly from the new opportunities created naturally supported the state. The result of these changes was to create not the integrated society which the early modern state in Europe forced into being, but what Furnivall aptly named the 'plural society'.[15]

In the plural society in Burma, Europeans, Indians and Chinese lived side-by-side with the indigenous Burmese in a 'medley of peoples', for as Furnivall wrote at the end of the colonial period,

> they mix but do not combine. Each group holds by its own religion, its own culture and language, its own ideas and ways. As individuals they meet, but only in the market-place, in buying and selling. There is a plural society, with different segments of the community living side by side, but separately, within the same political unit.[16]

Politically the plural society had

> three characteristic features: The society as a whole comprises separate racial groups; each section is an aggregate of individuals rather than a corporate or organic whole; and as individuals their social life is incomplete.[17]

Thus, he argued, not only was the plural society composed of three communities which only met in the market-place, but even within these communities individuals did not identify with others in the same group. Composed of a partially uprooted indigenous population along with transient immigrant labourers, few of whom intended to settle in the country, and equally uncommitted foreign businessmen and officials, the society lacked the social and cultural bonding of a settled, integrated political unit or nation. This lack of cohesion created a society which had no political will to control the economic forces of capitalist production, as its individual members felt no motive of self-sacrifice for the good of the whole. Social demand, the controls that integrated societies imposed upon economic forces through loyalty and shared concern for mutual welfare, was lacking. Price rather than value became the determining factor in decision-making by the individual, for it was only

15. Furnivall, *Colonial Policy and Practice*, pp. 303–12.
16. *Ibid.*, p. 304.
17. *Ibid.*, p. 306.

for his or her material wants that they became involved in society.[18] Thus:

A plural society is broken up into groups of isolated individuals, and the disintegration of social will is reflected in a corresponding disorganization of social demand. Even in a matter so vital to the whole community as defence against aggression, the people are reluctant to pay the necessary price. In religion and the arts, in the graces and ornaments of social life, there are no standards common to all sections of the community, and standards deteriorate to such a level as all have in common. And because each section is merely an aggregate of individuals, those social wants that man can satisfy only as members of a community remained unsatisfied. Just as the life of an individual in a plural society is incomplete, so his demand tends to be frustrated. Civilization is the process of learning to live a common social life, but in a plural society men are decivilized. All wants that all men want in common are those which they share in common with the animal creations; on a comprehensive survey of mankind from China to Peru these material wants, essential to the sustenance of life, represent the highest common factor of demand. In the plural society the highest common factor is the economic factor, and the only test that all apply in common is the test of cheapness. In such a society the disorganization of social demand allows the economic process of natural selection by the survival of the cheapest to prevail.[19]

In Furnivall's view, the new colonial Leviathan had only partially gained man in Burma release from the conditions of Hobbes's pre-Leviathan state of nature: life might not necessarily then be poor or short, but it most certainly remained solitary, nasty, and brutish; and therefore the colonial state had not fulfilled its promise to the people made by Maingy in 1825. Indeed, one cannot imagine a greater distinction than that between the anomic, economy-ridden, Darwinian plural society of colonial Burma, and the integrated, religiously-rooted communal-traditional society that the precolonial state had maintained, with its patronage of the arts and regulation of economic self-advancement. Despite Furnivall's romanticization of traditional society, especially at the village level, it is nonetheless true that the changes in society that the new policies and structures of the state allowed caused the destruction of the cohesion of Burma's precolonial social life.

Furnivall's idea of the plural society provides a graphic metaphor for the results of the colonial state's mode of government in Burma. But it is

18. *Ibid.*, pp. 308–9.
19. *Ibid.*, p. 310.

a stagnant image; a society that was acted upon, but which could not respond to the economic and other external forces which were imposed upon it. By analyzing the political workings of the plural society, it may be possible to grasp more fully the dynamic characteristics of Burma's society during the period in which the plural society and the bureaucratic state were created. Then it may be possible to better understand what has followed since. But before we can turn to study the relationship of the state to society in contemporary Burma, it is necessary to examine what kind of state it was that created the plural society and what kinds of class formations and politics existed within the plural society. This Chapter is devoted to the first of these questions, and the next Chapter to the second.

The Territorial Organization of the State

The rationalization of the state was partially a consequence of the territorial revisions which the British undertook. These were important both conceptually and administratively. Administratively, they further simplified the divisions of the state from the three types of territory recognized in the early modern state to two. These were 'Burma proper', which incorporated both the nuclear and the dependent provinces zones of the early modern period, and the 'excluded' or 'frontier areas' of the surrounding hills. Conceptually, they introduced the idea of firm territorial divisions of authority. It is beyond the scope of this volume to explore fully the implications of the development of firm borders with neighbouring states: China, French Indo-China, Siam and British India, but this too was part of the general process. In a sense, the colonial state did not just rationalize the map of Burma, it drew it, though incompletely.

The territorial pattern developed in the 1820s for the governance of Tenasserim and Arakan, borrowed from the British-Indian model, set the mould for the later development of the British state. All of Tenasserim from the time of the annexation was directly ruled by British officials, whereas in Arakan the practice was established of dividing the plains and hill areas into zones with different administrative patterns. While direct rule was implemented in the plains, in the hills a system of indirect rule relying upon the recognition of traditional chiefs was deemed appropriate. The British raj merely replaced the king of Burma as the suzerain to whom the chiefs paid allegiance through tribute. The

Karen population residing in the hills of Tenasserim, however, were immediately placed under direct British control. Tenasserim set the pattern for Burma proper. It was divided into three districts each under the supervision of a British Deputy Commissioner.[20] This figure was the linchpin between the British-dominated central administration and the largely indigenous local government officials throughout the colonial period.

The first Commissioner of Tenasserim began, albeit gradually, the process of disrupting the traditional pattern of local government. The hereditary *myo-thu-gyi* and *thu-gyi* were confirmed in their positions but the conception of their responsibilities and obligations was fundamentally altered from a personal, patron-client relationship to a territorial and impersonal one. The old Burmese township, the *myo* or *taik*, seen erroneously by the British as the same as the Indian village tract or circle, was redefined as a geographical unit in which all the residents were under identical obligations to the headmen.[21] Ignored were any distinctions between *athi* and *ahmu-dan* population categories living in proximity but with their own headmen. From the beginning the British instructed headmen to draw the territorial boundaries of their circles as if these administrative units were geographical concepts held to be meaningful by the local population.[22] The precise demarcation of administrative boundaries, a key aspect of the concept of the rationalized state, was being imposed in place of the complex non-territorial administrative divisions of the lowlands which the precolonial state's control of manpower had necessitated. Similar practices were followed in Arakan, but in the hill areas where the amount of revenue which could be raised from local taxes was too small to justify more than 'light administration' (one of the code phrases of the period), the British did nothing to change the responsibilities of the local chiefs. Here, until the twentieth century, the British seemed by and large to acknowledge the unimportance of precisely drawn administrative maps.

After the annexation of Pegu, the British extended the territorial organization established in Tenasserim and lowland Arakan to their new territory. The province was divided into five districts, each under a

---

20. *Ibid.*, p. 36.
21. Furnivall, *Colonial Policy and Practice*, p. 37.
22. *Correspondence for the Years 1825–26 to 1842–43 in the Office of the Commissioner Tenasserim Division* (Rangoon: Government Printing and Stationery, Burma, 1929), p. 19.

Deputy Commissioner with the same powers as their counterparts in the other areas of southern Burma. In 1862 the different terminology and adjustments which had developed in the practice of local government were systematized. The districts were divided into administrative townships under a *myo-ok* or township officer who was a junior version of the Deputy Commissioner.[23] Each township was in turn composed of a number of *myo* under a headman who administered one or more villages within his territory or circle.

The pattern of territorial administration in Burma proper was thus established before the completion of the British takeover in 1886. The structure was a tiered set of administrative relationships headed by a Chief Commissioner, later Governor, under whom served the Commissioners of what would eventually be seven Divisions. The latter in turn supervised the activities of the Deputy Commissioners or District Officers, usually called the 'DC', who administered the affairs of the township officers or *myo-ok*. The interface between the township and the district was where the colonial state had the most immediate initial impact on the rural population, for the District Officers were the men who ensured that central policy was carried out at the local level, and who controlled the appointment of subordinate officials and magistrates.

The colonial territorial redivision did not begin to affect the lives of the people to any significant extent until the period of the so-called pacification (1886–90), when order was restored through military and administrative methods following the rebellions which broke out after the deposition of King Thibaw. At this time a Village Act was passed under martial law regulations which had the purpose of breaking up the *myo/taik* administration level — thus further enhancing the role of the new-style township and placing greater responsibilities on the village headmen.[24] Before 1886 the British government had seen fit only to alter the traditional *taik* and *myo* jurisdictions by amalgamating or splitting them for reasons of administrative convenience and territorial rationality on a case-by-case basis. Now, under the Village Act, the government went further and abolished the *myo*, only in some cases to re-amalgamate villages later for reasons of financial viability.[25] The traditional social unit of the *myo* was obliterated and replaced by a non-

23. Donnison, *Public Administration*, pp. 23–4.
24. Ibid., pp. 31–2.
25. This process began in 1886 and apparently reached its peak in 1919 when 593 headmanships were abolished. In all, between 1909 and 1919 over 2,000 headmen were

organic administrative village which itself was 'little more than a cogwheel in the machinery of maintaining order and collecting revenue'.[26] The anomie of the indigenous sector of Burma's twentieth-century plural society had its roots in these territorial administrative policies.

In the hills, territorial adjustments did little to break down the traditional, organic social units. After 1886 the British state gained additional responsibilities as it assumed suzerainty over the extensive hill areas of northern Burma. This territory amounted to about half of the land area received from the Burmese king. Here the British followed the pattern established in Arakan of administering areas indirectly and leaving essentially untouched the pattern of relations they found. However, the existing units recognized, or in some cases created, were never considered intrinsically important and the government, especially in the twentieth century, was willing to redefine them for administrative reasons even though this often meant altering or ignoring promises given to the ancestors of the local authorities.

The Rationalization of Authority Relations

The colonial state imposed a formal bureaucratic structure on society which, while not completely abolishing the system of personal patron-client ties which had been the basis of the precolonial *myo*-centred order, complicated, amended, or ignored it by creating a pattern of systematic 'line of command' procedural relationships and obligations. The very language used to describe this change indicates its nature, for the rationalization of the state meant creating a 'sphere of government' separate from society and more clearly differentiated from other, less obviously coercive, aspects of social control. The process of this transformation was gradual in Arakan and Tenasserim but came more rapidly in Pegu. The policies pursued after 1886 speeded the process even more, so that by the turn of the century the relationship of the state with society through its local territorial and functional officials had been rationalized in a form similar to that of the modern European state of the

---

removed from their positions as villages were amalgamated on the criteria of sufficient size to provide an adequate financial base to pay the headman out of his revenue collections, but not too large as to make the exercise of his duties impossible. Furnivall, *Colonial Policy and Practice*, pp. 74–5.

26. *Ibid.*, p. 75.

same period. This transformation of authority relationships was a natural corollary of the rationalization of the territorial structure of the colonial state.

The first Commissioner of Tenasserim, Mr Maingy, and his three Deputies attempted to establish their notions of proper authority relationships quickly, but soon had to bend to local practices as they had neither the manpower nor the money to enforce rapid changes. They primarily confined themselves to the tasks of administrative re-organization and tax collection although they also assumed judicial responsibilities. Initially they were left to their own devices in determining how to carry out their tasks. However, like their counterparts in Arakan, they were required after 1832 to justify their actions to higher authorities in Calcutta in terms of the practice of the British Indian empire's bureaucratic regulations.[27]

Despite his desire to reform the government, Maingy recognized the utility of employing cooperative officials who had served the precolonial state and who, because of their hereditary positions, had personal influence over the local population. But he sought immediately to amend their personal authority so that it became more formal and under his control.[28] In his eyes, the old system was merely one of plunder and extortion which, even when regularized by placing officials in salaried positions, was still open to bribery and corruption as defined in his code of official conduct.[29] In the face of rising disorder, particularly what he called 'crime', Maingy was forced to 'swear in and employ as constables' sixteen of the old headmen on a fixed salary.[30] As the headmen were turned into salaried officials of the new state, they were no longer seen 'as local representatives but as government officials to be transferred from one charge to another as the convenience of administration might dictate'.[31]

The destruction of the headmen's personal authority and their ability to intercede between the demands of higher officials and the wishes of their former patrons initiated the decay of their ability to govern without the use of significant amounts of coercion. Thus, although the reinstatement in government service of the king's *thu-gyi* was intended to reduce the rate of crime, its effect was to increase the level of disorder as

27. Ibid., p. 36.
28. Selected Correspondence Tenasserim Division, p. 2.
29. Ibid., p. 3–4.
30. Ibid., p. 40.
31. Furnivall, 'The Fashioning of Leviathan', p. 46.

the traditional social bonds that had checked unsocial behaviour in the past were sapped of their vitality. The system, in some respects, nonetheless slipped back into the practices of the past, but without the social conditions that had made them effective means of social control. Patron-clientage was being replaced by bribery, corruption and force. While the old system may not have been as extortionate as Maingy believed, the system created by the British took on aspects of organized and state-sanctioned plunder by imposed officials.

Until the 1860s, and in most areas, the 1880s, the officials of the British state above the level of *myo-* and *taik-thu-gyi* were seldom able to penetrate directly into the villages. Poor communications, limited resources and the bureaucratic inertia caused by the perpetuation of the old but debililtated system of maintaining order and collecting revenue in the conditions of an expanding economy provided little incentive for thoroughgoing reform. 'The system, though in theory one of direct rule, was in effect a system of indirect rule through the circle headmen.'[32] In a sense, the early colonial state sat upon the traditional local administrative system in a more exploitative manner than the pre-colonial state had done, only interfering with its personnel recruitment and posting patterns.

Nonetheless, the territorial revisions and introduction of the township officer after 1862 had begun to transform the quality of local government authority relations to a further degree. The *myo-ok* was a new kind of official administering an additional bureaucratic tier. Some of the first recruited were *myo-* and *taik-thu-gyi*.[33] Those who got on best with the new regime learned English. The *myo-ok* became the link between the British officer or civilian who was Deputy Commissioner of the District and the *myo-* or *taik-*headman who administered the circle. Subordinate to the headmen were appointed police officers or *gaung* who also assisted in revenue collection. Subordinate to these officials were the village officers, the old *kyedangyi*, or largest taxpayer, who had had similar responsibilities under the kings but were often now no longer men of personal influence. They were responsible for the maintenance of law and order and the collection of revenue in their village.[34]

During the 1860s the personal authority of the headmen was further undermined by a variety of new regulations intended to raise the level of administrative skills of local officials. By the mid-1860s headmen had all

32. Furnivall, *Colonial Policy and Practice*, p. 42.
33. Donnison, *Public Administration*, pp. 23–4.
34. Furnivall, *Colonial Policy and Practice*, pp. 39–40.

their original powers removed except for the collection of revenue, and many of their police powers were assumed by a new centrally directed force under a British officer. In 1867 it was ordered that headmen had to be qualified land surveyors, and twelve years later a system of qualifying examinations for village headmanship was established similar to that which was already applied to township officers. Surveying, accounting, and knowledge of revenue law now became matters to be considered in making appointments of headmen as did 'hereditary claims, local influence, intelligence, and good character'. 'Impersonalization, specialization, and division of roles' now became the hallmark of the government system at all levels in Burma proper.[35]

The changes in the territorial structure of local administration which the abolition of the *myo* and *taik* level of government in favour of direct control of the village unit introduced after 1886 had a profound impact upon the relationship of the peasantry with the state. The effect of these changes in terms of authority relationships was essentially to abolish any remaining notions of local self-government and replace them with a system of tightly centralized district administration under the rigorous control of the Deputy Commissioner.[36] Whereas previously the *myo*- or *taik-thu-gyi*, even with his diminished powers, had been able to serve as an intermediary mediating for his community the demands of central authority in an informal manner, the new act placed directly upon the villagers collectively, through an emasculated village headman, the obligation to carry out the law or suffer collective penal sanctions enforced by the armed and mounted 'punitive' police of the central administration. The effect of this legislation was to abolish 'self-government over any unit larger than the village and, by converting the village from a social and residential unit into an administrative unit', it cut 'at the root of organized social life within the village', destroying the solidarity of the traditional community which was based on the *myo*. The position of the *myo*- or *taik-thu-gyi* was abolished and the village headman became the instrument through which the central government worked directly in the villages on a sustained basis.[37]

35. J.A. Mills, 'Burmese Peasant Response to British Provincial Rule, 1825–1885', in D.B. Miller (ed.), *Peasants and Politics* (Melbourne: Edward Arnold Australia, 1978), p. 94.
36. Hugh Tinker, *Foundations of Local Self-Government in India, Pakistan, and Burma* (Bombay: Lalvani, 1957), pp. 56–7.
37. Donnison, *Public Administration*, pp. 31–2; John F. Cady, *A History of Modern Burma* (Ithaca: Cornell University Press, 1958), pp. 141–4.

The implementation of this change was gradual, but by 1891 the old order was effectively gone. In its place, the British instituted officially nominated bureaucratic local bodies which were largely ignored both by the people and the civil servants. Known as circle boards, they were seen primarily as another mechanism for raising government revenue through their cess funds, half of which was used for the payment of the police.[38]

The precolonial system of patron-client ties and hereditary authority was now completely replaced by a system of salaried, appointed headmen who, though usually men from the local area, were appointed more for their knowledge of British procedures than for their vigilance in protecting local interests. Not only were they seen as cogs in the wheel of a regularized bureaucratic state, but they were very minor cogs at that, for many of the positive and less coercive functions of the state were soon assumed by specialist officials from the central administration. The development of the agriculture, education, sanitation and health departments and other functionally specific country-wide government services meant that each of these bureaucracies had their own personnel to carry out their own policies — though in ignorance of local conditions. These subordinate central government officials, given specialized tasks to perform, now involved themselves directly in the lives of the peasantry. Despite their welfare-type activities, many 'were regarded as agents of oppression, to be propitiated by petty bribes,'[39] for the village headmen were unable to intercede in opposition to their schemes.

The headmen were no longer the natural leaders of their communities, able to defend their client's interests against a rapacious state, but the salaried tax-collectors of that state providing the funds for the policies, police and courts which most of the people neither wanted nor believed they benefited from. In Burma as in much of the rest of Southeast Asia, the colonial state had undermined communities which had controlled their own internal affairs for generations. The efficiency that rationalization brought was at the cost of decivilizing the village; but turning the village into a revenue raising and administrative unit created systematic order and facilitated increased agricultural production. The rationalization of village administration became a central political cause of the growth of anti-state sentiments among the peasantry throughout the colonial period, and no amount of subsequent tinkering with its

38. Tinker, *Foundations of Local Self-Government*, p. 54.
39. Furnivall, *Colonial Policy and Practice*, p. 77.

form could either recreate the old order or cause satisfaction with the new.

In regard to the peoples living in the hill territories which first fell under British control, the new officials were less able or desirous of imposing their new system of authority relationships. Here, in a sense, the patterns of authority seemed to have been frozen from the early nineteenth century until the middle of the twentieth. However, as will be shown subsequently, changes with great political significance for the state in the middle of the twentieth century were underway. Initially, the British Commissioner of Tenasserim felt he knew too little about the people living in the hills, collectively referred to as Karens (and sometimes in the earliest years as Malays), to attempt 'to reduce them to any system' of rule.[40] Nothing was done to interfere with existing patterns of relations between these hill peoples and the lowland state authorities until the twentieth century, although there was a drift of people out of the hills to more prosperous and settled areas in the lowlands. It was from this pool of people living in the Karen hills, as well as from people in the plains who identified themselves as Karen, that the early conversions to Christianity were made by American Baptist missionaries. Many converts then became attached to the institutions of the British state.[41]

In Arakan, where the system of separate administrative patterns for the hills was established, the British did little to tamper with the so-called traditional authority structures they found. However, before formally guaranteeing the authority of an individual who was put forward, or more likely put himself forward, as the local leader, they ensured that he was amenable to their overall control.[42] It was not until 1871 that any alterations were made to the governing and taxation system the British found upon their arrival. Greater control was then introduced first by increasing the size of the police presence. Control of the population had to precede other efforts to 'reduce them to any system'. Following the establishment of police control, the system of tributary payments by chiefs was abolished and 'a uniform rate of one rupee for each hill clearing, and one rupee a house was imposed on all tribes alike'.[43] Rationalization inevitably meant monetization; and greater state intervention meant less authority for the tribal chiefs. Prior

40. *Selected Correspondence Tenasserim Division*, p. 7.
41. Cady, *History of Modern Burma*, pp. 137–41.
42. British Burma Political Department, *Report on the Administration of Hill Tracts, Northern Arakan, 1870–71* (Rangoon: Secretariat Press, 1872).
43. *Report on the Progress of Arakan Under British Rule from 1826 to 1875* (Rangoon: Government Press, 1876), pp. 14–15.

to these changes, the British administration had been represented only by a Superintendent over the chiefs who had 'administered [the law] in the simplest and most paternal form' and encouraged the growth of trade between the hills and plains.[44] In later years, especially after the annexation of northern Burma, the development of interaction between the hills and plains was discouraged for military and political reasons. Moreover the divide between Burma proper and the frontier areas became much more marked administratively and politically, with important consequences after independence.

More than administrative reform, it was the relative peace that British rule brought to the hill areas that caused political change there. Internecine conflicts between villages and tribes were largely halted by the threat of punishment of offenders by British-Indian troops, and, later, by the frontier force. Periodic flag marches by the colonial armed forces, the only significant evidence of the power of the state in many regions, nonetheless led in time to a weakening of the power of the tribal chiefs. Their power was based on the need of isolated cultivators to gather together for security. Once relative order was created in an area, it was more advantageous for people to live nearer their fields, and they tended to drift away from the larger village settlements and the control of the traditional leaders.[45] The decline of the local leaders' authority in turn led to the development of the idea of Chin, Kachin and other local ethnic identities, as local élites sought to create a separate identity for their people (and were encouraged to do so by the amateur anthropologists of the British-Indian army).

Financing the Rationalized State

The method of financing the precolonial state, the passing upward through the chain of patron-client ties and appanage arrangements of a proportion of revenue collected from villages, usually in kind and rarely audited, as well as providing corvée labour for public works, was largely rejected by the colonial state in the plains areas.[46] As far as the first British administrators were concerned, there was no effective financial system in

44. *Ibid.*, p. 19.
45. Khin Mya, 'The Impact of Traditional Culture and Environmental Forces on the Development of the Kachins, a Sub-Cultural Group of Burma' (unpubl. Ph. D. thesis, University of Maryland, 1961), p. 51.
46. Although Maingy continued to demand corvée in the early years in Tenasserim.

the traditional Burmese order. When, in Tenasserim, for example, Maingy attempted to find out the means by which local government officials were paid under the kings, he 'could not discover that they received any other remuneration besides the liberty of plundering and extorting from the lower classes'.[47] One of his first acts, therefore, was to attempt to rationalize the revenue collection system in order to raise auditable funds with which to pay a salaried class of government servants. He ordered that collectors of land revenues be appointed and that they should collect one-tenth of the grain produced.[48] This was in fact only a partial reorganization and reallocation of the tax burden of the previous system, for the Commissioner abandoned earlier levies on fruit trees and similar non-grain crops because at that time they were too difficult to assess. In fact, the new state probably reduced the overall level of taxation, thus perhaps lessening the proclivity of the recently colonized people to organize resistance to their new rulers. It was made clear, however, that this low rate of taxation would not be allowed to persist, and the peasants were repeatedly warned that the rate would increase in the future.[49] The abolition of the traditional controls on economic activity and the free export of rice at highly profitable prices, combined with the grain taxes, led to a substantial increase in the local price of grain in the towns. This, in turn, was one of the causes of increasing rates of taxation, as the servants of the government had to pay more for food and therefore had to receive higher salaries derived from local revenues.

The Commissioner's initial belief in his ability to reduce taxes was partially based upon his liberal assumptions that a more rationalized system, operating in a free market, would, as production increased, result in larger revenues for the state at a lower unit cost to the peasant. Indeed, the state's revenues did increase because of senior officials having a more complete knowledge of what was taxable, although in time the rate of taxation on the peasants, both direct and indirect, also rose. By appointing the *thu-gyi* on a salaried basis, the Commissioner believed that he would get accurate information about the amount of grain available to be taxed.[50] What he clearly failed to take into account was the fact that bribery and corruption would continue to ensure that headmen

47. *Selected Correspondence Tenasserim Division*, p. 10.
48. *Ibid*., p. 2.
49. *Ibid*., pp. 51–2.
50. *Ibid*., p. 40.

under-reported the resources of their villages, despite repeated threats to remove them for involvement in illegal pecuniary activities.[51] In fact, the failure of the early colonial state to establish a completely rationalized system of taxation meant that soon there was 'a return . . . to the Burman custom of paying [headmen] by a commission of their revenue collections'.[52] It was not until the introduction of a province-wide cadastral survey in the 1870s that it was possible effectively to make headmen salaried officials. When this was done, it was believed, land revenue receipts doubled.[53]

If the first British-appointed headmen were still able to keep land revenue which was legally due out of the coffers of the state, they were less successful in regard to the implementation of the capitation or head tax, which, at least in Arakan, was properly administered from the perspective of the British officials.[54] The introduction of such reforms was believed for many years to be one of the major achievements of the British state. The system of extortion and plunder that the first Commissioner of Tenasserim complained of was supposed to have been replaced by an impartial and incorruptible administration. The gap between theory and practice was great, for an 'incorruptible administration remained very largely an ideal throughout the British connexion'.[55] Bribery and corruption, the new name of the clientage aspects of local administration, now became a major administrative 'problem' for the state, as well as an additional financial burden upon the peasantry. It also became one of the practices that kept the system of local government from becoming more oppressive than it was.

Despite the fact that a large proportion of nominally state revenues continued to remain in or to flow to private hands during the British period, the government was more effective in taxing the land and people than the precolonial state had been. Increases in revenue were also in part due to the increased level of production. In Arakan, for example, between 1830–1 and 1868–9, before the boom in Burma's exports to Europe, the acreage devoted to paddy cultivation increased 139 per cent and the revenue on this land increased 213 per cent. During the same period the amount of garden and orchard land on which taxes had to be

51. *Correspondence for the Years 1825–26 to 1842–43*, p. 18.
52. Ibid., p. 1.
53. Ibid., p. 93.
54. 'Report on the Progress Made in the Arakan Division from 1865–66 to 1874–75', in *Report on the Progress of Arakan*, p. 2.
55. Donnison, *Public Administration*, p. 50.

paid increased over 1000 per cent and revenue went up more than 500 per cent. In all, total land revenue during the period increased 324 per cent. While the level of capitation tax was actually reduced, because 99 per cent more people were paying it in 1869 than in 1830, revenue increased 54 per cent, but the greatest increases in revenue were in new excise duties on spirits, toddy, and opium shops, which increased 96 per cent during the period.[56]

Nonetheless, financing the colonial state was never an easy matter. Its costs continued to rise as it assumed greater administrative and service responsibilities. The fact that the civil service élite were paid European salaries added significantly to the wage bill. Basic research on the finances of the colonial state remains to be done; it has been shown, however, that the country would have developed economically more rapidly had the colonial government not been an appendage of the Indian empire. From the earliest days, the government of India insisted that Burma be financially self-supporting and that no funds would be authorized from the central Indian treasury for its development.[57] However, when it did become a financially viable province of India following the development of the rice-exporting industry, there was always a shortage of funds for the development of roads and other infrastructure because of the system of 'provincial contracts' that existed until separation in 1937.[58] Even then, Burma had to assume a debt toward India and continue to pay for Indian army troops stationed in Burma.

The Shan States under the British

To illustrate a few of the points made earlier as well as to explain more fully the colonial state's organizational developments, an examination of the relationship of the colonial state with what came to be called the Shan states will prove useful here. Such an example is also illuminating for in this area, as in the other 'excluded' areas, the British were less intent upon introducing a rationalized administrative system. In the Shan states the colonial government initially followed the pattern of

56. *Report on the Progress of Arakan*, pp. 40–2.
57. Furnivall, 'The Fashioning Leviathan', p. 16.
58. Shein, *Burma's Transport and Foreign Trade*, p. 89; for an analysis of the provincial contract system and its impact on the finances of Burma, see Shein, Myint Myint Thant and Tin Tin Sein, ' "Provincial Contract System" of the British Indian Empire, in Relation to Burma — a Case of Fiscal Exploitation', *The Journal of the Burma Research Society*, LII, pt. II (Dec. 1969), p. 1–26.

political organization established near the end of the precolonial period at the lower levels of the political-administrative hierarchy, but it also began a process of rationalizing the administrative system from the centre which gradually permeated down to affect the lives of more and more of the population. In the case of the plains-dwelling peasantry this process, after a slow beginning in Arakan and Tenasserim, developed rapidly after 1886, so that by the time of the First World War few peasants had not been affected by these changes. In the hill areas, which the British governed by a separate system of 'indirect rule' and whereby they 'professed "to administer the chiefs rather than the people" ',[59] this process was much more gradual. And in the case of the peoples living in the Chin and Kachin designated areas, obvious administrative change did not occur until after independence.

For several reasons, this process was well underway before the Second World War in the Shan area as well as in the juridically but not administratively separate Kayah zone. One reason was that the British government shared the same concerns as the Burmese kings: that the Shan plateau and the mountains beyond posed the major strategic threat to the state for, historically, it was through or from these regions that invading armies attacked the Irrawaddy basin. A second reason was that the Shan states were, to use the language of the colonial state, the 'most politically advanced' of the hill areas. That is to say, they possessed an obvious class structure and had been governed in a more complex manner, on a larger geographical scale, than the so-called tribal communities of the Chin and Kachin regions, as well as those among the Karen. As discussed in Chapter I, in the Shan states the *Sawbwas* stood in a position comparable both to an independent sovereign paying tribute to the king at Ava, and as a *thu-gyi* or a *myo* under the administrative control of the centre. Therefore, it was easier to organize the region indirectly through the use of indigenous authorities than elsewhere in either the plains or the frontier areas. Finally, though it proved impossible to make the administration of the Shan states self-financing, it was thought possible to do so if the region was economically developed, because it possessed valuable teak reserves, potential mineral deposits and trade routes to the fabled markets of China. Thus, the developmental potential of the Shan states, coupled with the financial drain of their administration that the

---

59. Ba Thann Win, 'Administration of Shan States from the Panglong Conference to the Cessation of the Powers of the Saophas 1947–1959' (unpubl. MA thesis, Rangoon Arts and Sciences University, nd), p. 5.

British inherited from the monarchy, created the belief that the rationalization of their administration carried the promise of beneficial rewards for the state in trade, taxation and improved security.

But the economic potential of the region became exploitable only in the twentieth century. Initially, the British, like the kings, sought to control the area and its people as cheaply as possible through the utilization of the existing political authorities, the *Sawbwas*. Little was done to change this until new economic opportunities emerged. The British little understood the complexities of the Shan and other hill ecological zones they inherited. The simplistic pseudo-anthropology of the colonial world easily classified peoples and practices in an abstract and reifying manner, thus creating political problems of ethnicity and group relations for later generations. When taking over a new region, the British tended to accept and implement the advice they received from the existing local authorities who were most cooperative with them, and these figures, arguing their alleged historical grievances with the Burmese monarch, and by extension the Burman people, became the rulers recognized by the colonial state as the legitimate exercisers of authority in a particular region.[60]

In 1886 the British authorities sent letters to the *Sawbwas* explaining the principles that guided their policy. The chiefs 'were assured that there was no desire to interfere in the internal affairs of the State' which they governed, but they had to acknowledge British supremacy, maintain peace and not oppress their subjects. In exchange for the *Sawbwas* accepting these conditions and paying an annual tribute to the government of India's treasury, 'the British Government undertook to recognize the *Sawbwas* who were in effective possession, to uphold their rights, and to give freedom and open the way for commerce'.[61] In subsequent years, the descendants of the *Sawbwas* ruling in 1886 referred back to these undertakings to justify claims to semi-sovereign powers and privileges, but the British insistence on the fair treatment of the rulers' subjects and the opening of the states to free commerce gave them a pretext for increasing external interference in the states' internal affairs. Between 1886 and 1895 the *Sawbwas* pledged their allegiance to

---

60. Robert H. Taylor, 'Perceptions of Ethnicity in the Politics of Burma', *Southeast Asian Journal of Social Science*, 10, 1 (1982), p. 12.
61. Charles Crosthwaite, *The Pacification of Burma* (London: Frank Cass, 1968; 1st published 1912), p. 147.

the British crown, and after being forced to abandon any claim to control the borders of their domains were placed under the supervision of British Assistant Superintendents.

From the beginning, the colonial state attempted to limit the powers of the *Sawbwas* just as the nineteenth-century Burmese kings had done by insisting that the tribute levied upon their domains be calculated on the basis of the *thathameda* or household tax, levied under the supervision of central inspectors since Mindon Min's time. The *Sawbwas* wished to revert to an earlier system whereby they themselves determined the taxable resources of their states, thus allowing them to keep a larger proportion of revenues within their states. This was unacceptable to the British.[62] Nonetheless, in effect, but not in law, the *Sawbwas* were recognized as the heads of 'native states, with much the same status as the native states of India, and were placed under the personal supervision of the Chief Commissioner as Agent of the Governor-General [of India]'.[63] In law, the chiefs were British administrative agents permitted to maintain juridical and other rights over their subjects. Thus, despite some administrative rationalization, the egalitarian consequences of rationalized law were not to reach the Shan states until the 1950s.

Like the precolonial state, the colonial state denied the *Sawbwas* control over the forests, mines and mineral resources of their domains, but asserted proprietary control much more effectively through the granting of exploitation contracts (mainly to British firms). The towns which developed in the region during this period were also removed from the control of the *Sawbwas* and placed under local councils controlled by expatriates. The newly appointed Superintendents of the Northern and Southern Shan States who resided in their respective areas gradually increased their supervisory powers 'and there was a trend in the direction of extending to the Shan States the regulations which were in force in Upper Burma'.[64] This was because of the central state's desire that the *Sawbwas* 'adopt more orderly methods of government and more effective means of raising revenue'. The regulation of criminal and other law was increasingly standardized following the promulgation of 'a set

62. J. George Scott and J.P. Hardiman, *Gazetteer of Upper Burma and the Shan States* (Rangoon: Government Printing and Stationery, Burma, 1900), pt. I, vol. I, p. 300.
63. *A Study of the Social and Economic History of Burma (The British Period)*, pt. V: 'Burma Under the Chief Commissioners, 1886–87 to 1896–97' (Rangoon: Economic and Social Board, Office of the Prime Minister, roneoed, 1957), p. 6.
64. *Ibid.*, p. 12.

of rules, modelled on the Indian penal and procedural codes in a form adapted to a primitive people'.[65] The *Shan State Manual* came to supplement the customary law of the region as the guide to judicial behaviour for the *Sawbwas* (who remained the administrators of the law under the supervision of the Residents).[66] There was, however, no uniformity imposed on the region at that time.[67] The Superintendents also began to encourage the *Sawbwas* to regularize the management of their governments by having them 'submit rough budgets of proposed receipts and expenditures'.[68]

Though a few of the bureaucratic procedures of the rationalized state were imposed on the *Sawbwas* in the 1890s, little major change was attempted until the early 1920s, when political events elsewhere in British India and Burma necessitated the creation of new administrative arrangements. The colonial government maintained its control over the *Sawbwas* during the colonial period through the threat of the removal of their tenure or the abolition of their state if they did not comply with the Superintendent's requirements. In fact, fourteen states were abolished through amalgamation by not maintaining *Sawbwa*ships, thus making for larger and more efficient administrative units.[69]

Although the intention of the British was not to change the *Sawbwas*' traditional relationship with their subjects, in time the colonial administration 'tended to make the Chiefs think more and more of their own interests and less and less of their subjects who [could] no longer drive them out if found unsatisfactory or oppressive' because they were backed by the superior armed force of the colonial state.[70] For the *Sawbwas*, colonial rule made their task easier as long as they obeyed the British, but

65. Scott and Hardiman, *Gazetteer of Upper Burma and the Shan States*, pt. I, vol. I, p. 398; see also *Materials for the Study (British Period)*, pt. V, p. 1.
66. Interview with Sao Khun Khio, former *Sawbwa* of Mongmit, Cambridge, England, Jan. 1983.
67. Scott and Hardiman, *Gazetteer of Upper Burma and the Shan States*. pt. 1 vol. 1, pp. 316–8.
68. *Materials for Studying (British Period)*, pt. V, pp. 11–12; Scott and Hardiman, *Gazetteer of Upper Burma and the Shan States*, pt. I, vol. I, p. 311.
69. Changes are noted in *The Shan States Manual* (Rangoon: Government Printing and Stationery, Burma, 1933), pp. i–ii. See also Minutes of the 5th Meeting of the Committee on Scheduled Areas Held on the 15th Dec. 1942 in BOF M/4/2803 and Minute Paper Bo. 761/38, Burma Office: Proposed Amalgamation of the two lesser Shan States, by R.M.J. Harris, 11 Feb., 1938, in BOF 1506/37.
70. Minutes of the 5th Meeting of the Committee on Scheduled Areas held on the 15th Dec. 1942. BOF M/4/2803.

for their subjects the weight of the state became greater. This was especially the case as the more settled conditions created by the colonial regime led the *Sawbwas*, few of whom were really wealthy, to attempt to increase their tax revenues, an action which in areas where the people were not well-integrated into the traditional domain led to rebellion. By the mid-1900s, several *Sawbwas'* expenditures had outrun their incomes and they had to be removed or disciplined by the Superintendents for debt or extravagance. The monetization of the economy subsequent to increasing taxation also led to a growth in crime which caused some states to expand their police forces and to build better prisons.[71]

The formal administrative entity known as the Shan States was not created until the early 1920s. The decision to introduce the dyarchy system of partially responsible government into central Burma made it necessary, in the eyes of the British, to establish a Shan States Federation in order to protect the *Sawbwas* from the effects of a more democratic government and of Burmese nationalism. The intent was to remove the Shan states from the legislative jurisdiction of the soon to be formed Indian central and Burma provincial legislatures. Also, it was hoped that the creation of the Federation would ensure that 'in the course of time' the Shan states would not be a financial drain on the revenues of the central Burma state. This was because the introduction of elections in Burma proper would mean that the voting taxpayers there would have to subsidize the Shan states over which the elected ministers would have no control. But the Federation was far from a genuine federal government. It merely established a Council of *Sawbwas* to advise the Commissioner while simultaneously giving the British administration greater control over the financial affairs and economic development of the *Sawbwas'* states. Matters such as road construction and other public works were removed from the control of the states, though education remained their responsibility.[72] At the same time, a separate civil service known as the Burma Frontier Service was established to administer the Shan states as well as the other excluded areas.[73] Clearly, the establishment of the Shan States Federation was not intended to enhance the

71. *Materials for Studying (British Period)*, pt. VI, p. 1.
72. 'Preliminary Proposals for the Future Administration of the Shan States', by T. Lister, 6 March 1920. IOF L/PS/10/145. A copy is also found in BOF P&J(B) 396.
73. Letter, F. Lewisohn, Chief Secretary, Government of Burma, to Political Secretary, Government of India, 25 Aug. 1920. IOF L/PS/10/1073.

powers or status of the *Sawbwas*, but rather had the effect of bringing their areas under tighter British administrative control.

Despite the effect of British policy, which was to subsume the *Sawbwas* within a larger federation and to impose the strictures of the rationalized state upon them, the local rulers never gave up their desire to be recognized as the hereditary rulers of sovereign states under British protection. The final decade and a half before the Japanese invasion in 1942 saw the *Sawbwas* fight a rearguard action against the British to preserve and enlarge what had now become defined by them as their traditional and historic rights as independent monarchs. The *Sawbwas* were concerned about losing control over the internal affairs of their states as well as being absorbed into the larger political and administrative system of the central state. Both they and the British recognized that they were anomalies in the rationalized, formally democratic, and egalitarian structures of the central state. Financially, they were unable to fend for themselves either singulary — except for those states with extensively developed teak and mineral resources — or in a Federation, and thus remained dependent upon finance from Rangoon. Various compromises were reached between the *Sawbwas* and the government during the 1930s, but the *Sawbwas* never achieved their desire to be recognized as independent sovereigns like the Malay sultans and the Indian princes. Aware as they were of the nationalist demands of politicians in Burma proper, as well as some of their own subjects who had been educated in Rangoon, for the incorporation of the Shan states into a democratic and independent Burma, they sought to demonstrate their loyalty to the British before the war by organizing their own military forces for the defence of the country (a measure which also provided them with their own security forces).[74] At the same time they sought to ensure that the British would do nothing to alter their status after the war.[75]

The consequences of the Second World War on the nature of state power in the Shan states will be discussed in a subsequent chapter. After the impact of nationalism reached the Shan states and began undermining the authority of the *Sawbwas*, the process of incorporating the states — along with the remainder of the frontier areas — into the unified and uniform structures of the central state accelerated. But had the post-colonial authorities not changed the shape of the distribution of

---

74. Burma Defence Bureau Intelligence Summary no. 10, 28 Oct. 1939. BOF I 358.
75. Text of proposals of Representatives of Shan Chiefs to the Governor, 14 March 1941. BOF 1506/37.

power and the relationship of the Shan states with Burma proper during and after the Second World War, the British would have done so in any case. The British spent the war years planning how to consolidate the Shan states, reduce their number, make their government less autocratic, and link them to a federal Burma, thus completing the rationalization of their administration begun sixty years earlier.[76] The intent of these plans was to truncate the independence of Burma, but the effect would have been to further undermine the powers of the *Sawbwas*. No matter who won the war, no matter who took control of the central state of Burma, the imperatives of the modern state meant that the Shan states would in time become egalitarian and more firmly integrated into the political and administrative system of Burma proper.

Rationalizing and Expanding the Functions of the State

The changes in authority relations which occurred as a result of the new territorial and bureaucratic nature of the colonial state were not merely a function of foreign rule coupled with administrative rationalization. These changes were also a consequence of two other factors. First, the colonial state faced greater physical resistance to its authority which required it to develop stronger instruments of suppression and social control, and, secondly, the social changes consequent to economic change, urbanization, population growth, and new class formations, demanded that the state assume greater responsibilities in such fields as education, agriculture and public health. In an ironical manner, the British, who came with a pledge to free the people of Burma from the shackles of a state that denied a distinction between the public and private spheres of life, did the contrary by ensuring that the private sphere could be controlled and manipulated more directly and immediately by the public sphere. The shackles of custom were replaced by the fetters of regulation of personal choice by police, courts, and the beginnings of the modern state's control of private choice in education, occupation and lifestyle. The initial increase in the range of personal options that were apparent in the nineteenth century soon gave way to tighter regulation and growing resentment in the twentieth.

---

76. See correspondence in BOF M/4/2803.

State Security and Public Order The security of the colonial state rested primarily on the army, although by the close of the British period the government had developed more complex instruments of social and political control by the police, including an intelligence capacity which allowed it to monitor the plans of anti-state and anti-British movements and individuals. Such activities were, however, minor in the overall maintenance of the state. The army upon which the colonial state depended was that of the Indian empire; it was this army which had created the three British victories over the kings in the nineteenth century and supplied the personnel which established most of the initial colonial administrative order.

One of the reasons advanced in 1885 for the final annexation of northern Burma was the external threat to the security of India and British Burma which would be posed if France or some other power gained control of the upper Irrawaddy valley and the Shan plateau. However, after the 1893 agreement between France and Britain to neutralize the Chao Phraya valley in neighbouring Siam, there was no longer an obvious external threat to India and Burma from the east until the early 1940s. With China weakened by internal disorder and external penetration, Laos and Vietnam under French control, Siam for all practical purposes within the British sphere of influence, and India part of the same empire, few in Burma or elsewhere in the British empire felt there was any threat to the external security of the colony even after the rise of Japanese militarism and expansionism in the 1930s.

Therefore, 'the primary role of the Army in Burma' was 'Internal Security'.[77] After each of the Anglo-Burmese wars, troops from the British-Indian army were retained in Burma to garrison the towns and maintain control until civilian administrators could take over their tasks. When, after the 1852 annexation of Pegu, and more especially after the 1886 deposition of Thibaw, there was widespread disorder and rebellion against the new rulers, more troops were brought in to restore order.[78] During the twentieth century both regular British and Indian troops were always stationed in the country. In 1938 there were a total of 4,713 British soldiers plus 358 officers in the country as well as 5,922 Indian army or Burma army troops, of which more than half were Indian. The core of the British Burma army which was created only on April 1, 1937, by transferring units of the Indian army to the command of the

77. Notes on the Land Forces of Burma, app. III (n.d., [1938]), typescript, IOF L/WS/1/276.
78. See ch. III, pp. 156–60.

Governor of Burma, was the Burma Company of Sappers and Miners. This was made up of British officers and NCOs with 380 other ranks drawn entirely from the plains-dwelling population, and the Battalion of the Burma Rifles composed of British and indigenous officers and 715 indigenous other ranks, all of whom came from the hill areas.[79]

From 1887 until near the end of the British period, except briefly during the First World War, it was army policy not to recruit and train infantrymen from the plain and delta because, it was argued, they were too expensive to maintain in comparison to Indian troops and less prepared to accept the methods of discipline and training of the Indian army. Also, as a matter of political policy, it was thought imprudent to train and arm a large number of Burmans because they had only been conquered in the previous century and, being in the terminology of the British-Indian army a 'martial race', would perhaps be more of a hindrance than an asset to the maintenance of British rule.[80] Even after the rapid expansion of the Burma army between 1939 and 1941 when it was felt necessary to raise forces following the outbreak of the Second World War in Europe, as well as the fear of Japanese aggression in Asia, only 1,893 of the troops of the regular Burma army were classified as Burmans, in comparison to 2,797 Karens, 852 Kachins, 1,258 Chins, 32 Yunnanese, 330 Chinese, 137 others, and 2,578 Indians. Even the Territorial Army, a sort of home guard which was expanded most rapidly, contained after two years recruitment only 1,189 Burmans compared to 939 Karens and 940 Shans out of a total of 3,272.[81] The unwillingness of the army to recruit men from Burma proper was interpreted by Burmese nationalists as part of the 'divide and rule' strategy of the imperialists. The British government undoubtedly viewed using Indian and hill area-recruited troops as the safest method of controlling nationalist opposition in central Burma, for there was less likelihood that they would side with demonstrators or rebels they were sent to put down.

The regular Burma army as well as the British and regular Indian army were held as a reserve and only called out 'in aid of the Civil Power' at times of severe public disorder such as riots and major rebellions. The largest of these, the Hsaya San peasant rebellion in 1930-2, required more than 3,500 additional regular Indian army troops to be brought

---

79. Notes on the Land Forces of Burma, p. 2.
80. Furnivall, *Colonial Policy and Practice*, pp. 178-83.
81. Statement Showing by Class [i.e, ethnicity] the Strength (other than officers) of the Burmese Army and the Frontier Force on the 30th April 1941. BOF 66/41.

into the province from central India.[82] For the normal maintenance of internal security the British government relied primarily upon the Military Police, which had been created from units of the Indian army after the suppression of the disorders following the 1852 annexation, and expanded in the same manner after 1886. After the separation of Burma from India, the Military Police was divided into two units, one primarily for use in central Burma and under the control of the elected Burmese Home Minister, and the other, renamed the Burma Frontier Force, for use in the excluded areas (but available for deployment in Burma proper) under the control of the Governor. The troops of the Military Police, numbering 4,294 men in 1941, were almost entirely Indian and were under the command of British and Indian officers seconded from the Indian army. At that time, the 10,073-strong Frontier Force was composed of 7,376 Indians with the remainder coming primarily from the hill areas of Burma.[83]

The development of the Military Police, also referred to in the blunt language of the colonial state as the 'punitive police' because of their use in punishing entire villages for alleged acts of crime, followed from the inability of the unarmed civil police force to maintain order in the villages and towns. Initially, the British attempted to develop a local police service from the officials they inherited from the precolonial system. The *kyedangyi*, the largest taxpayer who assisted the *thu-gyi* in revenue collection and policing, was enlisted as an unarmed village constable. By the 1880s, if not earlier, these men were no longer figures of influence in their communities and the British found it increasingly difficult to recruit men for the post, despite increasing the salary which went with the job.[84] The bulk of the unarmed civil police were recruited in Burma proper and in 1938 nearly 71 per cent of all civil police were Burmans. However, nearly 11.5 per cent of the civil police were Indians and another 8.7 per cent were Karens, indicative of the state's continued reliance on minority and foreign personnel for maintaining law and order. Reflecting the largely Indian nature of the population of Rangoon, only about 26 per cent of the police in the capital were Burmans while over 67 per cent were Indians.[85] The senior police officers and most urban sergeants were British.

82. Cady, *History of Modern Burma*, p. 316.
83. Statement Showing by Class [i.e, ethnicity] the Strength (other than officers) of the Burmese Army and the Frontier Force on the 30th April 1941. BOF 66/41.
84. Mills, 'Burmese Peasant Response', p. 95.
85. Notes on the Land Forces of Burma.

From the 1880s onwards the British state devoted a larger and larger effort to maintaining and expanding the police force in a vain effort to control the growing social unrest and high rate of crime, including murder, in the country. Between 1871–5 and 1933–8, the rates of crime committed and reported to the police rose dramatically. Dacoity increased 41 per cent and the rate of murder 53 per cent.[86] Increases in crime in a district often led to the imposition of extra police, including Karen levies and punitive police forces, which were paid for out of taxes added to the villagers' normal land rates.[87] While in the early years of British rule it could have been fairly claimed that life and property were safer than under the king's rule,[88] this was doubtful by the end of the colonial period.

In summarizing the role of the police in maintaining internal security during the colonial period, one can do little better than cite the experiences of Tharrawaddy district in the reasonably quiet period between 1900 and 1912. When, in 1907, there developed 'another severe storm of crime . . . the regular police force was increased by 117 men and a punitive police force of 263 men was imposed . . . at a cost . . . which was recovered from the local inhabitants by a ten per cent cess upon land revenue.' This increase was on top of an earlier increase in the size of both police forces, so that by 1905 there was a ratio of 1 policeman for every 760 head of population compared to 876 per policeman five years earlier. As a former Deputy Commissioner of Tharrawaddy wrote in retrospect,

a marked feature of the modern history of the district is the frequency with which punitive police forces have been imposed; in the late nineties they were a regular institution in most of the townships. The increase of crime in 1906 and the repeated effect of an increased police force in diminishing crime suggest nothing so much as a spring compressed by the police and expanding at the slightest relaxation of their pressure.[89]

Courts and the Law The strong arm of the colonial state, the force provided by the military and the police, was justified in the name of the preservation of a system of law which was felt by the British to be more

86. G.E. Harvey, *British Rule in Burma 1824–1942* (London: Faber and Faber, 1946), p. 40.
87. S.G. Grantham, *Studies in the History of Tharrawaddy* (Cambridge University Press [for private circulation], 1920), pp. 17–18.
88. Furnivall, *Colonial Policy and Practice*, p. 53.
89. Grantham, *Studies in the History of Tharrawaddy*, p. 24.

fair and just than that which they had found upon their arrival in Burma. The administration of law and the courts were important to the colonial state; and the consequences of this change were crucial in shaping the relationship of the individual to the state during the colonial period. The growing depersonalization of the legal system, its increasingly complex and rule-bound nature, and its tendency to rely less and less on Burmese customary law and more and more on British-Indian codified law, meant not only a more expensive and less understandable legal system for the mass of the population, but also an increase in crime and litigation as the customary bonds of society were replaced with what seemed arbitrary and unjust dictates from the foreign-controlled state.

With the establishment of British rule in Tenasserim, the Commissioner began the introduction of the British-Indian system. British Burma's legal system remained under the supervision of courts in Calcutta until 1872. Under this system the executive officer of the government was responsible for all judicial functions including both prosecution and adjudication in civil and criminal cases.[90] Initially, the Commissioner in Tenasserim instructed his subordinates to apply Burmese customary law 'as far as possible', and gave them wide discretion in this.[91] It had been his original intention to re-establish Burmese courts, but he found their structure and principles 'so complicated' that to him the traditional courts were incapable of dispensing justice but were merely institutions of official extortion and arbitrary decision-making not untainted by bribery. It was therefore necessary for him 'to draw up a Code of Regulations for the Administration of Justice' making the Commissioner, or his deputy or assistant, the sole judge in all courts.[92] Nonetheless, these courts were to be advised, as he wrote at the time, by 'a person . . . skilled in the Burman laws and usages and well acquainted with the decisions that would have been given by the late Judges in cases similar to those that may be brought before the Commissioner, according to whose statement a judgement will be given so long as it be not cruel or does not militate against natural justice'.[93] In order to ensure that justice was done in the eyes of the Burmese as well as the British, the first courts used local juries, but when the British judges

90. Alan Gledhill, 'Burma', in vol. E. no. 7 of John Gilissen (ed.), *Bibliographical Introduction to Legal History and Ethnology* (Brussels: Editions de l'Institut de Sociologie, Université Libre de Bruxelles, 1970), p. 10.
91. *Selected Correspondence Tenasserim Division*, pp. 1–2.
92. *Ibid.*, pp. 9–10.
93. *Ibid.*, p. 11.

in Calcutta reviewed some of these decisions and found them unacceptable, being too much in the nature of Burmese arbitration and accommodation, as well as improvisation, than based upon a search for 'evidence and truth', the jury system was abandoned.[94]

It was through the courts as well as the gaols and police buildings that the British state first became permanently visible to most of the people.[95] Still, until the 1870s, most disputes between villagers and even villages were settled through the traditional system of arbitration conducted by the *myo-thu-gyi*. At the same time, however, the British appointed indigenous judicial officers to apply British-Indian law in the villages. Few of these law advisers were familiar with English which was the language of this law and many did not even have copies of the laws they were expected to interpret. In such circumstances, one can safely assume that in most cases Burmese practice in the courts as well as the tradition of avoiding the courts altogether continued to be followed, especially in civil cases.[96] However, once the colonial authorities decided that it was necessary to maintain law and order more systematically throughout their jurisdictions, they appointed the requisite legal officers to carry out the management of a full judicial system as then found in India.

In 1872 a Judicial Commissioner was appointed for Lower Burma 'who exercised most of the powers of an Indian High Court and for some purposes sat with the Recorder of Rangoon to form a Special Court'.[97] The involvement in judicial administration by the Chief Commissioner, until then the highest appeals officer in British Burma, had been scant, receiving no more than twelve appeals per year. The full-time Judicial Commissioner, having no other duties, managed by 1875 to generate 225 appeals and called on his own initiative 1,613 other cases to review. The effect of this typical bureaucratic behaviour was to weaken the authority of the lower courts. In time, 'almost no order was looked upon as final' because every decision was potentially open to review.[98] This was particularly the case after 1891, when a British Judicial Commissioner set aside a *myo-thu-gyi*'s decision for being contrary to indigenous law.[99]

The elaboration of the judiciary grew apace with the growth of the

94. Furnivall, 'The Fashioning of Leviathan', p. 24.
95. *Report on the Progress of Arakan*, p. 9.
96. Furnivall, *Colonial Policy and Practice*, pp. 38–9.
97. Gledhill, 'Burma', p. 10.
98. Donnison, *Public Administration*, p. 36.
99. Furnivall, *Colonial Policy and Practice*, pp. 75–6.

state in the twentieth century. A Judicial Commissioner was appointed for Upper Burma in 1890 and a new judicial service was formed in 1905 to relieve the Deputy Commissioners of all civil and some criminal cases.[100] The office of the Recorder at Rangoon was merged with that of the Lower Burma Judicial Commissioner in 1900 and a Chief Court of Lower Burma was formed with appeal and revisional powers throughout the southern regions. In 1923 a court with jurisdiction throughout Burma proper was set up when the Rangoon High Court assumed the duties of the Chief Court of Lower Burma and the Judicial Commissioner of Upper Burma. At the lower levels, as well, the judicial system became more elaborate and separate from the executive officers of government. Magistrates tried lesser crimes and Sessions Courts dealt with the more serious, as well as serving as the first court of appeal. The Sessions judges were also in charge of the new system of district courts which relieved Deputy Commissioners of judicial tasks in most areas of Burma proper.[101] However, this modern judicial system did not extend to the frontier areas.[102] There the traditional rulers under the supervision of the British Superintendents applied simplified British-Indian law or modified customary law as interpreted through the minds of British-trained officials.

The result of the changes in the judicial system introduced by the colonial state was not only growing litigation and crime, but also a weakening of the authority of local government officials, both indigenous and foreign. The replacement of customary law with British-Indian codified law became one of the most important grievances that Burmese nationalist politicians could cite in developing popular arguments for their movements. As one Burmese scholar of the subject has written, 'in Burma . . . under British rule, the judicial system became more and more the apparatus of a foreign government . . . there was a wide gap between law and life and to the common man the "rule of law" came to be almost synonymous with caprice.'[103] As that 'capricious' law was used as an instrument to remove peasants from their lands

100. *Ibid.*, p. 72.
101. Gledhill, 'Burma, pp. 10–11.
102. Donnison, *Public Administration*, p. 55.
103. Hla Aung, 'The Effect of Anglo-Indian Legislation on Burmese Customary Law', in David C. Buxbaum (ed.), *Family Law and Customary Law in Asia: A Comtemporary Legal Perspective* (The Hague: Martinus Nijhoff, 1968), p. 80. A similar assessment of judicial changes under the British is given in Cady, *History of Modern Burma*, pp. 144–8, and Harvey, *British Rule in Burma*, pp. 33–7.

in the twentieth century, the strength of negative feeling toward it cannot be underestimated.

Nonetheless, the utility of colonial law and its institutions and consequences justified its use for many Burmese as well as the state. The growth of the indigenous legal profession is one indicator of this. The development of a more complex economy and society which followed upon the imposition of the rationalized state made property law and procedural rules and norms vital for controlling the new social forces which were coming to dominate Burma's political community. Increasingly, for many urban and propertied segments of society, the law came to be seen as a tool rather than as a moral norm, a blessing if you could use it to advantage, a curse when you could not. Even peasants came to use the law when they were unable to gain protection or redress through more direct methods. The old proverb that 'a Tharrawaddy man comes to you with a law-book in one hand and a *dah* [common knife] in the other'[104] soon became true of most of the Burmese population.

State and Economy Under the prevailing liberal economic doctrine of *laissez-faire*, the economic functions of the colonial state were to have been kept to a minimum. Particularly during the nineteenth century, when the state assumed few economic responsibilities, Burma's traditional subsistence economy was transformed into an export-oriented, rice-production-based economy. Not assuming responsibilities, however, did not mean that the state lacked a keen interest in the trends of economic change and did not act to encourage those aspects it saw as politically and economically desirable from the perspective of its interests and external links. Measurement of economic growth became almost a fetish of the rationalized state. The consequences of the economic changes allowed to develop by the colonial state were, in terms of the development of contemporary Burma's social and political order, as important as the changes introduced by the state itself.

The key to the colonial government's economic policies in the nineteenth century was the encouragement of trade between Burma and India and further afield. Thirty years before the annexation of Arakan and Tenasserim, the Governor-General of India saw Burma as a potential market for British and Indian goods. Other British observers, sent to Burma in the first half of the nineteenth century, saw the Irrawaddy delta as a potential source of additional foodstuffs for India in time of

---

104. Grantham, *Studies in the History of Tharrawaddy*, p. 21.

famine, and as a 'safety-valve' for the overcrowded and famine-threatened masses of the subcontinent.[105] Indeed, after the annexation of Pegu, the government of India encouraged the migration of Indian labour to Burma to open up the sparsely settled delta. For ten years after 1876 the government subsidized the migration of labourers recruited by agents in India to travel to Burma,[106] but this scheme was abandoned in place of the 'laws of the economy' to provide sufficient incentive for the flow of labour from Bengal and southern India to Burma throughout the remainder of the nineteenth and the first four decades of the twentieth century. This business expanded and became so lucrative that the interests behind it lobbied long and hard to try to ensure that Burma remained a province of India and did not become closed to Indian labour by the imposition of immigration restrictions.

It was in the period between the final annexation in 1885 and the outbreak of the First World War in Europe that the economic structure of modern Burma came into being. Until then the British in the south and the kings in the north and central regions continued to preside over an economy that had only very loose ties with the larger world trade system. As was discussed in the previous chapter, Mindon and his officials were as keenly aware of the benefits of foreign trade and increased production for the strength of the state as their predecessors in the Toungoo and early Konbaung dynasties had been, and they had also been made aware of the advantages of economic reform in order to free resources for increased domestic production. However, the political environment in which they operated had made radical changes to the traditional system slow and difficult. Even in southern Burma, where none of these political inhibitions existed, the speed of change was not great and was limited to small areas and a few trade items (except perhaps in Arakan, which became closely tied to the more active trading zone of the Bay of Bengal). Indicative of the slow rate of change in the economy until the final three decades of the nineteenth century was the apparent fact that there was no money-based exchange economy of country-wide proportions until the 1880s. The late impact of an exchange economy on Burma was one of the factors in determining the consequences, in class

105. Michael Adas, *The Burma Delta, Economic Development and Social Change on an Asian Rice Frontier, 1852–1941* (Madison: University of Wisconsin Press, 1974), pp. 28–9.
106. N.R. Chakravarti, *The Indian Minority in Burma: The Rise and Decline of an Immigrant Community* (London: Oxford University Press for the Institute of Race Relations, 1971), pp. 8–9.

and ethnic terms, of economic development during the next seventy years.[107]

When the British first arrived in Burma, they perceived the traditional economy to be sluggish and the people to be insufficiently oriented to trade and commerce. It was the intention of the new rulers to change these conditions; for the wealth and security of their empire depended upon the lively development of trade and the state revenue it would provide to pay for their ruling institutions. As Mr Maingy, the first Commissioner of Tenasserim wrote less than a year after taking charge of his domain, the king's discouragement of unofficial exports was now abolished and his government had been able to open up a small but important trade between Tenasserim and Malaya, from whence Chinese merchants were coming to purchase sapan wood. Maingy, in a tone of self-congratulation, noted 'this may be considered as the first decided instance of the Burmese shaking off that indifference they have hitherto evinced about money, and it has been my utmost endeavour to encourage this feeling so that it may be extended to other branches of labour.'[108] He was only the first of many with this ambition.

Aware as Maingy was of the importance of trade for the development of his domain, he was not able to ignore the political necessity of controlling food supplies for his population — any more than the kings of Burma had been. Having abolished the king's prohibition on the export of all kinds of goods, he was forced to impose a control on rice exports from Tavoy in order to avoid political unrest in Mergui. Under the kings, Mergui had been a rice deficit area and had depended upon imports from Tavoy to feed the population. However, rice exports under Maingy's liberal regime had received 'such a spur from the large and unknown profits of a free foreign trade in grain that the love of gain was in danger of running away with a due regard to [the people's] own wants'. He then had to impose limits on this trade after determining first the supply and demand situation in his territories. 'In the balance of good and evil', he wrote, 'I preferred a deviation from Political Maxim [à la Adam Smith] to the misery of a starving population which seemed evident in the rage for exportation.'[109] This was the colonial state's first act of intervention in the free flow of commerce for the benefit of the stability of the society and the state.

107. Shein, *Burma's Transport and Foreign Trade*, p. 8.
108. *Selected Correspondence Tenasserim Division*, p. 43.
109. *Ibid.*, pp. 48–9.

Rationalizing and Expanding the Functions of the State 109

After the annexation of the Irrawaddy delta the state faced fewer such problems. The delta region was underpopulated when the British took control and its agricultural potential was thought to be very promising. What was most lacking was manpower to develop it, and this need was the reason for both the government's encouragement of migration from India, and, more importantly, for the migration of peasants from central to southern Burma who provided the bulk of the labour to open the frontier. The state provided very few inputs into this development although there was some expenditure on the development of bunds and flood-prevention devices to ensure the protection of lands from salination. The rapid growth of rice production in the delta meant that from 1851 till the 1920s, despite two or three periods of depressed prices, particularly in the 1890s and the late 1900s, the migrant cultivators of the region were, in comparison with what was to follow, relatively prosperous. There was plenty of land for development with little or no initial capital investment, and the international price of rice and the level of demand were both normally high. The quick profits to be made in the region attracted not only peasant cultivators but also indigenous land speculators and moneylenders who took advantage of the new protection of ownership and loan repayment that British law provided. Speculation in land and usurious interest rates provided easier profits than tilling the new paddy fields.

The phenomenal growth of the delta economy can be seen by comparing the total land under cultivation at the beginning of the period and at the end. According to the best available estimates, the delta region, also the granary of Konbaung Burma, contained over 662,000 acres of cultivated land in 1856–7. By correcting these figures and adjusting for other factors, Adas has concluded that at least 700,000 to 800,000 acres were under cultivation at that time. However, as little as fifteen years later, in 1871–2, 1,146,000 acres were under cultivation, and this was a mere fraction of the total reached by the mid-1930s, 8,702,000 acres.[110]

The inflow of internal labour into the delta to open the fields to cultivation left only one major obstacle to the full development of Burma as a rice-exporting nation. This was the lack of cheap and reliable means of getting the harvest from the fields and villages to the ports. It was in this area that the government first assumed major responsibilities by encouraging, and sometimes financing either directly or through

---

110. Adas, *Burma Delta*, p. 22.

subsidies and contracts, the development of a modern communications infrastructure. Until then the costs of transport made profitable rice export nearly impossible, at least on a large scale. In 1874, for example, the price of rice at Rangoon was three times what it was in Toungoo and other remote rice-growing areas, and the significant gap in prices between 'the growing and exporting centres discouraged any extension of cultivation'.[111] Only along the Irrawaddy river, where the new steam-powered boats of the Irrawaddy Flotilla Company operated with a form of hidden state subsidy, were transport prices low enough to justify export production. The cost of transporting grain from areas far from the river by slow bullock carts thwarted the development of new fields in these areas until the 1870s.

Therefore the development of roads, and more importantly, railways, was crucial for the expansion of the export trade. Internal security was the major reason for the government's desire to improve transportations, thus allowing troops to be moved more rapidly and cheaply to areas of disturbance and lowering garrison costs. Ultimately, the economic impact of the railways was to prove of greater significance.[112] The government saw the need to develop roads to lower transport costs, but was constrained by budgetary considerations as they had to be built out of current revenues. By 1870 there were only 709 miles of roads in British Burma and three years later there were still only 815 miles.[113] Railways, however, could be built with funds raised in capital markets and thus were easier for the government to finance. Between 1877 and 1886, 333 miles of railways were built in British Burma and by 1914 there were 1,599 miles of railways in operation.[114] Though crucial for the development of southern Burma, the expansion of the road and railway network in central Burma had less of an effect upon agricultural production. There the roads and railways were also built primarily for military purposes, subsequently becoming important for the export of minerals from the surrounding hills and the importation of foreign goods as well as rice from the south. By the end of the 1930s Burma was served by 4,100 miles of roads and 2,060 miles of railways, all built and maintained by the state.[115]

111. Shein, *Burma's Transport and Foreign Trade*, p.40.
112. *Ibid.*, p. 61–4.
113. *Ibid.*, p. 37.
114. *Ibid.*, pp. 41–2.
115. Harvey, *British Rule in Burma*, p. 7.

The Development of New State Functions Though the maintenance of internal security and the encouragement of trade and agriculture through *laissez-faire* policies remained the essence of the colonial state's responsibilities from the turn of the century until the First World War, the government developed other functions designed to improve the living standards of the population and raise the level of economic production and efficiency. The liberal reforms of the European world were then being extended to Burma and much of the rest of colonial Southeast Asia. Most of these new functions took their outward form in the shape of new government agencies and ministries.[116] Their impact upon the nature of authority relationships in the countryside was discussed earlier. The development of a fuller and more modern system of medical provision and public health began in 1899 when the prison administration was separated from the hospitals. A central administration for land settlement and cadastral survey was developed after 1900. Government concern for credit begun in 1904 with the creation of the Cooperative Credit Department. A Forest Department, first begun in the 1860s, reached its full form in 1905, and an Agriculture Department came into being in 1906 along with a Veterinary Department and a Fisheries Department. The Public Health Department emerged from the work of the Sanitary Commissioner who was first appointed in 1908.[117] These, along with the Public Works Department, which saw to roads, canals, the construction and maintenance of public buildings and the government-owned railways, were little affected in future years by the political and social changes that went on around them.

The introduction after 1923 of the dyarchy system of government, which gave elected Burmese ministers executive authority over most of these departments, had little effect on their purposes or modes of operation. Most departments were staffed by British and Indian officials at the upper levels and tended to become preserves of certain minority communities at the lower levels. For example, the medical service became largely dominated by Indians and the railways by Indians and Anglo-Burmans. Among the élite administrative services, including the Burma Agricultural Service (Class I), the Burma Forest Service (I), the Indian Medical Service, the Burma Veterinary Service (I), the top administrative personnel of the Education Service (I), the Public Works

---

116. Cady, *History of Modern Burma*, pp. 148–50.
117. Furnivall, *Colonial Policy and Practice*, pp. 71–3; Donnison, *Public Administration*, pp. 42–3.

Department, the Railways and the Posts and Telegraphs Department, in the late 1930s, non-Europeans held only about 25 per cent of all posts.[118] According to the 1931 census, although 87.9 per cent of the total participants in the country's labour force were indigenous by birth, only 62.9 per cent of those involved in public administration were locally born and only 47.2 per cent of those working in the police and other security agencies were indigenous. In comparison, 28.9 per cent of those involved in public administration were Indian (2.3 per cent born in Burma) and 45.5 per cent of those in security work were Indian (2.0 per cent born in Burma).[119] The rationalized state was largely a foreign institution in the eyes of most of the population.

Despite the growth of its functional agencies, the bulk of the state's expenses until the end of the colonial period were directed at administrative costs. The rationalized state was expensive compared to its predecessor and the importation of the Indian system made it difficult to lower these costs. As late as 1938–9, only 24.3 per cent of all government expenditure was on health, education and economic development activities, while the remaining 75.5 per cent was spent on 'purely administrative services'.[120] Efficient as it was in increasing revenue, the rationalized state consumed most of its funds simply to maintain itself. And, unlike the precolonial state, its perpetuation was not deemed to depend upon maintaining and enriching the cultural and spiritual life of the community.

Education It was in the field of education that the colonial state had its most dramatic impact upon the culture of the people as well as upon their political responses to rationalization. The precolonial education system had been designed to provide the rudiments of literacy to boys through the decentralized agency of the village monastery or *pongyi kyaung*. Higher education was also provided through the monkhood, and the educational responsibilities of the religious institutions were part of their hold on the community and their utility to the monarchical state. The British, however, first saw education less as a prop for the

118. European and Non-European Strength of the Civil Departments of Burma (carbon typescript), 25 March 1943. Clague Papers in the India Office Archives and Library, London.
119. Taylor, 'Relationship Between Burmese Social Classes and British-Indian Policy', table 8, p. 45, based on *Census of Burma 1931*.
120. *Fiscal Enquiry Committee Report, Second Report* (Rangoon: Government Printing and Stationery, Burma, 1938), p. 1; statistical breakdown on p. 16.

state and an agency of cultural continuity than as an instrument for the training of a cadre of English-speaking clerks to fill government offices and provide skilled labour for the trading offices of foreign firms. As Vernon Donnison, once Chief Secretary of the colonial state wrote, the education provided in government schools 'was an alien affair imposed from above, not an indigenous growth developed to meet modern needs'. The kind of knowledge imparted was largely 'artificial' and 'did not grow out of the experience and inheritance of the people'.[121] Nonetheless, the opportunities for well paid and comfortable employment provided by an English education made such schools highly popular among those few who could gain access to them; for, by the 1870s, their graduates 'would be worth Rs. 150 to Rs. 200 a month in a merchant's or Government office' in Arakan.[122]

Western education was initially provided primarily in missionary schools in Tenasserim and Arakan, and later in Pegu. Following the development of the province of British Burma, the government began to take a more direct role in education and a Department of Education was established in Rangoon in 1866. At first, the government attempted to use the *pongyi kyaung* as a medium for the introduction of Western learning to Burmese youths, but the monkhood was by and large uncooperative and the government then concentrated its efforts on developing government schools and facilitating the activities of missionary schools. In 1891–2 there were 4,324 government recognized monastic schools but still only 890 secular schools. Less than thirty years later, in 1917–18, there were 4,650 secular schools and only 2,977 monastic schools. A major cause of the decline in the number of monastic schools was the belief by parents that their children would get a better education in the secular institutions.[123]

Most of the secular schools were privately owned and only élite institutions were directly under government or missionary management. In the 1930s there were 5,582 secular schools teaching in the Burmese medium, of which 5,440 were privately run under the lax supervision of local education authorities. The standards of these schools were not high and the requirements for employment as a teacher

---

121. Donnison, *Public Administration*, pp. 46–7. A similar assessment was made by an American teacher at Judson College in the 1930s. See John F. Cady, *Contacts with Burma, 1935–1949: A Personal Account* (Athens, Ohio: Ohio University Centre for International Studies, Southeast Asia Program, 1983), pp. 1–37, passim.
122. *Report on the Progress of Arakan*, p. 10.
123. Cady, *History of Modern Burma*, p. 179.

minimal. Nepotism rather than knowledge was often important in gaining a post.[124] Advanced education, necessary for the gaining of government and commercial employment, including a knowledge of English, was provided in the English-medium and Anglo-vernacular (i.e. English-Burmese medium) schools found in the towns and cities. The growth of the number of students in these schools and in college-level institutions in the twentieth century was dramatic.

The tremendous growth in the enrollment of students in secondary and university education is indicative of the changing society of the first four decades of the twentieth century. Whereas in 1900 there were 27,401 students in government recognized secondary schools, by 1940 there were 233,543 students, almost an eightfold increase. In college and university education the increase was even more dramatic, the figure rising from 115 students in 1900 to 2,365 students in 1940, an almost twentyfold increase. However, the growth of enrollment in colleges and universities did not mean that the Burmese population was reaping comparable benefits in terms of gaining the knowledge, skills and wealth that such education was intended to provide. As in other areas of change induced by the colonial state, communities not indigenous to Burma gained disproportionate benefits.[125]

While the overwhelming majority of secondary students was undoubtedly indigenous, this was not true of university students. The percentage of indigenous students in colleges between 1900 and 1925 fluctuated around 55 to 65 per cent. By 1940, however, in all institutions of higher education in Burma, Burman and Karen students were only a bare majority, 1,298 students out of 2,465. In University College at Rangoon University, the most important college in Burma, the proportion of indigenous students never reached two-thirds of the student body — and sunk to a bare majority during the peak of the depression in the early 1930s.[126] Increased opportunities for education in Burma commenced with the founding of Rangoon University in 1920 and the later founding of a medical college, a teacher training college, an intermediate

---

124. *Report of the Education Reconstruction Committee* (Rangoon: Government Printing and Stationery, Burma, 1947), pp. 4–5.
125. Taylor, 'Relationship Between Burmese Social Classes and British Indian Policy', table 10, p. 57, based on *Reports* or *Quinquinnial Reports on Public Instruction in Burma*.
126. *Ibid.*, table 11, p. 58, based on *Education Reports, 1900 and 1925*; table 12, p. 59, based on *Education Report, 1940*; table 13, p. 58, based on *Education Reports, 1927, 1937, 1940*. (All official government documents.)

college at Mandalay, and an agricultural institute at Pyinmana as well as the Baptist Judson College affiliated to Rangoon University. These new institutions not only increased the opportunities for Burmese students to gain higher education, but also increased the likelihood that Indian and other non-indigenous youths would stay in Burma for their education and subsequent careers. Thus, to the educated Burmese, the expansion of educational opportunities, like the development of other opportunities for social and economic advancement under British rule, was a mixed blessing. While it increased their opportunities for careers in administration, the professions, and commerce, it also increased the number of Indians who could successfully compete with them for such posts.

State 'Legitimacy' and Constitutional Policy

As noted earlier, the great strength of the colonial state was its external sources of military power and administrative organization gained from Britain and India. The great weakness of the colonial state was its inability to sustain support, either active or passive, from the indigenous population. The precolonial state had persisted with relatively few physical coercive instruments because it had to support it a vast range of religious and customary norms: these created an environment where questioning its legitimacy or purpose was not only not encouraged, but was rarely encountered. Dissatisfaction, when it arose among villagers or officials, was directed toward a particular set of superiors or a particular ruler, including the king himself *in extremis*, but not at the system. Such a culture made government easier than it would have been had there existed countervailing intellectual and political currents. On the other hand, one of the key sources of the physical weakness of the precolonial state was its inability to mobilize support, except in times of great peril and then often too late to be of assistance. The second and third nineteenth-century defeats at the hands of the British-Indian empire each time resulted in a *post-hoc* rising of popular sentiments around the symbols and institutions of Burmese monarchical government, Buddhist religion and local autonomy. But the kings themselves had few mechanisms for mobilizing such popular support, as the only instruments at their disposal were the *ahmu-dan* population and the patron-client system which allowed them to use these relatively uncoordinated forces for their defence.

For the British, however, the question of legitimacy did not arise in the same way. It was, of course, impossible for them to assume the mantle of the kings and the carapace of authority that enshrouded them. The possibility of retaining the throne after the third Anglo-Burmese war was briefly considered but soon abandoned for direct rule as already practised in British Burma. The lack of reliable Burmese princes to put on the throne and the effectiveness of the new system in the south made the abolition of the monarchy an easy decision. Otherwise, the British might have introduced into Burma something similar to the two-part administrative system which the French installed in Vietnam; retaining a powerless monarch in the north while directly managing a more internationally oriented colony in the south. The degree of ethnic homogeneity that Burma proper had attained by the 1870s, however, would have made the justification of such a division difficult, but perhaps not impossible.

Initially, in a world which had yet to experience mass nationalism, the colonial authorities felt confident that the new economic and personal freedoms created by their state and its laws would be sufficient to ensure the loyalty and support of the Burmese population. This would result not merely from the economic prosperity they believed would be created, but also because of the 'character' of the people. As Maingy wrote soon after taking control of Tenasserim, 'The Burmese of Mergui are a lively, good natured and tractable race . . . little trouble will, I think, be required to strengthen the sentiments of respect and confidence they already entertain towards our Government'.[127] In fact in the small and isolated provinces of Tenasserim and Arakan during most of the nineteenth century, the British faced little opposition to their rule. Perhaps this was because the new state did little to interfere directly in the lives of the people, and perhaps also because the symbolic continuity of the monarchical state and its support for traditional culture was still maintained in its prestigious splendour across the permeable border between the British territories and the Burmese state.

However, following the annexation of Pegu and the increasing power of the colonial state to intervene in the lives of the people, growing discontent with foreign rule became apparent and the British began to institute reforms designed to build political support for the colonial order. The few Burmese who actively cooperated with the colonial authorities by serving the government were primarily from the minority communities, such as the Karens; migrant communities, such as the

127. *Selected Correspondence Tenasserim Division*, p. 14.

Indians; and from what the British throughout the colonial period called the 'respectable classes', the wealthier minority of townspeople who benefited from the economic and career opportunities that the colonial state had created. But it was obvious to the governors of British Burma by the 1880s that the 'majority did not set much store by British law and order', and the recalcitrant attitude of the peasant majority was the cause of the introduction of the punitive police force at that time. As J.A. Mills has written, 'it seems hard to escape the conclusion that by the 1880s the British government must have been regarded as an even greater evil than a Burmese government, with most of its vices but few of its virtues'.[128]

In addition to increasing its repressive power in the face of both active and passive resistance, the British state began the introduction of participatory institutions with which to gain the cooperation and collaboration of the prosperous minority of the population whose interests were wedded to those of the colonial state. Initially, steps were taken to establish institutions of urban self-government. As early as 1883 two-thirds of the Rangoon municipal government was elected. The nature of its composition is indicative of those interests which the British felt to be on their side and therefore amenable to collaboration with the colonial order. Of the seventeen members elected to the city council only five were Burmese and one was a Karen, while of the remainder, five were British, two were Chinese, two were Hindus, and there were two Muslims and one representative from the British-run Chamber of Commerce.[129] The plural society was now recognized officially. The extension of elected and appointed municipal and district boards designed to establish the rudiments of local self-government outside the capital was even less successful than in Rangoon. 'People could barely be persuaded to accept membership of municipal boards in Burma, feeling that Government was "getting at them in some way".'[130]

At the central state level in Burma proper, the British did little to introduce institutions designed to mobilize support for or increase the legitimacy of the state until the 1920s. The advisory Legislative Council created in 1897 was composed entirely of British officials except for two other Europeans representing business interests. Following the expansion of this body to 15 members in 1909, four Burmese, one Indian and

---

128. Mills, 'Burmese Peasant Response', pp. 96–7.
129. Tinker, *Local Self-Government in India, Pakistan and Burma*, p. 49.
130. *Ibid.*, p. 51.

one Chinese were appointed by the Chief Commissioner. Its size had been increased to 30 by 1920, of which 10 were Burmese and two were Indians and one was Chinese. (Business and government held the other positions.)[131] This body had no impact upon the political life of the country. Because none of its members were elected, and as it had no power, it remained what it was intended to be, a means of ensuring that the Governor consulted with the economically and administratively most influential members of the colonial society's recognized élite.

The absence of serious and effective institutions to ensure that the colonial state developed some semblance of legitimacy in the eyes of the Burmese population before 1923 does not mean that the government was unaware of the problem posed by its lack of popular support. The breaking of the connection between the state and the Buddhist faith and the growth of new forces and classes convinced leading British officials that there was a need to create positive feelings toward the colonial state. Intellectual and political trends abroad also influenced the thinking of many officials who were aware of the politically unsettling impact of nationalism, and later socialism, on the political stability and legitimacy of the remainder of Asia, as well as of Europe, around the time of the First World War. Perhaps the most imaginative of such attempts to counter these intellectual and political trends was the appointment in July 1916 by Governor Sir Harcourt Butler of a 'Committee to Ascertain and Advise How the Imperial Idea May Be Inculcated and Fostered in Schools and Colleges in Burma'. The committee, composed of eight leading British administrators, four missionary educators, and two Burmese, 'was charged with devising means of realizing through the schools and colleges a spirit of justice, co-operation, and sacrifice in the interest of national development, coupled with a sense of personal loyalty to the king-emperor and an appreciation of the imperial idea.'[132] The committee was to come up with a means to create both 'sentiments of national patriotism and imperial loyalty' by showing how 'Burma for the Burmans within the Empire' was the only effective means of developing the country. The conclusion drawn by one civil servant as to how this seemingly impossible goal was to be achieved reveals that the ideas of legitimacy of the colonial state, in the eyes of the colonial rulers, had changed little between 1826 and 1916. He wrote that the student,

131. Cady, *History of Modern Burma*, p. 152.
132. The following discussion is based upon *ibid.*, pp. 195–9, from which the quotations are also taken.

should be taught not to regard his people as a conquered nation but to understand that England had assumed the task of the education and government of his country not as a tyrant but as a trustee for civilization in order to . . . build up those conditions of liberty and opportunity of the individual in which the people can learn to govern themselves.

Textbooks published by the colonial government conveyed much the same message. *Burma Under Colonial Rule* by S.W. Cocks,[133] a standard set history throughout the late colonial period, emphasized the despotic nature of the Burmese kings and their thwarting of economic and personal liberty in contrast to the prosperous and free equality of life allegedly created by the colonial state.

From about 1915 onwards, British imperial pronouncements made the repeated promise that the burden of the colonial task in India was not merely trade, commerce and profit, but the creation of the conditions for the development of self-government and democracy under British tutelage; by the 1920s these ideas had to be applied to Burma as well. The irony of the situation is that by the late 1930s, Burma had been granted a constitutional form that provided a greater degree of internal self-government than India or indeed almost any other Asian or African British colony had received by that time. But in the early 1920s it was not believed that Burma was as 'prepared for self-government' as was India. It was the logic of British policy toward India that unintentionally determined British policy toward Burma. For the sake of political expediency it was necessary to make it seem that Burma was being treated on an equal footing with India.

From 1919 it had been the avowed purpose of British policy toward India to make the colony a fully equal self-governing member of the British Commonwealth at some unspecified future date. This promise of eventual dominion status was made most unequivocally in 1929 by the Viceroy, Lord Irwin (later Lord Halifax), in his remark that the natural issue of British policy in India, as implied in the preamble to the Government of India Act 1919, was dominion status. But when the 1919 Act was passed by the British Parliament, its provisions to establish the dyarchy system of tutelary democracy were not applied to Burma. The dyarchy system had been recommended by the Viceroy, Lord Chelmsford, and the Secretary of State for India, Edwin Montagu. No one concerned with preparation of the Montagu-Chelmsford reforms visited Burma, and at that time no one serving on the executive

133. S.W. Cocks, *Burma Under British Rule* (Bombay: K. & J. Cooper, 1st edn., n.d.).

council of the Viceroy had had any experience of Burma.¹³⁴ Several Burmese politicians did travel to see Montagu while he was on a visit to India. He 'summed up the Burman leaders who came to see him as "nice, simple-minded people with beautiful clothes. Complete loyalty; no sign of political unrest". '¹³⁵ The Montagu-Chelmsford report contended that there was no demand or need for political reforms in Burma and implied that the Burmese were politically less advanced than Indians.¹³⁶ The report thus gave rise to the belief among Burmese leaders that Britain intended to treat Burma less liberally than India. This was an idea that was not without foundation and was not put to rest until independence.¹³⁷

In lieu of dyarchy, the Governor of Burma, Sir Reginald Craddock, prepared his own schemes for constitutional change with an emphasis upon Burma's fiscal autonomy from India. These plans were complex, and proved unacceptable not only to the Burmese nationalist leaders but to the governments of India and Britain as well.¹³⁸ Whereas the Burmese nationalists viewed them as reactionary, since all power remained in the office of the governor, the government of India opposed them because they would have lessened its financial and legal control of Burma. Soon after the slights of the Montagu-Chelmsford report and the Craddock schemes became known, the nationalist movement began its first sustained campaign. While directed initially toward problems of education rather than governmental reform, the country-wide student strike of 1920 demonstrated to the British government that there was political activity in Burma which required institutional outlets. Political *pongyi* under the leadership of U Ottama, including many younger monks who subsequently were involved in the General Council of Sangha Sammeggi (GCSS), toured Burma encouraging the populace to resist the British.¹³⁹

134. Tinker, *Local Self-Government in India, Pakistan and Burma*, p. 112.
135. *Ibid.*
136. Great Britain, Parliament, House of Commons, *Sessional Papers*, vol. VIII for 1918 (Cmd. 9109), p. 198, in Cady, *History of Modern Burma*, p. 201.
137. Later, when the separation of Burma from India was being supported both by the British government in London and Rangoon and British business interests in Burma (but opposed by Indian economic interests with involvement in Burma), many Burmese believed their support for separation was an effort to hold back the constitutional advance of Burma relative to that of other provinces of India. Similar fears were expressed after the Second World War as India's independence became imminent.
138. Cady, *History of Modern Burma*, pp. 199–212, for details.
139. *Ibid.*, pp. 213–41, gives the details. These points are taken up again in ch. III.

London was so unaware of political conditions in Burma that these demonstrations came as a surprise.

When news of the widespread political agitation reached Whitehall, preceded by two delegations of Burmese politicians to argue for Burma's inclusion in India's constitutional reforms, the Secretary of State relented. In 1921 Parliament voted to extend dyarchy to Burma and a Burma Reforms Committee was sent to Burma to work out the details of the changes. The special significance of this committee is that it was sent not as an agent of the government of India but as an instrument of Parliament, even though there were no MPs on it. Never again would London consider policy toward India without giving thought to the consequences for Burma. The episode also shattered the imperial illusion that the colonial state was self-perpetuating because of its fairness and efficiency and the alleged passivity of the Burmese. The relative political stability of Burma after the mid-1890s ended in 1920 and was never restored again under the British.

Five years after the introduction of dyarchy into Burma, the British government appointed a commission under Sir John Simon to investigate the operation of this experiment in democratic 'tutelage'. In regard to Burma, the Simon Commission had not only to consider whether further extensions of self-government should be applied to Burma if granted to India, but also whether Burma should remain an Indian province. The government was not to make the same mistake it had made ten years earlier and ignore the effects of change in India's state structure on Burma's political future. The government of Burma, through the Governor and his officials, was asked to comment on the possibility of separating Burma from India and extending representative institutions and Burmese control to the central government. While the officials would not officially recommend for or against separation (they had no public objections to greater democracy), they clearly favoured separation for administrative, constitutional and political reasons. Separation, they thought, would better involve Burmese politicians in the management of the state and allow the civil servants of Burma to get out from under the domination of the central Indian administration. Other reasons for separation included the relative national unity of Burma in comparison with India; the fact that Burma's economic interests were divergent from those of India, especially as the Indian tariffs designed to protect nascent Indian industries hampered Burma's imports, and that Burma's attachment to India was a continual drain on the revenues of the state. The reasons for keeping Burma as part of India were essentially military, most notably Burma's reliance for internal security and defence upon the Indian army. There were also financial reasons, all of which could be overcome by administrative arrangements.[140]

In addition to the memoranda of the government of Burma, the Simon Commission also received a report from a committee of conservative and cooperative members of the legislative assembly.[141] All of the members of the committee favoured separation except for one Indian member who demanded immediate dominion status. The majority's reasons for advocating separation were similar to those of the government but emphasized factors of greater concern to the indigenous population. Political groups unwilling to cooperate with the Simon Commission would have made the same points but more forcefully. First, the connection of Burma to India has always been 'unnatural' as it had been achieved by armed force and maintained merely for reasons of administrative convenience. Secondly, attachment to India was detrimental to the development of the economy of Burma. Thirdly, there was apprehension that continued attachment would destroy the traditional composition of Burma by the continued influx of Indians. As the Burma Committee summarized the latter two points: 'Burma's political subservience to India has seriously jeopardised her financial and economic interests and even threatens to denationalise her.'[142]

The Simon Commission recommended the separation of Burma from India, but this was vigorously opposed by the government of India and Indian economic interests in Burma who saw the loss of the province as the creation of a separate state which could be able to control the flow of labour and capital across its borders. The complex politics of the ensuing five years demonstrated the economic and political power of the Indian community and the civil servants' need to limit their preferences in order to meet nationalist political pressures.[143] Despite electoral results in 1932 which could have been interpreted to mean that the Burmese electorate

---

140. 'Secret Memorandum on the Separation of Burma from British India [by the Government of Burma to the Indian Statutory Commission]', 7 Jan. 1929, Clague Papers.
141. 'Report of the Burma Committee', *Report of the Indian Statutory Commission*, vol. III, pp. 509–25, Cmd. 3568. As the major nationalist parties boycotted the visit of the Simon Commission, the Committee was composed of members of the minor and minority parties in the legislative council.
142. *Ibid*, p. 510.
143. Details are provided in Taylor, 'Relationship Between Burmese Social Classes and British-Indian Policy', pp. 102–49.

and politicians did not desire Burma's separation from India, the actual situation was the reverse. Along with the opposition to the colonial state that had developed because of its increasing interference in the lives of the people, there were the economic and national consequences of the country's integration into the capital and labour markets of India. Separation, it was thought, would halt and perhaps reverse this trend, although the superior economic and political power of India in the empire meant that Burma would have had to delay the full implementation of separate powers to regulate trade and immigration for several years.

The Government of Burma Act, 1935, which came into effect on April 1, 1937, was a significant document in the development of the modern state in Burma. Not only did it establish a system of parliamentary government similar in form to that of the Westminster model of British cabinet government, providing a means for Burmese politicians to involve themselves in the management of the central state, but if further legitimized in the eyes of many Burmese politicians the electoral institutions of the dyarchy government, including political parties. The rise of a stratum of politicians who were willing to cooperate with the British in turn led to the further development of organized nationalist opposition to cooperation with the colonial state.[144] Try as the twentieth-century colonial state might to create democratic and participatory modes of legitimacy through policies of progressively extended self-government, the contradictions between the British veto and national self-government, and the domination of external economic and military forces over a recalcitrant population, meant that the colonial state was never able to achieve the legitimacy of its precolonial predecessor. Until the end of British rule, people could always hark back, via selective historical memory, to the not too distant past when the king's state apparently demanded less of the people and they lived lives unaffected by international price fluctuations, foreign labour competition, alien landlords, debts and a punitive police force.

New Class and Ethnic Formations

The most obvious impact of the colonial state upon Burma's social structure during the late nineteenth and early twentieth century was the

---

144. To be discussed in ch. III.

development of new class and ethnic formations and interests as a consequence of the economic and administrative changes introduced and encouraged by the British. The social structure of the precolonial state, with its clear correlation of power with status and wealth, was replaced in the twentieth century and the political reforms introduced held out the promise of political power within the state to the new classes. Most dramatically, the colonial era saw the creation and rise to the centre of indigenous political life of a new class, a Burmese middle class, which became the main force behind the development of modern Burmese political nationalism. This class was largely urban and had grown out of the opportunities for Burmese to leave the villages and take advantages of the economic, educational and career opportunities created by the colonial order. It was this sector of society that became mobilized both as a prop for the new state and as a rival to the British and Indian interests which also benefited, disproportionately, from the new order.

From the 1870s and 1880s onward, the speed of economic and political change provided the opportunities for this new class to evolve; but it did so in conditions which worked against its developing into a fully independent class. By the 1930s, however, the class structure had evolved to its most complex form, and it was from this form that the class conflicts of post-independence Burma's politics were fought in the 1940s and 1950s. The class structure of the 1930s can be visualized as a three-tiered pyramid. At the apex was a very small group of British government officials and the managers of the major European trade, mineral extraction, and banking firms. Included in this group was a significant proportion of the Eurasian population which, for financial and psychological reasons, was dependent on the British for its position in society. This top group was of less importance for the internal politics of the colonial period than has been generally assumed. The second tier of the class structure was composed of the middle class. For purposes of analysis, the middle class can be divided into three sectors. First, there was the landowning sector, secondly, the commercial and trade sectors, which together are in some ways comparable to the European bourgeoisie. The third middle-class sector comprised independent professionals and government employees. It might be considered in Western terms the 'white-collar' middle class. The Burmese middle class, over a period running from about 1907 to 1930 or 1935, became increasingly urban and white-collar. Whereas in 1880 there was developing a prosperous class of Burmese traders, landowners, moneylenders, mill owners and the like, over time, and as a result of several interrelated problems of the internal and external economy of Burma, Indians began supplanting Burmese in these roles. Burmese in the middle class were losing their sources of independent wealth and were increasingly dependent on government or Indian financiers for their incomes. Even the expansion of university education in the 1920s and 1930s, as discussed above, did not imply an increasingly strong and vigorous middle class relative to the Indian middle class. This was because Indians in increasing numbers were settling permanently in Burma and were using the expanded educational facilities to maintain their relative competitive advantages over the Burmese.

Thus by the 1920s and 1930s the emerging Burmese middle class was already facing a crisis which was encouraged and compounded by the problems of the Burmese peasant population. As a result of the exigencies of agricultural production, especially during the depression of the 1930s, the number of landless labourers and insecure tenant cultivators was rapidly increasing. With the growing shortage of new rice lands in the delta and the growth of surplus labour in the countryside, more Burmese were competing with Indian workers in the cities and towns for jobs in trade, manufacturing and transportation. Simultaneously with this Burmese drive for unskilled urban employment, more Indians were remaining in Burma to compete for skilled positions in industry which until that time had generally been the prerogative of the Burmese. The result of these pressures is seen in the increase in urban and rural communal tension and violence in the 1930s.

The economic and administrative policies of the colonial state during the period up to the First World War created the conditions for the emergence of this class structure and of its attendant ethnic characteristic: the plural society. Not only was colonial Burma's society divided by various ethnic communities which remained isolated from each other except for purposes of the market: this horizontal division was further complicated by vertical divisions within each community between those who had superior skills and higher status, or controlled significant quantities of capital, and those who possessed neither of these advantages in the rationalized economy and commercially-oriented society. In such a society it was the middle class, Burmese and Indian, as well as the top group of Europeans, that served as the communicators among the ethnic communities. The bottom of the social pyramid held the overwhelming majority of the population, but it remained powerless to affect state policies in any positive manner, composed as it was of agricultural workers and a much smaller but strategically important group of industrial and transportation workers largely confined to their own communities. The colonial state was dependent upon the middle class to control and direct these elements.

Within each of the two main tiers of the class structure there was a variety of religious, ethnic, occupational, educational and geographic divisions, but these were sufficiently congruent that they can be discussed in terms of ethnic divisions. Indeed, because of the increasing hold on most important economic positions by Indians, and the consequent retreat of the Burmese middle class to white-collar positions, the main political questions in late colonial Burma were usually articulated in terms of ethnicity rather than class. For analytical purposes, however, it is necessary to combine class and ethnic categories in order to understand the social dynamics of the period. (As the changes in the class and ethnic structures of areas apart from the most economically dynamic areas were slight during the colonial period, they are omitted from the following analysis of colonial Burma's social structure.)

The migration of Indian labour into Burma from the 1870s onwards had the most visible effects in creating the plural society. The size of the Indian population grew proportionally larger from the 1870s to the 1930s. Although it has been estimated that the Indian percentage of the total population declined to 5.4 per cent in the 1941 census because of the effects of the depression in the early 1930s and anti-Indian demonstrations, riots and legislation in the late 1930s,[145] it is clear that the Indian population grew both in absolute and relative terms into the 1930s.[146]

The Indian population was concentrated in southern Burma: it first became significant in Arakan before spreading later to the other divisions. In the three remaining divisions of southern Burma the Indian population expanded and stabilized most rapidly in Pegu, i.e., the Irrawaddy delta, but was continuing to grow in Irrawaddy and Tenasserim. In Arakan, the Indian population was proportionately the

145. Chakravarti, *Indian Minority in Burma*, p. 18. The 1941 census was never published as almost all of its records were destroyed during the Second World War.
146. Chakravarti argues, as did the Baxter Report on Indian Immigration (*Report on Indian Immigration* [Rangoon: Government Printing and Stationery, 1941]), that for most purposes it is fairer and more appropriate to remove the Arakan division from any analysis of the size and growth of the Indian population, because of the land connection between Arakan and Bengal and because of the earlier conquest of Arakan. Chakravarti goes further and argues that the Indian proportion of the total population was much smaller because, at any one time, probably half of the

largest of any division. It also had the most Burma-born, with fewer than one quarter of the Indian population born in India, whereas in the rest of Burma this figure was slightly over 72 per cent.[147]

By 1931 over half of the population of Rangoon, the commercial and administrative capital, was Indian[148] (it seemed more an Indian city than a Burmese or Southeast Asian city).[149] The population remained in great flux into the 1930s. Having grown rapidly from a small port before the British conquest, Rangoon never became a settled city during the colonial period, and as late as 1931 only 35 per cent of the population had been born there.[150]

There was almost an inverse relationship between the size of the various ethnic groups and their hold on political and economic power during the late colonial period. The inclusion of the colonial state in the British-Indian empire was the cause of this. Because it entered Burma in the form and personnel of the government of India, the colonial state relied heavily not only on British but also on Indian and Anglo-Indian personnel. Also, the early economic development of British Burma, except for agriculture, was chiefly undertaken with Indian labour, with British and Indian capital, and with a smaller proportion of Chinese finance.[151] (Table 2.1. sets forth in gross terms the possession of political and economic power in pre-war Burma; it gives the population of Burma at the 1931 census by ethnic classification and should be read from the bottom up.) The five non-indigenous groups, or key elements

---

Indians in Burma were temporary residents seeking work and returning to India with their savings. By excluding Arakanese Muslims and an additional 150,000 Indians from the total, which Chakravarti considers the minimum number of temporary residents, the Indian proportion of the population is reduced from 4.8 per cent in 1911 to 3.5 per cent, from 5.5 per cent in 1921 to 4.3 per cent, from 5.8 per cent in 1931 to 5.4 per cent, and from 4.3 per cent to 3.3 per cent in 1941. (Chakravarti, *Indian Minority*, table 2.3, p. 18, and table 2.6, p. 22). While Chakravarti's figures are no doubt correct, they in no way lessen the size of the Indian population which was seeking work in Burma. In fact, because there were more single males in the Indian population in proportion to the total Indian population than among the indigenous population, the Indian labourers took more jobs from Burmese than a permanently settled population of the same size but with a more normal age and sex distribution would have done.

147. *Report on Indian Immigration*, p. 16.
148. Chakravarti, *Indian Minority*, table 2.4, p. 19.
149. B.R. Pearn, *History of Rangoon* (Rangoon: A.B.M. Press, 1939).
150. *Report on Indian Immigration*, p. 22.
151. D.G.E. Hall, *History of South East Asia* (London: Macmillan, 3rd edn., 1968), p. 786.

TABLE 2.1. POPULATION OF BURMA BY ETHNICITY, 1931

Ethnic categories	
Indigenous[a]	12,680,052
Indian	1,017,825
Chinese	193,589
Indo-Burman	182,166
European and Anglo-Indian	30,851
Others	3,039
Total	14,647,756

(a) Burma group 9,267,196; Mon 336,728; Karen 1,367,673; others 1,888,455.

Source: Government of Burma, *Burma Handbook* (Simla: Government of India Press, 1944), Table A, p. 6.

of them, despite being a small proportion of the total population dominated external trade, all banking except for petty finance, the police and military and the judicial system. The Europeans, mainly the British, with their closely allied groups, the Anglo-Indians and the Anglo-Burmese, dominated the legal, military, police and administrative positions. From a small proportion of the Indian population and a large proportion of the Chinese population came the groups which tended to dominate internal banking, trade and land ownership. The Europeans and Indians shared the external trade of Burma to the almost total exclusion of other groups. The ownership of industrial, mining, timber, refining, and other modern industrial operation was shared, albeit unequally, by the Indian and European groups. The bulk of the labour in these modern concerns and in internal and external transportation was Indian. The key positions in both the administration and the economy of pre-war Burma were held by non-Burmese.

While the Burmans — meaning the majority of the residents of the delta and central plains — and other indigenous peoples were at a disadvantage relative to the alien groups in political and economic terms, they were not powerless. Members of the Burman and other indigenous groups, especially the Mon and Karen, were traders and moneylenders, landowners, lawyers and other professionals, and held important positions in the administration and police. More important, however, for the power of the Burmese middle-class politicians, was the inability of the alien groups to govern and trade without the compliance, if not the support, of the indigenous population.

In a multi-ethnic society such as colonial Burma, the lingua franca was the language of the dominant group. Knowledge of English was a key determinant of one's status in society and place in the economy. It was also crucial for contacts in trade and politics outside Burma. The relative positions of the various ethnic groups can be further gauged by an examination of levels of literacy in English. Europeans, Anglo-Indians and Anglo-Burmans along with other tiny minorities were the most literate groups in English. With over 43 per cent of the males and 71 per cent of females literate in English, these groups, most closely tied in culture and sentiment as well as economic interests with Britain, far surpassed the next most literate group, Indians other than Hindus and Muslims. This group, probably mainly Christians, was also closely tied with the European group. Within the larger population groups, Indian Hindus were the most literate in English, followed by the Chinese population and Indian Muslims. The Burmans and other indigenous peoples were the least literate in English, neither group achieving the national average of 1.9 per cent literate in English. In absolute terms, however, the Burmese had the largest number of literates in English of any group in the country.[152]

The relationship between class and ethnicity in gross terms is further demonstrated by examining the occupational structure of Burma toward the end of the colonial period. Table 2.2. (p. 130) gives the participation of ethnic groups in different categories of employment. The Burman and other indigenous groups made up over 87 per cent of the total workforce. However, only in agriculture for the other indigenous peoples, and only in agriculture, industry, trade and the professional and liberal arts did the Burmans match or exceed their proportion of the total labour force. If the professional and liberal arts categories are used in the Western sense of the term, then the Burmans and other indigenous people's percentages are inflated, as the classification includes *pongyi* and other members of religious orders. This table shows the size of the alien hold on the modern sectors of the state and economy. Only in farming, industry, trade, public administration, and the professional and liberal arts do all the indigenous peoples combined have more than half of the positions in the country. Even in these occupations, the hold of the indigenous people was weakening and their relative economic standing declining during the period between the First and Second World War.

Other gross indicators of class and ethnicity in pre-war Burma's social structure are found in the figures for the payment of taxes on trade and

152. *Burma Handbook* (Simla: Government of India Press, 1944), table I, p. 12.

Table 2.2. LABOUR FORCE PARTICIPANTS BY ETHNICITY AND OCCUPATION, 1931 (%)

Occupations	Burmans	Other indigenous	Chinese	Indians born in Burma	Indians out of Burma	Indo-Burman	European	Anglo-Indian	Other
All	55.8	32.1	1.5	1.6	7.9	0.9	0.1	0.1	0.1
Agriculture & forestry	56.7	38.0	0.5	1.6	2.5	0.7	0.0	0.0	0.0
Mining	33.5	15.0	9.8	1.0	36.3	0.3	1.4	0.4	0.0
Industry	56.7	24.1	2.3	1.1	14.7	0.9	0.1	0.1	0.0
Transport	40.5	8.3	2.6	2.5	43.2	1.5	0.6	0.6	0.1
Trade	59.2	14.1	6.9	1.6	15.6	2.2	0.1	0.1	0.1
Military & Police	31.3	15.9	0.3	2.0	43.4	0.8	5.8	0.5	0.0
Public administration	37.4	25.5	1.3	2.3	26.6	1.9	0.8	1.7	0.1
Professional & liberal arts	67.1	24.8	0.7	0.8	4.4	0.8	0.5	0.6	0.1

Source: Adapted from Moshe Lissak, 'The Class Structure of Burma: Continuity and Change', *Journal of Southeast Asian Studies*, 1, 1 (March 1970), p. 61, who takes the table from Surider K. Mehta, 'The Labour Force of Urban Burma and Rangoon, 1953, A Comparative Study' (unpubl. Ph.D. diss., University of Chicago, 1959), p. 52. Mehta has prepared the percentages from the table on p. 134 of the 1931 *Census of Burma*.

TABLE 2.3. ETHNICITY AND INCOME/SUPERTAX PAYMENT IN RANGOON, 1931–2

Ethnic group	Total tax paid %
Burmese	0.52
Indians (non-Chettiar)	10.70
Chettiars (urban)	2.70
Chettiars (rural)	12.09
Chinese	3.49
Europeans	70.35
Others	0.23

Source: Appendix to Letter, R.G. McDowall, Reforms Secretary, Government of Burma, to D.T. Monteath, Assistant Under-Secretary of State, India Office, 16 Nov. 1933. BOF P&J(B) 15, part 1.

commerce and the use of the port of Rangoon. These are useful as they show the strength of the various communities in the most modern and highly monetized sectors of the economy. Table 2.3. indicates the relative size of the European, Indian, Chinese and Burmese involvement in trade and commerce, especially as the table omits tax paid by non-Chettiar Indians paying income taxes outside of Rangoon. The above figures do not include tax on income derived from property and therefore probably underestimate Burmese earnings from rents, but for the same reason they probably also understate the earnings of the Indian population, especially the Chettiars.[153] In any case, it is extraordinary that less than one per cent of the income tax and supertax paid in Rangoon on commercial incomes was paid by Burmese, whereas Indians paid over 25 per cent and Europeans 70 per cent of these taxes.

The strength of Indian interests in the economy of Burma affected the position of the peasant and middle-class Burmese population more than did the interests of British and other European traders and investors. In addition to mere size there were two other reasons for this state of affairs. First, Indians were more involved in the daily operations of the economy than were the other foreigners. This was particularly true in the retail trade and the provision of rural credit, though some Chinese were also active in these sectors. In these and other economic spheres they were in direct competition with Burmese interests. Secondly, the largest European firms were rarely in competition with Burmese firms. The former were part of the international economy which was beyond

153. The Chettiars were a banking caste from Madras and will be discussed more fully on pp. 142–5.

the control of either Indians or Burmese. Even if Burma had at that time been politically sovereign like Siam, the European firms, like the multinational corporations and banks of the present day, would still have determined prices and conditions in those sectors of the international economy in which they operated, especially in the rice trade and the timber and mineral markets. The European-dominated world economy of the nineteenth and twentieth century set the overall conditions within which the Burmese and other Asian middle classes developed.

At this point it is appropriate to examine in greater detail the characteristics of the class formations that developed in Burma between the 1870s and the 1930s. Not only were they the creations of the colonial state, but several of them were major factors in the conflicts of the 1940s, 1950s, and 1960s for dominance in the postcolonial state. The tiny but powerful top group of Europeans, mainly English and Scots, accounting for less than 0.002 per cent of the total population in 1931,[154] may be considered briefly. While the British had dominated the upper echelons of the colonial state from its formation, it was the intention of the imperial government after about 1920 that their positions in the civil service, military and police would ultimately be assumed by Burmese. And by the late 1930s non-Europeans including non-Burmese had been admitted to positions at all levels in the civil service, to a few lower-ranking military and police officerships, but not to any extent into the top management and direction of the largest financial, trade, timber and mineral-extraction firms which, like the exclusive British clubs of Rangoon, remained closed to the Burmese until the end of the colonial period.

Though the first non-official Europeans involved in the political and economic life of Burma during the nineteenth century were largely traders, during the twentieth century an increasingly large proportion came to be involved in the management of sizeable Western investments

---

154. Of the 30,851 Europeans, Anglo-Indians and Anglo-Burmese in Burma in 1931, only 7,819 had been born in Europe, the British Isles, Australasia and North America. Of that number, 6,426 had been born in the British Isles (*Indian Census, 1931, Burma*, pt. II, Imperial Table VI, Birth Place, pt. I). Of the British in Burma, almost 5,000 served in the army in non-commissioned officer rank or below, leaving less than 3,000 who could be considered members of the top group. Even if all the Anglo-Indians and Anglo-Burmese are included in the top group, along with the few Burmese in élite civil service and other senior posts, the group cannot have numbered more than 31,000 to 32,000, less than 0.002 per cent of the total 1931 population of over 14.5 million.

in banking, manufacturing, and especially mineral and timber extraction.[155] The total size of foreign investments in Burma tripled between the First and Second World Wars, chiefly because of the interest which developed in the exploitation of petroleum, rubber and certain metals, including wolfram (tungsten) and tin. These totalled nearly £40 million in value by the 1930s.[156] The three giants in Burma's oil industry were the Burmah Oil Company, the British Burma Petroleum Company, and Burma Shell, which between them controlled about 98 per cent of production. The largest mining company was the Burma Corporation, Ltd., which was 'one of the largest silver and lead producers in the world' and which also mined zinc, iron ore, copper and nickel.[157] British firms dominated the export of teak and hardwoods and the major timber companies also had sizeable interests in the rice trade, owning many of the largest rice mills; several also owned cement works, rubber estates, and oil refineries. These firms included the Bombay-Burma Trading Corporation, Steel Brothers, MacGregors, Foucar, and T.D. Finlay.[158] The total foreign investment in banking, trade and manufacturing in pre-war Burma is estimated at about £6,800,000, although if we exclude funds invested through Burma in neighbouring countries the figure is probably nearer to £5,500,000. Of these investments, 75 per cent were considered to be in British hands.[159] The major banks operating in colonial Burma were British or Indian owned.[160] However Indian investments, including loans to agriculturalists, probably exceeded British and other Western investments before the Second World War.[161]

155. Helmut G. Callis, *Foreign Capital in Southeast Asia* (New York: International Secretariat, Institute for Pacific Relations, 1942), p. 94.
156. Ibid., p. 89.
157. Letter, R.G. McDowell to D.T. Monteath, 16 Nov. 1933. BOF P&J(B) 1, pt. 1.
158. Callis, *Foreign Capital in Southeast Asia*, p. 91, provides an incomplete listing.
159. Ibid., p. 92. It is not clear in Callis's estimate whether he has taken into consideration the level of Indian investments in British firms operating in Burma. It is safe to assume that 10 per cent of the stock in most British firms in Burma was held by Indians. Chakravarti, *Indian Minority*, p. 92. Japanese assets in Burma immediately prior to the Second World War, including bank balances, did not exceed £150,000. They owned little real estate and most of their assets were trading capital. Telegram, Governor of Burma to Secretary of State for Burma, 24 Sept. 1941. BOF 286/40, pt. 13.
160. *The Burma Gazette*, 26 March 1938, in BOF C67/46; Tun Wai, *Burma's Currency and Credit* (Bombay: Orient Longmans, rev. edn, 1962), p. 24.
161. Furnivall, *Colonial Policy and Practice*, p. 190. See also Harvey, *British Rule in Burma*, p. 68.

The New Middle Class The purpose of the following discussion is to analyse the evolution of the Burmese middle class during the colonial period in order to highlight major aspects of social and political change during the period. From being essentially a non-existent class under the monarchical state, the Burmese middle class had emerged by the 1920s and 1930s into three analytically distinguishable groups: those involved in trade, commerce and industry; those involved in public administration,[162] the liberal professions and allied occupations; and those involved primarily in earning their living from land rents, moneylending and the provision of agricultural credit. As the middle class was a product of the colonial state and the economic forces it brought into being, its growth and strength was clearly a consequence of the new state structure. Unlike the evolution of the modern European state where the middle classes rose to challenge the authority of the absolute state, or India, where the new middle class, although created by the colonial state, became powerful enough to take control of the state from the British, in Burma the middle class was the child of the state and remained ultimately dependent upon it.

While an in-depth study of the economic and class transformations of modern Burma has not yet been done, it seems apparent that the middle class evolved somewhat along the following lines. Former officials of the precolonial government often received appointments in the British administration or, because of their English education (usually at missionary schools), were taken into government employ. With their earnings, or perhaps with money borrowed from Indian moneylenders, they often went into business or invested in land. Through the foreclosure of mortgages and further land speculation these families became wealthier and more powerful, and used their additional capital to send their sons to government schools and universities in India and England. After 1920 more of these students remained in Burma for their university education. It was from families with histories like this that the Burmese middle class emerged.

162. Cady, *History of Modern Burma*, p. 151, writes that 'the emerging Burmese bureaucracy constituted a new middle class (called *a-so-ya-min* or simply *min*), affiliated neither with the people generally nor with the British ruling group.' While it is quite correct to note that the indigenous government servants and, indeed, other members of the new middle class, did live in a style separate from the bulk of the peasant population, it is misleading to conclude that their lives were divorced from the welfare and prosperity of the rest of society. The Burmese middle class was not a deracinated intelligentsia.

The 1931 census revealed that 557,248 individuals were involved in trade. Of that figure, 73.3 per cent were listed as indigenous, 17.3 per cent as Indian, and 9.4 per cent from other groups. Despite the fact that the indigenous peoples made up over 85 per cent of the total population and 87 per cent of the total workforce, they held less than three-quarters of all positions in trade. Of the 10,914 persons engaged in larger businesses such as banking, insurance and import/export, Indians held 75.6 per cent of all positions.[163] In Rangoon in 1931, the indigenous population held only 13.2 per cent of all positions as traders and shop assistants.[164] As these figures indicate, what Burmese strength there was in the commercial sector of the economy was not in the more vigorous economy of the delta but in the more traditional economy further north.

The Indian middle class had the strongest hold on foreign trade of any group in Burma. Indian exporters ' . . . handled the majority of commodities exported from Burma though mineral oil, minerals and rubber were important exceptions.'[165] Of an estimated total annual export trade before the Second World War of Rs. 4,800 lakhs, it is estimated that Rs. 2,500 lakhs was in Indian hands. By the early 1940s, Indian firms had increased their share of the import trade to an estimated 50 per cent.[166] Because Indian merchants as well as European and Chinese traders had long secured control over Burma's foreign trade, the Burmese were unable to enter and compete to any large extent in this sector of the economy.[167]

Even though a majority of the traders in the internal market remained indigenous, their shops and holdings were smaller than those of many of their Indian competitors. As Chakravarti writes,

Indian participation in the local and domestic trade of Burma was . . . very

---

163. Chakravarti, *Indian Minority*, p. 34; Taylor, 'Relationship between Burmese Social Classes and British-Indian Policy', table 8, p. 45.
164. In the remainder of the delta, excluding Rangoon, they held 52.6 per cent of all such positions, *Report on Indian Immigration*, p. 37.
165. India's Interests in Burma's Trade and Industry, by R.T. Stoneham, 24 Jan. 1944. BOF 60/44.
166. It was estimated that Burma's import trade amounted to Rs. 2,200 lakhs before the war; and of this figure 1,100 lakhs were controlled by Indian firms, *ibid*. Chakravarti conservatively estimates that Indian firms controlled 20 per cent of Burma's foreign trade before the war, *Indian Minority*, pp. 78–9.
167. Adas makes this point relative to the external rice trade (*Burma Delta*, p. 177), though it could be made for other commodities as well.

extensive. Indian shops, particularly grocery, departmental, food and drug stores, could be seen all over Burma in urban and rural areas. . . . Most of the large shops in important centres of trade and in big cities such as Rangoon, Mandalay, Maymyo, Moulmein, Bassein, Pegu, and Akyab belonged to Indians and each and every district town, subdivisional town, and township centre contained several Indian shops. . . . Indian hotels, restaurants, food centres, jewellery shops, and cinemas were fairly well distributed in all important cities and towns. Most of the traders also owned land and buildings at their places of business.[168]

In Rangoon, Indian merchants were the largest property owners. This was due primarily to the fact that the money to pay for the development of the city centre after 1852 was raised largely from the sale of property — Indians had been the principal buyers.[169] By the 1930s Indians paid over 55 per cent of all municipal taxes in Rangoon while the Burmese paid only 11 per cent, Europeans paid 15 per cent and all other groups paid 18 per cent.[170] In the larger towns, including Rangoon, even much of the property owned by Burmese was under mortgage to Indian bankers and moneylenders.[171]

In the rural areas, most of the small shops were run by Burmese but most of their imported goods had to come via Indian wholesalers. Other than these shops, there were commercial opportunities for Burmese as rice brokers and grain merchants. Their numbers greatly expanded with the rapid development of the delta rice economy from 1852 to the First World War, but later decreased as a result of the decline of the value of the rice trade and increased competition from Indians and other non-Burmese groups. Whereas there had been 39,000 grain and pulse dealers in the delta in 1921, by 1931 there were fewer than 30,000 in all of Burma. While in 1921, 82 per cent of these dealers had been Burmese, by 1931, 77 per cent were Burmese.[172] As Adas notes, by the 1920s there was a struggle between the Burmese and the Indians for control of internal marketing and transportation in the delta rice industry which was generally 'overshadowed by the rivalry . . . in the rice processing

---

168. Chakravarti, *Indian Minority*, p. 79.
169. *Ibid.*, p. 7.
170. Riot Inquiry Committee, *Interim Report* (Rangoon: Government Printing and Stationery, 1938), p. 17; Chakravarti, *Indian Minority*, p. 91.
171. Especially Chettiars, N.C. Sen, *A Peep Into Burma Politics (1917–1941)* (Allahabad: Kitabistan, 1945), p. 71.
172. Adas, *Burma Delta*, pp. 176–7.

industry and among dock laborers in Rangoon harbor'.[173] By the 1930s the same struggle had extended to greater or lesser degrees to the rest of central Burma.

The inability of the Burmese middle class to compete in the ownership and management of manufacturing and industrial concerns during the colonial period reveals a similar story. Of the 1,031 factories in Burma in 1939–40, at least 303 were owned by Indians.[174] Indian firms owned mills and other factories in every major category of modern industry. Chakravarti estimates that the size of Indian investments in industry closely followed those of the British.[175] While Burmese owned a few more factories than did Indians, they were usually smaller, employed fewer workers, and were frequently capitalized by Indians. Similarly, Chinese industries were usually very small-scale operations. Two-thirds of the industrial concerns of pre-war Burma were owned directly by non-Burmese. Of the 792 rice mills in Burma in 1940, 45 per cent were owned by Burmese, 24 per cent by Chinese, 28 per cent by Indians, and only 4 per cent by Europeans. The few European-owned mills were by far the largest. Both internal and external transport were dominated by Indian and British firms or the state-owned railways. There were no Burmese-owned commercial banks and insurance companies in pre-war Burma. Most Burmese conducted such business with the Indian banks and insurance companies which had branches in Burma.[176] While Indians had substantial investments in British firms doing business in Burma, estimated, as noted above, at 10 per cent of total investments, there is no evidence of Burmese investment in British firms.

Though the indigenous population clearly benefited less from the economic opportunities created by the colonial state than the Indian or European communities did, in public administration and the liberal professions they did somewhat better, and it was in this sector that the Burmese middle class had its greatest strength. Here Burmese predominated over Indians in total number but not in proportion to the country's total population. Table 2.4. shows the composition of this sector of the middle class. Of those in public administration, which in 1931 totalled about 45,000 persons, 63.4 per cent were indigenous, 30.8

173. Ibid., p. 178.
174. Chakravarti, *Indian Minority*, p. 88.
175. Chakravarti contends that this is probably true for investments in mining, but this is doubtful.
176. Chakravarti, *Indian Minority*, pp. 86–7.

per cent were Indian and 5.8 per cent were members of other foreign groups. In the liberal arts and professional category, if the 128,280 members of religious orders or others primarily involved in religious activities are excluded, the indigenous peoples account for 80.6 per cent, Indians for 14.5 per cent and others for 4.9 per cent.[177]

Given the importance of the law in shaping the quality of the colonial state, the growth of the legal profession is an important indicator of social change. Of the 2,301 lawyers of all kinds in Burma in 1931, almost 77 per cent were indigenous, over 70 per cent being Burman.[178] Of the 20,658 persons in the category of instruction (other than in religious institutions) about 56 per cent were Burman and 23 per cent were from other indigenous communities. Whereas the Burmans and other indigenous peoples held over 75 per cent of the posts in law and teaching, in medicine, a more financially secure occupation, the Indian population held over half the positions in 1931. Almost 52 per cent of all doctors practising Western-style medicine were Indians born outside Burma and almost 7 per cent were Indians born in Burma. Only about 20 per cent of doctors were Burman and another 5 per cent came from the other indigenous peoples.[179]

The third sector of the middle class was composed of those persons who owned agricultural land and provided credit for the cultivators. It had been the policy of the government of India from the time of annexation to encourage cultivator-ownership in Burma as the most desirable means of organizing agriculture and creating a stable and peaceful society. Both utilitarian principles and the pre-British agricultural system convinced the government that it should protect and promote the interests of the smallholder.[180] The importance of continuing this policy was noted by the Land and Agriculture Committee in its reports

---

177. If the Europeans and Anglo-Indians are exluded from the 'others' category, on the assumption that all of them were members of the top group, then the Chinese proportion of the public administration and professions categories would be reduced to about half of the 'others' percentage noted here.
178. Over 2 per cent were Chinese, 14 per cent Indian (of whom almost 11 per cent were born outside Burma), 5 per cent Indo-Burman, slightly more than 1 per cent European, slightly less than 2 per cent Anglo-Burmese and 2 per cent from other groups. There were in addition to the lawyers, 2,148 lawyers' clerks, petition writers etc., who presumably would have been distributed in much the same manner as the lawyers.
179. *Census of Burma, 1931*, p. 139.
180. Adas, *Burma Delta*, pp. 32–4.

Table 2.4. EARNERS AND WORKING DEPENDENTS BY ETHNICITY IN MIDDLE-CLASS POSITIONS, 1931

Occupation	Total	Burman	Other indigenous	Indigenous %	Indian	Indian %	Chinese	Indo-Burman	Europeans and Anglo-Burman	Others %
Trade	557,248	329,079	78,366	73.3	96,211	17.3	38,419	2,249	1,466	9.4
Public administration	44,867	17,003	11,003	63.4	12,822	30.8	572	869	1,441	5.8
Professional & liberal arts	198,890	133,890	49,386	91.9	10,418	5.2	1,490	1,594	2,268	2.9
Members of religious orders, etc.	128,280	89,257	36,945	97.9	156	1.5	128	156	156	0.6
Professional & liberal arts excluding members of religious orders	70,630	44,533	12,441	80.6	10,262	14.5	1,362	1,438	2,112	4.9
Private incomes	7,167	3,497	813	60.1	1,829	25.5	175	370	456	14.4

Source: Census of Burma, 1931

in 1938–40, which held that the 'ownership of land by the small agriculturalists [was] the best suited to Burma and [the] one which [would] make for social and political stability since it [would] rest on the foundations of a comfortable, contented and independent peasantry'.[181] The Land and Agriculture Committee further felt that land should be owned by permanent residents who had 'a direct interest in the maintenance of law and order and in the stability of national institutions'.[182]

By the 1930s these principles bore little relationship to the reality of Burma's rural economy, especially in the delta, where there had gradually developed a class of landlords who invested in land for profit and rented their land to tenants. As early as 1880, settlement reports in Bassein and Henzada noted the passage of land into the hands of moneylenders and the trading class.[183] By the 1930s non-agriculturalists owned over half the agricultural land in principle rice-growing districts of deltic Burma.[184]

The pre-war decline of the cultivator-owners as a class in Burma was precipitous. In 1931 there were 39,000 male landlords (non-cultivating owners in census terms), whereas in 1921 there had been only 33,000 male landlords. Female non-cultivating owners decreased in this same decade from 41,000 to 31,000, but as most of these women were probably the widows of previous cultivator-owners what it indicates is not so much a reduction in the number of landlords as a decline in the number of small, family-owned farms. The number of cultivating-owners fell from 2,569,000 in 1921 to 1,248,000 in 1931, a decrease of more than 50 per cent. This is evidence of the decline of the more prosperous and independent segments of the agrarian population and the rise in wealth of a small number of landlords. The amount of land owned by non-agriculturalists in the principle rice-growing districts of the delta almost doubled between 1930 and 1938, which suggests that the number of cultivator-owners continued to fall rapidly after the 1931 census when the full impact of the depression on the rice economy began to be felt.[185] For all of Burma, similar generalizations can be made. In 1926, of the

181. *Land and Agriculture Committee Report* (Rangoon: Government Printing and Stationery, 1939), pt. I, p. 2.
182. *Ibid.*, pt. II, p. 1.
183. *Ibid.*, pt. I, p. 37; Mya Sein, *Administration in Burma: Sir Charles Crosthwaite and the Consolidation of Burma* (Rangoon: Zabu Meitswa Pitaka Press, 1938), p. 104, who adds pleaders to the list of new landlords.
184. *Land and Agriculture Committee Report*, pt. I. p. 39.
185. *Ibid.*, pp. 37–8.

18,271,818 acres of cultivated land, 14,799,950 acres were owned by agriculturalists, 1,012,505 were owned by non-agriculturalists who were residents of Burma, and 2,459,363 by non-residents. By 1937, of the 19,304,907 acres occupied, 12,862,874 acres were owned by agriculturalists, 1,465,164 acres by resident non-agriculturalists, and 4,976,869 acres by non-resident non-agriculturalists. Whereas land held by landlords domiciled in Burma increased by about 150,000 acres in this eleven-year period, landlords not domiciled in Burma increased their holdings by almost 2,500,000 acres.[186]

A further indication of the decline of cultivator-ownership is the decrease in the percentage of cultivator-owners in the male agricultural workforce between 1921 and 1931. From the time of the British conquest, when almost all land was effectively held by cultivators, to 1921, the proportion of cultivating owners had dropped to nearly half the total workforce. In the next ten years the proportion dropped to just under 37 per 100, while in the same period the number of landless agricultural labourers increased by 13 per cent.

The basic cause of the decline of the cultivator-owner in pre-war Burma, the class that both the British administrators and the Burmese political élite had looked to as a foundation upon which to build a stable political order and healthy economy, was the nature of the rice industry, especially the system of financing the rice crop. As Furnivall wrote,

In the capitalist system the weakest go to the wall and their share in the output tends to fall down or below the level of subsistence. Burmans were in the position of the weakest. Not only were they confined to agriculture but over large tracts where economic progress was most rapid, the peasantry was transformed into a landless proletariat.[187]

These conditions developed in the twentieth century. Before then conditions had been much different.

From 1852 to about 1907, the Burmese cultivator in the delta received a good price for his surplus produce and was able to spend his money on a variety of new imported products.[188] Few made enough profit to invest, and the consumer opportunities the new state introduced were apparently enjoyed. Many Burmese moved from the dry zone to the delta to develop new areas of rice production.

186. Ibid.
187. Furnivall, *The Economy of Burma*, p. 3.
188. Adas, *Burma Delta*, pp. 74–6.

In the last half of the nineteenth century, it was possible for an individual beginning as a landless labourer to work his way upward until he eventually attained the status of a large landholder. The number of persons who began as laborers and rose to become landlords was small, but large numbers of agriculturalists moved one or two notches up or down the social scale.[189]

During this period there was little competition between the Indians and Burmese as each group had its own functions, the Indians providing seasonal labour and some finance, with the Burmese doing the bulk of the work. When almost all available land in the delta had been brought under cultivation, the 'problems inherent in the nature of economic development in Lower Burma grew more intense and an era of apparent prosperity and content gave way to decades of conflict and unrest'.[190] In fact, the crisis in agriculture which was so apparent in the 1930s had begun in the first years of the twentieth century in some parts of the delta and had spread slowly.[191] The depression merely accelerated the decline of the Burmese cultivator-owner that had begun much earlier.[192] The doctrine of legal equality provided equal opportunity but provided none of the personal security of the precolonial state's economic order.

Much attention has been given in previous studies of rural Burma to the role of the Chettiars, because they were the single largest agrarian creditor group. The Chettiars were the most obvious targets for critics of the rural credit system because by 1938 they owned at least 25 per cent of the occupied land in the most important rice growing areas.[193] Before discussing the Chettiars, however, it is important also to note the role of other Burmese and Indian moneylenders.

In the first few decades after 1852, most agricultural credit required for the development of the delta was provided by friends, relatives, shopkeepers and indigenous moneylenders. In the earliest years friends and relatives were probably the most important single source of rural credit. Many entrepreneurs who prospered combined the functions of shopkeeper, moneylender and rice trader.[194] By the 1880s, when Chettiars had also started to operate in the delta, large landowners and established

189. *Ibid.*, p. 70.
190. *Ibid.*, pp. 128–9.
191. Grantham, *Studies in the History of Tharrawaddy*, pp. 31–2.
192. Adas, *Burma Delta*, p. 153.
193. *Land and Agriculture Committee Report.*, pt. I, p. 37.
194. Adas, *Burma Delta*, pp. 64–5.

cultivators took the place of friends and relatives.[195] Others who had been sources of rural credit and who, through foreclosures, became landlords, were traders, speculators, lawyers, government clerks, merchants, retired village headmen, school teachers and doctors.[196] All were individuals who had had an opportunity to take advantage of the relatively sudden monetization of the economy following the establishment of the colonial state. At the turn of the century many British officials felt that these Burmese moneylenders were greedier land grabbers than the Indians.[197] 'Agrarian debt tended to be the highest in tracts near large towns where moneylenders, paddy brokers and other credit sources were more accessible, and where holdings were generally larger.'[198] Adas has written,

throughout the last half of the nineteenth century land was the most secure, profitable and frequently chosen investment outlet for persons who had accumulated capital through trade, in the professions or in government service. The steady rise in the price of paddy was paralleled by a similar increase in the value of land. Wealth, status and local influence were the rewards earned by those individuals who were able to acquire substantial holdings of rich paddy land.[199]

The only areas of Burma where indigenous moneylenders were able to fulfil the domestic demand for agricultural credit in the 1920s and 1930s was in Akyab district.[200] This situation was principally due to U Rai Gyaw Thoo and Company, the only large Burmese moneylending firm. It also owned sizeable amounts of land in Akyab and was involved in other commercial activities.[201] The only European institution directly involved in the provision of rural credit was Dawson's Bank, which primarily made loans to larger Burmese cultivators in order that they would not have to borrow from Indian sources.[202] Efforts by the government to form a cooperative credit movement as an alternative source of loans was a failure. In addition to these sources of rural credit, Indians

195. *Ibid.*, p. 67.
196. *Ibid.*, pp. 71–4.
197. *Ibid.*, p. 119.
198. *Ibid.*, pp. 68–9.
199. *Ibid.*, p. 74.
200. Tun Wai, *Burma's Currency and Credit*, p. 58.
201. *Ibid.*, pp. 55–7.
202. Adas, *Burma Delta*, pp. 138–9; Tun Wai, *Burma's Currency and Credit*, pp. 71–2; letter, Mr Laurence Dawson to Under Secretary of State for Burma, 22 Sept. 1942. BOF E4173/46.

other than Chettiars participated in the moneylending professions.[203] However, between 1907 and 1942, although the majority of moneylenders remained Burmese, the greatest amount of capital for rural credit came from the Chettiars.[204]

The Chettiars were a caste of bankers and moneylenders from Madras. Their original homes were in Chettinad but their banking operations spread throughout India and much of the rest of Eastern Asia.[205] While many of the people who supplied rural credit to the Burmese cultivators from the 1880s to the 1930s were interested in land speculation and investment, and were thus eager to foreclose on mortgages, the Chettiars, being essentially bankers, did not wish to tie up their capital in land. The fact that by 1938 the Chettiars owned 25 per cent of the cultivable land in the great rice growing areas of Burma was undesirable not only from the perspective of the Burmese agriculturalists and the British administrators, but also from the point of view of the Chettiars.

This situation resulted from the great strength of the Chettiars' banking system relative to those of the indigenous middle class; the former were able to charge lower rates of interest than other moneylenders and were considered honest even by their creditors.[206] Naturally, they were able to develop a larger clientele than moneylenders with higher interest rates and poorer reputations for probity. The security of their finances was due to their 'connections with Western banks and joint-stock companies, such as the Imperial Bank of India and the Indian Overseas Bank, which provided them with sources of working capital which were not readily available to Burmese brokers, merchants and moneylenders'.[207]

Initially the Chettiars had not tendered loans directly to the cultivators but had remained in Rangoon and other towns where they provided loans to indigenous moneylenders. From the 1880s onwards,

203. Chakravarti, *Indian Minority*, p. 93.
204. Adas, *Burma Delta*, pp. 136–7.
205. For a fuller description of the Chettiars, see Adas, *Burma Delta, passim*; Adas, 'Immigrant Asians and the Economic Impact of the European Imperialism: The Role of the South Asian Chettiars in British Burma', *Journal of Asian Studies*, XXXIII, 3 (May 1974), pp. 385–401; Chakravarti, *Indian Minority*, pp. 56–69 and *passim*; Tun Wai, *Burma's Currency and Credit*, pp. 40–52; Usha Mahajani, *The Role of the Indian Minorities in Burma and Malaya* (Bombay: Vora, 1960), pp. 16–21.
206. Chakravarti, *Indian Minority*, p. 65, who cites the Report of the Government of Burma's Banking Inquiry Committee, 1929.
207. Adas, *Burma Delta*, pp. 114–15.

however, they expanded their operations into the delta and undercut the interest rates of the indigenous moneylenders.[208] Thus, 'while there were more Burmese moneylenders at the end of the 19th century than Chettiars, the Chettiars provided most of the capital and even some of that for indigenous moneylenders.'[209] Beginning with the depression in rice prices in 1907 the rivalry between Chettiars and Burmese moneylenders increased, so that by the late 1930s few indigenous moneylenders were able to borrow from Chettiars to finance their operations.[210] Following the great slump in rice prices in 1930 many Burmese cultivator-owners were unable to meet their payments, and the Chettiars, partly because of the pressure exerted on them by the great banks of India, were compelled to foreclose. From 1930 to the Second World War, the Chettiars did not attempt to expand their businesses but hoped merely to regain their capital and protect their investments.[211]

The sector of the middle class which owned the other half of the non-agriculturalist-held land in the delta were 'mainly indigenous moneylenders, rice merchants, successful Burmese cultivators, urban investors, and Indian merchants other than Chettiars, just as they had been in the preceding period'.[212] While the indigenous/alien proportion of this half of the delta landlords is not known, it is likely that Burmese owned less than 50 per cent.

Workers and Peasants As within the middle class, the working class was divided both ethnically between Indians and Burmese and occupationally in terms of the nature of their work and places of employment or income. Because of the way the economy developed under British rule, the alien sector of the working class was concentrated in industry while the indigenous peoples were concentrated in agriculture. By the 1920s, however, this ethnic division of roles was breaking down as the tenant-cultivators and cultivator-owners were pushed off the land. Simultaneously with the growth of a larger class of Indian landlords, Indians were moving into agricultural occupations, thus accelerating the flight of Burmese labourers from the land. The heightened competition for jobs and land resulted in greatly increased communal tensions between

208. *Ibid.*, pp. 66–7.
209. *Ibid.*, pp. 112–13.
210. *Ibid.*, p. 175.
211. Chakravarti, *Indian Minority*, p. 58.
212. Adas, *Burma Delta*, pp. 188–9.

the alien and indigenous workers throughout the 1920s and 1930s. In 1931, 96 per cent of the 4,321,356 persons working in agriculture and forestry were indigenous, compared to only 48.5 per cent of the 39,505 workers in mining and 80.8 per cent of the 664,376 in all types of industrial employment. In the largest and most important industries, the proportion of Indians and other aliens was much higher than that of the indigenous groups.[213]

Within the major industrial establishments, the total number of workers fluctuated during the year as more workers were taken on after harvests to process crops prior to marketing. In the larger industrial concerns Indian labour held an absolute majority of positions in all seasons and at each of two levels of skill.[214] With the growth in the size of the labour force between 1933–4 and 1938–9, the percentage of Burmese employed increased in every category — indicating the increasing competition between Burmese and Indian workers for industrial jobs.[215]

As noted earlier, in the 1870s and 1880s, the government of India adopted policies to encourage the immigration of Indian labour to Burma. With the termination of these programs, 'the recruitment of Indian labour for work in Burma naturally fell into the hands of two of the most unscrupulous types of people, namely the shipping agents of companies plying steamships between India and Burma, and the Indian labour contractors popularly known as *maistry*.'[216] The *maistry* were middlemen between the European and Indian employers and the labourers. They hired out gangs of workers recruited in India, and served as the gang paymasters, foremen, and housing and transport

---

213. Table 2.2 (p. 130) includes all workers and earning dependents in its calculations. If only wage earners are used to calculate the percentage of indigenous and alien workers in the labour force, the indigenous percentage decreases. Of the 2,704,427 male earners in the 1931 census involved in agriculture, 93.4 per cent were indigenous. Among the 435,293 unskilled and semi-skilled male earners in industry, 47.4 per cent were indigenous (*Report on Indian Immigration*, p. 36). In Rangoon, Indian accounted for 88.5 per cent of all unskilled and semi-skilled labour and 56.1 per cent of all craftsmen. Male members of the indigenous groups accounted for only 8.8 per cent of the unskilled and semi-skilled labourers and 26.2 per cent of the craftsmen. Excluding Rangoon, in the delta in 1931, Indians held 56.3 per cent of the semi-skilled and unskilled male labouring jobs and 20.8 per cent of the craftsmen position. *Ibid.*, p. 37.
214. *Ibid.*, table I, p. 62.
215. *Ibid.*
216. Chakravarti, *Indian Minority*, p. 43.

agents.[217] In India the labour gangs were normally organized on the basis of family or village of origin, and when vacancies in a gang occurred they were normally filled by another member of the same group, thus making it more difficult for indigenous peoples to gain employment.[218]

The port of Rangoon was the busiest in terms of immigration in the world after 1924.[219] Most of the Indian labourers stayed in Burma for only two to four years, depending upon how fast they could save enough to buy their return fare and have a little left over for their efforts. Most of them would then remain in India for a few months before returning to Burma for another two to four-year stay. Despite the low wages these men earned, they were in most cases sufficiently greater than what they could earn in their native provinces to justify their travel to Burma and long separation from their families.[220] It is estimated that between 200,000 and 350,000 of the more than one million Indians in Burma entered or left the country every year in the 1930s.[221] The consequences of this migration were not only the creation of the plural society, but also a growing level of tension and conflict between the indigenous population and the migrant labourers. The antagonism between these groups publicly expressed itself in the form of race riots and pogroms, and its political repercussions were still being felt in the 1980s.

This chapter has attempted to show the consequences of the nineteenth-century rationalization of the state by the colonial authorities on other institutions of Burma's society. Removing the fetters on economic growth that had been part of the political strength of the precolonial order made Burma an arena of fierce economic and social competition in the twentieth century. The resulting conflicts were the product of this structure, and it is to this that we now turn.

---

217. The *maistry* system and its attendant evils have been described in detail in Chakravarti, *Indian Minority*, pp. 43–55. See also A. Narayen Rao, *Indian Labour in Burma* (Madras: Keshari Press, 1933), and E.J.L. Andrew, *Indian Labour in Rangoon* (London: Oxford University Press, 1933).
218. *Report on Indian Immigration*, p. 55.
219. Harvey, *British Rule in Burma*, p. 70.
220. *Report on Indian Immigration*, p. 13.
221. Chakravarti, *Indian Minority*, p. 21.

CHAPTER 3

POLITICS UNDER THE RATIONALIZED STATE, 1886–1942

Introduction

The development of the rationalized state under British colonial auspices led to the emergence of a complex of factors in the political life of Burma which, though in some ways new, nonetheless shared important qualities and concepts found in the early modern state. Altering the forms and enhancing the secondary functions of the state was relatively easy, given the strength of the British-Indian empire. Developing indigenous ideas and organizations to respond to and to take control of the state was more difficult. But the process was remarkably rapid, and within fifty years Burma had created the private and public institutions normally associated with the modern state, including political parties, mass movements, and ideological constructs containing a justification for state intervention in social and economic affairs.

The formal organization of the colonial state is easy to recognize as it stands out against the background of the precolonial state and society upon which it was imposed. Consequently, the new state structures were often seen as more important and powerful than the old. Their novel qualities impressed both indigenous leaders and foreign observers throughout the twentieth century. The new aspects of political life which developed in the nineteenth and twentieth centuries, and the responses from the public which these elicited, should not, however, obstruct the importance of the background.

Among the political issues of the colonial period, the historical relationship of the central state with economically marginal but strategically important peripheral zones was one of the most important. But the power of the colonial order kept this question from coming to the top of the political agenda until the very end of the period, when external forces threatened to dislodge the British. More important, especially in the years between 1920 and 1940, was the relationship of the core population with the central state. Different segments of the new class structure had to concern themselves with different aspects of this relationship. For the peasantry there were the persistent demands by the state to pay taxes and rents in the face of declining levels of income and security.

For the middle class, and the political élite which emerged from it, the major questions hung on the issue of the degree to which cooperation with the British order had to be balanced against the long-term goal of regaining the independence of the state. For the creators of the colonial state and their bureaucratic successors, the problem hinged upon the maintenance of the state's authority and the interests which it served within a political context which denied their legitimacy and which often spurned their values as the creators of wealth and order. For the British, Indian and other foreign commercial interests which had been created under the colonial state the perpetuation, as cheaply as possible, of the existing order was paramount.

One factor which obviously distinguished the colonial state from its predecessor was the way in which its controllers sought to manage these issues. The limited development of bureaucratic and rationalized means of rule in the face of persistent local and patrimonial opposition to central extraction in the early modern system made the amassing of wealth and power more difficult for the monarchical state than for the colonial state. The colonial state's greater physical power and its methods of operation, in the end, however, could not halt the development of both passive and active opposition to it. In this we see the development of new political forms and the re-emergence of old political forces, as the institutions of the rationalized state were turned against it in the name of precolonial political norms and prerogatives often presented in new guises. But just as the colonial state did not replace the precolonial order instantly, and then only with a good deal of trial and error, anti-state and anti-British forces developed gradually and were much conditioned by the internal and external environment in which they had to operate.

What was the nature of politics under the colonial state and what was its basis? Previous analysts of Burma's politics have generally argued that colonial politics centred largely on opposition to British colonialism; and throughout a significant proportion of the population of Burma, or at least of central and southern Burma, this opposition took the form of nationalism. In tandem with this grew the idea that the Burmese people were one nation which had a moral right to self-determination and self-government, and that it was therefore illegitimate for Burma to be ruled by an alien people from another nation. This now strongly-held, emotive, and almost unquestionable argument, upon which the politics of the globe have come to be structured in the twentieth century, does provide in vast, if vague terms, an explanation for the development of anti-British forces in Burma during the twentieth, if not the nineteenth century. But such an argument assumes many things about human motivation and action in a large and heterodox population in which individuals faced different challenges and opportunities as a result of the existence not only of the state, but also of their own personal, class, religious and ethno-linguistic identity.

The development of the concept of the Burmese nation stems from a variety of factors, some old but reinterpreted in twentieth-century terms, others new and the consequence of modern developments. The existence since the Pagan period of a history of Burma and a simplified lineage of kings, in addition to the strength and continuity of the precolonial state, provided a semi-mythical but also historically-grounded claim that a state called Burma had long existed and was not therefore a colonial creation incapable of self-rule. The rapid homogenization of the population of the more important economic zones of the Toungoo and Konbaung polities had created a strong, if yet incomplete notion of an ethnic identity with the precolonial state. The importance of the Buddhist religion in terms of both the state-centred and ethnically-grounded notions of identity of the precolonial Burmese people provided an additional cultural tie for the majority with the notion of the Burmese nation.[1] The colonial state further strengthened these sentiments in both negative and positive ways. The colonial authorities' insistence upon racial distinctiveness gave ethnicity a greater centrality in political thought than it had previously had. The development of more rapid and easier means of travel and communications throughout southern and central Burma by new roads, railways and river steamers enhanced people's understanding of the commonality of their existence within Burma's territory. The growth of printing and publishing in Burmese, coupled with the development of nationalist newspapers and the Burmese novel, strengthened a notion of common identity. All of these came to provide a bond between the individual and those movements which claimed to speak for the Burmese nation. The growing assertiveness of Burmese nationhood, however, also enhanced the fears and apprehensions of those people, foreign and indigenous, who did not share these terms of identity.

In order to understand what the force of nationalism meant in colonial Burma, one needs to analyse further the factors which went together at different times to form the basis of the nationalist movement. Despite

1. Donald Eugene Smith, *Religion and Politics in Burma* (Princeton University Press, 1965), pp. 81–6.

Introduction

references to the historical glories of classical Burma, few nationalist leaders believed in the feasibility of re-establishing the monarchical state. The king's state had been no more a nation-state than the colonial state, and its virtues were seen as too few and its vices, much emphasized by the colonial rulers and conceded implicitly by Western-educated Burmese, to be too great, to be held up as a viable ideal. More importantly, the colonial state's rationalized features and its justification of production and efficiency had, by the twentieth century, been accepted by a significant proportion of the middle-class political leadership who sought to capture the state in the name of the Burmese.

The growth of the rationalized state also led to the development of what came to be called nationalism but which had its roots less in the desire to capture the state than in a wish to evade it. Among large segments of the peasant population, resistance to the greater demands of the modern state and the economic and social dislocation it created for them began to develop. Peasant perceptions of the consequences of the modern state led to the growth of a movement which did not intend to glorify the nation-state and make it an ideal with which to take power from the foreigners. Rather, their movement had, as its major purpose, the denial of the legitimacy of the demands of the modern state and all that it had created by its policies on taxation, regulation, economic enterprise and labour and capital mobility. Rejection or boycott of the state was the key to political action among many peasants. They saw the removal of the British as essentially the same as the removal of the modern state, for to them, the two were inseparable. If the cause of the modern state (the British) was removed, the modern state would go with them, it was believed.

The manner in which these two forms of opposition to the colonial state coalesced as the nationalist movement from their radically different premises provided much of the internal political dynamic of the colonial period, and made it possible for the British to maintain their position with greater ease than they might otherwise have done. The nation-state ideal called for the acquisition of state power, either by evolutionary, cooperative means, or revolutionary, violent means, while the boycott approach called for the rejection of the modern state by either passive or active means in the name of the nation, but also in the interests of local and personal privilege and identity. But the leaders of these movements were able to use to their advantage similar sets of ideas, grievances and symbols in the internal and external political argument that raged during the colonial period. The major issues they used included the role and nature of the Buddhist faith and its institutions, the concept of equity and justice for the indigenous population, and the place of foreign or alien capital and labour in the economy, as well as the place of the British in the management and control of the state. But the fundamental division between those who accepted the legitimacy of the purpose of the modern state, and those who did not, still runs through these arguments, and, in large measure, explains the absence during much of the colonial period of clear and concerted cooperation between the political élite and much of the peasant population in what, in the idiom of the modern state, was called the nationalist movement.

The crux of the problem was legitimacy, the legitimacy of the rationalized state and of the power of the élite which controls it. To those who accepted its utility in terms of its progressive, efficiency-oriented nature and the power thus created, and who viewed the life of the nation in terms of its external relations with other nations as well as of the internal problems of social control, economic provision and élite status, the modern state's existence in a world of similar states is justification for its power. For those who concerned themselves more with their own personal and local security and immediate prosperity, who thought primarily in terms of local issues and historical privileges, the state, or an anti-state movement, if it was to be supported, had to provide some rationale other than mere efficiency, productivity and national independence. It had to provide an aura of emotion, sentiment and personal bonding, an 'imagined community',[2] which a merely utilitarian movement or institution could not create. It was the skillful use of these sentiments, unconsciously reinterpreted to provide support for a power-seeking movement, which provided the means by which political leaders eventually developed a following among people whose utilitarian interest was to boycott the state. By making the power-seeking nationalist movement more legitimate than British rule, the political élite were able to combine with the peasantry to wrest control from the British in the name of ideals and interests contrary to those of the peasantry. The political upheavals in Burma after independence were the legacy of the nationalist movement and the class conflicts it temporarily submerged in the name of nation-state autonomy.

2. See Benedict Anderson, *Imagined Communities: Reflections on the Origin and Spread of Nationalism* (London: Verso, 1983).

Early Responses to the Colonial State

During the first sixty years of British rule, when the colonial state was small, incomplete, and made few demands upon the people, perhaps even fewer than the precolonial state had done in some areas, it was fairly easy for people to comply with the new rulers, and even, in some cases, cooperate with them. Those disenchanted with conditions under the kings in the north migrated to the south to take advantage of the economic opportunities developed there as well as of the abolition of corvée and military service obligations. The colonial state's unwillingness to recognize or sanction patron-client ties provided an incentive for those wishing to avoid their traditional obligations. Even so, the symbols of the old order and the identity they provided through the continued existence of the monarchy and the permanency of the Buddhist faith meant that there was little lost in terms of personal identity when taking advantage of these new opportunities. Especially in the period between the first and second Anglo-Burmese wars, the weakness of the colonial administration and its peripheral relationship to the core of the independent states' domains posed few problems to the heterodox population which remained under or migrated to British rule.

The establishment of British rule in Arakan and Tenasserim evoked little violent opposition after the surrender of the king's forces; there are a variety of reasons for this. Neither Arakan nor Tenasserim had been well integrated administratively or ethnically into the precolonial order. Arakan had been conquered by the Avan state only in 1784 and resistance to the central state had persisted, including a significant rebellion in 1797, which created one of the precipitative causes of the first Anglo-Burmese war. Tenasserim, too, was a peripheral region with a small population. The land had been fought over repeatedly by the kings of Burma and Siam and the people there seemed to take some consolation from the fact that, with the advent of British rule, they would be exempt from these inter-state rivalries.[3] Being marginal territories, both contained a significant proportion of people who had fled from one authority or another, who did not share either a religious or ethnic identity with the monarchical state, and indeed, who had little sense of loyalty to any state in the region.

3. *Selected Correspondence of Letters from and Received in the Office of the Commissioner Tenasserim Division from the Years 1825–26 to 1843–44* (Rangoon: Government Printing and Stationery, Burma, 1928), pp. 3–4; John F. Cady, *A History of Modern Burma* (Ithaca: Cornell University Press, 1958), p. 80.

Equally important in easing the way for the peaceful establishment of colonial rule in these two regions was the rapid agricultural and commercial expansion which took place. Within the first year of British rule in Tenasserim, rice production increased 34 per cent. The security which the British created allowed the cultivators to spread throughout the province and redevelop their fields.[4] Conditions were similar in Arakan, where the price of agricultural goods rose dramatically and the importation of inexpensive British cloth meant that more could be purchased with the new currency in circulation.[5] The individualism and legal equality fostered by British rule, coupled with the abandonment of the sumptuary laws of the precolonial state and the growth of wage labour and a money economy, made first Arakan and Tenasserim, and later all of British Burma, attractive areas for entrepreneurs seeking release from the constraints on consumption and investment that had maintained the precolonial state.

The rapid growth of population in these regions is indicative of their attractiveness. The population of Tenasserim grew by 50 per cent between 1835 and 1845 and by another 50 per cent between 1845 and 1852.[6] Lower Burma's population doubled in the first decade of British rule.[7] In the earliest years much of the population growth was due less to the migration of people from independent Burma to British territory than to migration from regions elsewhere in South and Southeast Asia, as well as China. The land connection between Chittagong and Arakan and the existence of the same government on both sides of the border encouraged the migration of Bengalis into the region. Early efforts to encourage Burmese to migrate in large numbers to Tenasserim were unsuccessful,[8] but the government brought in labourers from south India, including convicts, and encouraged the migration of Chinese from the west coast of Malaya. Both Tenasserim and Arakan soon took on the aura of international trading centres and settlements (which they still have).

Particular segments of the populations of Arakan and Tenasserim

---

4. *Selected Correspondence Tenasserim Division*, pp. 51–2.
5. *Report on the Progress of Arakan Under British Rule from 1826 to 1875* (Rangoon: Government Press, 1876), p. 47.
6. Cady, *History of Modern Burma*, p. 84.
7. *Ibid.*, p. 94.
8. *Ibid.*, p. 82.

were keener to cooperate with the British than others. This cooperation is normally explained in terms of the ethnic antagonism that was claimed by the British to exist between the Burmans of the north and the Arakanese, Mon and Karen populations. Great emphasis is given, for example, to the cooperation that Mons and Karens gave to the British forces during the first Anglo-Burmese war; these groups are claimed to have viewed the British as liberators from 'Burman' rule.[9] Many members of the Mon and Karen communities had not yet been fully integrated into the state structure of the precolonial order and therefore felt little if any sense of identity with the old state. Moreover, many Karens were not Buddhists and had been denied opportunities for advancement under the crown.

The British interpreted their behaviour in terms of ethnic antagonism, and thus set the pattern for subsequent foreign and indigenous interpretation. Particularly among the Sgaw Karen population there was a significant minority of individuals who turned to British officials and American Baptist missionaries for the opportunities they provided for a distinctive identity, and thereby developed an attachment to the new order. A notion of Karen identity separate from the precolonial state was encouraged by the missionaries, who had had little success in converting Buddhists to their cause, and by the British, who were seeking a pool of reliable recruits for state service. Many of the animist Karens thus gained not only a distinctive identity but also a distinctive religion, connected ideologically and personally with the growing power of the western world in southern Burma. 'Thus, especially among the Sgaw Karens, Christianity and pro-British Karen nationalism developed hand in hand'— the first Western-style voluntary political organization in Burma's history, the Karen National Association, was formed in 1881 by Karen Christians and their American mentors as a pressure group 'to promote a broader sense of unity among all Karen peoples and to provide spokesmen for them in political matters'.[10]

The ease of the establishment of British rule in Arakan and Tenasserim should not, however, obscure the point that there were individuals and groups who did oppose the new order. Though the independent state in the north could provide them with little support, the gentry in particular attempted to defend the privileges and power they had enjoyed

9. *Ibid.*, p. 73.
10. *Ibid.*, p. 99; J.W. Baldwin, 'The Karens in Burma', *Journal of the Royal Central Asian Society*, XXXVI (1949), pp. 102–13.

before the British arrived. After the second Anglo-Burmese war the extent of this opposition grew, for the British annexed not a peripheral region, but a nuclear area of the precolonial state which had provided new opportunities to officials and others from the core during the previous century.

The majority of the resistance leaders during the nineteenth century were former princes and officials of the precolonial state and their supporters, as well as Buddhist monks. It was the officials who suffered first. In Tenasserim, 'none of the higher Burmese officials were retained by the British administration'.[11] While the Commissioner, Mr Maingy, was confident that 'the lower and middling classes appear . . . mild, obedient, inoffensive people', and were 'attached' to the British, he was worried about 'some desperate gangs of thieves' who belonged 'to the party of the late Ye Woon, or Second Governor' who he had despatched from office.[12] From the start, the British government tended to see any opposition to their rule as the acts of thieves and dacoits, rather than in terms of economic, political or personal grievances against the colonial state and its masters, and thus denied such acts any justification.

In Arakan, there seems to have been no initial opposition to the assumption of British rule; however, within a few years resistance developed, and in 1836 there was a serious rebellion. 'Disaffection centred in men of property and social standing under the traditional order who were being denied influence under the new regime.'[13] But the strength of such opposition was not great and the improving economic conditions of Arakan, like Tenasserim, apparently undermined the support that the followers of deposed officials had previously given them. Others drifted back over the border into independent Burma.

Following the second Anglo-Burmese war, there was a period of widespread disorder, although it could hardly be defined as a national uprising. Nonetheless, it took more than three years for the British to feel confident that order had been restored. Here also the heart of the leadership of the rebellion was provided by officials and gentry of the precolonial state, especially *taik-thu-gyi*, many of whom had only recently received their appointments from the throne and had not yet

11. *Correspondence for the Years 1825–26 to 1842–43 in the Office of the Commissioner Tenasserim Division* (Rangoon: Government Printing and Stationery, Burma, 1929), p. 1.
12. *Selected Correspondence Tenasserim Division*, p. 23.
13. Cady, *History of Modern Burma*, p. 85.

established hereditary claims to office. Where an established *myo-thu-gyi* acknowledged the new rulers, presumably upon a promise of their continuity in office, turmoil rarely resulted.[14]

Still, as late as the final years of the 1850s, there existed organized bands of men opposed to British rule, though not all of these were led by officials who had served the monarchical state. The fact that people whom the colonial authorities called Mons and Karens were involved in anti-British activities and refused to comply with the new order caused officials concern. The statement of the Commissioner of Pegu in 1858, that some rebellious Mons 'would not acknowledge being Mons',[15] says more about British perceptions of ethnicity than of the nature of the resistance. By the beginning of the 1860s, however, the British-Indian forces had established a reasonable degree of tranquility. Less widespread opposition to the state from then until 1885 was labelled banditry and dacoity, and though the number of these acts continued to grow, they were dealt with by armed military police units. The ease with which this was done was in part a consequence of the fact that those individuals who had been influential under the old order had mostly been captured and removed from their areas of influence, or had fled north to live under the patronage of the court. By 1882 a British administrator could lament that 'not a single Burman could be found with interest, position, or influence' in the entirety of his district.[16]

Following the annexation of northern Burma and the deposition of King Thibaw, the British faced more intensive and extensive opposition. Unlike the first two annexations, the British now directly assaulted the personal identities of the majority of the population by removing the central pillar of the old state, the monarch, and denying the institutions he had supported, in particular the Buddhist faith, the backing of the state.[17] Disturbances first occurred in the core areas of the precolonial state, but eventually spread south as well. Rebellious activity was not suppressed in some areas of central and southern Burma until 1890. In the hill areas, however, some of which had already fallen out of

14. *Ibid.*, pp. 89–90; J.A. Mills, 'Burmese Peasant Response to British Provincial Rule 1852–1885', in D.B. Miller (ed.), *Peasants and Politics* (Melbourne: Edward Arnold, Australia, 1978), pp. 83–5.
15. Mills, 'Burmese Peasant Response', p. 84.
16. *Ibid*, p. 96.
17. Ni Ni Myint, *Burma's Struggle Against British Imperialism (1885–1895)* (Rangoon: The Universities Press, 1983), p. 156.

the grip of the central state before the British arrived,[18] or had had only a tributary relationship with the king, *pax Britannica* was not established for another five years. The extent of the resistance to the British and the intensity of feeling behind it might have been reduced had the decision not been made by the Viceroy of India to abolish the monarchy. This action made clear to the royalty, old nobility and the monkhood, that there would be no role for them in the future of the state, and they therefore felt they had little option but to resist.

Much of the initial opposition was led by princes who were able to organize substantial followings, some of up to a thousand or more men.[19] Their appeal for support was put in terms of the defence of the old order. For example, the Myinzaing Prince, in his call to arms, after noting his descent from the royal lineage and the power of his personage, issued a statement encapsulating their fears. It said in part,

> the heretics, savage and lawless *Kalas* [originally referring to Indians, but now generalized to include Europeans] have now entered Burma, and are destroying religious edifices, such as pagodas, monasteries, etc., held sacred by the people, the Buddhist Scriptures and the Priesthood. They have destroyed the accounts and records of royal ceremonies which were generally referred to by the Kings of old. And these *Kalas* are using in the profane way the white umbrellas and other insignia which belong only to royalty.[20]

Others whose claims to princely status were doubtful, including one who previously had served as a vaccinator under the British, raised the standard of royalty to rally support against the invaders, perhaps hoping to emulate Alaungpaya's founding of the Konbaung dynasty.[21] Though a few of the former officials of the court at Mandalay did join with some of the princes in rebellion, most stayed on to serve the state's new masters. Like the good bureaucrats that they were (servants of the state, not the ruler) 'the replacement of King Thibaw by the British at Mandalay became for them only a change of master'.[22] One of the princes even cooperated with the British, perhaps in the hope of receiving the nominal throne for himself, and helped induce 'the bulk of the *Wuns* and *Myothugyis* in some areas not occupied directly by the British officers to

18. *Ibid.*, p. 15.
19. *Ibid.*, pp. 45–51. Profiles of some of these leaders are given in app. G, pp. 198–201.
20. *Ibid.*, app. E, p. 194.
21. *Ibid.*, pp. 53–4.
22. *Ibid.*, p. 58.

carry on as officials of the new regime or to yield their places to successors appointed from Mandalay'.[23]

Though the British were able to enlist the cooperation of the head of the Buddhist order, the *thathanabaing*, who had served King Thibaw, to assist in maintaining order in both secular and religious affairs,[24] some of the resistance was led by monks; this happened mainly in southern Burma where monks had been outside the control of the central ecclesiastical organization since 1852.[25] Many of the leaders of the smaller rebel bands were headmen and other local officials of the precolonial state. Dacoit leaders also joined the conflict with the new state, though whether this demonstrated 'a nobility of aspiration' rather than a desire to make profit in the ensuing disorder is arguable.[26]

Though the extent of the opposition was great, requiring in the words of the Commissioner of British Burma 'the military occupation of a hostile country',[27] the lack of unity and cooperation among the rebel leaders eased the task of the British-Indian forces. 'Every village was a little republic', and without a single leader to rally these forces to a united purpose, 'Burma as a nation was broken up'.[28] This, at least, is the explanation given by twentieth-century Burmese writers. However the possibility of routing the British from the country, given adequate organization and leadership, did exist, because a little over a year after the annexation the British had to organize a force of 40,500 men to restore order.[29] The advantages the British had over their opponents were not only in manpower, organization and weapons. They also developed an effective strategy 'aimed at a close occupation of the country', quelling unrest with military force, followed quickly by the imposition of a civilian administration backed by the military police.[30] The commencement soon after of major public works projects, especially the extension of the railways from southern to northern Burma,

23. Cady, *History of Modern Burma*, p. 127; see also Ni Ni Myint, *Burma's Struggle*, p. 95.
24. Ni Ni Myint, *Burma's Struggle*, p. 97.
25. *Ibid.*, pp. 75–7 and app. G, pp. 209–11.
26. *Ibid.*, pp. 58–61, 77; app. G, pp. 205–8; app. H, pp. 218–21, lists a total of 71 prominent resistance leaders; see also Cady, *History of Modern Burma*, p. 134.
27. Quoted in Ni Ni Myint, *Burma's Struggle*, p. 66.
28. Lei Maung, *Myanma Naingnganyei Thamaing* (History of Burma's Politics) (Rangoon: Sapei Biman, 1974), vol. 1, p. 1; Maung Maung, *Burma and General Ne Win* (New York: Asia Publishing House, 1969), p. 2.
29. Cady, *History of Modern Burma*, p. 134.
30. Ni Ni Myint, *Burma's Struggle*, p. 86.

provided new opportunities for paid employment which further undermined the appeal of the disparate rebel leaders and helped end the uprisings.[31]

It took another five years for the British to 'pacify' the surrounding hill areas, for there it was more difficult to find figures willing to be placed in authority over the people, except in the Shan States.[32] Most of the resistance in the Chin and Kachin hills, except for that led by the Wuntho *Sawbwa*, was organized by local leaders who had had few if any relations with the old state other than through the payment of tribute. The British were able to get many of these leaders to accept their authority in exchange for a promise not to interfere with local customs and the chief's taxing powers over their subjects.[33] Where chiefs were not willing to abide by the colonial authority, the British exacted retribution with punitive raids which met with little resistance because of their inability 'to overcome local and sectional interests and mobilize wider loyalties'.[34] During much of the British period, the central state's authority in the more remote areas amounted to little more than periodic 'flag marches' in which the symbol of state supremacy was displayed and the promise of punishment for unruly behaviour was made.

But the heart of the precolonial state's territories were now firmly under the control of the new rulers, and the local inhabitants increasingly turned their attention away from attempting to resist the foreign rulers and more toward taking advantage of the opportunities being created. The migration of increasing numbers of people from the north to the expanding rice economy in the delta relieved political pressure on the new state as energies became concentrated on economic activities.[35] The massive human endeavour that went into building the new railways, roads, irrigation canals and bunds, and the clearing of the delta swamps for the rice industry partially explains the air of political and social quiet that settled over Burma for a generation after 1890.

The absence of effective and trusted leadership was another important factor. The British had removed the old élite from the central state and

31. Ibid., pp. 101–2.
32. Ibid., ch. 5, 6, and 7; app. G, pp. 211–17.
33. Ibid., p. 135.
34. Ibid., p. 137.
35. Michael Adas, *The Burma Delta: Economic Development and Social Change on an Asian Rice Frontier, 1852–1941* (Madison: University of Wisconsin Press, 1974), pp. 41–3.

exiled the king and his immediate family while pensioning off other members of the nobility and court officialdom. Those *myo-thu-gyi* and other gentry who had not rebelled against the British were absorbed into the new administration and were busy learning their altered tasks. The destruction of the old township system weakened the social and political bonds of communities larger than the village. However, underneath this outward calm, forces were at work which would begin to erase the feelings of remorse, resentment and helplessness that the older generation of Burmese felt in the 1890s and the early twentieth century.[36] The economic transformation of the country was creating the new class and ethnic structure discussed in the previous Chapter, and this would unleash massive peasant protests in the 1920s and 1930s, at first passive, later active. Yet, as there were still plenty of opportunities, the ethnic competition for jobs and land that became politically serious in the 1930s was not seen as a major problem.

Nonetheless, the growing prosperity of the people and their release from the constraints of the past were leading to new forms of social behaviour which threatened to remake Burmese culture and society. Established conservative interests, in particular the Buddhist monkhood, looked with displeasure upon these changes. Moreover, that the cause of many of these changes stemmed from the growing domination of the society by foreign capital and labour came to be increasingly understood by much of the population, especially those in the towns and cities where the impact of colonialism was most immediate. But in the villages, too, the intrusion of the state's new institutions, laws and police was felt, and resistance to the violation of accepted norms of fairness and order was developing a political form. Except perhaps for those tied most closely to the state, for the majority of Burmese at the beginning of this century there were aspects of change which were felt to be immoral and unfair, and while different individuals and groups could not always agree as to what these were, they could all agree that there was one cause: British imperial rule.

But what was to be done about it?

Unlike in Vietnam, where in Confucianism the culture provided a state-centred and essentially secular philosophy which could be used, or at least it was believed for a time could be used, in order to find a solution

36. Maung Maung, *From Sangha to Laity, Nationalist Movements of Burma, 1920–1940* (New Delhi: Manohar, Australian National University Monographs on South Asia no. 4, 1980), p. xvi.

to the colonial dilemma,[37] Burmese culture, and in particular Buddhism, provided no answer to the plight of the old élite nor the population at large. The challenge posed to Buddhist beliefs and institutions by the utilitarian ethic of the modern state and the international organizational power of Christian missionaries forced educated Burmese to rethink the basis of social and political action in terms appropriate to their transformed world. The institutions of the modern state and of Western religion, including elected leaders, committees, formal resolutions and voluntary membership, came to be seen as necessary instruments to be used to resist colonial rule. It was more than just the name that the founders of Burma's first countrywide voluntary organization, the Young Men's Buddhist Association (YMBA), adopted from the Young Men's Christian Association. In fact, this was the least important, for the organization's Burmese name, *Budda Batha Kalyana Yuwa Athin*, literally the Association to Take Tender Care of the Wholesomeness of Buddhism, shared little with the YMCA. Rather, it was the Christian body's organizational form, use of printing and propaganda, and efforts at mass education which were crucial to the development of a Burmese nationalist organization.[38]

But first a new élite aware of these models and lessons had to rise from the ruins of the old order via the institutions created by the new state. The first outward evidence of the changes experienced and the lessons learned between 1885 and the first years of the twentieth century was the emergence of a new political élite which claimed to speak for Burmese nationalism and was accepted as its voice by the British.

The Emergence of the Middle Class Political Elite

The new urban-based political élite which emerged with the development of the colonial state was the product of and the spokesman for the small and increasingly financially insecure Burmese middle class. Much of its behaviour can be explained in terms of an attempt to defend their class's position in society by taking advantage of the political opportunities that the British-Indian policy of increasing the role of liberal

37. See David G. Marr, *Vietnamese Anti-Colonialism, 1885–1925* (Berkeley: University of California Press, 1971).
38. See the general comments of S.J. Tambiah, *World Conqueror and World Renouncer* (Cambridge University Press, 1976), p. 213, on this point.

democratic institutions within the colonial state created. The new political élite saw itself as having a responsibility for protecting and enhancing the middle class's political and economic power by creating the conditions that would ensure that the state they would inherit from the British would guarantee the perpetuation of their class.

However, forces in society which predated the rationalized state and looked less favourably upon its social and economic consequences were also emerging and taking advantage of what opportunities they could to organize resistance not only to the British but to the state itself. Many of their grievances were, in fact, not the result so much of British rule but of the nature of the rationalized state (whoever managed it), which as a modern state was taking on responsibilities and enforcing rules which ran contrary to their interests, historical privileges and status. Especially important among these groups were the peasantry, the largest sector of the population, and the Buddhist monkhood, whose role in society was being undermined by the educational, judicial, administrative and economic policies and general secular orientation of the state.

Toward the end of the colonial period, another force, students and other youth, rose to challenge for the leadership of political life. These young men and women were disillusioned with what they regarded as the political élite's collaboration with the colonial power and were strengthened in their beliefs by new ideological constructs, especially the revolutionary rhetoric of Marxism-Leninism. But by then the middle-class élite was near to taking control of the state themselves, and was only stopped by foreign invasion in 1942. The politics of the end of the colonial period were thus dominated by rivalry between the youth who attempted to champion some of the interests of the peasantry, and the established middle-class political élite.

The membership of the political élite changed little throughout its rise to prominence. Many of the persons who were founders of the first parapolitical organizations in the 1900s and 1910s were ministers and senior officials in the 1930s and 1940s. The first widespread organization, the YMBA, formed the basis of many of the political parties of the 1920s, although its initial concerns were formally limited to cultural and religious questions. It was led by students and most of its membership was composed of young government officers and clerks,[39] all products of the new state. For example, the organizers of the YMBA's first nominally political act, the protest over the wearing of shoes by Europeans in the

39. Maung Maung, *Burma and General Ne Win*, p. 4.

precincts of Buddhist pagodas, were all among the top leaders of a political party in 1942.[40] The YMBA's successor, the General Council of Burmese Associations (GCBA), which was organized for more explicitly political and nationalist ends, was led by many of the same middle-class lawyers, businessmen, landowners and journalists.[41]

The new legal profession developed by the needs of the colonial state provided a natural recruiting ground for the political élite. Indeed, in the early 1920s it seemed that politics in Burma was the 'monopoly of barristers'.[42] This situation changed very little during the succeeding twenty years. Lawyers, who by training possess the bureaucratic, verbal and drafting skills necessary for party leadership, lacked the financial security of doctors, large landowners, and contractors. Burmese lawyers even lacked the financial security of Indian lawyers,[43] but they mostly worked in Rangoon, the centre of political life, and this gave them time for political activities. Because of their financially insecure positions, however, the party leaders often had to rely on others for financial support, not only for political but also for personal reasons. This made them especially vulnerable to outside financial manipulation, particularly by Indian financiers.

There were wealthy Burmese involved in colonial politics, but for the most part they tended to keep their money for use at the local level. At least until the late 1930s, relatively little flowed to Rangoon for the use of politicians and parties at the national level. One reason for this was that local leaders often felt that those involved in national politics did not need or deserve their financial support since they were in the capital, the centre of government, and thus able to live off the state as officials had under the Burmese monarchy.[44] The necessity of financing parties

40. *Ibid.*, p. 6; for a fuller discussion, see Smith, *Religion and Politics*, pp. 86–92.
41. Maung Maung, *Burma and General Ne Win*, pp. 8–9.
42. Maung Maung, *Burma's Constitution* (The Hague: Martinus Nijhoff, 2nd edn, 1956), p. 11. Of the 75 Burmese and Indian members of the 1932 Legislative Council, 33 were lawyers. The next largest group was businessmen, who held 18 seats, and landowners who had 12. Seven members were teachers or former government officials, or employees of foreign firms, and of the remainder, one was an engineer, who was Chinese, one a contractor, one a doctor, one a cultivator, and three for whom no occupational identification is known. Taken from 'Brief Notes on the Status and Political Leanings of Members Elected to the Burma Legislative Council', G.B.C.P.O. no. 387, Judl. Secy., 4 April 1933, BOF P&J(B) 1.
43. G.E. Harvey, *British Rule in Burma 1824–1942* (London: Faber and Faber, 1946), p. 36.
44. For example, Sir J.A. Maung Gyi, a leading politician of the 1920s, and in 1930,

which were not part of the government was not generally recognized as an obligation of local leaders. There certainly was no tradition under the precolonial state of individuals giving financial support to aspiring officials, at least willingly.

Related to this was the fact that the idea of political parties was very new to Burma. National organization was slow to develop, for although spontaneous support for a leader was easy to arouse, it was difficult to sustain a political body through the payment of membership fees and the like. The need for individuals to protect their own local interests often appeared paramount, especially in the uncertain political and economic conditions of the late 1920s and 1930s. Besides, with the relatively limited powers of the few ministers under the dyarchy system, and the dominance of local government bodies by civil servants, there was little in the way of concrete financial or political rewards national leaders could give local supporters. Indeed, some of the members of the provincial middle class had achieved their wealth through the existing autocratic administrative system (with its opportunities for corruption and the hoodwinking of uninformed and transient British administrators). Some did not wish to see the system change in favour of a new political élite which they did not know and might not be able to control if it gained state power. A review of the nature of local leadership in the colonial period may shed more light on some of these points and give a better sense of the kind of local political order the colonial state had created.

The elected and appointed membership of the town and city governing bodies, the municipal committees, provides one indication of the nature of local leaders in urban Burma. Of the 828 such persons for whom occupational data is available for April 1937, business people were the largest group among all the major ethnic communities. Among the Burmese, people in business or the owners of real property held slightly over half the posts.[45] Another way to understand the nature of the colonial middle class and its political leadership is to examine the pre-Second World War careers of people prominent in the 1950s. *Who's*

---

    acting Governor, became known as the 'eater of 5,000 kyats' because of his position as a minister in the government, much as pre-British officials were known as *myosa*. Nyo Mya, 'Profile: Sir Joseph Augustus Maung Gyi', *The Guardian*, (Rangoon) 2, 6 (April 1955), p. 11.

45. Robert H. Taylor, 'The Relationship Between Burmese Social Classes and British-Indian Policy on the Behaviour of the Burmese Political Elite, 1937–1942' (unpbl. Ph.D. thesis, Cornell University, 1974), Table 21, p. 155.

Who in Burma, 1961, includes 233 persons who had active careers in the 1930s. Their names are listed along with their fathers' occupations. Merchants and the owners of real property account for 104 or 45 per cent of the fathers of these élite individuals. Indicative of the élite's growing dependence upon the state, however, is the fact that individuals whose fathers were government employees accounted for the largest single group of these leaders.[46]

While such data suggests something of the nature of the middle-class leaders who were elected to public posts or had active careers in the 1930s (and were still influential in the late 1950s), it does not give an individualized picture of who the influential people in the colonial period were. The last pre-war Deputy Commissioner of Amherst District prepared a list of twelve important people in his jurisdiction for use by the reoccupying intelligence section of the British army after the war. While Amherst was not a representative district, being in Tenasserim rather than in the delta or central Burma, his list and description of these people gives an insight into the nature of local leadership under the late colonial state.[47]

First on the list was the member of the House of Representatives from Moulmein North, U Ohn Pe. He was described as 'one of the wealthiest and most influential Burmans of the District. Landowner, millowner, and owner of the Moulmein Electric Supply.' His brother was the prominent Rangoon civic leader Sir U Thwin, a member of the Senate and former head of the Burmese Chamber of Commerce. U Ohn Pe was 'reasonably cooperative with Government, but kept in with both sides and had friendly contacts with some of the leading *Thakins*,'[48] the most radical anti-British youths of the period. U Po Lun, the business manager of the Moulmein Electric Supply Company, was the second person on the list, but he was not known to be interested in politics.

The third person was Thakin Maung Gyi, an engineer at the Moulmein Electric Supply Company. He had been to England and had an English wife. Although an active nationalist in the early 1930s, he

46. *Who's Who in Burma, 1961* (Rangoon: People's Literature Committee, 1962), tabulated in Taylor, 'Relationship Between Burmese Social Classes and British-Indian Policy', Table 22, p. 157.
47. List of Influential Persons in Amherst District, by W.I.J. Wallace, 19 October 1943. (Wallace Papers in the India Office Library and Archives, London.)
48. *Thakin* was the title taken from the early 1930s by nationalists who wished to assert that they, rather than the British, who were normally addressed as '*Thakin*', like

later lost interest. U Toe Lon, the fourth person, was influential because of his wealth and standing as a timber merchant. He was very conservative, the Deputy Commissioner believed. Another influential older person was U Maung Nge, a Senator and wealthy landowner. Two persons of Sino-Mon descent were on the list of influential figures. One was a large landowner and the other ran the Modum Motor-Bus Association. Also listed was the President of the Moulmein municipal government, a Muslim lawyer, who had been born in Moulmein. The next three men listed were headmen who were also substantial landowners. The last man was the Township Officer of Chaungzon who 'had the support of the influential and wealthy Burmans, including U Ohn Pe of Moulmein, who were interested in seeing law and order preserved under whatever Government'.

The type of local leader who expressed disdain for the national figures and would have contributed nothing to support their political parties is described by C.J. Richards in *Burma Retrospect*.[49] In his account of U Kyan Aung, Richards, who was a British Deputy Commissioner, provides a description of one of the routes to local power and wealth in Burma in the 1920s and 1930s, if not earlier. Kyan Aung began by gaining the post of Revenue Surveyor; a 'badly paid and generally overworked' position which had ample opportunities for graft and corruption. A Revenue Surveyor was 'the first link in the administrative chain responsible for the amassing of something like one-third of the total Provincial Revenue of Burma'. Kyan Aung was responsible for assessing the tax that had to be paid on a cultivator's crop: obviously a position open to the influence of bribes or the application of unofficial coercion. In time his corrupt activities were discovered by his British supervisor, but he 'easily escaped prosecution for bribery,' as no one could be found to testify that he had been bribed by him, 'but Government discharged him for bad work'.

With his bribe money, plus twenty acres of paddy land he had inherited from his parents, Kyan Aung 'proceeded methodically to add various other holdings, partly by purchase, partly by foreclosure of mortgage, on money acquired through his exactions'. By the late 1930s, when land prices had risen again after the slump of the early 1930s,

---

'*Sahib*' in India, were the 'masters' of Burma, for this is what the word literally means. This movement, and the implications of its name, will be discussed below.
49. C.J. Richards, *Burma Retrospect and Other Essays* (Winchester, England: Herbert Curnow, The Cathedral Press, 1951), pp. 62–6, from which all the following quotations are taken.

'Kyan Aung was owner and mortgagee of something like a thousand acres, valued at something up to two hundred rupees an acre, most of which he had acquired at about one-tenth their worth'. He then expanded his activities by securing the 'leases of two neighbouring fisheries for a good deal less than they were worth, by the process of buying-out intending competitors, before the auctions took place'. He made further profits through paddy trading; something his neighbours with fewer liquid assets were unable to do. Kyan Aung also bought a bus and began a passenger and freight service to the township headquarters where he started a general store.

Having made his fortune through bribery and speculation, Kyan Aung decided it was time to make his mark in the political world, perhaps in order to protect his little empire and further diversify its activities. He stood for the District Council and ran against two other candidates, 'an obscure lower-grade pleader and a landowner of nearly U Kyan Aung's prominence, and it was thought that between these two there would be a close finish'. Several weeks before the election the other landowner candidate was shot through the head and his murderer was never apprehended. Safely elected as a member of the council, 'Kyan Aung had ample opportunities of graft among contractors and the like'. He was even tried for organizing robberies and dacoities while serving on the District Council but was acquitted. Doubtless blind justice could still feel a rupee in the hand.

Despite his local prominence, wealth and active political career at the local level, Kyan Aung expressed 'outspoken mistrust of advanced nationalism' of the type advocated by the national party leaders. 'Thus at a meeting of local celebrities, when a discussion of politics arose, U Kyan Aung remarked — "Personally I do not want Independence. I do not like the Law of the Jungle." There were some rather dark glances when he said this, but U Kyan Aung did not seem to notice them.' It would, of course, be a mistake to assume that most, or even a great many, local political leaders behaved in a manner similar to Kyan Aung. But it would equally be a mistake to assume that all local political bosses viewed the colonial state and the system it had created as an unmitigated evil to be got rid of at the earliest opportunity. Furthermore, Kyan Aung's behaviour as an official and an entrepreneur goes some way toward explaining the negative response of the peasantry to the state which gave him his chances and which could do little to protect them from his illegal acts.

However, before turning to an analysis of the villagers' response to

The Emergence of the Middle Class Political Elite   169

the colonial state, it is necessary to examine further the nature of the political élite and its institutions. The careers of several of the leading national political figures during the 1920s and 1930s indicates the consequences of the inability of the nationalist parties to draw funds from the local middle class to support their organizational activities. The career of U Chit Hlaing expresses this dilemma perhaps more than that of any other major figure of the 1920s and 1930s.

Chit Hlaing was born in October 1879, in Amherst district, an area that had known British rule for fifty-four years. His grandfather was said to have been a head constable who upon retirement set up as a timber merchant. The teak industry prospered in the early years of British rule through exports to India and the shipbuilding industry in Moulmein. His father continued in the timber business and diversified into moneylending. With such a prosperous family behind him, Chit Hlaing was able to study in England from 1898 until 1902, and became a barrister.[50] Chit Hlaing rapidly dissipated his financial legacy in support of the activities of the GCBA,[51] and by April 1932 was in hiding in Moulmein to avoid arrest for debt.[52] There is no questioning Chit Hlaing's political courage and dedication to the nationalist movement. In addition to using his own funds to support the nationalist cause, he was arrested for his beliefs on several occasions.[53] As a key figure in the early GCBA, serving as its chairman for several years, and nearly made president-for-life, he was widely regarded in rural areas as one of the leading Burmese national leaders.

This towering figure of the 1920s, touring the country in the style of a prince and possessing independent means and contacts with both the

50. Burma List no. 32, History Sheet of U Chit Hlaing, appended to letter, Government of Burma to Government of India, 4 April 1931, BOF P&J(B) 1. See also Sein Myint, *Hnit 200 Myanma Naingngan Thamaing Abidan* (Dictionary of 200 Years of Burma History) (Rangoon: Sapei Yathana, 1969), pp. 74–6. This volume is useful for providing potted careers of political leaders and has been consulted in the preparation of this chapter. Also, details of careers of political leaders have been taken from various files in the Burma Office as well as the standard publications noted in the bibliography, especially those by John F. Cady and the two Maung Maungs.
51. Cady, *History of Modern Burma*, f.n. 37, p. 367.
52. Appreciation of the Political Situation, by Sir C. Innes and T. Lister, 12 April 1932, BOF P&J(B) 1.
53. Burma List no. 32, History Sheet of U Chit Hlaing; N.R. Chakravarti, *The Indian Minority in Burma: The Rise and Decline of an Immigrant Community* (London: Oxford University Press for the Institute of Race Relations, 1971), p. 110.

Indian and Burmese nationalist movements, was in the 1930s closely tied to the financial interests of the Chettiars and several Indian firms, in particular the Scindia Steam Navigation Company, one of the major transporters of Indian labourers to and from Burma. Scindia's Rangoon agent, S.N. Haji, was notorious in the 1920s and 1930s for the misuse of funds to 'buy' Burmese politicians. Chit Hlaing's personal financial plight came simultaneously with the political controversy over the separation of Burma from India and his decision to participate in the colonial political system. When he attended talks in London on the separation questions he, like all the other Burmese politicians in the delegation, agreed on the desirability of Burma becoming a separate political entity. However, upon his return to Rangoon, he changed his mind and advocated Burma remaining an integral province of the Indian empire. From 1932 until the Second World War, he almost invariably sided in any dispute with Indian financial interests.

Thus, from the early 1930s U Chit Hlaing was never able to regain his national prominence, and his place was taken by two new politicians, Dr Ba Maw and U Saw. Ba Maw's career shows again the interplay between the strategies of popular appeal and Indian financing which tugged at the major political figures of the period. To get elected and mobilize popular support, a politician had to assure the Burmese peasant majority that he and any government he led would act to obviate the consequences of the rice-export economy, the indebtedness of the peasants to the Chettiars and other moneylenders, and the state's actions to protect existing contractual obligations. But to finance their political movements, they had to turn to the large financial interests, including the Chettiars, which could provide them with the funds they needed to finance elections, pay followers, and purchase votes in the legislature.

Born in 1893, the son of a former official in the court of King Thibaw, Ba Maw attended St Paul's English High School, Rangoon, took a BA with Honours from the Rangoon branch of Calcutta University in 1913, then an MA from Calcutta in 1917, before travelling to England where he studied at Cambridge University from 1922 to 1924 while simultaneously preparing for the bar at Gray's Inn, London, to which he was called in 1923. Forced to withdraw from Cambridge when the authorities there discovered his London studies, he went to France and took a doctorate from the University of Bordeaux in 1924. Entering politics in the ranks of the GCBA, while practising law in Rangoon, Ba Maw gained his early reputation by defending Hsaya San and other leaders of the 1930–2 peasants' rebellion at their trial. One of his British colleagues at the Rangoon bar subsequently described Dr Ba Maw at the Hsaya San trial as

an able advocate, and with a flamboyance and histrionic skill calculated to allure the gallery. . . . He was within the law, but seemingly on the side of the rebels. It was an attractive combination, and the Doctor was hailed as the champion of the oppressed.[54]

In preparation for the 1932 elections on the separation from India question, he organized one of the two Anti-Separation Leagues. Unlike the leader of the rival league, Chit Hlaing, Ba Maw was not then beholden to Indian interests, and made it clear that his anti-separation stance was intended for bargaining purposes with the British government. He always insisted that there would have to be a clause allowing for Burma's secession from India at whatever time the government of Burma chose. In 1934 Ba Maw accepted the post of Minister for Education in the dyarchy cabinet and in 1937 he became the country's first premier under the new constitution. By 1939, however, he was seen as an ally of Indian interests and a collaborator with the British by Rangoon University students, and when he was unable to rectify their grievances they organized demonstrations with rival politicians, including U Saw, which led to the downfall of his government. Having been elected as the leader of the reformist *Hsinyeitha* (Poor Man's or Proletarian Party), championing peasant causes such as land reform and the abolition of indebtedness, he only remained in office with the assistance of Indian votes in the legislature and Indian financial backing until politicians less encumbered with these obligations were able to create such public disorder as to cause his downfall.[55]

The politician who succeeded Ba Maw as Premier was Shwegyin U Pu. He was an independent man who apparently had few contacts with Indian interests during his career, although he did have Chinese financial support. Born in 1881, his parents were timber merchants in Shwegyin. He received a BA at Rangoon College in 1903 and was called to the English bar from the Middle Temple in 1908. While studying in London, Pu founded a Buddhist society and upon return to Rangoon became active in the YMBA and the GCBA. His career was very similar to that of another leading figure, U Ba Pe. Ba Pe, born in 1883 in a small

---

54. E.C.V. Foucar, *I Lived in Burma* (London: Dennis Dobson, 1956), p. 75.
55. See Taylor, 'The Relationship Between Burmese Social Classes and British-Indian Policy', chs. 4 and 5, for details.

town in Tharrawady District, was the son of landowners. He received a BA from Rangoon College in 1906, but being unable to afford study in Britain, took a job as a teacher at St Paul's English High School. In 1906 he was one of the founders of the YMBA and from 1907 to 1911 continued in a leading role in the YMBA while working as a government clerk. He left the government to found the Sun Press Limited, and his newspaper, *Thuriya* (The Sun), became the leading voice of Burmese middle-class nationalism throughout the colonial period. Ba Pe's varied career included being an editor and publisher, party leader, businessman, Education Minister under dyarchy, Home Minister in the 1939 ministry of U Pu and being jailed by Premier U Saw's government in 1941. He was for several years before the war the head of the Burmese Chamber of Commerce and as such served as one of the leading spokesman for indigenous business interests.

Shwegyin U Pu and U Ba Pe, though both able to achieve high office briefly, were never able to capture the public's attention in the way that Chit Hlaing and Ba Maw did. This was partially due to differences in personalities, neither having the histrionic skills of their opponents. Both were closely associated with the urban and business-oriented sector of the Burmese middle class which was increasingly dependent upon the colonial state. While probably more serious and orthodox Buddhists than Chit Hlaing (Ba Maw was a Plymouth Brethren), they were less capable of using religious appeals to gain public support because of their belief that monks should not be involved in political activities. Furthermore, because of their reliance on funds for their parties from Burmese and Chinese sources, they were never able to compete financially with their Indian-backed opponents.

Dr Thein Maung and U Saw were politicians who gained greater freedom of action than some of their contemporaries by not becoming reliant on Indian funds. Both were able to gain financial assistance from the Japanese consul in Rangoon at different points in their careers to maintain or enhance their independence, and Saw developed a following among the largest Burmese landowners. Dr Thein Maung was born in Paungde in 1891 and entered politics with Ba Pe's People's Party in the 1920s after completing a medical degree at Calcutta University. A staunch separationist in 1932, and a firm supporter of Burma's industrialization on a model similar to Japan, he left Ba Pe in 1937 to join Dr Ba Maw's coalition government and stayed close to Ba Maw after his government fell in 1939. In 1940 he travelled to Japan where he received Japanese assurances of financial support for Ba Maw's new Freedom Bloc organization which campaigned against Burmese cooperation with Britain in any future war.

The most successful politician of pre-war Burma was U Saw.[56] Although not adverse to taking Indian money, Saw was more independent of Indian interests than other leading politicians and seemed the best hope of the Burmese middle class. Born in 1900, the son of a well-to-do landowner in Tharrawaddy district, Saw was educated only in Burma and unlike almost every other member of the colonial political élite did not have a degree. His formal occupation was that of a third grade pleader, one of the lowest ranks of the new legal profession. Saw's political career began in the early 1920s, and until the founding of his own *Myochit* or Patriot's Party in 1938 he was a member of Ba Pe's party. Because of his support for the Hsaya San rebels, he was charged with sedition, although the charges were later dropped.

In 1935, Saw visited Japan, Korea and Manchuria, and was impressed with the efficiency and power of the Japanese. His account of his travels, *Gyapan Lan Nyunt* (Japan Points the Way),[57] describes the industrial and commercial prowess of the Japanese, their concern for cooperation with other Asians, and his belief that the Japanese model of economic development and cultural conservatism was appropriate for Burma. From the time of his visit to Japan, which was paid for by his hosts, until sometime shortly before he became Premier in 1940, he maintained close contacts with Japanese diplomats and agents in Rangoon, and, in the words of the governor of Burma, 'there was good reason to think that he accepted money from them'.[58] After cultivating the favour of the Japanese consul in Rangoon, he had sufficient funds to become the sole owner of the *Thuriya* newspaper in February 1938, and the next month began to organize his *Myochit* Party by leading ten legislators out of Ba Pe's camp. His views and growing power also attracted support for his party from among the wealthiest members of the middle class, who were increasingly aware of the consequences for private business of the growing class tensions and socialist rhetoric in the country. Among these were U Ba Tin (a leading supplier of railway sleepers to the Burma Railways), Henzada U Mya and Pegu U Sein Win, members of the House of

---

56. A fuller account is given in *Ibid.*, chs. 8 and 9, and in Robert H. Taylor, 'Politics in Late Colonial Burma: The Case of U Saw', *Modern Asian Studies*, 10, 2 (April 1976), pp. 161–4.
57. Saw, *Gyapan Lan Nyunt* (Japan Points the Way) (Rangoon: Thuriya Press, 1936).
58. 'Report on the Burma Campaign, 1941–42, by Sir Reginal Dorman-Smith, p. 8, Dorman-Smith papers in the India Office Archives and Library, London.

Representatives. The latter two were reputed to own in excess of 30,000 acres of land.[59]

The colonial political élite was comprised of very different men from its precolonial predecessor. Unable to rely upon the state and the appanage system to maintain themselves, they all developed careers in the new professions, using as a springboard the independent means of their parents. But their personal wealth was insufficient to pay the large costs of organizing and maintaining the political machines needed to win votes and gain access to office. Except for Dr Thein Maung and U Saw, all who reached the pinnacle of domestic power had done so on the backs of Indian financiers or by cooperation, even if grudging, with the colonial state. Consequently, only Thein Maung and Saw were not compromised in the eyes of the Burmese electorate.

It was the opportunities provided by the changing internal and external conditions that allowed Saw to break free of the dilemma that had trapped his political rivals. Japanese financing, the heightened class and national awareness of leading wealthy Burmese, and the political patronage provided to ministers who gained office under the 1935 constitution, allowed the late colonial political élite to become more independent both of the British, and, more importantly, of Indian capital. How had this situation come about? The British-Indian policy of introducing liberal democratic political institutions and the subsequent fostering of political parties was one factor, a second factor was the increasing development of anti-state, peasant-based non-cooperation movements. A third was the growing radicalism of the younger generation of the educated middle class; a group which had less of a financial stake in the existing economic order.

The Emergence of Burmese Political Parties

The idea of the political party as an institution for mobilizing support for aspiring politicians and maintaining their government once in power, as

---

59. The author is indebted to Dr Dorothy Guyot, who supplied this information from an interview she conducted on Sept. 26, 1962, with U Ba Maung, a House member in the 1930s and Saw supporter. Conversations between the author and U Aye, a close associate of Saw in the Myochit Party, held in Rangoon in January, 1975, further confirmed the details set out above.

well as for implementing widely-shared policy preferences with a justifying ideology, was totally outside the political experience of precolonial Burma. However once these voluntary organizations were formed by the new political élite they developed rapidly. The formation of such parties is explained by a combination of factors. Members of the élite had become aware of the party mode of popular organization during their travels in England and India. The creation in 1923 of the dyarchy Legislative Council and its attendant elections demanded the creation of some means of amassing votes for candidates and of presenting a national political programme. Meaningful opposition to cooperation in these elections required a means of communicating with the populace as well. The growing politicization of the village population, led often by politically oriented young monks, was another factor, for this new force provided the politicians with a ready following if they found symbols and policies with which to elicit support. Behind these obvious factors lay a growing belief among the new Burmese middle class that it was necessary to form some means of defending their interests and their perceptions of Burma's interests from the power and wealth, as well as from the social and cultural influence, of British rule, from Indian labour, and from both British and Indian capital. That the regaining of independence under middle-class leadership was ultimately the only means to protect their interests was obvious, but conditions were not yet deemed appropriate for that step, and the early political leaders had to work within the political community under the constraints imposed by the colonial state and the conditions of the evolving class and ethnic structure of society.

Nonetheless, the nature of the political parties in Burma evolved rapidly between the early 1900s and the late 1930s, reflecting both environmental changes and the growing sophistication of the political élite. The parties were never tightly-knit organizations during these thirty-five or so years, but over time they became increasingly national in scope and hierarchical in structure. For analytical purposes, there were three phases of party development. The first phase lasted from the mid-1900s to around 1920, the second from the early 1920s to around 1936, and the third from 1935 until 1942. The first phase was essentially one of urban, élite organizations which were marked by greater unity among the leadership than at any later period. The second was noted for great divisiveness at the top but also for mass support at the village level for those parties which espoused rejection of the colonial state. The third phase saw the beginning of both mass support at the base and more unified leadership at the top, but due to the brevity of the period the full implications of these trends were never realized.

The unity at the top in the first phase was a result not only of the small number of leaders in the initial years, but also of the lack of opportunities in this period of administrative rule. The repeated bifurcation of parties in the second phase was a result of both the opportunities for a limited number of leaders to gain political office under dyarchy and of the absence of sufficient indigenous funding for all the party organizations. Contentions over the proper role of political monks and of radical and often illegal peasant organizations were also a highly divisive influence. The third phase was conditioned by the existence of a great many more opportunities for patronage for party members from the controlling party in the legislature and cabinet, coupled with other sources of party finances not tied to Indian interests. The unity and strength of the parties from about 1936 on was also aided by a growing sense of class and communal consciousness on the part of the Burmese middle class. This consciousness increased as their position in society was increasingly challenged by Indian capital on the one hand and the Burmese peasantry on the other.

During these years the intellectual and ideological underpinnings of party life also evolved through successive short phases. The first nationalist leaders sought to save Burmese society from the corrosive effects of colonial rule and the new state. Later leaders sought to change and redefine society to regain national independence while preserving those traditional elements which were compatible with a rationalized economy and state. The eventual result was that nationalists began to reorient Burmese political thinking away from notions appropriate for a patrimonial society and monarchical state towards ideas of nationhood with economic and class interests and a world perspective relevant to modern party politics and mass movements.

As a consequence, Burmese political thought shifted from concern for religious honour, social respect and proper behaviour in the 1910s, to demands for explicitly political and economic reforms in the 1920s, to anti-imperialist, anti-capitalist sentiments and calls for action in the 1930s. However, the incorporation of new political ideas into Burmese political life was not a rectilinear process. Until the 1930s, and especially in the 1920s, there was incongruity between the content of political demands and resolutions and the format through which the leadership of the major nationalist organizations presented these ideas in conferences and meetings of their supporters. While the nationalist movement was essentially restricted to a few Rangoon-centred university graduates, teachers and government servants, the national organization was modern and secular in form: its programme was cautious, being both culturally and socially conservative. When the nationalist movement sought to widen its support in the 1920s, the leadership, increasingly under the sway of Buddhist monks, felt it had to present its still essentially conservative goals through religious and culturally recognized mediums and symbols. Only in the later years of the 1930s did the content and form of Burmese nationalism begin to coalesce. Nonetheless, the ideas of the 1930s were interpreted in the context of Burmese culture, which was the product of a thousand years of patrimonial rule justified by Buddhist philosophy.

It is perhaps a misnomer to refer to the predominant institution of the first phase of party development, the Young Men's Buddhist Association, as a political party. It was founded in 1906 as a religious, cultural and welfare-oriented group by a small number of Western-educated men. They 'basically accepted British rule as an unavoidable part of life in Burma, and began using western organizational and institutional forms in setting up various Buddhist associations, missions and schools.'[60] Having brought together under one umbrella disparate organizations of Buddhist laymen in various towns, the YMBA held conferences and debates on social and religious questions, but until 1916 the nearest it came to political activity was voting resolutions urging Burmese to use indigenous products and proposing a unified educational code.[61] In that year the annual conference passed a resolution demanding government action to ban the wearing of shoes in pagodas by Westerners, and the YMBA joined with monks in the organization of public protests against such acts of disdain for Burmese culture by non-Buddhists. Eventually in 1918 the government ruled that it was in the power of the head of a monastery to determine the standards of dress required for admission to their premises, marking the first instance in Burma's colonial history when the government conceded to public demands. This outwardly cautious and conservative action preceded a split in the organization in 1917 between the so-called radicals, led by

60. Maung Maung, *From Sangha to Laity*, p. xvi.
61. *Ibid.*, pp. 3–4; Maung Maung, *Burma and General Ne Win*, p. 5; partial translations of the YMBA conference resolutions may be found in Maung Maung, 'Nationalist Movements in Burma, 1920–1940: Changing Patterns of Leaderships: From Sangha to Laity', MA thesis (Australian National University, 1976), app. A., pp. 552–77.

YMBA founder U Ba Pe and other younger leaders, and an elder faction who had taken the organization over in the late 1900s, over the question of sending the delegation to Calcutta to discuss the future of Burma with Montagu and Chelmsford (who were then considering the outline of the dyarchy system for India). The organization and the majority of its forty-five branches remained with the younger group and prepared the way for the formation of the more explicitly political GCBA. The growing political awareness of the YMBA leaders was also reflected at the fifth conference when a resolution was passed objecting to the Governor's schemes to use the schools for the inculcation of the 'imperial idea' in Burmese youth. At the next conference proposals for the repeal of the capitation and *thathameda* taxes, reflecting the organization's concern with ameliorating the conditions of the peasantry, and for the formation of women's sections or a YWBA were also made.[62]

The second phase of party development began with the shattering of the remaining unity of the YMBA. This resulted from its efforts to get the British government to apply the Indian dyarchy reforms to Burma.[63] In 1919 the leadership divided over whether to accept the Craddock reforms or to continue to lobby in London for equal treatment with India, as well as over differences among the members over finances and *pongyi* involvement in politics. The elder faction was willing to accept Craddock's proposals but the younger group insisted on mounting a protest to the British government over Burma's exclusion from the dyarchy system.

The leadership of the younger majority formed the nucleus of the major parties of the second phase of party development. In addition to U Ba Pe and U Thein Maung, these included the leading political monk, U Ottama, and others such as U Chit Hlaing, Tharrawaddy U Pu and U Tun Aung Kyaw. In March 1920, at its fifth national conference held in Prome, the YMBA changed its English name to the General Council of Burmese Associations, and its Burmese name to the *Myanma Athin Chokkyi*, meaning 'the great Burma controlling group'. The newly named organization's policies and membership were much the same as

62. Maung Maung, *From Sangha to Laity*, p. 13.
63. The following discussion of the development of the parties up to 1932 relies upon the standard historical accounts noted in the bibliography as well as *Special Confidential Supplement to the Police Abstract of Intelligence*, no. 1, XXXVI, 17 Sept. 1932, no. 37, 'The Burma Political Tree', BOF P&J(B) 1; Maung Maung, 'Nationalist Movements in Burma', app. B, pp. 604–13, and Maung Maung, *From Sangha to Laity*, chs 3 and 4.

the younger faction of the YMBA, but it extended party activities to the districts and outlying towns and villages by bringing the 200 or so branches of the old YMBA into closer contact with the Rangoon leadership.[64]

With the change in style of party organization and the abandonment of the most conservative leaders in 1920 the GCBA began to involve itself directly in popular political protests and demonstrations. In doing so, it adopted the technique of the Indian National Congress under Gandhi, the boycott or *hartal*, as for example in the successful boycott organized by the GCBA in protest against the election of members from Burma to the Indian Legislative Assembly and the Council of State at Delhi in October 1920. Such an action appeared to British observers at the time as mere imitation of, if not infiltration by, Indian nationalists in Burma's previously tranquil political life.[65] This conclusion might be easily drawn on one level, for the Burmese political élite were certainly aware of the Indian nationalists' techniques and intentions and shared the same colonial opponents. Yet despite the fact that several of the most important early Burmese nationalist leaders, particularly Chit Hlaing and Ottama, had close relations with the Indian Congress and other groups, Indian organizational techniques, much less political agents, had little to do with the development of Burma's popular political organizations throughout the colonial period.[66]

The boycott of the central Indian elections of 1920 was a minor affair. Because the franchise was tightly restricted and the issue of no intrinsic importance very few people were involved. However, less than two months later the development of a country-wide student boycott added impetus to the development of the nationalist parties and demonstrated to the political leaders the depth of feeling and the potential support for anti-British actions which existed in the country away from the artificial atmosphere of colonial Rangoon. On December 4, 1920, the day now celebrated as 'National Day' in Burma, a few students from Rangoon College organized a protest against the government's plan to set up and develop Rangoon University as an élite institution designed to produce only a few qualified Burmese men and women who could take over the jobs then done by foreigners. This small group had little idea of the effect

64. Maung Maung, *From Sangha to Laity*, p. 19.
65. Cady, *History of Modern Burma*, pp. 215–17; Albert D. Moscotti, *British Policy and the Nationalist Movement in Burma, 1917–1937* (Honolulu: Asian Studies at Hawaii, no. 11, Hawaii University Press, 1974), p. 20.
66. Cady, *History of Modern Burma*, p. 193.

their action would have.[67] Within days most of the indigenous students at both Rangoon College and Judson College (run by American missionaries)[68] were boycotting classes, and by early 1921 the strike had spread to all government schools and some missionary schools throughout Burma proper.[69] The organizers of the strike were not 'radicals' set to oust the British from power,[70] but the support they received from their parents, older sections of society and the leadership of the GCBA demonstrated the potential for political pressure on the colonial government to modify its policies. For the long-term development of national organizations, the 1920 university boycott spawned another movement which provided an important outlet for nationalist energies. This was the national schools movement. GCBA branches and individuals in most towns and cities organized alternative, non-government schools during 1921 in order to maintain the strike and also to ensure their children's education for advancement in the new professions. Though lacking the resources of the state schools, they increased popular awareness of the potential of local organization in the face of state opposition. The national schools persisted into the 1930s, though on a much reduced scale, as the movement split over the issue of the acceptance of government funds.[71]

Thus began the mobilization of increasing numbers of people from various sectors of Burmese society into political and social action. Different groups responded for different reasons, but they did so under the cloak of nationalism. For the leaders of the GCBA, national independence meant their taking control of the state and protecting the economic status and prerogatives of the new middle class. For the students,

67. Moscotti, *British Policy and Nationalist the Movement*, p. 29.
68. Karen and Anglo-Indian students did not join in the strike, although at first Karen students at Judson College were encouraged to do so, as the government's initial plans for the new university had made no provision for the missionary college. Lu Pe Win, *History of the 1920 University Boycott* (n.p.[Rangoon?], the author, for the Organization for the Celebration of the Golden Jubilee of the National Day, November, 1970), p. 17.
69. Cady, *History of Modern Burma*, pp. 213–21.
70. Many of the leaders of the 1920 student boycott returned to the new university and later became prominent officials. Eleven entered the élite ICS, while seven joined the Indian Police Service and another seven the Indian Forest Service. Many others became teachers and government officials of lesser rank. Lu Pe Win, *History of the Strike*, p. 33.
71. Maung Maung, *From Sangha to Laity*, pp. 21–3; Cady, *History of Modern Burma*, p. 220.

most of whom were also from the middle class, expanding educational opportunities meant more jobs for teachers and lower standards of admission and graduation.

A third group, the monkhood, which had not involved itself in political activities since the rebellions of the 1880s, now became politically organized. As discussed in Chapter I, the monkhood had fulfilled important social and sometimes political roles under the precolonial monarchic order. These functions were now being absorbed in new institutions shaped by the needs of the colonial state. Education, a monopoly of the monks under the old order, was now either a state, missionary or state-supervised private secular activity, thus depriving the monkhood of one of its major claims to respect and authority in town and village life. The growth of British law and the development of the legal profession meant also that the monk's function as the interpreter of the meaning of the Buddha's moral law as the basis of the settlement of disputes was now receding.[72] The state also no longer provided the *sangha* with patronage or protection, and while it continued to maintain and support Pali scholarship[73] it jeopardised the monkhood's financial position by creating areas of investment for private capital belonging to the new, secular middle class which the monarchs would have confiscated and in part donated to the monkhood. The monkhood did receive substantial gifts from the middle class (who were more affluent than private individuals had ever been before in Burma), but this support had about it an air of conspicuous social display and private reward that the patronage of the royal court had never had.[74]

At the time of the formation of the GCBA a minority of the approximately 120,000 monks in the country began, wrote U Tin Tut, 'to take an interest in politics seeing ahead a result by which the Govern-

---

72. Smith, *Religion and Politics in Burma*, p. 31.
73. *Ibid.*, pp. 66–71.
74. One is struck in visiting important and less important pagodas and monasteries in Burma today by the large number of donation plaques erected in the 1920s and 1930s, as well as the 1950s, by individuals and families. These often include, in addition to the donors' names, their social status, such as landowner or owner of a shop or small commercial concern. However, throughout the colonial period there were no major new pagodas constructed. Buddhist monumental architecture had to wait until the return of independence for the government to undertake the construction of new, large complexes such as the Kaba Aye pagoda and its precincts in the 1950s.

ment of Burma would again become Burmese and the Order would again become associated with governmental power for the advancement of the religion and the people of Burma'.[75] In 1920, monks came together to form the General Council of Sangha Sammeggi (GCSS), parallel to the GCBA. As with so many organizations in Burma's colonial history, religious or secular, its founders were intent upon essentially moral goals. The uplifting of lay standards of Buddhist practice and the imposition of discipline upon the monkhood itself were pre-eminent among these as the absence of effective government control to maintain discipline meant that the *sangha* was becoming increasingly factionalized and lax in application of the rules of the *Vinaya*.[76] However, due primarily to the leadership of one monk, U Ottama, the GCSS soon became a major political force and turned itself and the GCBA in different directions from those its founders had intended.

U Ottama, who had travelled in India and Japan and had spent most of the first two decades of the century out of Burma, returned advocating an interpretation of Buddhism that quickly found favour with younger monks, though the established *sayadaws* who provided the *sangha's* hierarchy looked with much distrust upon his message and tactics. Ottama's simple argument had clear appeal, particularly to monks in the villages who shared the peasants' declining standards of living. He argued that since the well-being of the religion was dependent upon the well-being of the people who supported it, the monkhood, like the king who claimed to be a *Bodhisatta*, had to involve itself in secular affairs until such time as conditions were appropriate to resume purely religious obligations.[77] The symbiotic relationship of the state with religion was now recast in terms of a symbiotic relationship of the people with the religion, with the state the cause of distress to both.

At first U Ottama's message was largely ignored and criticized by the senior monks, but after his arrest and conviction for sedition in June 1921 the GCBA took up his cause[78] and the GCSS pledged to continue his agitational tours of the countryside, multiplying the number of monks preaching his message of non-cooperation with government. The GCSS founded a group of political monks known as *dhammakatika* who served as political leaders and tutors to the newly formed *wunthanu*

75. 'The Problem of the Pongyi', by U Tin Tut, 6 Nov. 1943, BOF 4811/38.
76. Maung Maung, *From Sangha to Laity*, p. 24.
77. *Ibid.*, pp. 14–16; see also Smith, *Religion and Politics*, pp. 92–107.
78. Moscotti, *British Policy and Nationalist Movement*, p. 32.

athin (village nationalist and self-defence organizations which were affiliated with the GCBA). There were an estimated 200 of these monks touring the country in the early 1920s,[79] spreading the nationalist messages of Buddhist protection and personal benefit to the population. The 12,000 branches of the GCBA assisted them in their work.[80] But the government's arrest of Ottama was only the beginning of the suppression of the political monks. Even among the most conservative Buddhists, who disapproved of monks becoming involved in politics, it created hatred of British treatment of the religion. Throughout the 1920s monks were arrested and imprisoned with little regard as to their religious status. One monk was killed in a demonstration in Mandalay in 1924. The extent of their involvement in what the government regarded as seditious activities was so great by 1928 and 1929 that over 120 monks were arrested, and one, U Wisara, fasted to death in a government gaol.[81]

The influence of the political monks soon gave them a controlling say in many of the activities of the GCBA and was one of the causes of the organization's eventual decline. The GCSS became subject, as it involved itself in secular activities, to the same factional tendencies found in the YMBA and GCBA, but the most militant faction of monks always stood with that group of lay leaders who refused to cooperate with the government by voting or by standing in elections to state bodies. By the early 1930s there were GCSS factions supporting at least four political offshoots of the original GCBA, although the largest remained with the staunchly pro-boycott leader, U Soe Thein, and was the only lay body never to enter into the colonial political system. Nonetheless, as late as 1937 most of the major political parties had some connection with *pongyi* groups. Dr Ba Maw's party, as well as U Chit Hlaing's and U Ba Pe's, had advisory boards of *sayadaws*. Critics of the monks' role in politics claimed that the party leaders had to clear appointments and policy decisions with these boards, although once in office, politicians felt able to ignore their monk supporters. Before then, though, the *sayadaws* support was crucial.[82]

79. Maung Maung, 'Nationalist Movements in Burma', app. C, pp. 614–8, provides a partial listing.
80. Moscotti, *British Policy and Nationalist Movement*, p. 32.
81. *Ibid.*, pp. 51–4.
82. For example, see *The All Burma Sangha Samaggi Orders of the Thetpan Sayadaw on the Question of the Policy of the G.C.B.A. in Respect of the Separation and Federation Issue* (short pamphlet) (Rangoon, Aug. 26, 1933), which expelled Dr Ba Maw from the GCBA; Taylor, 'Relationship Between Burmese Social Classes and British-Indian Policy', pp. 220, 222.

As part of the package of political reforms intended to prepare the population for what the British conceived of as responsible self-government, the government introduced in the early 1920s a system of circle boards to be elected at the district and township levels. These were to take control of the administration of education, roads and sanitation in 28 of Burma's 37 districts, although full powers were granted to only 17 of the boards.[83] Urged on by the GCSS and perhaps not wishing to be seen to lag behind popular sentiment, as had happened at the time of the university boycott the previous year, the GCBA leadership organized an election boycott. This proved distinctly successful. Only 6 per cent of the eligible voters participated in the election and nearly 600 of the 2,700 boards to be elected no candidate was put forward, while in another 800 or so only one candidate stood. The level of participation in these government-sponsored bodies was even lower in the 1925 elections and the experiment was considered a failure by the government.[84] It would seem that the only individuals who could see the advantages of such 'democratic institutions' were political rogues like U Kyan Aung. The GCBA was equally successful in organizing boycotts of the elections for the Legislative Council held in 1922. Less than 7 per cent of the electorate voted in 1922, but after a split in the movement in 1925, over 16 per cent voted. In 1928 still only 18 per cent were willing to vote.[85]

The development of the GCBA and the GCSS, coupled with the growing advocacy of the boycott by part of the political élite, is indicative of the radicalization of party politics during the 1920s.[86] The growing involvement of monks and villagers in political organizations enhanced the power of the nationalist movement by mobilizing increasing support for the central leaders. They were, however, caught in a serious dilemma, for on the one hand the British were holding forth to those members of the élite willing to cooperate with their constitutional policies the possibility of power. On the other hand, their ability to pressure the British to speed the transfer of more substantial degrees of

83. Cady, *History of Modern Burma*, p. 263.
84. Ibid., p. 265.
85. Ibid., pp. 241, 260. Cady (p. 245) notes that Karen Christians participated actively in the election of 1922; Maung Maung, *From Sangha to Laity*, p. 44.
86. At the 1921 GCBA conference the words 'within the empire' were deleted from the resolution demanding home rule. Translations and summaries of all the major GCBA conference resolutions are provided in Maung Maung, 'Nationalist Movements in Burma', app. A, pp. 577–601.

power to them was dependent upon the support they received from the mass of the population. The latter, encouraged by the political monks, viewed cooperation with the colonial state as a form of collaboration with the source of the economic and cultural ills of their class. The consequences of this dilemma were seen in the splits within the GCBA throughout the 1920s and to the end of its political effectiveness in the early 1930s.

In 1922 the GCBA suffered the first of these splits when it was announced that dyarchy would be extended to Burma. Although personal clashes and financial chicanery also lay under the surface of élite conflicts,[87] the political issue was over whether or not to cooperate with and participate in the elections for the Legislative Council. The faction willing to cooperate was known as the Twenty-One Party — after the 21 GCBA members who resigned to form the National Party to participate in the elections. Its central figure was U Ba Pe, who led it as well as its successor parties, the People's Party and the United GCBA. The party was considered to have more support from the educated middle class than its rival, the Hlaing-Pu-Gyaw GCBA; or perhaps, more accurately, the boycott-advocating GCBA had the support of the peasantry.

Taking its name from its three leaders, the Hlaing-Pu-Gyaw GCBA not only advocated non-cooperation in elections, but also demanded home rule outside the empire. Under the auspices of the Hlaing-Pu-Gyaw GCBA, the village and township movements created by the political monks (the *wunthanu athin*) became its local branches. Each was affiliated with the new higher party level through the payment of dues. Supported, and in time dominated by the GCSS, the conferences of the Hlaing-Pu-Gyaw GCBA were attended by thousands of delegates, and these increasingly forced the urban, educated leadership to bow to the demands of the local activists. The force of their demands led to another GCBA split at the time of the eleventh national conference in 1924, when the political *pongyi* forced through a resolution advocating a campaign for the non-payment of taxes as well as an election boycott. As will be discussed below, the strength of peasant feeling against the *thathameda* and capitation taxes was so strong at this time that even politicians who were cooperating with the British state attempted to get them repealed in the Legislative Council.[88]

---

87. Maung Maung, *From Sangha to Laity*, pp. 27–8. Chapter 3 of this work, entitled 'The Sangha Takes over the GCBA', is an account that follows closely the major histories of the period published in Burmese.
88. Moscotti, *British Policy and Burmese Nationalism*, pp. 50–1.

The question of *pongyi* involvement in party activities as well as the mismanagement of party finances resulted in another split of the Hlaing-Pu-Gyaw party in 1925. One of the new groups, the Pongyis' GCBA, was led by U Soe Thein, a chemist educated in Germany and America whose family had controlled oil wells before the development of the modern industry in Burma. The Pongyis' GCBA maintained the non-cooperation policy of the old Hlaing-Pu-Gyaw party, and was dominated by the monks who had control not only of policy but also of party funds. The other party remained under the control of Chit Hlaing and Tharrawaddy U Pu. Pu soon withdrew and formed the Home Rule Party, still advocating non-cooperation, while Chit Hlaing and his dwindling followers entered into the 1925 Legislative Council elections. From then on the GCBA as a national force diminished in influence and even the Pongyis' GCBA split in 1929.[89] Having cut themselves off from the political monks and peasant base of the original GCBA, the cooperating parties did not regain their national prominence until the late 1930s when they adopted a new middle-class base and a cooperative relationship with the colonial state.

Indicative of the lack of secure organizational bases for the parties was the fact that they organized and re-organized frantically in the run-up to elections. When the British announced that the 1932 Legislative Council elections would determine whether or not Burma would separate from India, there was a more than usual flourish of party activity. In addition to the Separation League, which was a direct outgrowth of Ba Pe's United GCBA, the two Anti-Separationist Leagues were founded in July 1932 (both were the products of the Free State League which had been formed in March of that year). In the 1932 elections, the success of the Anti-Separation Leagues, which received 529,127 votes to the separationists 293,042 votes, with a turnout of 40 per cent of the electorate,[90] is indicative both of the power that Indian financial support gave to political leaders (for the majority of them, as well as of the electorate, probably favoured separation) and of the crumbling of the boycott traditional among the party leadership.

89. In addition to the parties which developed out of the original GCBA, there were several other parties or factions. The most important in the 1920s was the Golden Valley or Independent Party. It took its name from the wealthy district of Rangoon in which most of its members lived. It provided most of the ministers of the governor's council until 1932. The party was led by an Irish barrister and a Burmese barrister.

90. Telegram, Governor of Burma to Secretary of State for India, 29 Nov. 1932, BOF P&J(B) 1.

The ineffectiveness of the Burmese political élite during the second phase of party development led to a large degree of cynicism and mistrust of the middle-class leadership among both the peasantry and the younger middle-class generation. The champions of the national cause of 1920 had, by the mid-1930s, become collaborators with the state and those foreign groups who most benefited from it. The majority of people in the districts did not look to the elected legislators as their leaders, spokesmen or protectors. When the Burmese ministers took office in 1937 under the new constitution, there was no expression of popular support for them, nor apparently did the ministers believe that the government was supported by the people. British and Burmese officials and politicians were aware of this situation and for that reason sometimes despaired of the possibility of making the democratic features of the 1935 constitution work. As one high official wrote, as long as it was known that the Burmese Ministers were kept in office with the aid of Europeans and Indians, 'the fight will be taken outside the Legislature on to the streets of Rangoon, Mandalay and elsewhere'.[91] Nonetheless the political importance of elections as a means of taking control of the state from the British was changing, and the political élite was intensely keen to gain access to office and to the privileges and protections that the mantle of state authority would provide them with in both their intra-élite conflicts and their contest with British officialdom. The strategy of boycotting elections had crumbled away further by the 1936 election, the only one held under the 1935 constitution, for approximately 52 per cent of the electorate voted on this occasion.[92]

The third phase of party development saw a struggle between two parties which had both rejected the earlier basis of party life. *Myochit*, led by U Saw, seized upon the opportunities provided by the 1935 constitution and the evolving international situation to develop a mass-based party which would defend and enhance the position of the middle class and regain Burma's independence by making its cooperation indispensable to the British. The other, the *Thakin* movement, sought similar political goals, but hoped to achieve them through the

91. Personal letter, James Baxter to D.T. Monteath, 4 April 1939, BOF P 106, part 1.
92. Based upon calculations made from Ganga Singh, *Burma Parliamentary Companion* (Rangoon: British Burma Press, 1940), election results statement on pp. 341–61. Dorothy Hess Guyot, 'The Political Impact of the Japanese Occupation of Burma' (unpbl. Ph.D. thesis, Yale University, 1966), table 2, p. 21, gives a turnout figure of 31 per cent.

subversion of the constitution and (perhaps) through a revolutionary struggle. The full flowering of this rivalry between that section of the middle class with a stake in the colonial state system and that section, increasingly socialist in its ideological orientation, without such a stake emerged just before the Japanese invasion in 1942.[93] This rivalry was temporarily submerged during the war years, but re-emerged in the internal politics of the post-war independence struggle, and culminated in the post-independence civil war.

Peasants and Politics under the Colonial State

One of the established myths about politics in Burma in both the colonial and the postcolonial periods is the so-called 'élite-mass gap'.[94] The development of such a conception is the consequence of taking insufficient account of the nature of politics under the precolonial state in terms of the people's relationship with the state, as well as of the unquestioning acceptance of certain folk statements, usually passed on by members of the élite, such as 'government is one of the five great evils to be avoided'. According to the myth of the élite-mass gap, the imposition of the modern state and the political élite who manage it meant that, over the past one hundred years, a vast gulf of misunderstanding and mistrust developed between the peasant population and the controllers of the state or the indigenous political leadership. This shaped the nature of both élite and mass responses to different political situations, making the Burmese polity less stable than it might otherwise have been. There certainly was, and remains, a gap in the perceived interests of the peasantry and the political élite, but it exists because these two groups *do* understand each other and their contradictory interests.

---

93. See Taylor, 'Politics in Late Colonial Burma'; also, James F. Guyot, 'Bureaucratic Transformation in Burma', in Ralph Braibanti (ed.), *Asian Bureaucratic Systems Emergent from the British Imperial Tradition* (Durham, NC: Duke University Press, 1966), p. 365. The growing power of politicians to interfere in administration during this period tended to undermine the authority of district officers and other civil servants as well as to add to their work load. F.S.V. Donnison, *Public Administration in Burma: A Study of Development During the British Connexion* (London: Royal Institute of International Affairs, 1953), p. 57.
94. Guyot, 'Political Impact of the Japanese Occupation', pp. 16–21; Josef Silverstein, *Burma, Military Rule and the Politics of Stagnation* (Ithaca: Cornell University Press, 1977), pp. 198–200.

An important corollary of the standard élite-mass gap theory is the assumption that the political attitudes and views of the mass of the peasant population have remained essentially unchanged from the time of the classical state, and that these are attitudes and views inappropriate for modern conditions. At the same time, the political élite, and the new urban or middle class generally, have lost any understanding they may have once had of their own social origins and conditions. The credence given to this theory has done much to obscure the lively political life of the rural population and its impact upon the behaviour of the political élite and the modern state.

While it is perhaps true that the colonial state of the nineteenth and early twentieth century, with its foreign rulers governing through a new bureaucratic structure and with the force of an empire behind it, had little need to relate with and understand the political and economic perspectives of the mass of the population, the same was not true of the indigenous élite which led the political organizations of the present century. The new state was making demands upon the peasantry in particular to which the élite was forced to respond. The replacement of patron-client ties with bureaucratic officials at the local level had altered the peasants' legal and fiscal relationship with state authority. The rapid development of the rice fields of the Irrawaddy delta demonstrates the Burmese peasants' clear and ready grasp of the profit motive and of the advantages of trade for the social advancement of himself and his family. The speed with which peasant political organizations developed in the 1920s, in league with, or in opposition to, the plans and programmes of the political élite, demonstrates their awareness of the opportunities available in altered circumstances. The apparent 'fact' that the political behaviour of the peasantry during the 1920s and 1930s had aspects of precolonial practices and beliefs does not invalidate the relevance of their response to the conditions in which it took place. All indigenous political movements are shaped by the culture in which they develop, and many of the political practices of the peasantry under the precolonial state were modified to meet the circumstances created by the colonial state.

Several factors motivated peasants to involve themselves in political action. The administrative, economic, geographic and demographic changes of the colonial period had ended the precolonial stability of the settled village, providing a population base that could be easily mobilized for political action. The colonial state's lack of legitimacy in the eyes of the population was a key psychological factor in encouraging individuals to strike out against the state: the deteriorating economic position of most peasants in the 1920s and 1930s merely compounded their sense of grievance. This growing sense of discontent, perhaps linked with the anomic conditions of the plural society, provided the political élite with an army of rank-and-file followers when the leaders could produce a programme and organization which addressed their perceived needs. The fact that the political élite's interests often ran counter to those of the peasantry provided much of the internal tension within Burma's domestic politics in the late colonial period.

As discussed in Chapter II, the closing of the rice frontier was one of the underlying factors contributing to the crisis of the Burmese peasant class during the 1920s and 1930s. The growing surplus of tenants and their weakened bargaining position led to widespread rural insecurity. Declining rice prices and rapid price inflation contributed to the peasants' plight. The rise in the number of indigenous landless cultivators and increasing competition by Indian labourers to gain land combined to heighten the insecurity of tenure of those who were able to remain cultivators. The rootlessness of the tenant class is indicated by the small percentage of cultivating tenants who lived on the same land for more than fours years. Short tenancy (a consequence of the growing competition among cultivators for land to till, leading inexorably under the prevailing economic situation to higher and higher rents) became a major feature in districts such as Tharrawaddy before the First World War.[95] After the collapse of the international rice market in 1930, the problem reached crisis proportions, leading to even greater communal tensions,[96] and reflected the complications and intermingling of class and ethnicity in colonial Burma's politics. The size of the crisis in the 1930s should not, however, overshadow the fact that for some cultivators personal dislocation predated the First World War and led to expressions of

95. S.G. Grantham, *Studies in the History of Tharrawaddy* (Cambridge: Printed at the University Press for private circulation, 1920), pp. 31–2.
96. In Insein District, for example, in 1933–5, over 22 per cent of all tenants had had the same land for 4 or more years, 10 per cent for 3 years, 21 per cent for 2 years, and 47 per cent for 1 year. Conditions were similar in Amherst, Pegu and Myaungmya. In districts further from Rangoon, security of tenure seemed to be greater. For example, in one Henzada tract in 1936–7, 63 per cent of the tenants had had their land for 4 or more years, 22 per cent for 2 or 3 years, and 15 per cent for only 1 year, *Land and Agriculture Committee Report*, part I, p. 15. Conditions were different in the delta compared to the dry zone. Whereas 47 per cent of all land was rented in 1938 in all of Burma, 58 per cent was rented in lower Burma compared to 33 per cent in upper Burma, *Ibid.*, p. 8.

peasant discontent and political action at least fifteen years before the Hsaya San peasant rebellion of 1930–2. Serious falls in the price of rice early in the First World War, coupled with general inflation at the time as imported consumer goods became scarce, began the absolute fall in the financial security of an ever-growing segment of the peasant class.[97]

The capitation tax in the south and the *thathameda* tax elsewhere contributed to peasant grievances toward the state.[98] While high rents and insecurity of tenure could be explained away as the consequences of the economic system, these taxes could not. Both were essentially head taxes, especially aggravating to the peasants, for as a fixed tax payable in cash they fell equally on the poor and the well-to-do. Though the *thathameda* was a precolonial tax carried over by the British, as a result of the efficiency of the modern state's collection system, it became a greater source of grievance because the headmen were no longer able to adjust it on an informal basis to fit changing economic conditions. The end of the sumptuary laws and the growth of obvious distinctions of wealth within the village made the tax even more galling, for the gap in the ability of different individuals to pay had become common knowledge. While other taxes, direct and indirect, may have actually taken more of the peasants' income, these taxes were annual reminders of the state's limitations to his freedom as well as a threat to his pride.

In the early years of the development of the rice industry growing prosperity and the absence or low rate of land taxes made the head taxes seem less onerous. Tenancy, too, was then seen by Burmese migrating to the delta as a step in the process of social advancement to cultivator-ownership. However, in the period after the First World War, tenancy became 'a dead-end for most agriculturalists or a temporary respite in their fall from cultivator-owners to landless labourers, rather than the avenue of upward mobility it had been in the nineteenth century'.[99] Political conditions, including the growing power of local administrators and bosses like U Kyan Aung together with the rise of land prices and the decline of paddy prices, combined to benefit the landlord class, so that class distinctions within the agricultural communities became more distinct. The corruption of subordinate employees

---

97. Cady, *History of Modern Burma*, pp. 187–8.
98. Ibid., p. 191; Maung Maung, *From Sangha to Laity*, p. 47; James C. Scott, *The Moral Economy of the Peasant, Rebellion and Subsistence in Southeast Asia* (New Haven: Yale University Press, 1976), pp. 99–102.
99. Adas, *Burma Delta*, p. 147.

of the Land Records Department by land-grabbing landlords[100] and the efforts of headmen to take more land for themselves meant that the peasants had less and less legal protection and came increasingly to see the agents of the state as the agents of their misery. The rapidity with which the pioneer peasants fell to the lowest categories of rural population can be seen by the fact that by the 1930s 'landless laborers became the dominant element in the population of many villages in lower Burma'.[101]

Next to the *thathameda* or capitation tax, the most irritating tax for the peasants was the land tax. Land tax was set at about 10 per cent of the cultivators' gross return, but this could amount to as much as 25 to 50 per cent of their net produce. In bad years, although it was intended that the tax be reduced or remitted by the Deputy Commissioner, this often did not happen, and the burden on the farmer could be even greater. In some instances, he had almost nothing to show for his year's labour. Though less regressive in form than the head taxes, the land tax was a greater burden on small cultivators than on larger ones, thus increasing rural economic inequalities.[102] Revenue from land tax formed the largest proportion of the colonial state's receipts.

The second most important source of government revenue was an indirect tax on rice production — which was initially less of a burden to the cultivator. This took the form of an export duty on the country's rice and was justified by the government in terms of keeping down the rates of land tax.[103] Its implications for peasants' incomes became apparent in 1918–19, when the government established a Rice Control Board to keep the domestic price of rice low for urban consumers in the wake of the rapid increase in the international price after the war. The government also hoped to limit the huge profits that would be made by the large rice exporting firms. However, the action drew clearly to the cultivators' attention the direct involvement of the state in the regulation of the price they could receive for their crop and thus was added to the head taxes and land tax as a source of peasant grievance toward the state.[104]

The peasants' political response was to form the *wunthanu athin*. These were intended to protect local interests, but became linked through the

---

100. *Ibid.*, p. 142–3.
101. *Ibid.*, p. 152.
102. Scott, *Moral Economy of the Peasant*, pp. 102–5.
103 Shein, *Burma's Transport and Foreign Trade*, pp. 129–30.
104. Cady, *History of Modern Burma*, pp. 221–3.

activities of the GCBA and GCSS which helped to set them up to the nationalist movement of the urban political élite. The term *wunthanu* came into common use as early as 1915. It was derived from Pali, and means 'supporting own race', and was used in the sense of 'nationalist' or 'patriotic'.[105] (*Athin* means organization.) The rapid growth of the *wunthanu* movement was a consequence both of the organizing activities of the political monks sent out by the GCSS and of the peasants' perceived need to have a voice in the growing nationalist movement.[106] Delegates from the village *athin* attended the major GCBA conferences and pressed for the increasingly radical resolutions passed there.[107] By 1924 there were *wunthanu athin* organized in almost every village in Burma.[108]

The effect of these organizations was to give the villagers a greater sense of their own power in their conflicts with the state and its officials. As U Maung Maung has written,

with an organized body holding them together, the people in the villages and towns became bold enough to refuse to comply with, or to complain against, unjust orders and ill-treatment by administrative officers, the police or the village headman. The signboard '*wunthanu*' on a placard (in Burmese) would be hung in every home and shop like a good luck charm. People purchased from shops with such signs.[109]

The initial importance of the *wunthanu athin* for the leaders of the GCBA was that through them they were able to organize the election and other boycott campaigns which were successful in protesting against the British government's unwillingness to give Burma home rule.[110] In this way they were able to link the national political goals of the urban élite with the interests of the villagers, who extended the idea to the organized general boycott of local state apparatus and its agents. The *wunthanu* organizations involved not only lay men but also women and monks, often as leaders, in their activities.[111]

105. Patricia Herbert, *The Hsaya San Rebellion (1930–32) Reappraised* (Melbourne: Monash University Centre of Southeast Asian Studies Working Paper no. 27, 1982), fn. 28, p. 15.
106. Moscotti, *British Policy and Nationalist Movement*, pp. 40–1; Maung Maung, *From Sangha to Laity*, pp. 28–32.
107. Cady, *History of Modern Burma*, p. 231.
108. Moscotti, *British Policy and Nationalist Movement*, p. 33.
109. Maung Maung, *From Sangha to Laity*, p. 20.
110. Moscotti, *British Policy and Nationalist Movement*, p. 41.
111. Cady, *History of Modern Burma*, fn. 66, p. 235.

The link between the village *athin* and the central executive committee of the GCBA paralleled that of the government established under the Rural Self-Government Act of 1921. Ignoring the state's plans for self-government, they set up their own with a hierarchy of village, circle and district boards.[112] Through these the *wunthanu athin* organized a variety of activities in defiance of the state. They encouraged the people and monks to refuse services, including food and religious ceremonies, to non-European officials — who were most vulnerable as they were dependent upon the communities in which they lived for their sustenance and authority. Headmen were especially singled out for this treatment and some were even killed.[113]

As part of their shadow administrative structures, the *wunthanu athin* organized their own courts, boycotting the state's legal system and reinstating Burmese arbitration techniques to settle disputes, often with the involvement of village monks.[114] They organized protests against specific legislation they found objectionable, especially the collective defence and punishment provisions of the Village Act.[115] After 1923 *bu* or 'No' *athin* were organized, often within the *wunthanu athin*, as the campaign grew more radical. These bodies organized boycotts of the state's auctions of fisheries and fallow lands and refused to acknowledge the state's right to control these resources; they encouraged villagers not to pay their taxes and to defy the orders of the headmen, and they attempted to thwart the legal sale of alcohol and opium.[116] Similar *sibwayei* (economy) *athin* were also organized, sometimes using violence in order to persuade Chettiars to lower debt obligations.[117] The height of the anti-tax campaign was reached in 1923–5, when the GCBA was most under the control of the radical delegates of the village *athin*.[118] They even succeeded in getting the 1924 GCBA conference to pass an

---

112. Herbert, *Hsaya San Rebellion*, p. 8; Moscotti, *British Policy and Nationalist Movement*, pp. 34, 42.
113. Moscotti, *British Policy and Nationalist Movement*, p. 33; Cady, *History of Modern Burma*, pp. 234–5, 253.
114. Moscotti, *British Policy and Nationalist Movement*, p. 42; Cady, *History of Modern Burma*, pp. 234–5.
115. Herbert, *Hsaya San Rebellion*, p. 11.
116. Maung Maung, *From Sangha to Laity*, p. 49.
117. Cady, *History of Modern Burma*, p. 252; Moscotti, *British Policy and Nationalist Movement*, p. 43.
118. Cady, *History of Modern Burma*, p. 253; Moscotti, *British Policy and Nationalist Movement*, pp. 41–2, 44.

illegal resolution authorizing the non-payment of taxes.[119] Though relatively quiet during 1926, the movement was revived after the release of U Ottama from prison in 1927.[120]

The formation of the *wunthanu athin* was part of the general process of the mobilization of the peasant population into the modern national political arena. Led by both the secular political élite and more traditionalist political monks, they provided the substitute for local leadership that the *myo* and village headmen had provided under the monarchical state. New forms of collective action, based upon traditional patterns of avoidance of unjust or exorbitant demands by the state and its officials, precolonial or colonial, were used not only as methods of self-defence but also of political expression. A tradition of resistance through avoidance was added to forms of direct political action in the face of the greater power of the colonial state which the indigenous political élite initially encouraged and the colonial officials could not ignore. The wide range and intensity of these non-cooperative forms of behaviour were difficult to assess and have been little discussed in the literature, but they provide the background to the political behaviour of other elements in the state and society throughout the colonial period.[121] Though after the Hsaya San rebellion the *wunthanu athin* movement as an organized force was suppressed, the tradition of boycott or avoidance of the state had been re-established under modern conditions.

The *wunthanu* movement itself lived on in popular memory as a reminder of the political potential of the peasantry and of the linkage between local political interests and the national political élite. If that élite was to increase its power through the support of the mass of the people, it would have to attune its policies and ideas to their interests and views. As Maung Maung makes clear in *From Sangha to Laity*, when the leaders of the GCBA abandoned the boycott movement in order to participate in the dyarchy elections of the colonial order, they lost the support of the peasants. The latter then drifted under the control of Soe Thein's Pongyis' GCBA and eventually into the Hsaya San rebellion.[122] When neither proved effective in rectifying their grievances, the peasantry was

119. Moscotti, *British Policy and Nationalist Movement*, p. 45.
120. Ibid., pp. 46, 51; Cady, *History of Modern Burma*, pp. 232, 260.
121. Andrew Turton, 'Limits of Ideological Domination and the Formation of Social Consciousness', in Andrew Turton and Shigeharu Tanabe (eds), *History and Peasant Consciousness in South East Asia* (Osaka: National Museum of Ethnology, Senri Ethnological Studies no. 13, 1984), p. 65.
122. Maung Maung, *From Sangha to Laity*, pp. 62–4.

briefly cut off from the national élite until the organization of new movements in the 1930s which gave them an opportunity to express themselves in organized political action.

The ideas of the *wunthanu* movement organizers were consonant with the views of the peasants themselves. *Wunthanu Rethkita*, which was written in 1924 for the use of the political *dhammakatika* monks as they toured the villages organizing the *wunthanu athin*, expressed these ideas well. Its author, C.P. Khin Maung, an ardent boycottist in the Hlaing-Pu-Gyaw GCBA, demonstrated in his *Wunthanu Rethkita* (National Principles) that the ideas of the *wunthanu* movement were moral and just, as they were 'in accordance with the Buddha's wishes'. He further pointed out the differences between a good state and the then existing state which they were to boycott. The good state of the Burmese kings and their officials, he argued, 'had to observe certain principles and duties and swore to act for the people's good'. The king's ministers, the *wun-gyi*, bore 'the king's burden and the people's burden and these are that the king should make no errors, that there should be no conflict and opposition with the people, and that the country should be populous and pleasant and the people tranquil and contented'.[123] These are ideas which reappear in the ideological justifications of every successful political organization in modern Burma's history and which have their roots in the precolonial state's ideology.

Despite the widespread support and deep commitment to the *wunthanu* movement in the villages and its link with national politicians, the colonial state was able to amass sufficient force and law to keep the movement under control. Existing legislation such as the 1887 Village Act, the Anarchical Revolutionary Crimes Act or Rowlatt Act of 1919, the Habitual Offenders Restriction Act (1919), Section 144 of the Criminal Procedure Code, and new laws specifically drafted to deal with the boycott movement, the Criminal Law Amendment Act (1922), the Criminal Tribes Act (1924) and the Anti-Boycott Act, were used by the state throughout the 1920s.[124] The *bu athin* were declared illegal and banned in 1923.[125] Military police units were sent in to punish recalcitrant villages, and they even, on occasion, razed buildings.[126] Coercive

---

123. Herbert, *Hsaya San Rebellion*, pp. 8–9.
124. Moscotti, *British Policy and Nationalist Movement*, p. 34; Maung Maung, *From Sangha to Laity*, pp. 42–3; Cady, *History of Modern Burma*, pp. 233–4.
125. Moscotti, *British Policy and Nationalist Movement*, p. 42.
126. Maung Maung, *From Sangha to Laity*, p. 46.

measures were used to collect taxes in the face of peasant opposition; in 1923–4 2,802,000 rupees were collected in this way.[127] The form of these coercive tax collections only served to reinforce the peasants' dislike of the state and of those who benefited from its methods:

> The *myooks* came with the military police, an armed Indian sepoy force, and a few Indians in business or a butcher in the neighbouring town. The *myook* held court and upon failure of the residents to pay taxes due, the properties of the delinquents were auctioned off . . . the villagers would not buy each other's property; but the Indian business man was there to pick it up at the cost of the dismantled material alone. The villager's animals, his means of earning a living, his bullock carts, and other movable property were also disposed of in the same manner.[128]

The *myo-ok* himself often profited from these actions, which sometimes went as far as selling the food in the villager's home.[129]

Far from ignoring the consequences of the state's actions in putting down the boycott movement of the *wunthanu athin*, the indigenous political élite, including those who cooperated with the Legislative Council, attempted to halt or ameliorate the actions of the officials and thus regain the support of the peasantry. The Nationalist Party under U Ba Pe attempted in the Council to halt the imposition of communal fines on villages and opposed the outlawing of the *bu athin*. In a creative political act, the politicians 'almost succeeded in passing a resolution (37 to 39) to lift the emergency ban against allegedly subversive *athins*' providing that only 'legislative councillors acquainted with the problem certify that the assumed emergency no longer existed.'[130] This resolution, had it been passed, would have removed from the officials and placed in the hands of the elected representatives a significant degree of political power within their constituencies, and given the politicians who worked within the state's structures evidence to demonstrate that cooperation was actually beneficial to the indigenous population.

The suppression of the *wunthanu* movement, coupled with the growing agrarian crisis after the 1930 depression in rice prices and the increasing competition for jobs and land, led to a significant rise in communal and class tensions in the towns and cities of Burma, as well as to the most widespread peasant uprising of the colonial era. The first major

---

127. Moscotti, *British Policy and Nationalist Movement*, p. 45.
128. Maung Maung, *From Sangha to Laity*, p. 48.
129. Herbert, *Hsaya San Rebellion*, p. 10.
130. Cady, *History of Modern Burma*, p. 249.

demonstration of these growing tensions was two weeks of rioting in May 1930 in Rangoon, between Indian dock workers and Burmese labourers who had been used as strike-breakers. After the strike by the Indian workers was settled the Burmese were fired; they took their anger out on the returning Indians. There were seveal hundred reported deaths and many more injuries. The rioting spread from Rangoon to surrounding towns, 'and especially to the Hanthawaddy district towns of Kayan, Thongwa, and Kyauktan, where a concentration of Indian landowners and tenants had gained footholds among the predominantly Burmese lands'.[131]

In December the Hsaya San peasants' rebellion broke out. Hsaya San, a district leader of the GCBA who had grown frustrated at the inability of the élite politicians to alleviate the peasants' conditions, had in 1928 secretly begun to organize associations to resist the collection of the capitation tax following the government's suppression of the anti-tax campaign of 1927.[132] In addition to the anti-tax issue, he also developed peasant support for opposing the state's restrictions on the use of timber and bamboo by the villagers, a traditional privilege which the colonial state had appropriated as a monopoly. When the acting Burmese governor, Sir J.A. Maung Gyi, refused to remit or reduce taxes following the dramatic decline in paddy prices of 1930, an apparently spontaneous peasant revolt broke out at the end of December in Tharrawaddy district. By early January it had spread to surrounding areas, especially the delta. The initial anger of the peasants was directed at the village headmen, and within two days four had been killed. In the 18 months of the rebellion, a total of 38 headmen were killed and 150 others attacked and wounded. The government, initially unprepared for the rebellion, brought in additional troops from India, and before the rebellion was suppressed killed over 1,300 rebels and arrested, captured or received the surrender of another 9,000.[133] While at the time the government explained the Hsaya San peasants' rebellion as the last gasp of the dying traditionalism of the Burmese peasantry (a view shared by many commentators subsequently), it can be more appropriately seen as a consequence of the inability of the *wunthanu* movement and its national

131. Maung Maung, *From Sangha to Laity*, p. 73; see also Moscotti, *British Policy and Nationalist Movement*, pp. 55–6.
132. Moscotti, *British Policy and Nationalist Movement*, p. 57.
133. The fullest account is Maung Maung, *From Sangha to Laity*, ch. 7, 'The Peasant Revolt', pp. 83–107.

level GCBA leaders to ameliorate peasant grievances to any significant extent.[134] The government's suppression of the *wunthanu athin* had demonstrated to the peasants the failure of nonviolent political action and suggested that force was their only resort. The rationalized state had also effectively abolished the option of avoidance that the peasantry had had under the monarchical state. That the rebellion was eventually put down by the massive armed force of the state taught them two further lessons: that for the time being there was little they or the national leaders could do to protect themselves, and that independence was the only way of gaining a state that might listen to them.

The extent of communal discord that existed in Burma in the early 1930s was further displayed by an outbreak of anti-Chinese rioting in Rangoon in January 1931, at the start of the peasants' rebellion. Fourteen deaths occurred in Rangoon and many Chinese fled the city.[135] The rioting spread to parts of Toungoo, Pegu and Hanthawaddy districts.[136] Though the Chinese population of Burma was then relatively small, and relations between Chinese and Burmese had never suffered from the cultural and economic strains that affected Burmese-Indian relations,[137] the indigenous population felt a mounting hostility toward any group which seemed to be prospering during the current conditions. In areas not directly involved in the Hsaya San rebellion, Burmese and Indians took the opportunity of the state's preoccupation with the urban riots and peasant rebellion to attack each other (as occurred in Syriam, Thongwa, and Kyauktan townships around Rangoon in April, May and June, 1931).[138]

The last major outbreak of communal conflict before the Second World War started on July 26, 1938, when there began five days of anti-Indian rioting which extended to almost all of southern and central Burma. The rioting began in Rangoon and spread through the districts, reaching Mandalay on the 30th. In the words of the

134. Herbert, *Hsaya San Rebellion*, p. 7.
135. Moscotti, *British Policy and Nationalist Movement*, p. 120.
136. Maung Maung, *From Sangha to Laity*, p. 74.
137. In contrast to other Southeast Asian countries, there has been very little written on the place of the Chinese in Burma's politics and society. This is primarily due to the small size of the community and its reasonably easy and rapid integration into Burmese society, and their being dwarfed by the importance of the Indian community. The best short summary is found in Victor Purcell, *The Chinese in Southeast Asia* (London: Oxford University Press, 2nd edn, 1966), pp.41–80.
138. Maung Maung, *From Sangha to Laity*, p. 74.

government-appointed committee which investigated the causes, the riots 'spread . . . almost in concentric circles radiating from Rangoon as fast as news of what had happened there could travel by means of Burmese newspapers, passengers, and other carriers of information and rumour'.[139] The ostensible cause of the riots was the publication of an anti-Buddhist tract by a Burmese Muslim. The book had been originally published in 1931 but its existence was publicized in the anti-Ba Maw press only in July, 1938, as part of the campaign to bring down his government by demonstrating that it could not maintain order. Monks took a leading part in organizing the agitation against the book.[140] On September 2, another outbreak of anti-Indian rioting occurred in Rangoon. Although somewhat less severe and restricted primarily to the capital, the disturbances lasted six days.[141]

These disturbances were orchestrated by political opponents of Dr Ba Maw, both from the established parties, particularly U Saw's *Myochit*, and from the younger nationalists of the *Do Bama Asiayon*. Burmese entrepreneurs were encouraged by the belief that Indians might be forced to leave Burma as a result of the widespread anti-Indian sentiment then so forcefully apparent throughout the country. Plans were made to establish Burmese cooperative stores and a Japanese-owned trading firm was asked to advise.[142] The government's official inquiry into the riots concluded that they were caused by discontent among peasants over land tenure and related matters, anti-Indian feelings, the consequences to the rights of Buddhist women who married Muslim men, and the political campaign to bring down the Ba Maw government.[143] Under the relatively open political system of the late colonial state, opposition forces could always champion one or another of these problems in order to create political instability, personal insecurity, and, perhaps, to bring down a government.

Even in what would be called normal periods of political and communal peace during the colonial period class and communal tensions were always apparent. A review of just a few months in 1939 will

139. Riot Inquiry Committee, *Interim Report* (Rangoon: Government Printing and Stationery, 1938), p. 9. See also Smith, *Religion and Politics*, pp. 109–14.
140. Riot Inquiry Committee, *Interim Report*, p. 8; Cady, *History of Modern Burma*, pp. 393–4; Burma Monthly Intelligence Summary, vol. II, no. 7, for July 1938, 1 Aug. 1938, BOF I 37, part II.
141. Cady, *History of Modern Burma*, p. 394.
142. Burma Defence Bureau Intelligence Summary no. 9, 26 Sept. 1938, BOF I 358.
143. Riot Inquiry Committee, *Interim Report*, pp. 11–12, 22, 28–9, 33–7, and *passim*.

suggest their nature and extent. In March 1939, for example, there were communal and agrarian troubles in Shwebo and Myaungmya of sufficient importance to be called to the attention of the governor.[144] Later in the same month additional Military Police units had to be sent to Myaungmya because of Burmese attacks on Indians. Military police were also patrolling Shwebo and parts of Katha in the north because of attacks by Burmese on Muslim and Zerbadi (Indo-Burmese Muslim) villages. Some of the Zerbadi villages were being armed by the state for self-defence.[145] The troubles were spreading to Tharrawaddy district as well. From there one official reported that,

in Minhla and Okpo . . . payment of rents has left many persons with hardly any food to live on. In fact, my firm conviction is that the basis of half of the Tharrawaddy trouble consists in the exorbitant rents charged by the Chettyars and moneylenders. This rent will have to come down if we are going to expect even comparative peace here. In fact these Chettyars who live safely in Rangoon and come to the district only to screw the last basket of paddy out of the tenants are the direct cause of crime and should be made to pay for the results.[146]

By April the troubles had spread to Pyapon, Bassein, Pegu and Lower Chindwin, as well as Shwebo and Myaungmya. In Myaungmya, because of the large number of Indian tenants, more military police were sent in an effort to stop a rick and hut burning campaign that was being conducted in an effort to drive off Indian tenants.[147]

Not all the conflicts were communal in nature, and some clearly indicated the class basis of much of the unrest. In one instance, 'where the culprits in an attack on a field hut of an Indian tenant were caught red-handed, they proved to be all Indians who resented the fact that the victim had accepted a tenancy on the landlord's terms.'[148] By mid-May the level of attacks had lessened, but the tenants stepped up their program of organizing cultivator's associations so as to present a united front before the landlords when the time came to prepare new leases.[149] The burning of hayricks and field huts continued mostly in Pegu and Irrawaddy divisions. The Home Secretary wrote,

144. Governor's Confidential Report no. 6, 16 March 1939, BOF P 39, part II.
145. Burma Defence Bureau Intelligence Summary no. 3, 27 March 1939, BOF I 358.
146. *Ibid.*
147. *Ibid.*, no. 4, 25 April 1939. Home Secretary's Fortnightly Report, first half April 1939, 26 April 1939, BOF P 39, part II.
148. Governor's Confidential Report no. 9, 2 May 1939, BOF P 39, part II.
149. *Ibid.*, no. 11, 17 May 1939. Home Secretary's Fortnightly Report, first half May 1939, 26 May 1939, BOF P 39, part II.

The crimes are not communal but are committed to intimidate tenants who have renewed their leases at the old rates. Armed patrols are now operating in the effected areas and where no evidence is obtainable against the culprits, the villagers are being called to show cause why fines should not be imposed under the Village Act; prosecutions are being instigated where possible.[150]

Communal conflicts, abetted by class tensions, often called 'agrarian outrages', continued throughout June and July.[151] As the conflicts continued into August, especially in Irrawaddy Division,[152] the Commissioner of Police drew official attention to the fact that there had been 'unusually large demands for revolver licences, particularly on the part of landowners'. It was also noted that rent collectors were becoming more common in the delta as Chettiars' fears of collecting their rents in person increased.[153]

With the resumption of cultivation, tensions diminished as the farmers returned to their work. In the next year apparently the landowners gained the initiative in the struggle. It was reported that because of the intensified competition among would-be tenants, landlords were having an easier time getting contracts, and that in Akyab and Tharrawaddy the Landlords' Association was causing more trouble than the cultivators' associations.[154]

Youth and Students in late Colonial Politics

From the 1920 students' strike over the formation of Rangoon University until the Japanese invasion in 1942 the importance of secular youth in colonial politics increased. In the latter half of the 1930s, every political leader had to take account of student politics. Politicians in power were generally keen on restricting student activities, but those out of power were interested in aiding and abetting student anti-government and nationalist activities. The contacts that student leaders

---

150. *Ibid.*; reports of these events were published in British newspapers. See, for example, *The Daily Telegraph*, 22 May 1939.
151. Burma Defence Bureau Intelligence Summary no. 7, 27 July 1939, BOF I 358.
152. Home Secretary's Fortnightly Report for second half July, 1939, 9 August 1939, BOF P 9, Part II.
153. Burma Defence Bureau Intelligence Summary no. 8, 26 Aug. 1939, BOF I 358.
154. Extract from Home Secretary's Fortnightly Report, second half March 1940, 9 April 1940, BOF E 1241/46, Home Secretary's Fortnightly Report for first half May 1940, 27 May 1940, BOF P 39, Part III.

had with the colonial political élite increased their own sense of power and importance and led to a growing belief on their part that they would, in a few years , succeed the current leadership with a purer and more principled anti-colonial movement.

Although student and youth politics was a national phenomenon by the 1930s, Rangoon remained the centre of student politics. Here was the capital of the state and the site of Rangoon University, the largest and most prestigious centre of higher education in the country. The emotional and intellectual impact of Rangoon — with its large foreign communities and businesses — on youth coming to the University from the districts, as most Burmese students did, was very great. Before they went to Rangoon the students of the 1930s may have intellectually apprehended the meaning of their country's dependent status and have experienced national or racial slights at the hands of Indian merchants or British officials, but the visual impact of Rangoon could not help but boldly underscore the structure of power in the country.[155] Coupled with this was the availability to students in Rangoon of various forms of leftist literature, especially tracts on imperialism, much of which was imported from Britain. This literature, more than the students' formal study of European history and law in the University, provided them with a theory to explain their country's and their class's historical dilemma.

If these factors stimulated youthful nationalist feeling, the political, economic and constitutional ferment of the decade suggested to the students that concrete political action might be of use in freeing Burma from British rule and from Indian money. The Hsaya San rebellion showed young people that the national spirit still existed among the peasants, and the general interpretation of the meaning of the rebellion provided a romantic link back to the military and political achievements of Burmese kings and generals. Moreover the constitutional reforms of the 1930s led to heightened interest and opportunities for participation in electoral politics. The party leaders, especially Dr Ba Maw in the 1936 election and U Saw in his 1939 campaign to bring down Ba Maw's government, had sought and encouraged student assistance. After Ba Maw's fall from power, he once more allied with the major youth leaders to form the anti-war Freedom Bloc. Perhaps even more than these

155. The flavour of the period is delightfully portrayed in Thein Hpei Myin, *Asheika Neiwunhtwetthe Bama* (As Sure as the Sun Rises in the East) (Rangoon: Hpyanchiyei Dana, Myat Sa Pei, 1974, and other editions). The title is taken from a line in Burma's national anthem, the old *Do Bama Asiayon* song.

specific political events, the economic crisis of the 1930s made students see the direct importance of political and nationalist action for their generation.

Up to the 1930s young Burmese with education and ambition had been able to secure adequate if not always lucrative positions with the government or with foreign firms. New positions for clerks, pleaders, barristers, civil servants, teachers and the like generally became available as the economy of the cities developed. In the 1930s, however, two events limited such opportunities. First, the effects of the world-wide depression put an end to the expansion of government and private employment, and retrenchment caused some already in employment to lose their jobs; secondly, the number of university graduates multiplied rapidly. Youth coming from rural areas saw their families' fortunes sink as the financial impact of the depression on Burmese agriculture took its toll even on the better off Burmese peasants, landlords and shopkeepers. In contrast to the generations of the 1910s and 1920s, that of the 1930s saw their parents' and their own opportunities for prosperity and advancement receding.

Such factors help explain the increased political involvement of the middle-class youth who came to lead some of the newer political movements, but they were supported in their endeavours by the increasing politicization of younger and less privileged students in towns and villages. As many of the university students were themselves from these districts, making contact with those who remained behind was easy. The increased interest of youth and students outside Rangoon in politics was manifested in the proliferation of youth movements, volunteer corps, student unions and local level *Thakin* organizations in the late 1930s.[156] The following data indicates not only the extensive nature of such movements, but also their organizational instability, as youth sought effective outlets for their political energies. In April 1937, British military intelligence reported that twenty-two new clubs, corps, etc., had been formed, of which three were considered political: one students' union and two *Thakin* branches.[157] In May of that year there were

156. The Burma Defence Bureau Monthly Intelligence Summaries under the heading 'Youth Movements' listed large numbers of new organizations. They also made a distinction between political and non-political youth organizations. Although it was not made explicit what criteria were used for making such distinctions, in all probability, groups which formally acknowledged affiliation with a political party or anti-government movement were labelled political, and those which either supported the official government appeared to be neutral and were considered non-political.
157. Extract from Intelligence Summary no. 4, 24 April 1937, BOF I 20.

thirty-two new clubs, corps, etc., of which fifteen were political: three students' unions and eight *Thakin* branches.[158] In January 1938, there were fifty-three new organizations, forty of which were political. During the next month another twenty-eight new clubs, twenty-three of which were political, were formed.[160] Reports for subsequent months contain similar figures.

In the first six months of 1938 there were over 230 such organizations formed, of which over 160 were considered to be explicitly political. Such a large number of new groups would indicate that while they were relatively easy to form, there being a great deal of youthful energy seeking organizational outlets, the groups did not last long. This was for the simple reason that there were few activities for the groups to engage in after the initial details of the organization had been completed: the members would slowly drift away and perhaps join other, newer groups. Another indication of the amount of youthful political energy in Burma in the late 1930s was the large number of meetings and parades conducted each month.[161] These youth meetings, parades and the like were certainly not all anti-government in inspiration or character. Many were not concerned with the struggle against imperialism but instead expressed a general but unspecific sense of national pride.[162]

The various volunteer corps organized to conduct these parades and rallies in the 1930s, often referred to somewhat grandly as private armies, were the most organized mass groups in pre-war Burma. Every major political party had its own volunteer corps as did the All Burma

158. *Ibid.*, no. 5, 26 May 1937.
159. Burma Defence Bureau Intelligence Summary no. 1, 26 Jan. 1938, BOF 1 358.
160. *Ibid.*, no. 2., 1938.
161. These, like youth organizations (see fn. 156 above), were tabulated in the monthly intelligence summaries. For example, in January 1938, there were 170 parades and 122 meetings, 74 of the meetings being held by *Thakins* (*Ibid.*, no. 1, 26 Jan. 1938) In February 1938, there were 166 parades, 105 conducted by volunteer corps affiliated with political parties and 61 by volunteer fire brigades. In the same month there were 164 meetings, 140 promoted by *Thakins* (*Ibid.*, no. 2, 23 Feb. 1938) In March 1938, there were 365 parades but nearly 300 of these were conducted by fire brigades. Of the 161 meetings that were held, 121 were held by *Thakins* (*Ibid.*, no. 3, 26 March 1938) In May 1938, there were 302 parades, 201 conducted by members of the Green Army, the *Dahma Tat* of Dr Ba Maw's party and the *Bama Letyon Tat* of the Students Union. Of the 275 meetings held, 202 were organized by *Thakins*. (*Ibid.*, no. 5, 27 May 1938).
162. Maung Maung, *From Sangha to Laity*, pp. 76–8.

Students' Union and the Hindu, Muslim and Chinese communities. The oldest of the volunteer corps, the *Ye Tat*, usually referred to in English as the Green Army, was founded by conservative politicians in 1930 but did not become politically involved until after the introduction of the 1935 constitution; the successes of fascism in Europe in the 1930s provided part of their inspiration. While they could be used to terrorize political opponents, the volunteer corps were rarely used to break up meetings and public speeches. They were not armed but did have uniforms — usually khaki shorts and shirts of distinguishing colours from which they took their popular name. Their most important function was usually the extortion of money from wealthy individuals through the threat of a beating or the destruction of property.[163] There were occasional clashes between the different 'armies' but they were never a serious threat to domestic order.[164]

Linking the relatively sophisticated, politically active students of the university and the students and other youth of the towns and districts by the end of the 1930s were the All Burma Students' Union (ABSU) and the organization of the *Thakins*, the *Do Bama Asiayon*. These two groups, often working together so closely as to be indistinguishable, were the primary focus of the energies of nationalist youth. Their leadership, often overlapping and almost identical in perspective on many issues, came from the youth of the Burmese middle class, but their behaviour, often in violation of traditional codes of conduct for young people in Burmese culture, led them into conflict not only with the political authorities but also with the older generation. In the first years of the 1930s some young people who felt a great deal of frustration with the inability of the older politicians to dislodge the British from Burma established study groups and other bodies to develop discipline and principle among themselves in order to avoid both the temptations of office and the apparent apeing of British ways by many youths in

---

163. Interview with F.S.V. Donnison, I.C.S. (retired), London, 14 Dec. 1971.
164. For example, 'A party of Dobama Red-shirt Volunteer Corps, while patrolling Kyaukpadaung [Myingyan] by night came into collision with the local Green Army. Blows were exchanged with the result that a number of Red Shirts are now "off parade". It was the "Red Shirts" however who laid complaint at the Police Station.' Extract from Intelligence Summary no. 4, 24 April 1937, BOF I 20. In mid-1938 there were clashes between U Saw's Galon Tat and parties of *Thakin* in central Burma. Burma Defence Bureau Intelligency Summary no. 6, 26 June 1939. BOF I 358. For a fuller discussion of the development and use of the private armies, see Taylor, 'Burmese Social Classes and British-Indian Policy', pp. 184–91.

Rangoon at that time. A Youth Improvement Society of this type was formed in 1930[165] followed a few years later by an All Burma Youth League. This small group contained several of the most important political leaders of the 1950s, including U Nu, U Ohn and U Thi Han.[166]

Emerging out of the first efforts of the 1930s generation to organize politically, the *Do Bama Asiayon* was the political grouping which provided many of Burma's government leaders of the 1940s and 1950s with their first political experience at national level. The name '*Do Bama Asiayon*' means 'We Burmans' or, more literally, 'Our Burma Association', and has its parallel in the *Sinn Fein* of Irish nationalism. '*Do Bama*' was also the slogan called forth by many of the Burmese involved in the anti-Indian riots of the early 1930s. The organization was criticized by Marxist nationalists in the late 1930s for being racist and sectarian because of its original narrow appeals to Burmese Buddhists. The name *Thakin* which the members of the *Do Bama Asiayon* adopted is an old Burmese word meaning 'master', and, like *Sahib* in India, was the title by which Europeans were addressed by subordinates during the colonial period. By taking the title for themselves Burmese nationalists were demonstrating that they were the masters of Burma; but also, perhaps unconsciously, the élite youth who appended the title to their names were telling other Burmese that they were the emerging governing élite.

The *Do Bama Asiayon* was formally organized on July 4, 1933, but it did not rise to prominence until it was taken over by the former leadership of the ABSU, including Thakin Aung San, in 1938. The ABSU, with its affiliated student unions at secondary schools and centres of higher education in Mandalay, Pyinmana and Rangoon was one of the groups seeking to organize politically interested youth. Initially it concentrated on matters directly affecting students — it had indeed grown from the efforts of the Rangoon University Students' Union to enlist the support of other students for the 1936 strike against the University Act, the cause of the first student strike in 1930 — but by the late 1920s it had become involved in political action touching all aspects of the life of the peasants and workers.[168]

---

165. Maung Maung, *From Sangha to Laity*, p. 75.
166. *Ibid.*, pp. 78–9.
167. *Ibid.*, p. 120.
168. See *Ibid.*, pp. 122–40; also, Cady, *History of Modern Burma*, pp. 378–83, for accounts of the 1936 students' strike.

Because of the earlier importance of students in Burmese politics before they were organized on a national basis, the formation of the ABSU was the cause of much concern to British officials responsible for internal security. One of them wrote in September 1937, 'this new tendency to combine unions and to accept orders from extremist organizations in Rangoon is pregnant with danger and the next school or university strike will probably be much more troublesome than any in the past.'[169]

The concerns of the annual conferences and other meetings of the ABSU reveal its interests and the nature of its political activities. At the third annual conference held in 1938 there were 53 delegates from schools in southern and central Burma as well as 250 other persons, including two of the four members of the House of Representatives from Bassein town district where the meeting was held. 'The background of the dais on which the President's chair [occupied by Aung San] was placed was decorated with a large picture of the famous Burmese General Maha Bandoola on horseback receiving the salute of a British army officer.' The meeting passed resolutions calling for free compulsory elementary education, technical and vocational education for those who passed the primary level, the sending of state scholars abroad for technical and vocational education, and a pledge not to assist the British in the event of war.[170] At the annual conference held in December 1940, over 4,000 persons attended an illegal ceremony honouring the eighty-nine students who had been injured in the anti-Ba Maw and anti-British demonstrations held in Rangoon during 1938–9, and a bust was unveiled of Maung Aung Gyaw, a student who had been killed by the police in these demonstrations.

At its ideological and political training classes the ABSU leaders encouraged students to read and discuss the implications for Burma of the various Marxist and Marxist-derived books and articles then in common circulation. Many of these volumes were written by leaders of the *Do Bama Asiayon* and were easily available through the *Nagani* (Red Dragon) Book Club run by Thakin Nu and others. Thakin Soe's *Socialism* and Thakin Ba Hein's *The Capitalist World* were among the most widely read volumes in Burmese, and Lenin's works were also much

169. Burma Defence Bureau Intelligence Summary no. 9, 25 Sept. 1937, BOF I 20.
170. Maha Bandoola was a Burmese officer who led several successful battles against the British Indian army in the first Anglo-Burmese war. *Ibid.*, no. 5, 27 May 1938, BOF I 358.

sought after.[171] The Marxist-oriented leaders of the ABSU, having graduated from student politics, if not always from the university, took over the *Do Bama Asiayon* from its more conservative and older leaders in 1938 and elected Thakin Thein Maung President and Thakin Aung San Secretary-General. Before then the organization had been led by men whose ideological views tended to be somewhat closer to the moralistic principles of the founders of the All Burma Youth League and the other student self-strengthening movements of the early 1930s from which it had developed. The man who was the inspiration behind the *Do Bama Asiayon* and who gave it its name, Thakin Ba Thaung, was the author of several tracts urging Burmese to have greater self-respect and to avoid involvement with foreigners and the purchase of foreign-made goods.[172] The political leader of the 1930s who bridged the gap between the *Do Bama* leaders of the early 1930s and the Marxist leaders of the late 1930s better than any other was Thakin Nu, the man who became Prime Minister at independence.

The dominance of Marxist-oriented students in the leadership of the *Do Bama Asiayon* led to a split within the organization after the 1938 conference; the majority remained with Aung San and the old ABSU leadership which had the patronage of one of the oldest Thakins, the essayist and poet Kodaw Hmaing. This outward split was only one manifestation of the divisions that existed within the organization and the youthful political group more generally. Though they were able to arouse widespread popular support from peasants and workers for anti-government campaigns in the late 1930s, the leaders were constantly torn, as the previous generation had been, between those who wished to work with the British state structures in order to regain independence and those who sought to subvert them, or at least boycott them, on the assumption that without collaborators the colonial state would collapse. By this time, however, the situation was more complicated, as the changing international order, particularly the development of Japanese

171. This is discussed further in Robert H. Taylor, 'Introduction: Marxism and Resistance in Wartime Burma', in the author's *Marxism and Resistance in Burma 1942–1945: Thein Pe Myint's 'Wartime Traveller'* (Athens, Ohio: Ohio University Press, 1984), pp. 2–3.
172. Tin Htun Aung, *Myanma Naingnganyei hnit Thahkin Ba Thaung* (Burma's Politics and Thakin Ba Thaung) (Rangoon: Sapu U Sa Pe Hpyanchiyei, 1980). App. D(1) of Maung Maung, 'Nationalist Movements in Burma', pp. 619–28, contains translations of Ba Thaung's first two '*naingnganpyu sasu*' or 'national building' articles.

militarism and the Chinese Communist Party, as well as the growing strength of the Indian National Congress, suggested to some leaders of the *Do Bama Asiayon* that outside support, perhaps even arms, would be made available to assist them.[173]

In the four years prior to the Japanese invasion the *Do Bama Asiayon's* young leaders were searching to find ways to solve their political dilemma. While it was clear to many of them that the existing political system did provide opportunities for personal advancement and even power, it did not allow for the kind of revolution that they felt was necessary in order to establish a more just distribution of economic and political power. An examination of the records of the period suggests that in searching for a solution the leaders were unable, under the existing order, to act upon their often creative and potentially effective ideas. Like the first generation of national leaders they were caught in the web of the state, and only its destabilization as a result of external change could create a situation where they might seize power and alter the nature of the state.

The stresses of the period laid bare the disorder among the younger political leaders. Within the *Do Bama Asiayon* there were socialists, militarists and reformers, and those who looked to Japan or the Soviet Union or the British Labour Party for inspiration. Various committees and divisions of the organization became enclaves of these differing perspectives and a great deal of time was spent in fairly academic debate. The first conference of the *Do Bama Asiayon*, held in Yenangyaung in 1935, had about it the flavour of the old GCBA conferences of the 1920s.[174] Following the second conference in 1936, a parliamentary branch, the *Ko Min Ko Chin* (One's Own King, One's Own Kind) party, was established. With its formation, the *Do Bama Asiayon* entered into electoral politics and competed in the 1936 general election. This action, which placed the *Asiayon* on the same footing as the political parties which cooperated in the state's structures, was followed soon after the inauguration of the new constitution by an announcement that echoed the boycott and non-cooperation movement of the *wunthanu athin* and the original GCBA. In July 1937, *Do Bama Asaiyon* leader Thakin Tun Ok was reported to have indicated

---

173. Taylor, 'Marxism and Resistance', pp. 8–11.
174. App. D(2) of Maung Maung, 'Nationalist Movements in Burma', pp. 629–43, contains translations of the resolutions of the five *Do Bama Asiayon* conferences.

that the ultimate aim of the Thakin Party is to establish a system of administration parallel to the existing Government system, and that the first step toward this end will apparently be to undermine the present system of village administration and the authority of the village headman. The idea apparently is that the . . . system of government from the village headman upwards would have its counterpart in the appointment of Presidents of village, township and district Asi-ayons, with the Central Baho Dobama Asi-ayon at the head of the organization.[175]

The following January it was reported in Bassein that the idea of a parallel administration was to be put into effect.[176] While occasional references to this scheme appeared from time to time subsequently, it seems it was never attempted on any broad scale.

The new generation of political leaders recognized that the modern state could not be ignored and that the gaining of independence would not mean the restoration of the economic and political practices of the precolonial era. The postcolonial state would have to be used to transform Burma, and from the time the young Marxists took control of the *Do Bama Asiayon* its rhetoric and policies were cast in the mould of the modern state. The clearest statement of this new view is found in 'The Manifesto of the *Dobama Asiayone* . . . Its Policy, Its Explanation, Its Future Work' prepared by the Fourth Working Committee of the organization under the leadership of Aung San.[177] The novelty of the organization's ideas and behaviour had created a good deal of opposition to it from established sectors of Burmese society; this was acknowledged at the beginning of the Manifesto. Stating that 'it has met with imperialist and bureaucratic repression', it went on to say,

for a time and still among a section of the public, it is regarded as a socially evil phenomenon. Its members are virtually ostracized. With political persecution on the one hand and social tyranny on the other, it has undergone innumerable trials and tribulations which are but the signs of its birth pangs.

Turning to explicitly political matters, the Manifesto described the organization as 'anti-imperialist and democratic'. The *Do Bama Asiayon* stood for 'full *"Ko Min Ko Chin"* a free democratic republic'. The

---

175. Burma Monthly Intelligence Summary no. 4, for month ending 31 July 1937, BOF I 37, part I.
176. Burma Defence Bureau Intelligence Summary no. 1, 26 Jan. 1938, BOF I 358.
177. Translated in CID Burma, Intelligence Branch Department no. 694R/C, 11 July 1939, BOF P 39, part II. The manifesto was reprinted in *The Guardian* (Rangoon) in 1959 during the time of the first military government.

details of the policy included the abolition of the Government of Burma Act, 1935, and the drafting of a new constitution by a constituent assembly exercising full self-determination. 'Mass struggle' was the strategy with which to accomplish this. Among the available tactics was parliamentary action. On the question of accepting political office the Manifesto noted that this was merely a question of tactics, but doubted whether accepting office would be of any use under the existing constitution, which did not allow for effective means of solving Burma's problems. Neither the experience of India nor Burma under the 1935 constitution offered any convincing evidence to the contrary. The strategy of mass action entailed four main tasks:

1. To raise the social and economic consciousness of all toilers of the land on their day to day needs, local, municipal, economic, cultural, etc.
2. To resist any encroachment upon our civil liberties and democratic rights.
3. To introduce effective measures which will ultimately turn the Dobama Asiayon into a full-fledged organ of the people's will — a united democratic national front against Imperialism, for freedom and democracy.
4. To hold a Plebiscite in regard to the constitution on every Anti-Constitution Day [April 1].

To achieve this strategy organization was needed 'to purify, regulate, extend and strengthen' the *Asiayon*. Also needed was a 'properly equipped and well-regulated headquarters and its staff.' The Working Committee felt that half of that goal had already been achieved.

The *Do Bama Asiayon* was often accused by British officials and more conservative Burmese of being a Communist organization and of being corrupt. It sought to defend itself against such charges as it did in the Manifesto.

To many the ideology and character of our Asiayone has not been clear. The . . . vested interests call our Asiayone communistic in origin. But everyone who knows something of a Communist Party would laugh at the suggestion. No, the Dobama Asiayone is not a communist organization. What is it then? Of course, unlike reactionaries and vested interests, we are not alarmed by 'the Spectre of Communism.' Within our organization, communists, socialists, nationalists, others, all can exist, provided they will sincerely fight for and live and die for freedom.

Now there is another criticism that our organization is corrupt. But this is such a big bluff for any sensible man to swallow. Whether it is corrupt or not will be more and more clearly seen. After all, some members of it may be corrupt. This is not peculiar to the Dobama Asiayone alone. But this is no reason why the whole organization should be condemned. This is however a good propaganda of our political opponents.

In addition to its broad policy goals of independence, self-determination and anti-imperialism, the *Do Bama Asiayon* adopted a variety of other specific goals which it attempted to get the existing government and parties to implement. These policies were directed toward the amelioration of the conditions of the masses, which, according to the *Do Bama Asiayon* constitution, were composed of 'labourers, cultivators, students, shopkeepers, hawkers, traders, brokers, clerks and working people'. The purpose of these other policy goals was not to promise the masses 'heaven and earth all of a sudden', but to indicate what an independent state led by them would achieve in governing Burma.

Though the groups defined by the *Asiayon* as the masses accounted for the overwhelming majority of the population, the peasantry was the most important sector to which all the parties had to appeal. On the questions of peasant indebtedness and landlessness the moderate policy of the *Do Bama Asiayon* suggests a certain ambiguity in its position. While at times advocating a militant pro-landless cultivator and even pro-revolutionary line at the rhetorical level, at the practical level the national leadership followed a reformist line suggesting an internal conflict of interest between the organization's need for political support and its leaders understanding of their interests within society.

Indeed, the *Do Bama Asiayon*'s policy was much in keeping with the policies of the major parties in the government. In the July 1939 Manifesto the goals of the *Do Bama Asiayon* were not greatly different from those of the Legislature's Agrarian Inquiry Committee or of the British policymakers who had been advocating small-scale peasant proprietorship since the 1880s. 'The agrarian problem will, we are afraid, for some time come to absorb most of our attention, because [the peasants] form the core of our national economy for the time being. Our policy in this connection is to create a prosperous peasant population.' While the *Do Bama Asiayon* expressed dissatisfaction with the terms of the government's agrarian policies, it also said it would 'give them full trial'.

The Central *Do Bama Asiayon*'s reformist policies in agriculture were demonstrated in 1939 when, during a spate of rick and hut burnings accompanied by Burmese-Indian communal tensions and clashes, the *Thakins*' central leadership urged the cultivators to abide by the law and to cease such activities.[178] However local *Thakins* working with the peasants apparently paid little heed to this advice and encouraged them to begin ploughing in areas where no contracts had been signed with the landlords, as happened in Myaungmya district in June of that year.[179] Local actions of this kind, in keeping with the old *wunthanu* methods, were opposed by the President of the *Do Bama Asiayon*, who called upon the peasants to abandon their non-payment of tax campaigns and urged them to work through legal procedures for a lowering of taxes and rents. He further suggested that the peasants were behaving precipitately in their efforts to throw out the British.[180] The central leadership 'brought to the notice of its rural branches the provisions of the Tenancy Act and . . . urged them to impress on their members the necessity for complying with the provisions of the Act and behaving in a law abiding manner.'[181]

The *Thakins*' central leadership, perhaps in the belief that only industrial workers could lead a progressive movement, spent a great deal of effort in trying to organize factory workers and labourers in the oil fields at Yenangyaung and Chauk.[182] Here one of the major problems they faced was the fact that most of the industrial labourers were Indians who were wary of the implicit pro-Burmese attitude and leadership of the *Asiayon*. Its labour program included the abolition of the *maistry* system and the establishment of a Labour Exchange Department run by the state to replace it. The most complete statement of the *Do Bama Asiayon*'s labour policy was made in a May Day manifesto signed by Thakin Soe, Burma's premier Marxist theoretician, and Thakin Kyaw Sein. (Its distribution was banned by government order.) Among other things, it called for a 35 per cent increase in wages, a forty-hour week, and the improvement of working and living conditions through government action.[183] Their organizational activities, along with the ABSU leadership, enabled them to gain the support of many oil workers during the 1938 strike.[184] The *Thakins* also made appeals for support from

178. Governor's Confidential Report no. 11, 17 May 1939, BOF P 39, Part II.
179. Home Secretary's Fortnightly Report for the 2nd Half May, 1939: 10 June 1939, Governor's Confidential Report no. 13, 16 June 1939. BOF P 39, part II.
180. Burma Defence Bureau Intelligence Summary no. 4, 25 April 1939, BOF I 358.
181. Governor's Confidential Report no. 12, 5 June 1939, BOF P 39, part II.
182. Report of an Officer of this Department (CID), 15 Aug. 1939, BOF P 233.
183. Extract from the May Day Manifesto to be issued by the DAA, 1940, BOF P 39, Part III.
184. For a discussion of the 1938–9 oilfield workers strike see Taylor, 'Relationship

members of the police, army and civil service, and their success was sufficient to cause the government concern.[185]

The *Thakins'* claim that the organization was not Communist was clearly correct: their policies were too eclectic and their hope to work through existing institutions of the state indicates their ambivalent attitude toward revolution. There were several reasons for this, one of which was the origins of their socialist ideas. There were a variety of sources, none coming directly from any of the internationally recognized centres of revolution. Rather, the *Thakins* learned their socialism from popular British and Indian tracts, particularly the publications of Gollancz's Left Book Club and the writings of people such as Palme Dutt and John Strachey. As the leading Eastern European student of Burmese ideological practices has written, the *Thakins* 'tended to accept some Marxist principles in a dogmatic and simplifying manner', and this 'produced a contradictory response among the *Thakins*'. The ideology was appealing to some because of its connection with the rapid development and power of the state in the Soviet Union, but for others its value was found in its 'explanation of the nature of colonialism and imperialism'. Most of the *Thakins* saw Marxism as 'a mere instrument in their anti-colonial struggle'.[186]

The ideological inconsistencies of the *Thakins* can also be explained by examining their social backgrounds, most of which were to be found among the landowning, commercial and government service sector of the state-dependent middle class. While full information on the class positions of the *Thakins* is not available, it seems apparent that most of the leaders and perhaps many of the district leaders, like the student political leaders of the period, came from the declining landowning and trading class of the rural areas. Of the nineteen persons listed in *Who's Who in Burma, 1961*, who were active *Thakins* in the 1930s, and whose father's occupation is given, only one was an agriculturalist. Most of their fathers were traders and merchants, four were landowners, two were timber and rice mill owners, and two were government employees. Thakin Aung San's father was a pleader, Thakin Tun Ok's father was a

---

Between Burmese Social Classes and British-Indian Policy', ch. 5. The Burmese literature on this period, often known as the 1300 Revolution, is extensive.
185. Burma Defence Bureau Intelligence Summary no. 12, 31 Dec. 1941, BOF I 358.
186. Jan Becka, *The National Liberation Movement in Burma during the Japanese Occupation Period (1941–1945)* (Prague: Oriental Institute, Dissertationes Orientales, vol. 42, 1983), p. 38.

landowner and Thakin Hla Pe's was both a landowner and a miller. Thakin Tun Shein was the son of a trader and Thakin Nu's parents were landowners and shopkeepers. Other prominent *Thakins* were the sons of contractors, merchants and landowners.[187]

Thus, the *Do Bama Asiayon* was a new force in Burmese society and politics, and it was based upon the youngest generation of the middle class. Generational differences determined their complaints against the older parties and leaders more than did ideological goals. While they used the language of Marxism, they were no more, and no less, anti-imperialist than the older party leaders. They may have seen the strategic possibilities of the anti-imperialist campaign in Burma in the late 1930s differently, but not necessarily more correctly. Their generation had not witnessed the defeat of the Hsaya San rebellion; it just remembered it as a glorious attempt to throw off foreign rule. The Indian population, as far as they could remember, had always been in Burma, and while they may have not liked to compete with Indians for employment, they had a different perception of India's relationship with Burma than did their seniors. Moreover the *Thakins* did not look upon King Thibaw as the king who could not fend off the British, but rather as the Burmese king that the British had arrogantly deposed.

These differences altered the world views of the two rival generations of political leaders in pre-war Burma. It affected their perceptions of what they could do and what they should do to regain the state's independence and remove policymaking from control by the interests of foreign capital and labour. It did not, however, change to any significant degree what they wanted Burma to become once it was again free of foreign rule and economic domination. Conflicts over the goal of the independent state were to occur in another decade, when independence was imminent and the consequences of internal class conflict made themselves felt. The ideas of the student political activists of the 1930s persisted after the fall of the colonial state to shape the present; but so did their legacy of political mobilization, which achieved success as the state was dislodged from its dominant relationship with civil society.

---

187. Guyot, 'Political Impact of the Japanese Occupation', app. I, pp. 419–21; Nu, *U Nu — Saturday's Son* (edited by U Kyaw Yin and translated by U Law Yone (New Haven: Yale University Press, 1975), p. 10.

CHAPTER 4

THE DISPLACEMENT OF THE STATE, 1942–1962

War, Revolution and the State

The relationship between the state and civil society in Burma was radically altered in the period between 1942 and 1962. As a result of the Second World War and the civil war which followed independence, the state was displaced as the creator of political order and economic direction and lost its hegemonic position. No longer able to determine many of the conditions of social and economic life, the state became a rival object for control by groups possessing different perceptions of what kind of society Burma should be. After independence from Britain was formally granted on January 4, 1948, these groups sought to dislodge those who had been bequeathed the shell of the state in order to reconstruct society in accordance with their own concepts of politics and morality. For twenty years capture of the state's carapace became the purpose of almost all political action, and as no group was willing to grant the state and its personnel pre-eminence a stalemate ensued. The state remained enfeebled, and a generation came of age in a society where non-state institutions were often perceived as more powerful than the state.

It has usually seemed logical to divide analyses of the 1940s and 1950s into reasonably distinct periods of four or five years. This implied that the primary objectives, leading personnel and perhaps even the purpose of politics during these years changed from one reasonably discrete unit of time to the next. These periods are: the Second World War, 1942–5; the regaining of independence, 1945–8; the post-independence civil war, 1948–52; the government of the Anti-Fascist People's Freedom League (AFPFL), 1951–8; the military 'caretaker government', 1958–60; the return to civilian rule under U Nu, 1960–62; and the military coup of 1962. Viewed from the perspective of the evolution of the state *qua* state, these twenty years are better seen as a whole, during which the state, denied the support of the British-Indian empire and briefly and ineffectually backed by the Japanese empire, disintegrated and was displaced. The two decades after 1942 can be conceived of as years of contest between competing groups over which would resurrect the state, in what form, and in whose interest. Because of its complexity, it is difficult to deal with the period chronologically and still grasp meaning from the passing events. The only significant change in the nature of that contest came in the months between October 1946 and January 1947, when, after the British had made it clear that independence would be granted within one year, the basic issues became fundamentally domestic or internal rather than imperial or international.

Many of the interweaving strands of political and economic developments during these twenty years have pre-war roots. As argued in Chapter II, the rationalization of the state under colonial auspices altered the nature of the society in many ways. However in the realm of popular ideas and symbols, many political and moral ideals of the precolonial order persisted in people's minds. When the Japanese invaded, only fifty-six years had elapsed since a Burmese monarch had reigned in Mandalay. While very few people in 1942 expected that it would be possible to return to political structures and state relations comparable to those of the late Konbaung dynasty, many looked forward, more in nostalgia than in clear memory, to a new version of the alleged order and justice of the precolonial state. Some felt there should be no return to the 'feudal' past and that Burma would have to 'skip historical stages' in order to 'catch up' with the modern world. Others, making less sweeping assumptions about the plasticity of the state and society, sought merely to guide the state along familiar paths. The struggle of the political groups holding these conflicting views and the interests they represented, together with efforts by local leaders to fend off the demands of the centre, form the essence of Burma's politics from 1942 until 1962.

The larger the number of attempts made to reorganize the state in a particular period, the more obvious does it become that its controllers are trying to reassert its position. Whereas the Burmese kings only reorganized their state system upon the founding of a new dynasty and the British merely elaborated the institutions of the colonial state, in the twenty years after 1942 incumbents attempted to restructure the state nine different times. Not all of these attempts were fundamental in intent, but all forced the ruling élite to rethink the nature and purpose of the state in order to construct institutions which would last. The range of options for state reorganization was limited by the experiences and knowledge of the dominant political group and by what they thought would be acceptable to their subjects. Conceptions of reorganization ranged from 'traditional' kingship to 'modern' ideas of socialism, and from Western notions of liberalism to varieties of militarism and statism as found in Japan or the socialist world. Crucial in shaping ideas for reorganization was the belief that some 'new' form of state was necessary to demonstrate that the ruling élite was not captive to the old order, but was creating an order which would deal with social and economic issues more effectively than their predecessors or rivals.

The question of the nature of the state had been a factor in the ideological debates of the nationalist movement throughout the 1930s. Politicians nearest to state power realized that even if the British were not defeated by the Axis powers in a major war it was unlikely that British would remain the master of Burma for much more than another decade or two. The political evolution of India, the relative decline in the economic power of Britain and the successful operation of the 1935 constitution by politicians such as U Saw were factors favouring the attainment of full and genuine internal self-government by leaders from the new middle class. The apparent rise of anti-capitalist left-wing movements as well as the continuing threat of peasant unrest demonstrated to the more far-sighted British officials and politicians the desirability of placing the social control functions of the state in the hands of Burmese officials and politicians whose interests were linked with the British Empire/Commonwealth. If nothing else, the maintenance of the internal order upon which Britain's economic interests depended necessitated a steady evolution of the identity of the state with the interests of the most conservative state-centred classes and groups in Burmese society.

The efforts of groups which opposed the policies and institutions of the colonial state and refused to identify with it had also grown during the inter-war decades. It was their strength, especially when they were able to mobilize support from the peasantry and from the youth, which most seriously challenged the attempts of the indigenous political élite after 1947 to assert the dominance of the state. The economic and ideological issues which motivated peasant and worker discontent were little touched by the transitions of power after 1942. While day-to-day rivalries monopolized political attention, the underlying issue of the state's ability to provide the focus of individual identity and social order (and thus dominate anti-state forces) was not resolved. Order remained uncertain, and extra-state agents of coercion and control continued to play a large role in the lives of the population.

The continuing grievances of the peasantry provided a motivation for political mobilization on the part of the majority of the population. The last pre-war government had attempted to improve the conditions of the peasants by introducing moderate tenancy and land reform legislation, but no solution was possible which both dealt with the massive level of peasant indebtedness and preserved the capital of politically powerful foreign and indigenous moneylenders and landlords, the *sine qua non* for political success under the late colonial order. Land tax also remained a complaint of the peasants, though the first government under the 1937 constitution had abolished the capitation and *thathameda* taxes. But with a large proportion of the peasant population landless, anti-state groups had a ready supply of the discontented to mobilize against the state.

As the political dilemma of peasant indebtedness indicates, the promise of internal political power and greater control over external affairs held out by the British to the indigenous political élite did not provide a solution to the middle class's major economic problems, including competition with Indian and, to a lesser extent, Chinese businessmen. As long as the credit system and the internal economy remained largely in foreign hands it was impossible for the indigenous middle class to feel assured that the political power which its leaders held was secure and would be used in the interest of political stability and indigenous economic advantage. The problem of Burmese professionals was easier to resolve through the passage of legislation requiring that individuals be citizens in order to pursue particular occupations such as teaching or the civil service. But comparable legislation in regard to trading, moneylending and other commercial activities could be easily circumvented.

A fundamental issue which remained unresolved between 1942 and 1962 was the legitimacy of the state. In the eyes of most of the urban middle class, political parties, elections and the rhetoric of nationalism and populism were sufficient to legitimize the state in the modern world. But as the heirs of the colonial state and the victors over their Communist colleagues in the independence movement, the wielders of state power in the 1950s, led by U Nu and the Socialist group, were uncertain of their own legitimacy[1] and perhaps that of the postcolonial state itself. To many others, including the culturally more conservative members of the middle class and of the Buddhist *sangha*, the state ought to have been rooted in older Burmese idioms and symbols. Despite

---

1. Khin Maung Kyi, 'Patterns of Accommodation to Bureaucratic Authority in a Transitional Culture (A Sociological Analysis of Burmese Bureaucrats with Respect to Their Orientations Towards Authority' (unpubl. Ph.D. diss., Cornell University, 1966), pp. 106–7.

acceptance of the colonial-style state with its advantages for political control by the middle class, the majority of the population received few of the permanent advantages that were commonly believed would follow from independence and the end of foreign exploitation. The departure of the British did not mean an end to the modern state and its concomitant economic and social institutions.[2] Nor did the achievement of independence make it possible for peasants and others to gain redress for their grievances (as allegedly occurred under a righteous king whose moral order limited the excesses of his state and its officials). The development of a legitimizing myth which combined a justification for the activities of the modern state with Burmese rather than British notions of justice had not occurred, and the state provided little focus of identity for much of the population.

These fundamental issues in the life of the state were largely irrelevant prior to 1942 because the external power of the British-Indian empire was sufficient to maintain the dominance of the state despite its perceived illegitimacy. The initial consequence of the Japanese invasion, of course, was to remove the British armed forces. The British civil servants and many of the Burmese politicians who had managed the late colonial state were immediately replaced by Japanese army officers and civilians and by Burmese politicians and officials who, for reasons of idealism, opportunism, or a degree of compulsion, cooperated with the new regime. Many, like Thibaw Min's officials at the time of the British conquest, felt obligated to continue to serve the state regardless of its master.

The Japanese invasion set in train other economic, social and political processes which undermined the state. Two major factors were at work. First, the removal of British power meant that many of those individuals and interests associated with the colonial order and ultimately dependent upon it either left the country or sought protection from indigenous or other foreign forces. Secondly, mass political groups were organized and mobilized in support of Burma's independence. With the encouragement of the Japanese military there arose a new, indigenous power in the form of the Burma Independence Army (BIA), which briefly assumed power as the British withdrew. There subsequently

---

2. These feelings of loss and betrayal are portrayed fictionally in Thiha, *The Chindits and the Stars* (London: Regency, 1971) and in the post-independence stories in *Selected Short Stories of Thein Pe Myint*, trans. and edited by Patrica M. Milne (Ithaca: Cornell University Southeast Asia Program Data Paper no. 91, June 1973), pp. 47–105.

developed other groups opposed to the Japanese fascists, often calling themselves Communists or Socialists, or acting in the name of the Karen community, willing to cooperate with the British to remove the Japanese. While the Karen leaders sought to bring about the return of the British, the Marxist-oriented groups wished to ensure that imperialists would play no role in the future of Burma. Both the BIA and the undergroud leftists, who formed a Communist Party in 1943, received the support of students and peasants who believed that they would benefit from the creation of a new and indigenously managed state. For the Karen Christian leaders and for the 'traditional' authorities recognized by the colonial state as its agents in the hill areas the threat of a new state form based upon egalitarian principles and indigenous rule meant an end to their protected positions.

The Reorganization of the State

The terminology used in a discussion of the displacement of the state tends to make the subject seem abstract and remote from the lives of individuals. In fact the resulting turbulent conditions directly affected the lives and property of most of the population. For many, the upheavals that resulted from war and revolution brought opportunities as well as difficulties. The uncertainty of these years can be gathered from talking with people who lived through them and from studying various written accounts. For example, one left-wing nationalist wrote of a group of villagers who at the time of the British withdrawal were primarily worried about the unchecked activities of dacoits in their area and who lamented that 'the government is no more'.[3]

The sudden dislocation of the state in 1942 provided opportunities for individuals on the periphery of colonial society to acquire positions and wealth or to settle old scores unhindered by established and recognized authorities. Property abandoned by fleeing British, Indian and Chinese businessmen fell, at least temporarily, into indigenous hands. For those seeking local administrative control the departure of the colonial state's personnel provided opportunities for office, and individuals acted alone or in groups to assume the mantle of authority.

---

3. Thein Pe Myint, *Wartime Traveller*, in Robert H. Taylor, *Marxism and Resistance in Burma, 1942–1945: Thein Pe Myint's Wartime Traveller* (Athens, Ohio: Ohio University Press, 1984), p. 122.

Governing roles were quickly taken up by audacious or by more authoritative individuals. In particular, *Thakins* and members of the BIA took it upon themselves to administer local areas and to establish new township and urban governing committees, often in conflict with each other, as well as with older politicians or the Japanese army. The committees dominated by youths saw the departure of the British as 'the dawn of a new Burmese era', in which traditional values could be resurrected and Western cultural influence eradicated. Many of their actions, however, were merely symbolic, such as the renaming of streets and public buildings.[4] They had too little time and too little authority to do more.

The chaos of local government was mirrored in the confusion and disorder of the central state. The political leaders in the capital often believed that if they could correctly organize their central institutions the disorder below them would be eliminated by new laws and edicts and by the example they set. The first wartime attempts at reorganization came immediately in the wake of the Japanese invasion. A *Baho* or Central Administration was established by the Japanese and nominally headed by Thakin Tun Ok. Pleading the exigencies of war, its leaders merely attempted to maintain functions equivalent to the British administration. From its beginning in early April the *Baho* administration, recognizing its relative powerlessness, made little attempt to guide local administrative bodies, seeking 'only to review local policies after they had been made'.[5] Indeed, for a brief period, Burma again became a series of little republics, as the central state's authority extended to little more than the capital. Given the uncertain authority of Burmese officials in their relations with both the Japanese and the initially autonomous township and town committees, the central administrators fell back on the forms of the old order.[6]

Faced with an inept and nearly powerless indigenous administration, in August 1942 the Japanese created a new order which would relieve the occupying army of administrative tasks. The *Baho* administration was replaced by a government led by Dr Ba Maw which invited civil servants and politicians who had worked with the

---

4. Jan Becka, *The National Liberation Movement in Burma during the Japanese Occupation Period (1941–1945)* (Prague: Oriental Institute, Dissertationes Orientales Volume 42, 1983), p. 90.
5. Dorothy Hess Guyot, 'The Political Impact of the Japanese Occupation of Burma' (unpubl. Ph.D. diss., Yale University, 1966), p. 143.
6. *Ibid.*, pp. 144–5.

British to join it; the autonomous committees of the BIA and other local bodies were suppressed and replaced with centrally sanctioned authorities. The Ba Maw administration was greatly hampered, however, by poor communications and by the existence of rival centres of authority, especially the Japanese army.[7] The indigenous authorities were left only the functions of law and order, justice, and revenue collection, while the Japanese managed major economic enterprises and the means of transport and communication necessary for the prosecution of the war. Local government officials, especially district officers, using the same organisational methods as their pre-war predecessors were forced to make administrative decisions without central supervision. More than two-thirds of the district officers had no experience of such autonomy. At the centre most of the administrators were also former British employees, except in newly created departments such as labour, war cooperation and religion, which were filled with political appointees. Perhaps the major innovation in the procedures of the state during the war was to change the official language to Burmese, though English-language manuals and forms were still the norm.[8]

Despite their reliance upon British procedures, the administrators under Ba Maw made great efforts to show that the state they were creating was radically different from the one it had displaced. Though the state's goals of security, order and economic well-being remained the same, the terminology used to explain these goals was altered to make the purpose of the state seem new and laudable. 'National unity' and 'strength' became the state's avowed purposes, and these were to be achieved in the first instance by the re-organization of the administrative machinery 'to make a fit and proper instrument for the service of the new State'. The initial problem to be dealt with was the composition of the state's personnel. This was vital, Ba Maw argued,

> especially when a State is defending its very existence. At such a time a State must be completely assured of the loyalty, integrity, competency and discipline of its servants or else it cannot survive. A house divided against itself must fall sooner or later. This is proved by what happened in the last days of British rule in Burma . . . when one of the contributory causes of the British defeat was a sudden breakdown of the administration. Such a contingency must be avoided

---

7. *Ibid.*, pp. 145–6.
8. James F. Guyot, 'Bureaucratic Transformation in Burma', in Ralph Braibanti (ed.), *Asian Bureaucratic Systems Emergent from the British Imperial Tradition* (Durham, North Carolina: Duke University Press, 1966), pp. 386–7.

at all cost in the new State by the means of timely action. Furthermore, there cannot be a sound and stable State if its administrative services are unsound or unstable.[9]

Every attempt to resurrect the state since that time has placed equal emphasis upon the need to ensure the loyalty of the state's officials and agents. While the British sought to ensure that there was a pool of trained manpower to staff the administrative services, the loyalty of officials was ensured by the unique foreign origins of those at the top and by the relatively munificent salaries they and their subordinates were paid. An indigenously based, impecunious state could afford neither of these options, and was forced to rely upon staff training that emphasized unity and loyalty. But without the centrality of the Buddhist king to provide a focus of loyalty, and with the existence of many powerful alternative symbols appealing for the allegiance of individuals, it was intended that the state and the nation it claimed to represent would become the focus of loyalty. Ba Maw's call for 'One Blood, One Voice, One Command' was not so much the order of a dictator, as an appeal for a nation-state-centred sense of loyalty of a kind that the state in Burma had not encouraged before; nationalism had now become official.

The constitution installed with the Japanese grant of independence in August 1943, like the British-drafted constitution of 1937, reflected more the ideas of its foreign sponsors than of the state's leading personnel. Intended to provide a means to carry out the government's New Order Plan, the constitution was similar to the 1889 Meiji constitution of Japan, placing ultimate authority, including control of the armed forces, in the hands of the head of state. The Minister of War, however, was always to be a serving senior military officer.[10] This was the constitutional basis of the position in the cabinet of General Aung San as the head of the Burma National Army (BNA), and was the beginning of a pattern of political equality between the head of state and the head of the army in the state which lasted till 1962. Below the head of state there was a Planning Board as well as an embassy in Tokyo, a supreme court, and the cabinet. There was no role for bodies such as a legislature or for local self-government as attempted under the British. However, in the most important aspects of state administration, the constitution followed the

---

9. Ba Maw, 'A Review of the First Stage of the New Order Plan', *Burma* I, 1 (Rangoon: Foreign Affairs Association, Burma, Sept., 1944), pp. 110–11.
10. Abu Talib bin Ahmad, 'Collaboration, 1941–1945: An Aspect of the Japanese Occupation of Burma', unpubl. Ph.D. diss., Monash University), p. 240–2.

pattern of the colonial state. For example, 'local administration was put under the Home Ministry with the exception of the Shan States which were administered by the Prime Minister's Department'.[11]

The divergent treatment provided for the Shan states within the organization of the wartime state was a continuation of colonial state practices. Little distinction was made though between the administration of central Burma and the western and northern frontier areas known subsequently as the Chin and Kachin states. Although these were nominally under the control of the central administration, as they were zones into which British and American military units made forays, they remained under Japanese military control. In the eastern areas the Japanese initially maintained a system of 'indirect' rule similar to that of the British. The Shan *Sawbwas* individually came to terms with the Japanese and in the process succeeded in ensuring that troops of the central state did not enter their domains.[12] The most eastern Shan state, Kengtung, was ceded by the Japanese to Thailand, but the other Shan states, as well as the Wa and Karenni states, were under central control after December 1943.[13] For the first time in Burma's history most of the country was, in theory, under a uniform administrative sovereign.

Upon their return in 1945, one of the conditions the British insisted upon before granting independence was that the leaders of the Shan states and of the hill tribes had to agree to cede their territories to an independent government in Rangoon. Barring such an agreement, Burma would be truncated between an independent central Burma and a surrounding horseshoe of sparsely populated mountains remaining under British sovereignty. Such a scheme had little rationale other than as a bargaining point in 1946 and 1947 between the British government and the leaders of the nationalist united front, the Anti-Fascist Peoples's Freedom League (AFPFL).

Once the British had decided that they had to leave Burma as expeditiously as possible, means were found for doing so with the 'consent' of the hill tribes' leaders. As called for in the 1947 Aung San-Attlee agreement, the Shan *Sawbwas* and 'leaders of the Chins and the Kachins' with delegates from the Supreme Council of the United Hill Peoples

11. Ibid., pp. 248–9.
12. Ba Maw, *Breakthrough in Burma: Memoirs of a Revolution* (New Haven: Yale University Press, 1968), p. 200.
13. 'The Address of His Excellency Thakin Mya, the Deputy Prime Minister, at the Third Session of the Privy Council on Monday, the 20th March 1944', *Burma*, 1, 1, p. 129.

(the traditional leaders' organization) agreed to join Burma in a 'federation'. This agreement was ratified by a British House of Commons special committee in April and the way was paved for Burma's independence as a federal Union.[14] The constitution of independent Burma, later ratified by a constitutent assembly in 1947, delineated the federal state but in reality provided for a centralized governmental system. The states, eventually numbering five, had no substantial legislative powers and little say in taxation or state finance. The Shan, Karenni, and Kachin States together with the Chin Special Division, which had less formal internal arrangements, were created in the initial constitution and a Karen state was created later by constitutional amendment. The drafters of the constitution had had no intention of establishing a federal system similar to that of the United States or Switzerland. Something more like the relationship between Scotland and the British government in London was intended.

Though in theory Burma in 1948 came under one legal authority, in fact this was not the case. In certain respects, such as the criminal law, the Shan States and the other former reserved areas remained outside the central state system until 1962. It could be argued that independence, rather than establishing the principle of nationalism as the basis of the state (as formally enunciated in the preamble of the 1947 constitution), actually reversed the egalitarian trend of the British period by increasing the powers and privileges of the Shan and Karenni *Sawbwas*.

The amalgamation of the federated Shan States in 1948 occurred when there was a shortage of personnel and of political will at the centre to impose a single government on the region. The *Sawbwas* had, by their cooperation with the non-Communist AFPFL leadership in accepting inclusion within the new order, gained a degree of recognition for their continuing political utility. After 1948 the *Sawbwas* were able to maintain their own budgets, police forces and local tax regimes, as well as appoint their own officials, but without the supervision of central civil servants as the British had insisted upon.

The democratic principles of the 1947 constitution logically required the abolition of the hereditary 'traditional' leaders of the frontier areas. Though the constitution called for the establishment of a socialist and egalitarian society, it provided the state with few means of carrying out social reform, for it was based upon a political compromise between the

---

14. Maung Maung, *Burma's Constitution* (The Hague: Martinus Nijhoff, 2nd edn, 1961), pp. 79–80.

central AFPFL leadership and the frontier area leaders. To have abolished their positions would have been a genuinely revolutionary act, but that was not to occur for another ten years.

This review of the constitutional evolution of the Shan states and other peripheral territories during the 1940s highlights an aspect of the displacement of the state. The post-independence constitution was framed upon the same liberal principles of government that had been the basis of the 1935 British Government of Burma Act. The bureaucratic structures of the colonial state which had not been destroyed by the war or had been rebuilt by the post-war British military administration were retained. Legislative powers were lodged in a bicameral legislature in which the upper house, the Chamber of Nationalities, served as a brake on the radical democratic possibilities of the lower house which was organized on the basis of one-person-one vote and therefore held out the prospect of influence for the peasantry. The Chamber of Nationalities was created in order to serve the interests of the 'traditional' leaders in the frontier areas rather than those of urban wealth and status, as did the colonial upper house. The governor was replaced by a nominal president possessing few effective veto powers. State power now became constitutionally lodged in the cabinet led by a prime minister, but because of the maintenance of the Secretariat structure between the ministers and the operative departments ministers were still dependent upon the willingness of the permanent officials to carry out their orders.

The establishment of this political order within the independent state was not an inevitable process. The constitution was written by the conservative interests which had won an internal power struggle within the AFPFL during the period between the autumn of 1946, when the British government decided to grant independence, and mid-1947, when power was handed to the non-Communist groups. The losing elements in that struggle were excluded from state power and formed the core of the groups in rebellion both during and after the four-year civil war. What differentiates the state before 1942 from that after 1948 was that after independence the incumbent political élite tried to control the country through the institutions of a liberal constitution while lacking the coercive force of their British predecessors. The consequence was perhaps inevitable. Forces unwilling to accept their exclusion from state power in 1948 launched the civil war in an attempt to achieve political power. The following section briefly analyses the nature of the contestants for state power during the late 1940s and 1950s.

The Contestants for State Power

During the six years between the Japanese invasion and the formal departure of the British there arose a variety of political organizations and groups which sought to seize control of the authority of the state either in all or in part of the territory internationally recognized as Burma. The most important of these groups, the Anti-Fascist People's Freedom League (AFPFL), the Burma army, the Burma Communist Party (CP[B] or BCP), the Karen National Union (KNU), as well as many less well known groups, all worked assiduously to organize and maintain popular support for their leaders and their policies. The most effective period of mass mobilization was during the war,[15] but the most dramatic and lasting consequences are seen in the politics of the post-war independence contest and the resulting civil war. The leaders of the various groups formed during the war years, secular and religious, Communist and non-Communist, each vigorously disputed the legitimacy of those who received the carapace of state sovereignty from the British.

The leaders of the most vehemently anti-British groups, most of whom had worked together in the nationalist and student political movements of the 1930s, believed that success in driving out the foreigners would mean that state power would accrue to them. In contrast, the leaders of various minority communities, especially the Christian Karen and the Shan *Sawbwas*, were aware that their influence would be diminished if independence were won in the name of the Burmese nation-state, and thus they sought to mobilize support as a countervailing power to that of the state-centred nationalists. Many of these leaders were able to find allies and friends in foreign communities resident in Burma or in governments and political movements outside. For this reason, indigenous minority leaders often had a greater feeling of power and support than they actually possessed.

Representing so many conflicting interests and ideologies, and backed by followers intent on achieving or maintaining their goals, the leaders of the different groups found it impossible to reach compromises with each other and still retain their supporters. To defend themselves against rival leaders within their own organization, incumbents often escalated demands to prove their militancy and dedication. The multiplicity of

---

15. See the discussion of the mobilization of groups during the war in Guyot, 'Political Impact of the Japanese Occupation'. A summary is provided in Table 13, Wartime Mass Organizations, p. 275.

political movements in the 1940s and 1950s and the cumulative sacrifices that their followers made prevented leaders from accepting compromises which could have lead to their incorporation into the state. The resultant political confusion was made worse by the existence of multiple offers of political alliance or collaboration, resulting in temporary liaisons between ideologically incompatible groups. The emotional atmosphere often bred unrealistic expectations, making leaders prisoners of their own rhetoric. Failing to win a place in the formal distribution of state power after 1948, opposition leaders felt they had no alternative but to resort to arms, either to carve out a separate state, or to seize state power.

The conflicts which underlay the civil war did not erupt until independence was assured. As long as the possibility of external control remained, the majority of internal groups were willing to submerge their differences. The defeat of the Japanese in Burma between February and late May 1945, three months before the surrender of the imperial Japanese government, created an illusion for individuals and groups attached to the colonial state that the return of the British would lead to a restoration of the political *status quo ante bellum*. This was the intention of the government in London and the governor-in-exile in India, and of those within Burma who had prospered under the colonial state. The returning British-Indian army was instructed to prepare the way for a return to civilian government under the pre-war governor (with temporarily enhanced administrative powers) until pre-war economic and political 'normality' could be restored. That was not to be, however, for between May 1945 and October 1946 the major internal political groups gathered together under the umbrella of the AFPFL maintained sufficient cohesion to apply pressure on the British to depart. The AFPFL persisted with its threat of rebellion, and once it had been made clear to London by the Indian National Congress that the British-Indian army was no longer at the disposal of the colonial authorities to suppress 'freedom movements', there was no viable alternative to granting independence. The British Labour government recognized that to attempt to hold on to power in the face of widespread nationalist armed resistance, even if Britain could muster a military force for an unpopular and expensive colonial war, might result in victory for the Burma Communist Party. Such a result would have undermined Britain's remaining strategic and economic interests in South and Southeast Asia, as well as in Burma.[16]

16. See Robert H. Taylor, 'Burma in the Anti-Fascist War', in Alfred W. McCoy

Once independence was assured following the Aung San-Attlee agreement of January 1947, the energies of all the political groups in Burma turned to a internecine struggle for a place in the new order. Nationalist unity now took second place to political advantage. Though all the major contending groups had their origins in Burma's pre-war political history, the forms they took in the late 1940s were new. Some of the parliamentary-style parties of the 1920s and 1930s had had their own 'pocket armies' but had been forced for the most part to accept the conditions of electoral politics within the order upheld by the colonial state. Under that order, groups who cooperated were guaranteed rights and privileges which were denied those who voiced revolutionary opposition. But unlike in India, where the same laws had applied, none of the political parties of the colonial era survived other than in name into the postcolonial political world, and extra-state coercive capacities became necessary for political survival after 1948.

During the war years, although the government of Dr Ba Maw attempted to develop a monopolistic political organization, *Maha Barma* (Greater Burma), out of the pre-war *Thakin* movement and the *Hsinyeitha* party, this grouping had little effect on the political life of the country other than to provide a cover for activists in underground resistance cells. The absence of electoral politics and the creation of a one-party pseudo-fascist state by Ba Maw and his associates, coupled with the economic and social dislocations caused by the war, provided no focus for political loyalty and little opportunity for individuals with organizational skills who sought to operate under state auspices. But below the surface of *Maha Bama* and officially sanctioned subordinate organizations there developed the politicized officer corps in the Burma army, the sizeable Marxist-oriented movements calling themselves Communist or Socialist, and the religious/ethnic minority political and paramilitary organizations exemplified by Christian Karens who worked closely with British wartime intelligence bodies. All of these groups emerged at the end of the war to collude briefly but uneasily in the AFPFL. But the people they mobilized — to oppose first the British, then the Japanese, and again the British — were turned against each other in the civil war, which lasted longer and was far more destructive than the struggle against British and Japanese imperialism.

(ed.), *Southeast Asia Under Japanese Occupation* (New Haven: Yale University Southeast Asia Studies Series no. 22, 1980), pp. 162–3.

The Army The core of the Burma army, though the longest established armed group at the start of the civil war, was formed only in July 1942 when the Burma Defence Army (BDA) was established under Japanese supervision from the 23,000 or so youths who had made up the Burma Independence Army (BIA). The BIA had swollen in number during the previous four months as young nationalists rallied to the call of the 'Thirty Comrades' whom the Japanese had trained to lead an anti-British force. Only 5,000 were selected to form the 'professional' BDA. Renamed the Burma National Army (BNA) in August 1943 at the time of the grant of nominal independence by the Japanese, the army was then a small infantry force used primarily for garrison and ceremonial duties. Its first officer training school, founded in 1942 at Mingaladon north of Rangoon, provided a large proportion of the politicized officer corps which split between supporters of the AFPFL government and the Communist party soon after the beginning of the civil war.[17]

The BIA had provided a model of youthful adventure and independent political action, especially as its leader, General Aung San, already well known among the student population for his leadership of the student union and *Thakin* movements in the late 1930s, had spurned the prevailing wisdom about what was politically possible under the colonial state, creating a style of political daring that many others were to emulate during the succeeding twenty years. The BIA grew out of the desire of leading *Thakins* and students to find a source of foreign assistance that would provide arms and training for the raising of a force to drive out the British. The approach of the Second World War, together with the progress of the Chinese Communist revolution, led nationalists to look to Japan or China as possible sources of such aid. On August 8, 1940, Aung San and another *Thakin* sailed from Rangoon in search of Chinese Communist assistance, but in the meantime Ba Maw and his party made contact with Colonel Suzuki of the Japanese Imperial Army. Through their discussions it was arranged that the Japanese should find Aung San in Amoy and take him to Japan. This was done and he returned to Burma in February 1941 to recruit a band of colleagues for training as the officer corps for a new Burmese military force. By July 1941 thirty men had been assembled on Hainan Island under the Japanese,

---

17. This section is based upon a fuller discussion of the development and political role of the army in Robert H. Taylor, 'Burma', in Zakaria Ahmad and Harold Crouch (eds), *Military-Civilian Relations in South-East Asia* (Singapore: Oxford University Press, 1985), pp. 13–49.

and these formed the core of the BIA which was raised in Bangkok and southeastern Burma in December 1941 and January 1942.

The BIA was different in character as well as in purpose from the army of the colonial state. The bulk of the colonial state's indigenous forces were recruited from various hill-peoples living along the borders with China and India or from among the Karen community. Lowland troops other than those designated as Karen were not recruited except for a brief period during the First World War and immediately before the Japanese invasion. The British force disintegrated as the Japanese advanced and the much larger regular British-Indian army retreated to India. However, some of the troops, especially Karens from the eastern border regions, remained in the country and towards the end of the war played leading roles in the formation of an anti-Japanese Karen resistance force while working with the BIA to lessen communal tensions in the delta.

The BIA was nationalist in the narrowest sense. It did not pass through the major frontier zones as it advanced into the country with the Japanese, and therefore its recruits were mainly from the most highly commercialized regions of southern Burma. Excluded from its ranks were members of the major immigrant communities as well as the hill peoples. Most of the officers of the BIA as well as their successors were from urban communities and many had achieved secondary, and in some cases university, educations. The ordinary soldiers were youths, disproportionately drawn from groups other than the peasant class until the final mobilization against the Japanese in 1945.[18] Given its narrowly nationalist basis and social origins, it is not surprising that the BIA officer corps tended to perceive Burma's political problems primarily in cultural and ethnic terms, rather than in terms of class or ideology.

The post-BIA officer corps which became the core of the Burma army after July 1942 developed careers within the confines of a small and corporately self-conscious organization. For those on the fringes of wealth and power in colonial society the army served as an important route of social mobility. Its popularity as a liberating force was, however, short-lived, and within a year of formation officers had to seek means of regaining popular support. As the army became identified with Japanese brutalities and the economic hardships of the war, officers, including Minister of War Aung San, sought to alter the attitude of their troops toward the civilian population while seeking a political alternative to the

18. Guyot, 'Political Impact of the Japanese Occupation', p. 334.

Japanese alliance. The army's unpopularity had become so great by the middle of the war that it was difficult to recruit additional men to expand the force to its authorized size of 10,000.

During the war the BNA developed two characteristics. One was its officers' and men's loyalty to the notion of Burmese independence and the necessity of having the support of the people. The other was that the army felt it necessary to involve itself in politics in order to compete with other political groups and to achieve the officer corps' notions of a correct social and political order. The wartime officer training school graduated five classes, passing out 791 officers. These men received a thorough Japanese-style military education, but many secretly studied Chinese and other Communist writings on the nature of a 'people's army' made available to them by cadres from the underground Communist Party. Professionalization was thus combined with a political and populist purpose encouraged by leading officers.

The BNA faced a serious external threat to its existence in 1944–5 as Japanese power began to wane relative to the force of the Allies in India and China. In the eyes of the British, the BNA in 1944 was a 'quisling' organization which could on moral grounds be denied any role in postwar Burma; the BNA was guilty of treason against the King/Emperor and would be punished accordingly. The BNA leadership had thus to search for a means not only of redeeming their political popularity in Burma but also of making themselves acceptable to the Allies if they were to have a role in the post-war campaign for Burma's independence. Such a means appeared in the form of a coalition with the Burma Communist Party. The BCP had made contact with the Allies in 1942 and since that time had been organizing the peasantry in Burma to oppose fascism and take power in an anti-imperialist revolution. The Anti-Fascist Organization (AFO), formed under the leadership of General Aung San and Communist leader Thakin Soe, in August 1944, was the answer to the BNA's dilemma.[19]

When the army, secretly renamed the People's Army, marched out of Rangoon on March 27, 1945 to fight the Japanese as the armed force of the AFO united front (renamed the AFPFL), it helped to guarantee the officer corps a role in the future of Burma. In so doing it demonstrated its patriotism to the population and its power to the British. The army also

19. See Robert H. Taylor, 'Introduction: Marxism and Resistance in Wartime Burma', in Robert H. Taylor, *Marxism and Resistance in Burma 1942–1945: Thein Pe Myint's 'Wartime Traveller'*, pp. 51–69.

managed to make itself seem indispensable as an armed force to the civilian political leadership, including the Communists. March 27, now celebrated annually as Army Day or Resistance/Revolution (*Towhlanyei*) Day, marks the army's position as a major force in Burma's politics.

The success of the army in assuring itself a political future was the result of the astute political leadership of Aung San, who until his assassination at the age of 32 in July 1947 was able to lead the Communist-inspired AFPFL national front in negotiations with the British, while reassuring the growing conservative elements within the League that the Communists would not control the post-independence state. After the return of the British, Aung San concerned himself with ensuring the integrity and political loyalty of the army to the AFPFL — of which he became President in May 1945 in place of Thakin Soe. Abandoning an initial demand that the British recognize the AFPFL as a provisional government and the BNA as an allied army, Aung San, in collaboration with Thakin Tun Tun, who replaced Soe as leader of the Communists at this time, settled for a compromise with the newly established British Military Administration. The essence of the agreement allowed for the continuation of the role of the army by placing it legally under the control of British military law while maintaining a popular and anti-British force in the form of the People's Volunteer Organization (PVO), a veterans' body primarily loyal to Aung San but with ties to various other officers serving in, or demobilized from, the BNA.

The Kandy agreement, as the deal struck between Aung San and the British Southeast Asia Commander, Admiral Mountbatten, became known, was viewed as a threat by many in the officer corps who feared that the disarmament of most of their troops and the command of the remainder by British officers would allow the Communists to take control of the independence movement. It had been the policy of most of the leading Communists since 1944 to cooperate with the returning British, and anti-Communist officers interpreted this strategy as directed as much against them as against the Japanese fascists with whom followers of Thakin Soe said they were aligned. Nonetheless, Aung San conceded in September that the army was not the legal force of an independent state as he had claimed in May. In the long term, however, the Kandy agreement was distinctly to the advantage of those officers and men who sided with the British.

The Kandy agreement provided the AFPFL with a body of men loyal to it yet within the British colonial army, thus allowing the independence movement to penetrate a main pillar of state power. But the army was then placed in a position to side with the British against the state's rivals, especially the Communists. In time, the British became increasingly dependent upon the former BIA troops as regular British and Indian troops were withdrawn. The former People's Army was engaged in pursuing Communist guerrillas and dacoits in the area around the oil fields of Yenangyaung during 1947. Called 'Operation Flush', it was the first major campaign conducted by a wholly indigenous state force since 1885. The force which carried out the operation was the 4th Burma Rifles, under the command of Lt.-Colonel Ne Win.[20]

The civil war of 1948–52 provided the army with important corporate experiences. In 1942 and again in 1945–6 it had been forced to shed some politicized officers and men in the interest of discipline and order, as required by the Japanese and the British. In 1948–9 the army experienced a third major shedding of personnel, but this time many officers and men went voluntarily, deserting to join one or another of the paramilitary organizations which took up arms against the state. By mid-1948 three battalions of the army along with more than half of the PVO's, known as the White Band, had joined the Communist side. The only units to remain loyal to the AFPFL government were Ne Win's 4th Burma Rifles and Karen, Kachin and Chin units which the independent state had inherited from the British. In December 1948 the 3rd Battalion Karen Rifles along with many Karen military and civilian police joined the rebellion of the Karen National Union, and the following month they were joined by the 1st Kachin Rifles.

The remaining officer corps drew two lessons from these experiences. The first lesson was the necessity of keeping party factionalism out of the army by maintaining corporate loyalty over ideological or party loyalties; the second was the necessity of ensuring that extra-military ethnic loyalties were not encouraged by organizational structures. The British practice of organizing troops on the basis of ethnicity had been perpetuated after 1945 at the insistence of the AFPFL leadership in order to ensure the loyalty of former BNA troops to them. During the civil war, this policy greatly weakened the solidarity of the state's armed forces.

The army's military and political experiences, both domestic and international, were crucial in shaping the officer corps' attitudes and policies in subsequent years. Faced by a plethora of enemies, Communist

20. Maung Maung, *Burma and General Ne Win* (New York: Asia Publishing House 1969), pp. 180–4.

and ethnic separatist, and supported by a weak and uncertain civilian government, the army leadership developed the ability to function independently of civilian control. The fact that the civilian government was unable to gain any significant external aid or equipment for the army during the most perilous years of the civil war, coupled with the backing that the Chinese Nationalist KMT troops in the Shan States received from Taiwan, Thailand and the United States, convinced the army leadership of the necessity of self-reliance.[21]

The inclusion of army Supreme Commander General Ne Win in the cabinet in April 1949 as Deputy Prime Minister and Minister for Home Affairs as well as for Defence[22] made official for a brief period what was unofficial throughout the first fourteen years of Burma's independence. All civilian governments were dependent upon the army for office, for it was only the loyalty that the army gave the civilian leadership and the norms of the constitution that kept one or another of the rival insurgent groups from seizing state power. Despite its formal adherence to the principles of the constitution between 1948 and 1962, the army remained a politically involved group even after Ne Win left the cabinet in September 1950. Several officers maintained close personal and political ties with the leading Socialist group in the cabinet. And political ambition, the motivation for joining the army in 1942, had not evaporated with the development of a regular state army. Many of the non-commissioned and commissioned officers recruited in the civil war and after joined for political reasons, and many NCO's who had joined in the anti-Communist and anti-KNU struggles were given commissions as the army rebuilt after the civil war.[23]

The Communists The Communist movement in Burma was never a well organized political force like the Communist Party of Vietnam. Its roots lie very late in the colonial period: the first 'party cell' was formed by Aung San, Soe and other *Thakins* in 1939, and the first underground 'party congress' was held in 1943 by Soe and one or two others. It had few articulated institutional structures and its pretentiously named

21. For details of the KMT affair and its effects on the politics of Burma, see Robert H. Taylor, *Foreign and Domestic Consequences of the KMT Intervention in Burma* (Ithaca: Cornell University Southeast Asia Program Data Paper no. 93, 1973).
22. Maung Maung, *Burma and General Ne Win*, pp. 214–6, 222.
23. Moshe Lissak, 'Social Change, Mobilization, and Exchange of Services between the Military Establishment and the Civil Society: The Burmese Case', *Economic Development and Cultural Change*, XIII, 1, pp. 5–6.

central committee was little more than a rallying-point for local enthusiasts. Nonetheless, the Communist movement soon assumed a major role in the political life of the country throughout the 1940s and 1950s, and its leaders thought themselves to be near to taking state power in the period between 1945–8. The strength of the Communist movement stemmed from the importance of its leaders in providing the ideas and formal organizational structure of the national united front after 1944, and from the power they appeared to demonstrate through the support of workers and peasants in opposing the policies and programmes of the Japanese, the British, and the AFPFL controlled government. Internal party feuding contributed to the decline of the Communist movement in the 1960s, but by then much of its programme had become less relevant and its ineffectual leadership had led to a decline in the respect which it had previously enjoyed.

The leadership of the Communist movement centred upon a few intellectuals and activists from the pre-war *Do Bama Asiayon*. Though assisted by others the key figures, Thakin Soe and Thakin Than Tun, were the focus of the movement. Soe, the most important left-wing polemicist in colonial Burma, was largely responsible for introducing Marxist-Leninist political concepts through the idiom of Burmese Buddhist thought to politically active students and others before the war. Convinced of the political and moral correctness of current international Communist strategy he did not believe in 1940–41, as did the leaders of the future army, that it was possible to enter into an alliance with the Japanese fascists in order to gain Burma's independence from the British imperialists. Taking a longer view of the political situation inside and outside Burma and sharing the beliefs of left-wing political forces in much of the world at that time that fascism and militarism were the primary enemy of colonial liberation movements, he argued that it was necessary first to attack the Japanese in collaboration with the British and other capitalist allies then in alliance with the Soviet Union. Despite its initial unpopularity at the start of the war, the Communist Party's ideological and strategic views of 1941–2 were interpreted as having been correct in 1944–5 (in contrast to those of the army and civilian leaders who had worked with the Japanese), and their advice on political strategy and tactics at the end of the war was thought to be grounded in an historically valid theoretical perspective.

Furthermore, untainted by collaboration with the Japanese Soe and other Communists spent the war years travelling the villages, setting up anti-fascist units and teaching the peasants Soe's particular understanding of Communism and the importance of organization in ending foreign rule and achieving revolution. The fact that the Communists were able to maintain contacts with the outside world through India via their association with the British intelligence organization Force 136 (the Asian section of the intelligence and sabotage agency established by the British war cabinet, the Special Operations Executive) also gave them a superior knowledge of international affairs; this proved an advantage in political debates. At the end of the war, accepting the advice of the Indian Communist Party and its interpretation of the wartime 'Browderist line' (which advanced the view that an anti-imperialist revolution would not be necessary after the war in order to achieve national independence and socialism because the United States and other capitalist states would be forced to come to terms with new, radical world-wide class forces), the Communists were able to join with the army and cooperate in the speedy defeat of fascism, which would lead, they thought inevitably, to independence under the guidance of left-wing forces.

The other major Communist figure was Thakin Than Tun. Although less of an intellectual than Soe he was a superior organizer. During the war he served as Minister of Agriculture in Ba Maw's cabinet and achieved a reputation as an effective administrator with a good understanding of agrarian problems. In that capacity he toured the countryside, meeting with peasants and making himself known as their champion. Toward the end of the war he joined with Soe and the Communist Party (Burma) (CP[B]) in circulating the underground propaganda of the anti-fascist national front. In mid-1945 he succeeded in ousting Thakin Soe from the leadership of the party over issues of strategy as well as of personal behaviour. From then on Than Tun was considered to be, along with General Aung San, one of the two most important political leaders of the country. Than Tun's removal of Soe from the leadership of the CP(B) set in motion a split between them and their followers which eventually made it easier for the anti-Communist forces to halt their drive for power.[24]

Both before and after the defeat of the Japanese the Communists gained a great deal of influence among the peasantry because of their advocacy of popular agrarian policies, especially the non-payment of rent and taxes and the abolition of peasant debts. Many of their local leaders

24. A detailed discussion of this period is found in Taylor, *Marxism and Resistance in Burma*, 'Introduction: Marxism and Resistance in Wartime Burma'.

were first mobilized as cadres of the Japanese-sponsored East Asia Youth League,[25] but at the end of the war they continued to agitate for the redress of peasant grievances. Their efforts were emulated by other groups, all of which adopted leftist slogans and symbols. As an American diplomat made clear in a report written in March 1946, the Communist programme was the most appealing to the peasantry, and even politicians such as General Aung San who did not consider it sound felt they had to accept it. Echoing the programme of the *wunthanu* and *bu athin* of the 1920s, the Communists after the war

> advocated cancelling agricultural debt (owing mainly to Indian Chettyars), establishing cultivators as owners of their land, and reserving the country's oil, timber and mineral resources for the benefit of the Burman. Not all of the Peasants' Unions were Communist led, but the most effective appeal everywhere was to denounce landlords, moneylenders, and rice exporters, mostly Indian, who under protection of British rule had despoiled the Burman people. . . . Cultivators must unite to forestall the repayment of Government loans and to obtain cancellation of land rents and taxes for the current year. Aung San acquiesced in the program for political reasons. . . .[26]

The popularity of such an appeal was obvious and no political leader wishing to demonstrate his ability to maintain mass opposition to the British could afford to stand against it until he was assured state power.

In the organization of peasant support for the nationalist movement, and the maintenance of an air of political uncertainty and revolutionary fervour, the Communists were the most visible political force in the three years between the end of the war and the formal grant of independence. Their leaders, however, were gradually squeezed out of the leadership of the anti-imperialist national front after the AFPFL's non-Communist leaders amended its constitution in May 1946 to exclude political parties.[27] When the British offered control of the Governor's executive council (the effective cabinet) to Aung San and the AFPFL in October 1946, the BCP refused to cooperate because the Labour government in London had yet to promise independence — a prerequisite for cooperation with the imperialists stipulated in AFPFL resolutions for

---

25. Guyot, 'Political Impact of the Japanese Occupation', pp. 296–8.
26. John F. Cady, 'The Character and Program of the Communist Party in Burma' (Rangoon: American Consulate General, 26 March 1946), p. 2.
27. Walter D. Sutton, 'Aung San of Burma', *The South Atlantic Quarterly*, vol. XLVII,1 (Jan., 1984), pp. 1–16.

over a year.[28] According to Than Tun's version of events during 1947, before and after the assassination of Aung San the BCP continued to seek to cooperate with the League in order to ensure independence, and to limit the degree of control that right-wing and imperialist forces could gain over the soon-to-be-independent state. They were, however, rebuffed in these efforts.[29]

Thus, when independence came, the Communists were denied any role in the state other than that of a loyal but powerless opposition. The CP(B) split in January 1946 between the smaller Soe faction, the Red Flags, and Than Tun's newly named White Flag Burma Communist Party (BCP) over collaboration with non-Communist groups and the passive revolutionary strategy of Than Tun. Subsequently, the major civilian group within the AFPFL stood by and watched politicians who had worked with the British before the war or with the Japanese during it form the first independent government of Burma since 1885.

After the expulsion of the Communists from the League, the CP(B) and BCP agitated to undermine the legitimacy of the AFPFL-led state because of its leaders' abandonment of the goals of the anti-fascist revolution. The Communists opposed the government both for its agrarian policies and for its post-independence agreements with the British, including the government's acceptance of a. debt obligations to Britain, b. the maintenance of a British military advisory mission in Burma, and c. British rights to use staging bases in Burma for military action elsewhere in Asia.[30] Believing that their popular support was wider than it apparently was, the two Communist factions claimed that they would bring down the government; Soe's by armed revolution and Than Tun's by mass organization. Soe's group had been declared illegal by the British in 1946 but Than Tun's party remained a legal organization into the early 1950s. However, on the night of March 27, 1948, the

---

28. San San Myint, 'Hpa Hsa Pa La Hkit Myanma Naingnganyei Thamaing' (Political History of Burma in the AFPFL Era) (unpubl. MA thesis, Rangoon Arts and Sciences University, pp. 73–4, citing *Pyithu Ana Gyane* (*People's Power Journal*), vol. 3, no. 1 (2-10-46), p. 4. See also Sein Win, *The Split Story* (Rangoon: Guardian Press, 1959).
29. *Hpa Hsa Pa La — Konmyunit Apyanahlan Peisa* (*AFPFL-Communist Correspondence*) (Rangoon: Pyithu Ana Punhnat Taik, 1947), pp. a–b. Introduction written by Thakin Than Tun.
30. *Hpa Hsa Pa La — Konmyunit Apyanahlan Peisa*, pp. c–d; San San Myint, 'Hpa Hsa Pa La Hkit', p. 206, p. 211. See also, John F. Cady, *Post-War Southeast Asia: Independence Problems* (Athens, Ohio: Ohio University Press, 1974), pp. 63–4.

government ordered the arrest of the BCP's leaders. Having been tipped off by Party sympathizers in the bureaucracy (for the state apparatus was riddled with supporters of various political groups), the Communists went underground.

Despite their organizational weaknesses, at the beginning of the civil war the Communists were probably the most popular political party in large sections of the country, especially the rice growing areas. Loyal to them were between 15,000 to 20,000 armed troops, mostly veterans of the anti-Japanese resistance movement. In addition, they were joined by about 9,000 former BNA troops in the White Band PVO and several hundred troops from the government army in mid-year.[31] The Communists had their greatest success in areas where they had been active during and after the war, such as the delta and around Pyinmana. As early as 1946 the Communist led Peasants' Union in Yamethin district claimed to have enrolled 33,000 members; its activities greatly overshadowed the organizational efforts of the peasants' groups which supported the AFPFL and its Socialist Party leaders. The Socialists had lost what support they had among the peasants by their advocacy of cooperation with landlords and of the payment of rents and taxes.[32]

But the Communists were unable to sustain their drive against the government's forces, especially as they were short of equipment and ammunition. Some Communist forces rallied to the government in early 1949 when the Karen National Defence Organization (KNDO) also went into rebellion. The Communists' lack of organization and their inability to provide protection for peasant families or to implement policies in the face of the government's refusal to recognize their actions negated much of their initial support. Even though a good portion of the public thought the Communist leaders had been denied state power by the scheming of the Socialists,[33] support drifted away from them in the early 1950s because they lacked the organizational structures and military power to sustain their campaigns. Nonetheless, a great deal of sympathy for the Communist agrarian programme and the Party's leaders persisted into the 1950s. The fact that they had come close to taking power twice in Burma's post-war history, once peacefully in 1947–8 and once by arms in 1948–50, gave the Communists a degree of

---

31. San San Myint, 'Hpa Hsa Pa La Hkit', p. 211.
32. Cady, 'Character and Program of the Communist Party in Burma', p. 3.
33. Khin Maung Kyi, 'Patterns of Accommodation to Bureaucratic Authority', p. 107.

prestige that they would not otherwise have had. Much of the electoral support given to anti-AFPFL left-wing legal political parties in the 1950s reflected the continuing popularity of the Communists long after they had been declared an illegal organization.

Non-Communist Movements and Political Parties Throughout the two decades of the contest for control of the state there emerged a variety of other political parties and movements beside the army and the Communists representing various ideological perspectives, class or sectional interests, and religious and ethno-linguistic groups. A few of these movements were developed by the controllers of the government of the day, such as the *Maha Bama* movement of the Second World War or the National Solidarity Association founded by the army during the 1958–60 'caretaker' period. These were not of lasting significance, but the model of political organization they provided was often emulated by more autonomous movements.

Some of the more important political parties and movements had their roots in the colonial period. The oldest was the Karen Central Organization (KCO), which, though formed only in 1945, was a lineal descendant of the Karen National Association which had been established in 1881 and was Burma's first modern political organization.[34] The KCO divided in 1947 when the Karen National Union (KNU) was founded. Others had much shorter lineages. The AFPFL can perhaps be traced back to the pre-war *Thakin* movement, but its organizational form emerged in August 1944, and between then and 1947 it lost its two formative members, the Communists and the army, and was after 1948 a rump organization.

Many minor parties sprang up at the time of elections. The Patriotic Alliance, for example, formed in the early 1950s and composed of a motley collection of older politicians and a few new ones, made little impact on the political scene. Other parties were founded by leaders of minority communities in the border areas which were drawn into state-centred politics for the first time. These served as the vehicles for the political support of various traditional leaders and groups, such as Kachin *Duwas*, and Shan and Karenni *Sawbwas*. The People's Economic and Cultural Development Organization, for example, was founded in 1953 by the Buddhist Sima Duwa to rival the power of the Christian-

34. J.W. Baldwin, 'The Karens in Burma', *Journal of the Royal Central Asian Society*, XXXVI (1949), p. 108.

oriented Kachin National Congress headed by Duwa Zau Lawn. The United Hill People's Congress was founded in 1947 by Shan *Sawbwas* to counter the growing influence among their subjects of the egalitarian and Rangoon-focused Shan State People's Freedom League.[35]

When it became the basis of the first government of independent Burma under the leadership of Thakin Nu in 1948, the AFPFL was a very different organization from the one which had led the fight against the Japanese and the British in 1945. The AFO was expanded under the name of the AFPFL in March 1945 by including in its nine-member executive committee three representatives of the People's Revolution group, the forerunners of the post-war Socialist Party. Like the BIA in 1942, in 1945 local AFPFL leaders assumed administrative powers in areas abandoned by the Japanese before the returning British Military Administration could take control. The League's cooperative policy with the British, despite opposition from some regional leaders and army commanders who argued that they were abandoning a chance for genuine independence, was carried out on orders from the central army and Communist leadership in Rangoon.

The policy of cooperation with the British and the consequent opening of membership in the League to conservative nationalist leaders and groups led to the first major fracture of the Communist Party and hence of the AFPFL. Subsequently, the League became increasingly heterodox in membership, with smaller groups joining such as some of the pre-war organizations for women and youth. Although they had little impact on its level of support among the public generally, their leaders demanded a say in policy, lessening the AFPFL's revolutionary potential as it adapted to less radical urban and middle-class interests. The Socialist leaders were keen to use the support of the older conservative elements in order to lessen the power of the Communists, and this was one of the reasons for their opposition to the no-rent/no-taxes appeal of the Communist-led peasant unions.

However, until the removal of Thakin Than Tun as League General Secretary, the AFPFL remained under strong but politically moderate Communist and left-wing influence. The Communist candidate for succession to Than Tun, Thein Pe, lost the leadership struggle in June 1946 by one vote to the Socialist leader and future deputy prime minister

---

35. A fuller discussion of political parties during this period is found in Robert H. Taylor, 'Burma', in Haruhiro Fukui (ed.), *Political Parties of Asia and the Pacific* (Westport, Conn.: Greenwood Press, 1985), vol. I, pp. 99–154.

Kyaw Nyein. After the Communists were expelled from the League five months later, the best organized leftist groups remaining within it were the PVO, the Trade Union Congress-Burma (TUC-B), and the All Burma Peasants' Organization (ABPO). The PVO was badly factionalized and the majority joined with the Communists in the civil war. The TUC-B and ABPO both lost many members when the Communists were expelled from the League and rival Communist-led organizations were established.

As the civil war raged in the months immediately after independence, the AFPFL government of Prime Minister Nu exercised little influence outside of Rangoon. The government relied increasingly on non-AFPFL support from various groups besides the army and the bureaucracy and on foreign aid to remain in power. The last ardently radical members of the League were expelled in December 1950, when left-wing Socialists quit the Socialist Party to form the Burma Workers' and Peasants' Party. In their view, the AFPFL government and its Socialist ministers had abandoned the goals of Burma's revolution by shifting away from Marxism-Leninism, by accepting United States aid and the American position on the Korean war in the United Nations, and by 'the enactment of legislation dealing with religion', specifically the Buddha Sasana Council Act. This act 'created a state-financed agency for the promotion and propagation of Buddhism', the purpose of which, according to the Prime Minister, was to 'challenge openly other ideological forces [but not other religions] at work in the country'.[36] The League's loss of popular support following independence made it increasingly reliant upon the instruments of the state to remain in power. As the state was weak, the League's ability to control affairs remained tenuous. Nonetheless, the League remained the country's major legal political party until it split in 1958, for no other group was able to directly tap the patronage and fiscal powers of the state during that time.

As it abandoned its founders and their Marxist ideology, the AFPFL lost its initial unifying set of beliefs. The heroism and martyrdom of General Aung San and the story of the independence movement provided the symbols and ideals which were its main asset (along with the charisma of U Nu). The leaders of the League, with the exception of Nu, were mainly members of the Socialist party and espoused a variety of welfare socialism similar to that of the British Labour Party in the 1940s

---

36. Donald Eugene Smith, *Religion and Politics in Burma* (Princeton University Press, 1965,), pp. 126-7.

and 1950s. The League increasingly based its strength on its control of the state bureaucracy. AFPFL ministers and cadres closely involved themselves in administrative decisions to ensure that their supporters were rewarded and their opponents denied preference. League organizers directed vital programmes such as land reform by supervising the work of the village land committees and the granting of annual government crop loans. Import/export licence awards were a mainstay of the League's support from the business community, where, despite attempts at creating government monopolies and encouraging Burmese entrepreneurs, Indian businessmen still played a large role. The executive committee of the League was the real centre of decision-making, not the government cabinet room.

The power of ministers came from the personal influence they had over key subordinate organisations of the League and the government. Ba Swe, a deputy prime minister through much of the 1950s and briefly Prime Minister, was vice-president of the AFPFL, head of the Socialist Party and head of the Trades Union Congress-Burma. Thakin Tin, holder of the agriculture ministry, was head of the All Burma Peasants' Organization. Kyaw Nyein, a deputy prime minister and secretary-general of the League, forged a power base from the great influence he wielded through the Home Ministry, with its control over the police, especially the Union Military Police, and the judicial system.

Local units of the League had little influence upon the centre; they were largely moribund between elections. The active units were often riven with factionalism between supporters and opponents of the Socialists. Most local leaders worked for the organization in order to gain access to the patronage and favours that their patrons at the centre could provide. Though the leaders claimed that there were 1,287,290 members of the League in 1957, many of these were nominal, for membership came automatically with enrollment in one of the subordinate organizations such as a labour union. So uncertain of their support within the League were the leaders that they failed to hold a national congress between 1947 and 1958; the 1958 congress was held only because by then the leadership had become so factionalized that they wanted to determine which group had the support of the rank-and-file.

In its thirteen years of existence, the AFPFL faced three nation-wide elections. The first, held in April 1947, was for the election of the constituent assembly to draft an independent constitution: 255 members were elected, 210 in 'Burma proper' and the other 45 in the former 'frontier areas'. The AFPFL or affiliated organizations won all but seven of the seats. The victory was less impressive that it seems, for the two principal opposition parties, the BCP and the KNU, urged voters to boycott the polls as the *wunthanu athin* had done in the 1920s. Nevertheless, seven independent Communists were elected against AFPFL candidates. The League and its associates in the PVO controlled the machinery of the election because many of their members were by then employed in government service and staffed large sections of local government. In some areas of central Burma, Indian, British and Burmese troops were used to maintain sufficient government control to allow campaigning and polling to proceed. The AFPFL dominated assembly elected at that time served as the parliament until 1951.

The national elections held in 1951 were conducted in three stages because of the continuing civil war. Out of 8 million eligible voters only 1.5 million cast their ballots, a turnout of less than 20 per cent, little more than during the boycotts of the 1920s and less than in 1936. The AFPFL was the victor in this election also, winning 147 seats out of the total of 250 in its own name and gaining the support of another 50 or so candidates from affiliated organizations. The remaining seats were won by independents and left- and right-wing parties. But despite its sweep of the legislature, the League actually received only about 60 per cent of the votes cast.

The League next faced the voters in 1956. At that time the major legal opposition parties banded together in a coalition, the National United Front (NUF), in an effort to break the AFPFL's domination of the government. Issues such as inflation, social stability and corruption were prominent in the campaign. More than twice as many voters cast their ballots in 1956 as in 1951. Again, the AFPFL won control of the legislature, with the NUF winning only 48 seats. The AFPFL's share of the popular vote, however, fell to about 48 per cent.[37] The decline of popular support for the League accelerated through the 1950s and its leaders became increasingly distrustful of each other as they fought over the spoils of power for distribution to their factional supporters. The result was not only a split in the AFPFL but also the collapse of the government in 1958, threatening a 'Civil War among the anti-Communists'.[38]

---

37. Maung Maung, *Burma and General Ne Win*, pp. 226–7; Josef Silverstein, *Burma, Military Rule and the Politics of Stagnation* (Ithaca: Cornell University Press, 1977), p. 69.
38. Richard Butwell, *U Nu of Burma* (Stanford University Press, repr. 1969), p. 205.

Following the splitting of the AFPFL earlier in the year Bo Min Gaung became Home Minister and thus gained control of the Union Military Police. The Socialist leaders, Ba Swe and Kyaw Nyein, both close allies of senior army officers, including Brigadier Maung Maung and Colonel Aung Gyi, sought the support of the army to return to power. Ba Swe had claimed publicly that their faction, referred to as the 'Stable AFPFL', had army backing, and Nu's so-called 'Clean AFPFL' faction claimed that a coup was imminent.[39] By September 1958 the capital was surrounded both by troops of the regular army and by the Union Military Police. In order to forestall armed conflict between them and thus re-open the possibility of the Communists taking power, Maung Maung and Aung Gyi convinced Prime Minister Nu to hand over power to a six-month 'caretaker' army government headed by army commander General Ne Win.[40]

The military caretaker government attempted to 'clean up' the country and its politics. After remaining in power for eighteen months it conducted a national election. In the campaign the radical Marxist and Socialist rhetoric of the 1940s and early 1950s was largely forgotten, except by minor party or non-party independent candidates such as former Brigadier Kyaw Zaw, who attacked the continued role of the United States in backing the KMT in the Shan State, or by the candidates of small leftist parties which did not possess the financial backing of the two major parties. The major parties' campaign slogans centred on the relationship of religion, especially Buddhism, to the state, and on the issue of whether the nominally ethno-linguistic states created in 1947 should be increased in number and granted autonomy. The continuing role of foreigners in the economy was also raised, but this was played down by U Nu and his followers because of their continuing contacts with foreign businessmen.[41] The election was won by Nu's 'Clean' faction, soon renamed the Union Party, despite or perhaps because of the support that the army had given to the 'Stable' faction.

The political scene in Rangoon was no more settled after the elections. Though the split of the AFPFL in 1958 might be seen, at least by

39. Louis J. Walinsky, *Economic Development in Burma, 1951–60* (New York: Twentieth Century Fund, 1962), pp. 247–8.
40. Butwell, *U Nu of Burma*, pp. 204–5; 'Parliament Meets', *Burma Weekly Bulletin*, vol. 7, no. 30 (6 Nov. 1958), pp. 258–9; Maung Maung, *Burma's Constitution*, p. 48; Nu, *U Nu — Saturday's Son* (New Haven: Yale University Press, 1975), pp. 326–7.
41. Silverstein, *Burma: Military Rule*, p. 70.

the League's sincere supporters, as a tragedy, the factionalisation of Nu's Union Party had, by mid-1961, assumed the proportions of a farce. His party and government were held together by little more than the name of one man, and when Nu threatened to resign after the next election a scramble for succession commenced. By early 1962 the ruling party had lost what little popular support it still retained.[42] But the increasingly chaotic politics of the political élite during the late 1950s and early 1960s was not merely a function of leadership and spoils rivalries.

The politics of this period were symptomatic of the condition of the state. Rather than determining the political agenda the state largely responded to demands made upon it by often contradictory political interests enunciating first principles as non-negotiable and axiomatic. Calls for ethnic autonomy and religious freedom were countered by demands for a unitary state and for support for the faith of the majority. Demands for socialism and a workers' state were countered by demands for the opening of the economy to foreign capital and for an end to state regulation and economic planning. With no clear ideals or institutions to guide them, state managers in the 1950s operated as best they could. The charismatic appeal of Prime Minister Nu was crucial for the perpetuation of the state, but his behaviour was too erratic to allow respect and loyalty to the state to become routine.

Old and New Functions of the State

Evidence of the displacement of the state between 1942 and 1962 is most clearly seen by the fact that it was much less capable of carrying out the minimal functions of maintaining order and regulating non-state institutions than the state had been under either the kings or the British. In addition, many of the functions the state assumed during the colonial period in the spheres of health, education and human welfare were carried out only with considerable inefficiency. Despite the widely-held belief that the functions of the state would change with the achievement of independence and the placing of power in the hands of indigenous leaders, one of the major consequences of the displacement of the state was the increased attention given by state managers to the functions of law and order and social control. In the meantime, repeated claims were made upon the state by political leaders and by others to assume even

42. *Ibid.*, p. 66.

greater responsibilities in regard to the management of the economy in the name, first, of wartime exigencies, then in the name of nationalism, and, finally, in the name of socialism. Ironically, the abandonment of the professed *laissez-faire* of the colonial state for the planned economy of the socialist state coincided with the collapse of the state power necessary for economic management.

Law and Order The displacement of the state from 1942 onwards was first experienced when the police and the military were unable to maintain social control during the Japanese invasion. The departure of nearly half a million people with the British was not the consequence solely of the change in administration and related personnel. Many, if not most, of the Indian and other non-European population who fled to India did so because of the breakdown of the control mechanisms of the state. The chaos of invasion led to a near collapse of the police and other instruments of order which had made life possible for the immigrant populations of colonial society. It has been estimated that about 1.5 million persons 'had their lives disjointed by military action'. From one-half to four-fifths of the remainder of the population 'were adversely affected by the breakdown of administration'.[43] The most telling figures on the breakdown of social control at this time are provided by the estimates for the rate of murder and dacoity. It is thought that more than 500 acts of murder per one million inhabitants occurred between February and June 1942. This compares with 73 per million in 1940. Dacoities during the same period probably reached more than 2,000 per million, compared to 41 per million two years previously.[44]

Though Dr Ba Maw's government did little to change the organization and functions of the police from those which had been created by the British, one of its first acts was to increase their number. By 1943 the force had been 'increased by 20 per cent over its pre-war strength or to 15,900 officers and men'. Men who had served both the British and new personnel were recruited 'in equal proportions'.[45] Nonetheless, the police remained ineffectual, and the most important coercive force in the country during the war was the Japanese army, especially the Kempetai (military police), which replaced the 'punitive police' of the colonial period as the most feared organization in the country. Even so, the costs

---

43. Guyot, 'Political Impact of the Japanese Occupation', p. 86.
44. *Ibid.*, Table 3, p. 152.
45. Abu, 'Collaboration, 1941–1945', p. 203.

of the indigenous police tripled during the war years while the total government funds devoted to law and order increased from about one-third to about one-half of the state's budget.[46]

During the British interlude between 1945 and 1948 efforts were made under both the British Military Administration (CAS[B]) and the civilian governors to restore the effectiveness of the police. Elaborate plans to ensure a better policed society had been drawn up by British officials while in exile in India. Their efforts were, however, largely in vain. After the war the police became highly politicized and strikes by the Rangoon police force in 1946 were among the events which prompted the handover of power from the governor to the AFPFL. In the first three months of 1947 the crime rate was higher than at any time for which records were available, except for the actual months of the Japanese invasion in 1942. The murder rate was more than double that of 1940 (180 per million population) while the dacoity rate was up from 41 per million to 1,260 per million.[47]

Such statistics become increasingly rare after independence, another indication of the state's declining control over society. The civil war resulted in widespread disorder, with violent death rates probably higher than at any time in modern Burma's history. Then, after the civil war subsided, the police were in many areas the least important of the agencies of social control. The army had responsibility for order, often assumed by local officers rather than authorized by the civilian ministers, and in some areas, as will be discussed below, local political bosses of the ruling AFPFL became the effective enforcers of whichever laws they found useful for maintaining their political base. The state continued to apportion a large percentage of its budget to law and order. In 1956, for example, 23 per cent of capital expenditures, the largest single capital heading, was devoted to law and order and defence.[48] In the first six years of independence military expenditure grew at an average rate (in constant price terms) of 35 per cent[49] and reached a peak equalling 6.7 per cent of gross domestic product in 1954.[50]

46. Guyot, 'Political Impact of the Japanese Occupation', Table 9, p. 212.
47. *Ibid.*, Table 3, p. 152.
48. *Economic Survey of Burma 1958* (Rangoon: Government Printing and Stationery, 1958), p. 120.
49. Stockholm International Peace Research Institute, *SIPRI Yearbook of World Armaments and Disarmament, 1968/69* (Stockholm: Almqvist and Wiksell, 1969), Table 1A.12. Far East: Constant price figures, pp. 208–9.
50. Stockholm International Peace Research Institute, *World Armaments and Disarma-*

Those responsible for the maintenance of law and order in the 1950s often looked back with some nostalgia to the colonial days when the state was able to maintain public order and thus allow a greater degree of public political activity. After the army caretaker government had worked for nearly eighteen months to suppress the private armies of local political bosses, General Ne Win, as commander of the armed forces, noted that under the British, even though there had been a great deal of internal political conflict, 'the factional struggles did not end up in violence and bloodshed. The British Government could afford to stay neutral, the entire administration kept aloof. Hence the fight was contained in a narrow arena.'[51] The postcolonial state was never removed to the same degree from political struggles because it did not possess the power of the colonial state to contain 'in a narrow arena' what had become stronger and ultimately more important political antagonisms.

As discussed earlier, one of the major changes in the state during the colonial period was in the nature of law and the courts. Arbitration was replaced by codified law with an emphasis upon written documentation, established precedent and a search for justice based upon 'facts' in order to determine legal rights. The peasantry in particular felt that the colonial legal system provided inadequate protection of their interests and rights in society. The emphasis of the colonial state on the rights of property against those of the person was felt not only to be morally wrong, but designed intentionally to ensure that the poorest had no chance of achieving justice. Since the poorest were the peasants, there was a clear wish on their part to see the system changed. However, little was done between 1942 and 1962 to alter the nature of the colonial legal system. The independent state after 1948 continued to enforce the same codes of law as had been imposed by the British in the nineteenth and twentieth centuries, and court procedures, rules of evidence and other aspects of the British-Indian legal system remained in place. The only major change was that appeal at the highest level to the Privy Council in London was abolished at independence and a new Supreme Court was installed to interpret the meaning of the constitution.[52] To most

---

ment *SIPRI Yearbook 1976* (Stockholm: Almqvist and Wiksell, 1976), Table 6A.19. Far East: military expenditure as a percentage of gross domestic product, pp. 160–1; *ibid.*, 1977, Table 3A.4, p. 234; *ibid.*, 1984 (London: Taylor and Francis, 1985), Table 3A.4, pp. 280–4.

51. Quoted in Maung Maung, *Burma and General Ne Win*, p. 25.
52. Alan Gledhill, 'Burma', in John Gilissen (ed.), *Bibliographical Introduction to Legal*

Burmese the continuation of the British-style legal system after independence was a clear sign that the nature of the state had not changed despite the departure of the colonial masters.

Economic and Financial The displacement of the state in the economic sphere was camouflaged by the greater attention state institutions appeared to devote to economic planning and regulation in the name of nationalism and socialism. While the state's control of some economic functions did increase during these two decades, this came about primarily because the state assumed responsibilities for many economic operations previously owned by foreign capitalist enterprises rather than through the development of new economic functions. Even at the end of the fiscal year 1961–2, the bulk of agriculture, accounting for 26 per cent of gross domestic product (GDP), and more than half of trade, accounting for 29.3 per cent of GDP, were in private hands, though the state had assumed greater regulatory control of these activities. Only in the major capital intensive areas of the economy which had been controlled by the state before independence (power generation, construction, communications, and social and administrative services) did the state have a major share of GDP in 1961–2.[53]

Between 1942 and 1962, planning became a substitute for the economic management which was beyond the state's capability to implement. During the war planning was intended to increase production for the war effort; throughout the period of the British military administration and up to independence planning was intended to restore the economy to the conditions that existed before the war; with independence, the purpose of planning was to create a more prosperous and equitable socialist society. In each period planning was seen as a shortcut to economic management, but given that the state had little control over the institutions of the economy it failed to meet the goals set. The first attempt was made in 1942–3 with the issuance of the 'New Order Plan', which was intended to provide a means of 'concentration, of power and control of action, of means and ends'. With the proper administrative structures Dr Ba Maw and his associates thought it would be possible to use the civilian and military manpower of the state

---

History and Ethnology, vol. E, no. 7 (Brussels: Editions de l'Institut de Sociologie, Université Libre de Bruxelles, 1970), p. 11.

53. *Report to the Pyithu Hluttaw on the Financial, Economic and Social Conditions of the Socialist Republic of the Union of Burma for 1977–78* (Rangoon: Ministry of Planning and Finance, 1977), Tables 9 and 10, pp. 21–2.

to meet the demands upon it and thus create a new order justifying independence.[54]

Though the state's managers in 1943 had ideas with regard to economic planning, these remained rather vague, as did all subsequent plans. Their rhetoric and style were belied by the state's inability to implement its plans for lack of both economic resources and coercive power. Planning became a talisman. Ba Maw argued in 1943 that the plan itself would create power for the state:

> All planning is concentration, of power and control, of action, of means and ends. Looking at it as a structure, a plan just follows this theory logically to the end and by doing so generates its own power. The ground-elements in planning are really concentration in one form or another, mass organizations, national unity, mobilization of wealth and labour, collective action, leadership, and so on.
>
> The basic unit is human energy, human labour and its values. It is radically different from the old democratic plan [sic] which was based upon vote-value instead of labour value. A real plan, that is a revolutionary plan now-a-days, must be built upon labour-value whether it gets the votes or not. . . .[55]

After independence, however, 'vote-value' was resurrected, and though the economic planners and the politicians were aware of the contradiction between the rhetoric of their planned economy and the realities of the political system, they later did not want to jeopardize their chances for re-election by demanding sacrifices in immediate consumption for long-term investment as required by their economic plans.[56]

The objective of state planning during the war was 'to create a personal stake in the State as well as in the war among the masses'. The state's managers argued that the threat of once again losing independence to the British was the initial stake in the war effort shared by the masses. But Ba Maw argued that it was necessary to 'create a more material stake than that'. One way of doing this was land redistribution, giving priority to those who served the state. The other was to give 'preferential consideration' in the granting of employment, leases, licenses, contracts and the like to those who had served the state.[57] Planning was replaced in practice with the power of patronage and with the construction of a political machine. By the 1950s, the most politically articulate

---

54. Tin, 'Commentary on the New Order Plan', *Burma*, 1,1 pp. 17–18.
55. Ba Maw, 'Burma's New Order Plan', *ibid.*, p. 105.
56. Khin Maung Kyi, 'Patterns of Accommodation to Bureaucratic Authority', p. 101.
57. Ba Maw, 'Review of the New Order Plan Stages', *Burma*, 1,1 pp. 118–19.

sectors of society under the AFPFL — small shopkeepers, small businessmen, and farmers other than rice cultivators — were protected from taxation and enforced economic direction to ensure their continued support for the state's managers.[58]

The decline of the state's economic capacity after 1942 is revealed by examining decreasing government spending. The average level of government expenditure in the period 1937–41 was 158 million rupees. Despite the massive inflation of the wartime economy actual government expenditure in 1943–4 was only 30 million rupees. Calculated in rupees at their 1937–41 value actual expenditure in 1943–4 was only 5 per cent of the prewar level. Budget estimates for 1944–5 put government expenditure at 3 per cent of the prewar level.[59]

The cause for the precipitate decline in state expenditure during the war was the dramatic fall in revenue as the state lost the ability to tax. The Japanese military preempted revenues from customs, business income tax and forests which had together amounted to 42 per cent of government income under the British. Land tax, which had accounted for 30 per cent of tax revenue before the war and had been a major cause of peasant discontent, became the wartime state's major financial base, but the collapse of the administrative system meant that only 12 per cent of prewar land taxes were collected. This decline was partially due to the fact that the domestic agricultural economy collapsed because of a lack of export opportunities.[60]

The state's ability to tax the peasantry directly through land revenue was never subsequently revived and indirect taxation on exports became the major source of state income after independence. By 1956–7, land tax revenue amounted to only 4 per cent of tax revenue and 2 per cent of all state income. By that time non-tax revenues in the form of earnings by ministries and departments, state trading boards and Japanese war reparations amounted to 38 per cent of all state revenues, with customs making up another 25 per cent of income. Only income tax, paid largely by state employee, as most individuals in the private sector did not pay taxes,[61] provided the other significant revenue source (22 per cent).[62]

58. Khin Maung Kyi, 'Patterns of Accommodation to Bureaucratic Authority', p. 101.
59. Guyot, 'Political Impact of the Japanese Occupation', Table 8, p. 208.
60. *Ibid.*, pp. 209–10.
61. Khin Maung Gyi, 'Patterns of Accommodation to Bureaucratic Authority', p. 101.
62. These percentages are calculated from Table 37: 'Union Government Budget Receipts, 1956–7 actuals', *Economic Survey of Burma 1958*, p. 54.

An underlying basis for the weakness of the state *vis-à-vis* the economy was the destruction of productive capacity caused by the Second World War and by the civil war. Real GDP, in 1970–1 prices, stood at Kyat (Kt) 5,483 million in 1938/9 but fell to Kt 4,663 million in 1947/8 and to a postwar low of Kt 3,983 million in 1948/9, the first year of the civil war. Production then steadily rose to Kt 7,758 million by 1961/2.[63] This increase was primarily due to an average rate of GDP growth between 1952 and 1960 of about 5 per cent per annum.[64] Growth rates fluctuated markedly during the period as the economy was highly dependent upon trade, especially in rice, timber and other primary products. In the early 1950s due to the boom in primary products caused by the Korean war export earnings grew rapidly, though mainly to the benefit of the state, as the price which farmers received for their crops remained under its control. But the downturn in trade caused GDP at constant prices to decline an estimated 3 per cent in 1958, the year of the political crisis which led to the installation of the military caretaker government.[65]

Despite the state's expressed goal of improving the economic well-being of the population through planning and the reinvestment of profits in the country (instead of losing these to foreign owners), the incomes of most individuals remained through the 1940s and 1950s well below what they had been at the end of the depression in the 1930s. Real per capita GDP in constant 1970/1 prices in 1938 stood at Kt 395.3 but fell 45 per cent because of war destruction to Kt 218.1 in 1947/8. But despite the growth of the 1950s, this figure had still only reached Kt 335.4 in 1961/2.[66] Per capita consumption also declined in 1947/8 to 84 per cent of it 1938–9 standard and fell to 72 per cent of the pre-war level in 1953–4. By 1960–1 per capita consumption had risen to 94 per cent of the pre-war level.[67] The failure of the state's economic promises was one of the causes of its inability to counter the political cynicism that greeted the platitudes of the authorities.

63. David I. Steinberg, *Burma's Road Toward Development: Growth and Ideology Under Military Rule* (Boulder, Colo.: Westview Press, 1981), Table 5.1, per Capita GDP, p. 78.
64. Mya Maung, 'Socialism and Economic Development of Burma', *Asia Survey*, IV, 12 (Dec., 1964), p. 1199.
65. *Economic Survey of Burma 1958*, p. 1.
66. Steinberg, *Burma's Road Toward Development*, Table 5.1, p. 78.
67. Frank N. Trager, *Burma: From Kingdom to Independence* (New York, Praeger, 1966), Table 3, Gross Domestic Product, Per Capita Gross Output and Consumption in 1947–48 Prices, p. 160.

The most obvious aspect of the state's enlarged economic role after the Second World War was its management of enterprises formerly run by private British firms. Many of these had been taken over by the British Military Administration in 1945 and were already operating under partial state management when nationalized after independence. The Irrawaddy Flotilla Company became the State Inland Water Transport Board, and the various timber extracting and exporting firms were nationalized under the State Timber Board. Rice purchasing and export became a monopoly of the State Agricultural Marketing Board (SAMB). More technically complex foreign-owned endeavours, such as the oil industry, became the subject of joint venture agreements between the state and their mainly British owners. Many other enterprises were also nationalized and placed under government-appointed boards which were intended to manage them as businesses, returning a profit which would accrue to the state rather than to British or Indian shareholders. However, the majority of state enterprises ran at a loss and depended upon state subsidies in the 1950s.[68] Furthermore, the government organizations, with the exception of several of the larger export-oriented boards, especially SAMB, were run in a way which was politically beneficial to the ministers to whom they were responsible, and many managerial appointments were made on the basis of political patronage.[69]

The major exceptions to this pattern were the economic enterprises managed by the Defence Services' Institute (DSI), which had been established by the army in the early 1950s to provide inexpensive consumer goods to members of the forces, but which expanded later to incorporate a wide range of economic activities. By the time of the 1958 caretaker government it had become the country's largest economic enterprise.[70] With the return to civilian rule in 1960 the DSI was renamed the Burma Economic Development Corporation and, despite its nominal position under the prime minister, remained in effect under army control.[71]

68. Aye Hlaing, 'Observations on Some Patterns of Economic Development', *Burma Research Society Fiftieth Anniversary Publications No. 1* (Rangoon: Burma Research Society, 1961), p. 10.
69. H.V. Richter, 'The Impact of Socialism on Economic Activity in Burma', in T. Scarlett Epstein and David H. Penny (eds), *Opportunity and Response, Case Studies in Economic Development* (London: C. Hurst, 1972), p. 225.
70. Walinsky, *Economic Development in Burma*, p. 261.
71. Lissak, 'Social Change, Mobilization', pp. 15–16.

One of the main problems the state faced in attempting to develop the economy was capital formation for investment. The initial nationalization programme resulted in an annual average net private capital outflow of Kt 14.3 million per year between 1951 and 1954, but this trend was reversed from 1955 to 1959 when there was an annual net private capital inflow of Kt 11.3 million. In the following year, 1960, however, there was a net private capital outflow of Kt 50.0 million and an additional Kt 13.0 million outflow in 1961.[72] Domestic capital formation was more successful after the civil war in both the private and state sectors, but never achieved the targets drawn up by the economic planners. State gross capital formation exceeded private gross capital formation in the years from 1953/4 to 1956/7 when they reached parity, but after that year until 1959/60 private capital accumulation exceeded that of the state.[73] This reflected the more settled economic conditions of the later period as well as declining government export revenues and reduced adherence to socialist policies.

The emphasis placed upon the development of a domestic manufacturing base was indicative of the desire of the independent state to make itself less dependent upon the outside world. In addition to investment in import substitution industries, a large amount of capital was directed toward power and transport development.[74] Between 1952/3 and 1959/60, 9.4 per cent of all capital expenditure was devoted to the industrial sector and another 12.8 per cent was directed toward power generation. The only sectors to receive a larger proportion of capital expenditure were construction and law and order.[75] This emphasis upon import substitution and the development of the industrial sector was reflected in a reorientation of imports. Whereas in 1938/9 only 22 per cent of all imports were for capital goods, in 1955/6 33 per cent of

---

72. Frank H. Golay, Ralph Anspach, M. Ruth Pfanner, and Eliezer B. Ayal, *Underdevelopment and Economic Nationalism in Southeast Asia* (Ithaca: Cornell University Press, 1969), p. 162.
73. Trager, *Burma: From Kingdom to Independence*, Table 4, Capital formation, Planned and Actual, p. 162.
74. Khin Maung Kyi, 'Modernization of Burmese Agriculture: Problems and Prospects', in Institute of Southeast Asian Studies, *Southeast Asian Affairs 1982* (Singapore: Heinemann, 1982), p. 116.
75. Trager, *Burma: From Kingdom to Independence.*, Table 2, Allocation of Capital Expenditure Spent, p. 159; Walinsky, *Economic Development in Burma*, Table 56: 'Percentage Distribution of Public Capital Expenditures by Economics Sector, 1952–3 to 1959–60', p. 354.

imports were for capital goods.[76] However, the state could not further reduce the importation of consumer goods so as to allow for more capital goods imports because of the political protests this would have caused among influential small shopkeepers and businessmen. Indeed, before the 1956 general election the government, with its limited foreign credits, purchased Kt 1,500,000 worth of consumer goods from India with Indian credits in order to replenish shops with consumer goods then in short supply.[77]

The events of the two decades between 1942 and 1962 resulted in relatively little restructuring of the economy despite the intentions of the state's leaders. According to their plan, the size of the government's share in economic activities should have increased dramatically in all spheres in the 1950s compared to the 1930s. As Table 4.1 shows, only in the sphere of government expenditure itself was there a significant change in the state's share of the economy from before the war to the end

Table 4.1 DISTRIBUTION OF GROSS DOMESTIC PRODUCT

	1938–9	1959–60
Agriculture and fisheries	38.6	34.5
Forestry	7.3	7.1
Mining and quarrying	5.5	2.3
Rice processing	3.7	2.9
State marketing	12.8	9.2
State transport	2.4	1.6
State banking	0.0	0.3
Other public utilities	0.6	1.0
General government	3.1	11.3
Rental value of housing	3.3	4.1
Other industries and services	22.7	24.7
GDP	100.0	100.0

Source: Calculated from Louis J. Walinsky, *Economic Development of Burma* (New York: Twentieth Century Fund, 1962), Table 57, Gross Domestic Product in 1947–48 Prices, 1938–39 to 1959–60, p. 355.

76. Frank N. Trager, *Building a Welfare State in Burma* (New York: Institute of Pacific Relations, 1958), Table 2: 'Imports by Value', pp. 28–9.
77. R.J. Kozicki, 'India and Burma, 1937–1957: A Study in International Relations' (unpubl. Ph.D. diss., University of Pennsylvania, 1959), pp. 403–4; Nu, *U Nu — Saturday's Son*, p. 228. Nu records that the goods were provided as a loan; Kozicki states that the loan funds were not used. See also Guyot, 'Bureaucratic Transformation in Burma', p. 393.

of the 1950s. Even in the state marketing and transportation sectors the independent nationalist state had control over a smaller proportion of all activity than had the colonial *laissez-faire* state.

External Relations With the end of colonial rule Burma's state managers had to develop new external relations. As with all states their primary goal was to establish and maintain the security of the state, but that security had both internal and external aspects which interacted upon each other. In as much as state managers often saw their personal or institutional political longevity as identical with the security of the state, external security decisions were often made for internal reasons, and economic aspects were often as important as political ones in the making of foreign policy.

Burma's external relations may have begun formally on January 4, 1948, but state managers and would-be state managers had been conducting external political relations for centuries under the kings, and, in the context of the European state system, since the 1920s. The negotiations that British officials in Rangoon conducted through the Governor with Calcutta, Delhi or London over immigration, defence and financial relations in the 1930s were the beginning of more formal relations after independence. These 'imperial' external relations came together when Premier U Saw, in order to secure his political position at home, journeyed to London in 1941 to try to gain a pledge of post-war formal independence. When the Churchill government refused to cooperate, Saw broke out of the imperial framework that had determined external relations from 1886 to 1941 and went as a head of government to lobby Washington for support against the British. Failing to get support from the Roosevelt administration, Saw then turned to the Japanese. State managers seek their friends where they can find them, and by the end of the British colonial state the premier of Burma was attempting to conduct external relations like any other head of government.[78]

As the rising power in East and Southeast Asia in the late 1930s, Japan was an important focus of attention for Burmese political leaders. Several Burmese travelled to the country, and while Japanese assets in Burma were small, Japanese military and trading interests were considerable. But Japan's primary interest was strategic. The imperial Japanese Army's 1942 invasion of Burma was intended to close the Burma Road

---

78. Robert H. Taylor, 'Politics in Late Colonial Burma: The Case of U Saw', *Modern Asian Studies*, 10, 2 (April, 1976), pp. 161–94.

which was the major supply link to Japan's enemy, the government of Chiang Kai-shek. But having occupied Burma and having promised Burmese nationalists an independent state, Japan had to attempt to buttress the power of the state *vis-à-vis* domestic society in order to gain the cooperation of Ba Maw and other leaders in the war effort.

Thus the Japanese recognized the autonomy of the state in Burma, which, weak as it was, was the only institution through which they could work to achieve Japan's economic, political or strategic goals. Similarly, after 1948, the fact that the state did not have effective control over society meant that other states' demands had to be tempered by a recognition of the state's limited ability to implement its policies. Occasionally, foreign assistance was needed to shore up the state and support it financially.

The ambivalent relationship between Japan and Burma in the 1940s is indicated by the means by which heads of state or leading political figures were elevated to office in that decade. Ba Maw was made head of state in 1942 like Thakin Tun Ok before him because he was thought the best man for the job by the Japanese army commander. The elevation of Aung San to the position of Burma's leading nationalist figure over Than Tun or Saw was a consequence of his being accepted by the Japanese as the formateur of an anti-British armed force. Similarly, Aung San was viewed by the Supreme Allied Commander Southeast Asia, Mountbatten, as the man to cultivate in order to maintain peace in Burma. When Aung San was assassinated, it was the British Governor who chose Thakin Nu to succeed him. This is not to argue that these men lacked support in the country; it is merely to suggest that in the balance of political power within the state during the 1940s external relations were crucial in determining the allocation of leading positions.

Formal independence modified but did not bring to an end the ability of external states to effect the functioning of the state and its leading personnel. However, the instruments through which such efforts were made had to be altered. The rhetoric of the AFPFL leaders called for external relations to be conducted in such a way as to avoid entering into alliances which would compromise Burma's independence. On the other hand sentiments of loyalty and existing economic and political ties, as well as treaty commitments made before independence, linked Burma to Britain and to India. The Aung San-Attlee and the Let Ya-Freeman agreements reached in 1947 obligated Burma to repay debts to Britain and to allow British forces to use bases in Burma in exchange for the receipt of British military aid and training facilities.

Thus the military and economic position of the state in 1948–9 pointed toward forming close external links with the West. It was also from the West that military and economic assistance could have been expected to come to shore up the state's position in regard to its multiple internal opponents. By mid-1949, when the government was dominated by conservative ministers from the pre-war political and administrative systems as well as from the army, thought was apparently given to entering into relationships for defence and economic cooperation with the West, but the idea of a formal treaty commitment, which would have raised a great deal of opposition within the country, was subsequently dropped. Instead, established but technically informal relationships with old imperial connections were allowed to provide the beleaguered state with a modicum of military and economic aid at the height of the civil war. Both India and Britain provided Burma with 10,000 small-weapons each and arranged with other Commonwealth countries, including Australia, Ceylon and Pakistan, to provide a loan of £6 million in the 1950s to tide the state's treasury over until the insurgent forces could be suppressed.[79] At the same time the United States, the rising hegemonic state in the region, was asked by Prime Minister Nu to provide $50 million in aid. This resulted in an aid agreement worth from $8 to $10 million.[80]

The outbreak of the Korean war provided an object lesson in the state's external relations and served to reinforce neutralist attitudes about security and foreign affairs. The initial United Nations response to the alleged North Korean aggression was viewed by the non-Communist state managers in Burma as a guarantee that if they were attacked by another state, and China was the state they thought most likely to do this, the world organization would come to their assistance. Subsequently, as it became increasingly apparent that the actions of the United Nations were being determined primarily to further United States' cold war policies towards the Soviet Union and China, Burma's leaders began to question the extent to which they could rely on the UN for support.[81] The subsequent recognition of United States' support for

79. Kozicki, 'India and Burma, 1937–1957', pp. 310–14; Evelyn Colbert, *Southeast Asia in International Politics 1941–1956* (Ithaca: Cornell University Press, 1977), pp. 107–8.
80. Moses Than Aung, 'A General Study in the Economic Development of Burma with Special Reference to Economic Planning (1948–1958)' (unpubl. MA thesis, Rangoon Arts and Sciences University, 1973), p. 13.
81. Colbert, *Southeast Asia in International Politics*, pp. 154–5, 157, 159.

the activities of Chinese Nationalist (KMT) troops in northern Burma, raising the prospect of a Chinese People's Liberation Army incursion into Burma's territory, underlined more strongly the position that Burma's government would have to develop its own independent foreign policy if it was to avoid entanglement in the Asian cold war.[82]

Burma's leaders recognized that siding with either the United States or the Soviet Union and China would raise greater threats to state security than abstaining from involvement in the major Asian international conflict of the early 1950s; this recognition, aided by the Korean war, was to later evolve into state policy. The increase in Burma's export earnings in the Korean war years gave the government financial latitude to pursue an independent foreign policy and even to order a curtailment of United States aid because of American assistance to the KMT troops in Burma. By the end of the war, when commodity prices declined, Burma's external financial position became much more perilous and it sought external assistance where it could without publicly compromising the country's independence. Thus the practice of seeking aid from a multiplicity of sources was established.

Burma's policies on the acceptance of aid in the latter half of the 1950s reveal the dilemmas the state's managers faced. Capital accumulation was difficult and the nation's economic prospects were in a state of gradual decline in the mid-1950s. The state's ability to import consumer goods was especially at risk immediately prior to the holding of national elections in 1956, and the government of India came to Burma's assistance with a loan of $42 million. As hard currency earnings became more difficult the state entered into barter agreements with the Soviet Union, China and Eastern European socialist states for development resources while once more accepting United States and British Commonwealth aid. Soon, Japan's war reparations became a major source of aid, enabling it to establish preeminence among those countries active in the economy.[83]

In the 1950s Burma's efforts to establish a neutralist foreign policy made necessary the development of an independent defence policy. By declaring neutrality Burma was tacitly siding with one of its two largest neighbours, India, without at the same time antagonizing Communist

---

82. Taylor, *Foreign and Domestic Consequences of the KMT Intervention.*
83. See the discussions in Walinsky, *Economic Development in Burma*, pp. 507–45; Trager, *Burma*, pp. 305–43; John D. Montgomery, *The Politics of Foreign Aid: American Experience in Southeast Asia* (New York: Praeger, 1962), *passim.*

China in the way in which an alliance with the United States would have done. But the state did enmesh itself into a web of informal economic relationships with the external world. Unable to raise adequate revenues internally, by 1957/8 the state had come to rely 'upon foreign grants and loans for 46 per cent of its capital expenditures, and this dependence rapidly increased to 74 per cent in 1958/9 and then to an estimated 82 per cent in 1959/60'. By 1959, it has been suggested that 70 per cent of the state budget was financed by external loans and aid.[84] The financial weakness of the state was threatening to make it dependent on the outside world by the end of the 1950s.

The Rise of Alternative Authorities

The collapse of state power after 1942 is clearly evident in the way that many individuals could, with relative ease, circumvent the institutions of the state and ignore the orders of its officials. The most ambitious individuals could find means of achieving power and wealth outside the structures of the state as the society regrouped itself on the basis of local centres and paid little heed to the capital. Unlike under the precolonial or colonial orders, there were for twenty years frequently used routes to power and wealth outside the structures sanctioned by the state. The expansion of dacoit gangs and insurgent bands is the most obvious example: influence and loot accrued to their leaders through the coercive power they possessed.

For others, however, there were more lasting ways of gaining power and wealth. Politics was the most promising of these and the descendants of the U Kyan Aungs of the colonial period (described in Chapter III) came into their own in the 1950s. Then, in exchange for the authority that acting in the name of the state provided, local bosses offered the centre the promise of keeping their areas under control. The central state in turn sought such alliances in order to re-establish some partial control over society at the least cost to itself. In effect, the displacement of the state resulted in local leaders being able to dictate conditions to the central authorities and thus inverted the relationship of state and society which had been the norm since the nineteenth century.

Though the colonial state's authority collapsed with the departure of

---

84. Montgomery, *Politics of Foreign Aid*, p. 31, though published government sources do not reveal such a large figure.

the British, many subordinate indigenous officials remained in post as servants of the new regime. During the war, because they were no longer the agents of a powerful state able to protect or coerce the population these officials lost much of their influence.[85] At the same time, there developed the phenomena of private individuals assuming for themselves responsibilities of administrative and political control. Sometimes this was done by local 'elders', but often by upstarts or individuals with personal connections with local BIA commanders.

After the war, the British Military Administration and the returning colonial civil service, staffed largely by the same personnel, attempted to resurrect the prewar system. However, the political and social mobilization of the war years and the resulting upheaval, coupled with widespread political opposition to the British, made this extremely difficult. One obvious problem was a shortage of personnel familiar with the old state system and still willing to work for it. Only 70 per cent of Burmese and 60 per cent of British and Eurasian officers returned to duty in 1945. As more of these officers were required to take on new administrative responsibilities relating to reconstruction and the distribution of consumer goods, their places were taken by subordinate officials. The result was a rapid turnover of personnel which made it nearly impossible to revive the more ordinary administrative routines of the pre-war period.[86] The loyalty from its personnel which the state had developed in the colonial period was now destroyed and opponents of the British permeated the administration. For example, the stenographer in the Governor's office made copies of his papers for the leadership of the AFPFL.[87]

The top of the bureaucratic order which had held the colonial state together was further eroded in the months immediately before and after formal independence. Between October 1947 and April 1948, nearly 58 per cent of top grade civil servants resigned along with 84 per cent of the police service, 50 per cent of the civil medical officers and 78 per cent of the senior public works officers.[88] The result was rapid promotion for officers from the subordinate services and the recruitment of many new, junior civil servants.[89]

85. Guyot, 'Political Impact of the Japanese Occupation', pp. 204–5.
86. Guyot, 'Bureaucratic Transformation in Burma', p. 383.
87. Leslie Glass, *The Changing of Kings: Memories of Burma, 1934–1949* (London: Peter Owen, 1985) p. 201.
88. Guyot, 'Bureaucratic Transformation in Burma', Table 4, p. 420.
89. *Ibid.*, p. 421.

By the 1950s, district officers were by and large unable to command respect in their regions. Power had passed to the politicians and army commanders on the spot who held the real authority over the local populations. The newly independent state's plan of using the colonial administrative system for economic development and the advance of social welfare proved impossible.[90] The district officers and their staffs had their authority limited not only by the interposition of new, local, extra-legal agents, but also by the state's intention of introducing a more participatory form of local government. The prevailing notion in the 1950s was that it was necessary to turn the centrally appointed state officials into servants of locally elected councils capable of representing local demands. However, the councils rarely operated as intended; rather than representing the local people, they became the fiefs of political bosses and but another arena for factionalism to be manifested.[91] The bureaucratic procedures required of local officials in order to satisfy both their central employer and their local boss multiplied by a factor of six or seven. They soon became overwhelmed with office work and the authority which the colonial administrators had shifted to members of the central legislature, to the nearest military commanders, or even, in some cases, to local insurgent leaders.[92]

The situation in Arakan in the early 1950s illustrates the loss of central state dominance. After independence, the Arakan branch of the AFPFL took control of the region. The expanded police force was filled with recruits from the demobilized forces of the PVO, but when the civil war broke out and the government declared the pro-Communist White Band PVO to be an illegal organization, many members of the police joined the insurgents. A local AFPFL leader was then appointed as Special Deputy Commissioner to oversee the police and administrative system, but his authority disintegrated after his main political opponent, a conservative Arakanese and former élite civil servant, U Kyaw Min, won a by-election in 1950. Kyaw Min then became the boss of the region[93] and, being unable to accept the socialist pretensions of the AFPFL leadership, formed his own political party, so-named to imply that it represented the people of Arakan.

90. *Ibid.*, p. 418.
91. *Ibid.*, pp. 415–6.
92. *Ibid.*, pp. 416–8.
93. ASMI, 'The State of Arakan', *The Guardian*, 1/10 (Aug., 1954), pp. 28–9, 1/11, (Sept., 1954), pp. 21–3, 1/12 (Oct., 1954), pp. 17–20.

One Burmese analyst has noted how the collapse of the state's administrative power in the districts allowed the rise of local *Bo*.[94] These men rose to leadership in their districts during the civil war by 'defending their own towns' when the armed forces of the state proved unable to do so. They were subsequently recruited by the AFPFL leadership as parliamentary representatives and they 'controlled the districts with their own para-military bands. They enjoyed their power independent of the legal authority' of the state.[95] Managing local affairs on their own, or running 'a government parallel to the bureaucracy' and arbitrating disputes and enforcing 'their decrees with their own power',[96] the local *Bo* became states within the state. Their authority was further enhanced by the wealth they accumulated and used in the construction of pagodas and other acts of Buddhist merit, and they developed their own networks of patron-client ties which made them increasingly independent of the state.[97]

During its attempts to re-establish order in the districts between 1958 and 1960 the military caretaker government worked to eliminate the power of the *Bo*. It was the army's intention to reinstate the authority of the village headmen and the district officers. The effect was to increase the opposition of the civilian politicians within the AFPFL toward the army[98] because the attempt to resurrect the dominance of central state agents in the districts undercut the power-bases of the party machine. The army also organized National Solidarity Associations as part of its psychological warfare programme during the caretaker period. These were under the leadership of headmen and local officials and were intended to develop within the public a willingness to resist the power of the local *Bo*.[99] At the end of the caretaker period the military felt they had successfully disbanded the *Bo*'s pocket armies.[100] Much of the military's success in restricting the power of these extra-state bodies came from the centralization of district responsibilities in the hands of security and

---

94. *Bo* is a term used to refer to military officers and also to Europeans. In time it has come to mean any strong figure in an area.
95. Khin Maung Kyi, 'Patterns of Accommodation to Bureaucratic Authority', pp. 110–11.
96. *Ibid.*, pp. 123–4.
97. Silverstein, *Burma: Military Rule*, p. 65.
98. Lissak, 'Social Change, Mobilization', p. 13.
99. Butwell, *U Nu of Burma*, p. 211; Lissak, 'Social Change, Mobilization', fn. 51, p. 16.
100. Maung Maung, *Burma and General Ne Win*, p. 24.

administrative committees, which had the effect of placing the power of the army and the police behind the local administrative officers.[101]

The army caretaker government not only attempted to resurrect the central state's power in the district administrations of central Burma where the AFPFL *Bo* had their power-bases, but also in the surrounding hill areas where the 'feudal' powers of the traditional leaders had been perpetuated. As Silverstein has written,

> in the states located on the nation's frontiers, the [army] government recreated a form of administration used originally under the British [sic]. The Frontier Areas Administration assumed direct jurisdiction over remote border areas and took responsibility for security and improvement in services to the peoples in those areas. As a result of these changes a more centralized administration was developed throughout the nation, and internal security was improved. At the same time, control by the states over their own territories was weakened, and their peoples were tied more closely to Rangoon.[102]

The authority of several of the *Sawbwas* had first been undermined and partially superseded during the civil war and the subsequent occupation of parts of the Shan states by the Chinese Nationalist troops which had crossed the border from Yunnan Province in 1949 and 1950. Earlier, Karen National Defence Organisation troops had passed through the territories of some of the *Sawbwas*, and the rulers' forces were unable to maintain control in the face of the insurgents. Martial law was then declared so the central army could reimpose order. According to a Burmese historian who had access to government records, the authorities felt that the consequence of unrest in the Shan states in the early 1950s would be the creation of a Communist government in collaboration with the forces of the Kachin insurgent Naw Seng (the former commander of the colonial army's 1st Kachin Rifles), who had fled across the Chinese border. Government officials alleged that if the army had not taken over the inefficient governments of the *Sawbwas* would have fallen to the Communists.[103] (Former *Sawbwas* have privately suggested that the army overstated the level of insurgent activities in order to have a pretext for intervention.)

The primary consequence of the civil war for the Shan states was the undermining of the position of the *Sawbwas*. On September 13, 1952, a

---

101. Silverstein, *Burma: Military Rule*, p. 78.
102. *Ibid.*
103. Ba Thann Win, 'Administration of Shan States', pp. 109–10; interview with Jimmy Yang, Rangoon, August, 1984.

state of emergency was declared in the state. At the end of November 1952, military administration under the control of General Ne Win was imposed in all areas. The state and the *Sawbwas'* police forces were amalgamated during the same period. The minister responsible in the central cabinet in Rangoon announced at a meeting in Taunggyi on October 28, 1952 that upon the termination of the military government, the *Sawbwas* would be replaced with a form of democratic government (the *Sawbwas* having agreed to the abandonment of their traditional powers at a meeting two days previously).[104]

Nonetheless, the politics of the situation were so complex that little was actually done to replace the *Sawbwas* with an elected government before central military rule was withdrawn on September 10, 1954. The Shan State Military Co-ordination Committee did not meet for six months after the establishment of army rule. In fact, it appeared that the administration was merely imposed on top of the state and *Sawbwa* administrative systems.[105] However, the military government did manage to implement some reforms, strengthening the power of the centre and weakening the position of the *Sawbwas*. Police powers had been concentrated in the Shan states' government, as had all revenue collection. Principles of democratic local administration were enunciated with the removal of the *Sawbwas'* power to appoint village headmen (who were subsequently to be elected). Also, a uniform code of law was introduced in the state, removing the *Sawbwas'* individual judicial powers. But theory was one thing, fact another. As no administrative mechanisms had been created to implement these reforms, the central government had to ask the *Sawbwas* to continue to function in its place.[106]

Nonetheless, the *Sawbwas* realized they could soon lose their positions, and in order to defend themselves established a political party, the Social Democratic Party, in May 1955.[107] They remained in control of all the seats in the two houses of the central legislature in the election that year, thus demonstrating their power to the central authorities. The contradiction between their powers and the egalitarian principles of the constitution provided a continuing ideological problem for the central state. In June 1957 it was rumoured that the Shan states would choose to secede from the Union under a clause in the 1947 constitution providing for such an option after ten years, and, furthermore, would allow the establishment of a United States air base in northeast Burma

104. *Ibid.*, pp. 119–27.
105. *Ibid.*, pp. 128–33.
106. *Ibid.*, pp. 152–6.
107. *Ibid.*, p. 157.

opposite China.[108] The central state thus felt obliged to act in order to preserve its sovereignty, territorial integrity and neutralist foreign policy.

The military caretaker government completed the formal process of ending the powers of the Shan and Kayah *Sawbwas* with a handover of power to the state on April 24, 1959 in exchange for sizeable pensions and payments.[109] However, the *Sawbwas* continued to exercise a great deal of authority (as well as dominating the electoral process) in their former states, thus guaranteeing continued political influence and safeguarding their 'traditional' positions.

Upon the return of civilian government in 1960, conditions in the countryside began to return to their pre-1958 condition. The government of U Nu attempted to rely once more upon local politicians and parliamentary representatives but, as many of these had sided with his opponents or had had their power undermined by the reforms of the caretaker government, the power of the state in relation to society was further undermined. In the Shan and Karenni areas where the power of the central state was no longer mediated through traditional authority the growth of anti-state insurgency under the leadership of the families and officials of the former *Sawbwas* was also weakening the power of the centre.[110]

Economic and Social Change

Although there was no fundamental change in the economy, the displacement of the state led to changes in Burma's social structure and domestic economic relations during the 1940s and 1950s. These changes reversed some of the trends begun by the colonial state and eventually facilitated the reassertion of the state's dominance over other institutions. But the process was uncertain, especially in the 1940s, when change was almost entirely the consequence of forces and pressures out-

---

108. *Ibid.*, p. 193.
109. 'Dawn of a New Era in the Shan State', *Burma Weekly Bulletin*, 8, 4 (21 May 1959), pp. 25–40.
110. See Jon A. Wiant, 'Insurgency in the Shan State', in Lim Joo-Jock and S. Vani, *Armed Separatism in Southeast Asia* (Singapore: Regional Strategic Studies Programme, Institute of Southeast Asian Studies, 1984), pp. 81–110; Bertil Linter, 'The Shans and the Shan State of Burma', *Contemporary Southeast Asia*, 5, 4 (March 1984), pp. 401–50.

side the control of the state. The political leaders of the 1950s had specific ideas about the restructuring of Burma's ethnic and class composition, but these were only partially implemented as extra-state forces protected powerful elements in the existing order.

Rapid social restructuring had commenced with the Japanese invasion and the departure of the British and other communities most closely dependent upon the colonial state. In little more than a few months, the British withdrew in a manner quite unexpected only a few months before. Between January and June 1942, 600 government employees, 3,600 businessmen, 170 missionaries, and 500 professionals who, together with their families, totalled 12,000 people, left for India. They were accompanied by more than 400,000 other less exalted individuals, including nearly half of the Indian and Anglo-Indian or Anglo-Burmese population; 9,000 Burmese also joined the exodus.[111] The cities were most dramatically affected. Rangoon's population fell from half a million to only 150,000 between the first Japanese bombing in December 1941, and the end of February 1942.[112]

The loss of such a sizeable proportion of the Indian population had a dramatic impact on the structure of society, especially in terms of employment and the distribution of economic functions. Many professional, transport, industrial and trading roles became vacant and were either left unfilled or taken up by Burmese. Apparently, only a small proportion of those who fled in 1942 returned after the war, though other Indians came to Burma in 1945 through 1947. Consequently, the Indian population, which stood at over one million in 1931, was reduced to about 700,000 in 1947–8.[113] After 1947 it was no longer possible to re-establish the colonial immigration pattern between South Asia and Burma.

Limitations on large-scale Indian immigration, long sought by Burmese politicians, were made law in June 1947, when the British Governor promulgated the Burma Immigration (Emergency Provisions) Act requiring visas for entry into Burma.[114] Furthermore, the unleashing of previously controlled antagonisms during the civil war made the country an uncertain place for South Asian migrants, and at

---

111. Guyot, 'Political Impact of the Japanese Occupation of Burma', p. 103; Golay et al., *Underdevelopment and Economic Nationalism*, p. 213.
112. Guyot, 'Political Impact of the Japanese Occupation of Burma', pp. 94–6.
113. Kozicki, 'India and Burma', p. 225.
114. *Ibid.*, p. 222.

the height of the conflict the rate of departures increased, so that in 1949 80,995 Indians left Burma but only 32,676 arrived by sea.[115] Together with entrées by those travelling by land routes, there was a total of 118,382 departures and a total of 65,414 arrivals, giving a net population decrease by emigration of 52,968 in 1949. Net movements resulted in a loss of 3,538 in 1950, but with the restoration of control over the cities and central sections of the country conditions once more encouraged Indian immigration. From 1950 until 1955 there was a net increase in population caused by immigration each year, with the exception of 1954. After 1955 recorded departures surpassed recorded entries for every year, with particularly large upswings in net departures in the politically uncertain years of 1958, 1959 and 1960.[116]

Despite the many family and business connections between Burma and India, immigration had become more and more difficult. Greater restrictions were placed on the activities of Indian businessmen in the name of socialism and nationalism, and their lives and property became increasingly uncertain. Nationalized property was often 'compensated for' in the form of government non-negotiable bonds redeemable only in Burma. As the President of the Indian National Congress stated in 1950 when discussing the problems Indians were having in repatriating money from Burma to India, 'sometimes we are told that we can enjoy [our prewar] money in Burma itself, but one does not know how long . . . by people who cannot feel a sense of peace and security in living there as they used to once during the British regime.'[117]

The Peasantry For the peasantry the political cataclysms of the 1940s and 1950s provided unplanned and uncertain relief from the problems of landlessness, tenancy and indebtedness that had developed during the colonial period. The insecurity and confusion caused by war, revolution and partially implemented government land reform and credit schemes made their positions no more secure than under the colonial state. The high expectations of relief from economic insecurity and predatory landlords, moneylenders and state officials that peasants had shared in the 1920s and 1930s were not fulfilled after independence, but the weakness of the state in the 1940s and 1950s did provide opportunities for revolt or

115. *Ibid.*, pp. 316–7.
116. Golay *et al.*, *Underdevelopment and Economic Nationalism*, Table 13: 'Recorded Movement of Population (Sea, Air and Land)', p. 214.
117. Quoted in Kozicki, 'India and Burma', p. 354.

withdrawal which some peasants were able to exploit. The state's leaders were very uncertain of their ability to control the peasantry and could not ensure that the majority of the population, often under local leaders, did not, by noncompliance or violence, destroy their plans for social and economic change.

The partial exodus of Indians in 1942 included most of the alien landlords and moneylenders to whom the peasantry were beholden. The collapse of the state's judicial system during the war years also meant that land rent and debt repayments owed to indigenous landlords were ignored as these obligations could not be enforced. Consequently, very few indigenous landlords were able to collect rents from their tenants during the war.[118]

For the bulk of the peasantry, however, the war period provided little of benefit and the advantages of being free of landlords, indebtedness, rent payments, and often land tax, were outweighed by the disadvantages of the collapse of the economy and of social order. Disease spread among the peasantry and the standard of life declined generally. The availability of imported consumer goods was greatly reduced and items such as textiles and soap became scarce and expensive. Prospects for achieving even depression level returns from the cultivation of export crops collapsed because of the curtailment of the international rice trade and because of a severe shortage of shipping to Japan and the rest of the East Asia Co-Prosperity Sphere. More than half of the draught cattle in the country were lost during the war due to disease and Japanese requisitioning. Peasants were also obliged to provide transport, construction and other labour services, often for little or no payment, for the Japanese army. The 'Sweat Army' of the Japanese era was only the most notorious of the forced labour gangs organized from among the peasantry.[119]

Many peasants adjusted to the precipitous decline in their conditions by undertaking only subsistence agriculture. As a result, half of all the pre-war paddy acreage was left uncultivated. Yields per acre fell by a third or more. In the face of this decline in production the state attempted to alleviate the peasants' conditions and to increase output, but its actions had little effect. In 1943 a 50 per cent reduction in rent was ordered in a largely meaningless effort to improve rural wages and

118. Becka, *National Liberation Movement in Burma*, pp. 110–12; Golay et al., *Underdevelopment and Economic Nationalism*, p. 223.
119. Becka, *National Liberation Movement in Burma*, p. 111.

to increase cultivation. The state also became a major purchaser of paddy in 1942 and 1943 in an attempt to keep prices and production up.[120]

The peasantry in the export-oriented delta suffered more during the war years than did those in the north. Many peasants in central Burma, because of their more diversified agriculture, were actually able to improve their economic positions, in particular by paying off their debts with increasingly worthless Japanese currency.[121] The government encouraged farmers to diversify away from paddy to cotton and jute in order to provide supplies of raw materials for the manufacture of goods no longer importable from abroad such as gunny sacks and cloth, though without much success.[122] The reason for this failure was probably the collapse of the credit system of the colonial period which had provided peasants with the means of planting. Without state assistance or private credit, the cost of diversification was prohibitive.

At the end of the war the returning British military administration and its civilian successors made the revitalization of the rice industry a top priority. There was then a world-wide shortage of food and not only the colonial authorities but also the leaders of the AFPFL set a high premium on Burma's ability to help feed the world. But for the peasantry the return of the British meant a return not only to the international market but also to increasing attempts by the state to control the production and marketing of the agricultural surplus. The programmes introduced by the British in 1945–6 to strengthen state control of agriculture in order to increase harvests and regulate prices were the basis of subsequent state attempts to control the production and profits of farmers. *Laissez-faire* in relation to the mainstay of Burma's economy ended in 1942, not at independence six years later.

The initial policies of the postwar British administration were successful inasmuch as rice production and the system which supported it returned to a relatively high level of efficiency in a very short period. Soon, planted acreage rose to a level more than two-thirds that of the prewar period and yields per acre increased. By 1949/50 total paddy production was about five-sevenths of the prewar level.[123] The government

120. Abu, 'Collaboration, 1941–1945', p. 209.
121. Becka, *National Liberation Movement in Burma*, p. 110.
122. Abu, 'Collaboration', p. 210–11; Golay *et al.*, *Underdevelopment and Economic Nationalism*, p. 223.
123. John S. Ambler, 'Burma's Rice Economy under Military Rule: The Evolution of Socialist Agricultural Programs and Their Impact on Paddy Farmers' (unpubl. paper, Cornell University, 1983), Table 1: 'Paddy Acreage, Production, Yield and Population Estimates — Burma, 1940/41 to 1961/2'.

regulated the price of paddy through a state agricultural purchasing organization and in the immediate post-war years set the official price below the cost of production. At the same time the colonial state apparatus which enforced payment of rent and taxes was resurrected, though apparently the peasantry had been led to believe this would not occur until economic conditions had improved. Even in areas where the economic well-being of the peasantry was not acute, the Communist-led peasants' union received widespread support for its campaigns attacking the state's rice policy.[124]

Recognizing the support the Communists received for their 'no rent' and 'no tax' campaigns, but also faced with the problems of raising revenue and capital and protecting property rights, the AFPFL was able to persuade the colonial authorities to introduce ameliorating legislation. Improvement in the security of tenure was one of the objects of the AFPFL's programme. The 1947 Tenancy Standard Rent Act limited paddy land gross rents to twice the level of land tax and placed the burden of land tax payment on the landowner rather than the tenant.[125] This allowed the state to determine the value of land, but placed the burden for the extraction of funds for the payment of tax onto the landlord. The government thought (mistakenly) that this arrangement would provide an alternative to the need for rural credit, as the lowered rents would allow sufficient savings for tenants to finance their own annual crop.[126]

Some legislation introduced to further peasants' rights and to undercut the appeal of the Communists' agrarian policies had the effect of putting the cultivators more under the control of both the state and the landlord. For example, the 1948 Disposal of Tenancies Act made security of tenure dependent upon the payment of rent, the cultivation of the land and the repayment of agricultural loans. Other legislation was more helpful to the peasants and alleviated some of their prior obligations. The 1947 Agriculturalists' Debt Relief Act cancelled all pre-war debts and obligated only the repayment of the principle loan agreements entered into between October 1946 and the date the legislation was passed. Though in theory these acts provided peasants with 'security of tenure,

---

124. Cady, 'Character and Program of the Communist Party in Burma', p. 4.
125. Golay et al., *Underdevelopment and Economic Nationalism*, p. 223. The amount of rent payable was reduced to the same as the rate of tax by an amendment to this legislation in 1954; *Ibid.*, fn. 47, p. 223.
126. *Two Year Plan of Economic Development for Burma* (Rangoon: Supt., Govt. Printing and Stationery, Burma, 1948), p. 10.

nominal rents, and reinstated the titles of many cultivators',[127] given the breakdown in the administrative system it is doubtful whether many peasants were in a position to extract support from the state in gaining their newly-acquired rights.

After independence more radical legislation was enacted in the form of the 1948 Land Nationalization Act. According to the government in 1948 there was a total of 11,120,343 acres of land in cultivation in the delta. Of this land, slightly less than 52 per cent was held by peasant proprietors, about 9 per cent by resident landlords and the remaining 42 per cent by non-resident landlords. In central Burma the situation was very different. There, nearly 87 per cent of the 8,203,498 acres in possession was held by peasant farmers and only 7.5 per cent was held by alien landlords.[128] The purpose of the Land Nationalization Act was to return the land held by foreign and indigenous landlords to the tenants who worked it. The act was implemented in only one township and then abandoned. The reason advanced by some for the failure of land reform in 1948 was the distractions of the civil war; others have blamed the absence of sufficiently well trained administrative personnel to implement the bill.[129]

However, given that one of the rallying points of the Communists against the state was that the AFPFL favoured the landlords over the peasants, it would appear to have been in the interest of the government to implement the act expeditiously in order to regain the support of the majority of the population which was then fighting with or aiding the Communist insurgents. The reasons given by J.S. Furnivall — at that time an economic advisor to the government — for the failure of the act were 'favouritism, mistakes and bribery. The whole plan was ruined by the incompetence and corruption of the politicians and officials who used it for their own benefit.'[130] Another obstacle in the way of the implementation of the 1948 Land Nationalization Act was the interference of the Indian Ambassador to Burma, who was demanding full compensation for the nearly 5 million acres of land held by Indian and other foreign landlords. The Ambassador, Dr M.A. Rauf, was the brother of the AFPFL's Housing Minister and a leader of the Muslim community in Burma, M.A. Raschid.[131] Thus it appears that the weak

127. Golay et al., *Underdevelopment and Economic Nationalism*, p. 224.
128. Than Aung, 'General Study in the Economic Development', pp. 79–80.
129. Golay et al., *Underdevelopment and Economic Nationalism*, p. 224.
130. Quoted in Than Aung, 'General Study in the Economic Development', p. 80.
131. *Ibid.*, p. 81; Golay et al., *Underdevelopment and Economic Nationalism*, p. 224.

political structure of the independent state and the interests of its managers combined to make complete land reform impossible.

A second Land Nationalization Act was introduced in 1954. Like its predecessor it was not intended to introduce socialist forms of ownership and production as land reform in China and Vietnam in the same period did, but rather to redistribute land ownership from foreign and domestic landlords back into the hands of tenants. The revised legislation provided for the compensation of the Chettiar and other landlords, but at only a fraction of the value they set on the land and largely in the form of fifteen-year, 3 per cent, non-negotiable, non-transferable government bonds of little genuine value unless used for investment in Burma.[132] Between 1953–4 and 1957–8, when the caretaker government halted the administration of the act, 17 per cent of all cultivated land had been nationalized.[133] Its implementation had been very slow. By late 1955 about 6 per cent of the target of 10 million acres had been reached,[134] and only 59,627 peasant households had been affected.[135] Assuming most of the 3,357,000 acres eventually nationalized was paddy land, this represented about 25 per cent of this category of land. Of these 3,357,000 acres, only 1,480,000 was actually redistributed to 178,540 previous tenant cultivators, while more than half of the resurveyed land was confirmed to be in the control of 305,490 households.[136] The implementation of the act, which included surveying work of a kind which had been largely neglected since before the war, did provide the state with an opportunity to improve its control of land usage and taxation. The ultimate failure of the land nationalization programme is indicated by the statement that as late as 1963, tenants were still paying rent to 350,000 landlords, one third of whom were aliens.[137]

A study of the consequences of land redistribution in one area has shown that the programme was more beneficial to the better-off members of the peasantry than to the poorer sections. Tenants who had been landowners were more likely to be granted land than were previously landless labourers, because to be eligible for a land grant, a farmer had to possess the means to cultivate the land. Many landless

---

132. Kozicki, 'India and Burma', pp. 347, 350.
133. Golay et al., *Underdevelopment and Economic Nationalism*, p. 224.
134. Than Aung, 'General Study in the Economic Development', pp. 82–3.
135. Kozicki, 'Indian and Burma', p. 349.
136. Silverstein, *Burma: Military Rule*, p. 75.
137. Golay et al., *Underdevelopment and Economic Nationalism*, p. 225.

labourers were too poor to own either draught cattle or ploughs.[138]

In the 1950s, government schemes to assist the peasants also tended to help the better-off in other ways. One of the government's major organizations which helped cultivators was the State Agricultural Bank (SAB). The SAB was developed as a means of providing credit to farmers in order to avoid the necessity of becoming once again indebted to Chettiars and other moneylenders. Research conducted by an American anthropologist in the 1950s revealed that in the delta better-off cultivators who did not need cheap credit borrowed from the SAB and then reloaned at higher rates to poorer peasants who could not meet the SAB's conditions for the granting of credit. Such practices did not occur in villages near Mandalay in the central dry zone.[139]

Tampering with the margins of the land distribution and credit systems probably had less effect on how peasants saw their relationship with the state and the economy than did the government's monopolistic practises in the purchase and export of paddy. Following the practice of the British military administration, the independent state assumed direct responsibility for the management of the rice trade. The Socialists in the AFPFL changed the scheme's public justification from increasing production to increasing peasant welfare, but the effect was to benefit the state.

Rice purchasing and resale was the source of a large proportion of the state's revenue and foreign exchange and it served, effectively, as a form of indirect taxation on cultivators. In years of high international rice prices during the Korean war, as much as 40 per cent of all state revenue was provided by the state rice trade.[140] All the profits of the State Agricultural Marketing Board (SAMB), first a monopsonistic and then monopolistic purchaser of rice, accrued to state revenues. The purchase price set by the SAMB was the minimum price in the domestic market regardless of other economic factors. Throughout the 1950s, the SAMB purchase price never varied though the average annual export price of rice and rice products varied from Kt 446 to Kt 838 per ton (f.o.b). 'The SAMB buying price for paddy, as compared with prewar, remained

138. Ambler, 'Burma's Rice Economy', p. 15, citing David E. Pfanner, 'Rice and Religion in a Burmese Village' (unpubl. Ph.D. diss., Cornell University, 1962), p. 241.
139. David E. Pfanner. 'A Semisubsistence Village Economy in Lower Burma', in Clifton R. Wharton, Jr., *Subsistence Agriculture and Economic Development* (Chicago: Aldine, 1969), p. 58; Ambler, 'Burma's Rice Economy', p. 18.
140. Richter, 'Impact of Socialism', p. 229.

below parity with prices of other goods.' In the face of criticism of the unfairness of this arrangement, as well as its denial of 'market forces', the government maintained that the cultivators were actually better off than before the war because of its land reform programme and because of reductions in rent, taxes and interest rates.[141]

After independence, the failure of the State Agricultural Bank to provide adequate credit for the bulk of the peasantry led to the re-emergence of the class of indigenous moneylenders. Wealthier members of villages who under the state's tenancy legislation were unable to invest in land turned their surplus cash to moneylending. There appeared in the 1950s a form of local credit not unlike that of the precolonial period, unsanctioned by law and parallel to the official controls on the economy.[142] As early as 1949–51 the absence of state legal protection for mortgages had led to a rapid drop in the registration of mortgages,[143] but it is not possible to assess the effect of these changes on the broad mass of the peasantry.

Urban Classes For the relatively small indigenous working class, social change and state policies during the two decades between 1942 and 1962 provided a new level of security. One reason was the return to India of many urban labourers and a consequent lessening of job competition in the cities, especially in the transportation and processing sectors. Another reason was the greater power that unions developed under the AFPFL government because of the influence the TUC-B had as a major constituent of the ruling front. However, during the war years the situation was initially far less positive. Unemployment grew rapidly, especially in manufacturing and the extractive industries including mining, oil production and the timber business. Many previously organized labourers migrated back to the villages in search of subsistence. The urban proletariat which had begun to develop under the British was thus dispersed during the war years.[144]

Nevertheless, organized urban labour was of critical importance after the war in maintaining immediate political pressure on the British to

141. Golay et al., *Underdevelopment and Economic Nationalism*, p. 242.
142. There are no complete studies, but see Pfanner, 'Semisubsistence Village Economy', p. 58.
143. Kozicki, 'India and Burma', f.n. 49, p. 342, citing the *Report on the Administration of the Registration Department in Burma During the Three Years 1949 to 1951* (Rangoon: Government Printing and Stationery, 1954), p. 4.
144. Becka, *National Liberation Movement in Burma*, p. 110.

grant independence. Strikes, especially by government employees, were very effective in 1945, 1946 and 1947. As inflation increased, the power of the strike was used after independence by government employees to defend their incomes from government fiscal stringency. The state's employees developed a great capacity for bargaining with the government because of their strategic positions in the administrative system of the capital and elsewhere. The need to ensure the support and loyalty of the lower ranks of the administrative services seriously weakened the government's ability to impose labour discipline on the economy, especially before elections. The political power of the state sector of the workforce had also increased as nationalization provided workers with higher rates of pay and greater job security than they had received in the private sector. The result was low productivity and high labour turnover as workers moved from job to job in search of the best conditions.[145]

The middle class, which should have benefited most from independence, was placed in a highly ambivalent position after 1942. During the previous twenty years it had developed uneasy relationships with the groups which strove for state power. The political élite was dependent upon the administrative and economic skills of the members of the middle class and it enunciated ideas of liberal democratic rule which would eventually have given the middle class a dominant position in relation to the state and to other classes. But the military requirements and socialist or statist ideological beliefs of most of the major political leaders after 1942 meant that policies which would have encouraged the growth of a large indigenous bourgeoisie were rarely enunciated, much less implemented. Rather, the middle class remained dependent upon the state, regardless of who controlled it, just as it had been before the war.

During the Japanese occupation, although indigenous businessmen no longer suffered from competition from Indian and British shops and companies, they were greatly restricted by the monopolistic activities of the Japanese trading firms.[146] The state attempted to come to their assistance in 1944 by making regulations limiting the ownership of property in Burma to citizens and by requiring 60 per cent indigenous equity in all companies. These rules, however, did not become law until almost the end of both the war and the Ba Maw government in 1945.[147]

Indicative of the ambivalent relationship of the middle class with the

145. Aye Hlaing, 'Observations on Some Patterns of Economic Development', p. 11.
146. Becka, *National Liberation Movement in Burma*, p. 112.
147. *Ibid.*, pp. 131–2.

post-independence state was the policy of maintaining the government monopoly over rice trading. While the colonial state's managers had perceived no objections to using state economic and social policy to assist the development of an independent, entrepreneurial middle class, the socialist ideology of the post-independence state managers viewed such a development with misgivings. The State Agricultural Marketing Board, in the process of replacing the Indian and British middlemen, placed this large sector of external trade not in the hands of indigenous businessmen but under the management of state employees. For those entrepreneurs who were permitted to work in the interstices of the state monopoly as millers and brokers, the many restrictions placed on their operations by the state meant that profits were small.[148] As a result, wealth which might have gone toward the middle class and strengthened its independence was drained off by the state.

In smaller trading activities, indigenous businessmen benefited more. However, even after independence, less than 40 per cent of all commercial dealers were Burmese. The predominant position of Indians and Chinese in trading concerns of all sizes, including the smallest, was not seriously disturbed by the social change that followed war and independence.[149] In private industry the indigenous middle class did rather better and by the end of the 1950s Burmese owned over 90 per cent of all firms while foreigners owned only 3.5 per cent.[150] However, the largest industrial and processing concerns were jointly owned by the state and foreign, mainly British, companies, who controlled top managerial posts. When the government lost enthusiasm for the state-owned firms in the mid- to late-1950s because of their inefficiency and high costs, attention was given to turning the nationalized industries over to private hands. The army caretaker government of 1958–60 opened rice exporting to private enterprise with preferential treatment given to Burmese firms, but its concern for economic rationality and the expansion of domestic and indigenous trade did not stop it from placing an increasingly large part of the import trade in the hands of quasi-government corporations.[151] In those areas where the government wished to encourage the growth of private indigenous enterprises (banking, pawnshops,

---

148. Golay et al., *Underdevelopment and Economic Nationalism*, p. 243.
149. Ibid., Table 23, Dealers [any seller after the importer] Registered by the Commercial Taxes Service, November 1949 through May 1951, p. 252.
150. Ibid., p. 232.
151. Ibid., p. 263.

moneylending and insurance) it was unsuccessful, for foreign competition remained strong and Burmese entrepreneurs were unable to enter into trade satisfactorily.[152] The result was often further nationalization, the threat of which made it difficult for large commercial or manufacturing investments to be made.

Paradoxically, the displacement of the state meant that the state became increasingly important as a source of middle-class employment. Many factors were at work in increasing the public sector workforce. One was the increasing use of the state bureaucracy as a source of reward for political followers. This was a trend which predated the Japanese occupation, but which in the less restrained administrative atmosphere of the 1950s grew apace.[153] Another reason was the increasing range of activities the state attempted to undertake either in the name of socialism or of economic planning.

The state had been the largest single employer under the British, and this situation was perpetuated in the 1950s. Between 1930 and 1953–4, the total number of public service employees in the country increased by 75 per cent, from 88,100 to 154,432.[154] By the end of the 1950s, nearly 250,000 people worked for government departments, boards and corporations, compared with 56,400 in 1940.[155] Growth was less rapid in the professional and technical services to which individuals from the old middle class were especially drawn (55 per cent in the period between 1930 and 1953–4).[156] The most rapid growth was in positions for top-level managers and directors of various governmental organizations. These increased nearly three fold from thirty-five in 1940 to ninety-six in 1957, of which thirty-five were government boards and corporations.[157] Highly prized and well paid posts in the central secretariat increased 233 per cent between 1940 and 1957, with senior positions numbering 130 in 1957, compared to 39 in 1940.[158] The size of the civil service and its leading figures' influence in the state at the height of the civil war was such that they even attempted to install a government without polit-

152. *Ibid.*, pp. 212, 258.
153. Richter, 'Impact of Socialism', p. 225.
154. Khin Maung Kyi, 'Patterns of Accommodation to Bureaucratic Authority', Table IV–1, Increase in Public Service Employees in Burma, p. 92.
155. *Ibid.*, p. 398.
156. *Ibid.*, p. 92.
157. *Ibid.*, Table IV–2, Growth of Government Organizations, p. 93.
158. *Ibid.*, Table IV–3, Growth of the Secretariat, p. 94.

icians.¹⁵⁹ However, their dependent position and lack of any independent power limited their political effectiveness. The middle class and its leading bureaucratic elements were in fact no more powerful than the weak state they served.

The greatest sources of influence the urban middle class had with the state was its proximity to the political élite and its hold over policy as a result of the ballot. Because small shopkeepers and businessmen were more politically vocal and articulate than the majority peasant population, they were able to be heard more easily within the leadership of the AFPFL and the bureaucracy. The urban middle class during the 1950s also increased its buying power as a result of public expenditure on development projects, and the government was forced to spend scarce foreign exchange on the importation of luxury goods to offset inflationary pressures. The wives of many political leaders were themselves involved in 'trade' and were keen to see their interests protected. 'Very few taxable persons in urban areas paid income tax' because of the influence they had and because the government was unwilling to attempt to tax them for fear of the political backlash this would cause.¹⁶⁰ The weak state could only tax the least influential group in society, the peasantry, and then only indirectly.

The Search for Legitimacy

The search for a set of ideas and symbols to provide the state with the seal of legitimacy and thus abet its perpetuation was a constant concern for political leaders after 1942. Nationalism alone proved insufficient to justify the continued exactions of the modern state, so the state stood exposed as an immoral and perhaps even exploitative instrument of a narrow ruling group. The constant experimentation with alternative legitimizing symbols and political slogans during the 1940s and 1950s stands in stark contrast to the consistency of the legitimizing myths of the precolonial state and even of the colonial state. The legitimacy claims of the state under Dr Ba Maw between 1942 and 1945 were based on the contention that by siding with the Japanese in their battle against European imperialism in Asia Burma was on the side of an

---

159. *Ibid.*, p. 120.
160. *Ibid.*, p. 101.

obvious and just historical trend. 'Asia for the Asiatics' and the 'Greater East Asian Co-Prosperity Sphere' had about them an aura of righteousness which wartime experience under the Japanese military eventually made hollow. After the August 1943 declaration of independence Ba Maw chose for himself the title of *Adipati Ashin Mingyi*, a title with an historical resonance going back to the Burmese kings. He then claimed that the state he led, based upon the contemporary dictatorial and nationalistic slogan, 'one voice, one blood, one nation', was in keeping with not only authoritarian trends in German, Italian and Japanese politics throughout the 1930s and 1940s, but also with expectations in Burma. Popular Burmese newspapers and magazines in the 1930s frequently posed the question of who would be Burma's Mussolini or Hitler. The reality of the war years, however, made these claims increasingly derisory and there were few who felt that a legitimate government had been overthrown when Ba Maw fled the country in April 1945.

The opposition to the Japanese-backed state was based on claims put forward by the Anti-Fascist Organization at the time of its formation in August 1944. The AFO began its appeals with round condemnation of the evils of Japanese fascism and militarism before proposing to create a free and fair society. Subsequent statements called for economic reforms and for the amelioration of the conditions of the workers and peasants after independence was gained. The language of these claims had a Marxist ring to it. Following the gradualist line that they were pursuing at the time, the central Communist leaders of the AFO and then the AFPFL, with the exception of Thakin Soe, were careful not to set forth radical economic plans until after independence. After the AFPFL fell under more conservative leadership the ideological claims of the League were expressed essentially in nationalist terms. The first AFPFL congress in 1947 stated that its economic and social policy would encourage private enterprise and that foreign, including British, economic interests would be able to continue to function — though in the interests of nation. The ideological statements of the AFPFL before and after 1948 were based upon the equality of all peoples within the country and on economic reform for the benefit of all nationals. The AFPFL did not publicly appeal in the name of any specific ethnic or religious community, though much of the organized opposition to the League was couched in terms of the protection of the special rights or privileges of Muslims, Christians, Buddhists or of the Karen and other minority groups.

The Search for Legitimacy

The preamble to the 1947 constitution sets forth the liberal basis of the claims to legitimacy by the postcolonial state, and represents the thinking of the conservative leadership of the League after the ouster of the Communists. It began thus:

WE THE PEOPLE OF BURMA including the Frontier Areas and the Karenni States, determined to establish in strength and unity a SOVEREIGN INDEPENDENT STATE, to maintain social order on the basis of the eternal principles of JUSTICE, LIBERTY AND EQUALITY and to guarantee and secure to all citizens JUSTICE social, economic and political; LIBERTY of thought, expression, belief, faith, worship, vocation, association and action; EQUALITY of status, of opportunity and before the law . . . ADOPT, ENACT AND GIVE TO OURSELVES THIS CONSTITUTION.[161]

Echoing later clauses in the constitution, the independent government's first major economic statement indicated that the state's managers also believed that the state had important economic functions, and that these, too, were the basis of its legitimacy. As stated in the initial *Two Year Plan*, the government was seeking to lay 'the foundations of a planned economy and to transform Burma into a country where the Welfare of the common man constitutes the main motive of State activity'.[162] The civil war, however, revealed how meaningless these doctrines were to much of the population, except the most westernized individuals such as the authors of the constitution and the government's first economic planners.[163] To many others, ethnicity, religion or Communism inspired more loyalty than did the state.

Claims to protect the rights of ethnic minorities had been one of the bases of the legitimacy of the colonial state. As discussed in Chapter II, individuals who referred to themselves as Karens were given special rights of employment and representation under the British, and the leaders of the communities in the hill areas and the Shan state were guaranteed a role in the state. The intellectual justification of this policy

---

161. The 1947 constitution and its amendments are reprinted as appendices VII, VIII and IX of Maung Maung, *Burma's Constitution*, pp. 258–313.
162. *Two Year Plan of the Economic Development of Burma*, p. 2.
163. See Robert H. Taylor, 'Burmese Concepts of Revolution', in Mark Hobart and Robert H. Taylor (eds), *Context Meaning and Power in Southeast Asia* (Ithaca: Cornell University Southeast Asia Program, 1986), pp. 72–92 for a discussion of the underlying notions of revolution in the thought of Burma's state managers in the 1950s and 1960s.

survived into the politics of twentieth century Burma. By using ascriptive notions of ethnicity common in nineteenth-century Europe, and by claiming that the Karens, Shans or other groups were ethnic categories embodying living social formations with unique and independent histories, ethnic labels became reified into claims for the existence of political nations within Burma other than that recognized as the 'Burmese state'. Of course, the state *qua* state has no ethnicity other than that which may be given to it by its subjects. In the modern age of nationalism, almost all states have ethnic labels which may incorporate within them one or more non-political ethnic groups.

The prevailing mood of nationalism in the 1930s and 1940s gave emotional and intellectual credence to claims for a unique national status for the 'Karen', 'Karenni', 'Chin', 'Kachin' and 'Shan' which the British had nominated as ethnically (or in those days 'racially') distinct from the 'Burman' who lived in the plains. Even Burma's Communists, borrowing from Stalinist doctrines about national races, accepted the legitimacy of these labels and it was their ideas, along with notions about nationality common in liberal thought at this time, that shaped the 'federal' nature of the Union of Burma set forth in the 1947 constitution.

The experiences of the colonial period, compounded by stories about the oppression of the 'Burman kings' toward the minorities before the British came to rescue them in the nineteenth century, and by conflicts between communities in the delta during the Second World War and civil war, heightened perceptions of ethnic distinctiveness in the post-war period. The British requirement that leaders of the 'hill tribes' and the Shan states indicate their willingness to join with the government in Rangoon in an independent Burma, culminating in the 1947 Panglong Agreement, meant that ethnicity became part of the independence process itself. In several cases, individuals sought to put themselves forward as ethnic leaders in order to increase their influence in the government. The growing perception that the state could not protect the Karen Christian community and that the Karens thus owed a higher loyalty to their ethnic label than to the state was the basis of one prong of the post-independence civil war.

The establishment of egalitarianism as a principle of the state, 'the eternal principle of equality' as stated in the constitution's preamble, and the implementation of universal suffrage, meant that the unique privileges created by the colonial state were denied to some groups after independence. Especially for the leaders of the Karen Christian community, the denial of ethnicity as a political principle in an all-Burmese order meant an end to their unique power not only within the state, but within their own communities, for they had no 'traditional' claims to authority (their influence having come from their ability to gain special treatment for their followers from the state). Similarly, the principle of equality meant that in the frontier areas, the 'feudal' powers of the *Sawbwas* and other rulers were now in contradiction to state principles. The constitution in its details, however, skirted this issue by allowing the Shan and Karenni state rulers to remain in office. The constitution's authors had no choice but to obfuscate the issue of ethnicity, for there is no logical limit to nationalist claims.[164]

The perception of an illegitimate grab for power by the non-Communist leaders of the AFPFL provided the basis for the other, Communist, prong of the civil war. The popularity of the Communist leadership and of their organizational activities after 1943 was only part of the basis of the support they received. The failure of the government to implement many of the egalitarian promises made by the AFPFL before independence was another factor. The state's search for legitimacy in the face of rival claims of politicized ethnicity and Communist ideology initially centred on several options: these included an extension of the federalist front to the unitary constitution with the creation of a Karen state and the placement of leading cooperating Karens in important positions in the state's structures. The initial promise of a socialist programme, including land reform, was intended to remove support from the Communists. However, during the 1950s, religion, especially Buddhism, became the most important element in the state's search for legitimacy.

Though Aung San and the Communist founders of the AFO were ardent believers in the separation of politics from religion,[165] their successors in the leadership of the AFPFL, particularly Prime Minister Nu and many of the older, more conservative figures in the government, believed that the state had an obligation to support the Buddhist religion just as the precolonial state had done. Others, such as the Socialist leader Ba Swe, argued that Marxism and Buddhism were actually comparable

---

164. A fuller elaboration of this argument can be found in Robert H. Taylor, 'Perceptions of Ethnicity in the Politics of Burma', *Southeast Asian Journal of Social Science*, vol. 10, no. 1 (1982), pp. 7–22.
165. Aung San, *Burma's Challenge* (South Okkalapa: Tathetta, 1974), pp. 61–5.

doctrines and that good Burmese could equally support both. What distinguished the Socialists from the Communists, they argued, was that the Communists were opposed to religion.[166]

The extent to which the state's leaders in the 1950s consciously used Buddhism as a religious weapon against the state's rivals and how far they genuinely believed that the faith should be upheld by the state can not be known. Nu and others certainly believed, however, that strengthening Buddhist beliefs among the population would prevent the Communists from coming to power.[167] Devout Buddhists had long been opposed to Communism and in the 1930s the colonial authorities had considered how they could use the monkhood to stop the spread of radical ideas. By the end of 1945, the Buddhist hierarchy had begun a program of its own, criticizing the Communist Party for being anti-religious; Burmese language newspapers also attacked the BCP for being not only opposed to private property but also to racial distinctions, thus allegedly making it impossible to oust Indians from Burma's economic life.[168]

Formal action was taken as early as 1949 with the passage of the Ecclesiastical Courts Act to use the state to support Buddhism. In 1950 Nu introduced into parliament legislation to establish a lay Buddhist Sasana Council, and a Ministry of Religious Affairs was established to implement legislation dealing with religion.[169] Not only did the Council support Buddhism among the existing members of the faith, it also undertook missionary work to encourage the development of Buddhism among animists and others living in the hill areas, under agencies such as the Society for the Propagation of Buddhism.[170] Other legislation passed in the early 1950s established a Pali University and continued the colonial state's practice of supervising examinations for Buddhist scholars. In October 1951 Nu announced the holding of the Sixth Great Buddhist Council to correct and maintain Buddhist texts. Government funds were used not only to construct the great artificial cave in which the proceedings of the council were conducted but also to build adjacent to it the Kaba Aye (World Peace) pagoda. This council, like the last one held

166. Smith, *Religion and Politics in Burma*, pp. 128–9.
167. John Everton, 'The Ne Win Regime in Burma', *Asia*, 2 (Autumn, 1964), p. 3.
168. Cady, 'Program and Character of the Commuist Party', pp. 4–5; Than Htun, *Pyithu Sit Pyithu Ana* (People's War, People's Power) (Rangoon, publisher unknown, 1946), pp. 28–9.
169. Smith, *Religion and Politics in Burma*, pp. 117, 148.
170. *Ibid.*, p. 154.

under the auspices of King Mindon, served to link the state clearly with the support and propagation of the faith.[171] The socialization of youth into Buddhist beliefs was also sought through the introduction of Buddhist instruction in schools, but this, like other state actions to support Burma's majority religion, provoked strong opposition from the leaders of other religious communities.[172]

The attempt to use Buddhism as the basis of the state's legitimacy was opposed not only by Christian, Islamic, Communist and animist leaders, but also by Socialists within the government. During the colonial period the previous consensus about the state's role as a supporter of Buddhism had been shattered, and although leaders like Ba Swe and Nu argued that socialism and Buddhism were compatible politico-religious doctrines, when they came to discuss the epistemological and moral bases of the two doctrines they were forced to differ.[173] After the split of the AFPFL in 1958, Nu was no longer constrained in his use of Buddhism as a source of political legitimacy. Given a completely free hand, he went even further and revived *nat* worship (a popular but non-Buddhist-derived practice), which he had conducted privately since 1948.[174] After 1960 Nu made *nat* worship almost an official state ceremony, once ordering the construction of 60,000 sand pagodas as a means of establishing peace in the country.[175] He also instituted the use of the Buddhist lunar calendar, abolished cattle slaughter and reinstituted many Buddhist support programmes which the military had dropped after 1958.[176]

Nu's attempt to create state legitimacy on the basis of the symbols and beliefs of the Burmese monarchs failed partly because the society upon which he attempted to impose these ideas was much more religiously

171. *Ibid.*, pp. 117, 165. See also E. Michael Mendelson, *Sangha and State in Burma, A Study of Monastic Sectarianism and Leadership*, edited by John P. Ferguson (Ithaca: Cornell University Press, 1975), pp. 270–6.
172. Mendelson, *Sangha and State in Burma*, pp. 178–80.
173. *Ibid.*, pp. 128–33.
174. Butwell, *U Nu of Burma*, p. 71.
175. Smith, *Religion and Politics in Burma*, p. 171.
176. Winston L. King, 'Contemporary Burmese Buddhism', in Heinrich Dumoulin (ed.), *Buddhism in the Modern World* (London: Macmillan, 1976), p. 92. Of course, during 1958–60 in an attempt to halt the spread of Communism the army itself had used the cry that Buddhism was in danger as a major part of its psychological warfare programme. The resultant public response is said to have been one of the main reasons for the pious Nu's election triumph in 1960 (against the wishes of the army). Smith, *Religion and Politics in Burma*, p. 135.

and educationally diverse and sceptical than that of the nineteenth century and before. It failed also because the state lacked the power to impose its control upon the Buddhist monkhood and because, unlike the strong kings of the past who were able to use the *sangha* and its institutions to prop up the state, in the 1950s mobilized factions within the monkhood used the state for their own political purposes. The continuing sectarianism of the monkhood was a reflection of the fact that the state could not enforce 'purification' upon them by championing one sect and its interpretation of the *Vinaya* over the others. The AFPFL thus became riven with the same sectarian feuds as the monkhood,[177] and factions within the monkhood supported different leaders of the League. The holding of parliamentary elections during the 1950s in particular increased the power of the monkhood over the state, for influential sect leaders could often sway votes toward one party or another.[178]

The controversies that surrounded the state's legitimacy were not lessened but rather exacerbated by the policies that Nu implemented. Nu's final desperate acts, seen to be politically expedient rather than serious efforts at national consensus by his critics, reveal how the state's legitimacy was largely dissipated by the early 1960s. In keeping with his campaign promises Nu introduced legislation amending the constitution and making Buddhism the official state religion. In the face of protests from other religious communities he then introduced another constitutional amendment guaranteeing freedom of religion. Neither act achieved anything in terms of creating a legitimizing doctrine for the state, but rather kept the issue of the state's legitimacy at the centre of public attention. Furthermore, in order to attempt to end ethnic separatist insurgency, in the 1960 election Nu promised to create more ethnically designated states for the Mon and Arakanese. As with the creation of the first five ethnic states, this proposal created no autonomy for the ethnic leaders, for their states were fiscally and militarily tied to the centre. But the promise, as well as its nonfulfillment, also kept the question of ethnicity and the basis of the legitimacy of the state at the centre of public attention. Twenty years after the collapse of the colonial state, no new basis for the state had been developed.

177. Mendelson, *Sangha and State in Burma*, pp. 25–6.
178. Smith, *Religion and Politics in Burma*, p. 138.

CHAPTER 5

REASSERTING THE STATE, 1962–1987

The Consequences of the March 2nd Coup

The ouster of the civilian government of Prime Minister Nu and his Union Party by a military Revolutionary Council headed by General Ne Win on March 2, 1962 was not seen at the time to be a particularly momentous event. Foreign observers saw the coup as a reassertion of the disciplined government of the 1958–60 caretaker period, and therefore primarily as an attempt to restore order in an increasingly chaotic political situation.¹ It evoked no outward manifestations of public opposition in either Rangoon or in the central and peripheral regions of the state. The coup, conducted with the loss of one life, began with the arrest of the President, Prime Minister, five other cabinet ministers, the Chief Justice and some thirty politicians and former *Sawbwas* from the Shan and Kayah States. Though it took place during a strike by Rangoon's importers and retail traders against government plans to turn more trade over to citizens,² this apparently had no bearing on the decision by the army to replace the civilian government.

Rather, the army justified its action in the name of ensuring the continued unity of the nation. Nu's policies since 1960, especially the establishment of Buddhism as the state religion, the organization of administrations for new Mon and Arakan States, and the continuing negotiations with politicians from the Shan and Kayah States over increasing regional autonomy, raised the prospect to the army and to many others of increasing disunity in the state and of the possible loss of independence. The examples of Laos and South Vietnam, both then riven by civil war and consequently under foreign domination, were very much alive in the minds of many people, including the coup leaders.³

1. John Everton, 'The Ne Win Regime in Burma', *Asia* (Autumn 1964), p. 6.
2. Frank H. Golay, *et al.*, *Underdevelopment and Economic Nationalism in Southeast Asia* (Ithaca: Cornell University Press, 1969), pp. 249–50.
3. Richard Butwell, *U Nu of Burma* (Stanford: Stanford University Press, 2nd printing, 1969), quoting Brigadier Aung Gyi at a press conference on March 7 1962.

The issue of federalism and the possibility of trying to apportion state sovereignty were intimately related to other central questions. The granting of greater autonomy to the states would have allowed them to pursue different patterns of economic development and would have further undermined socialism, which was of decreasing importance to Nu anyway.[4] The possibility of the secession of the Shan and Kayah States raised the prospect of independent foreign policies for these regions and, should they have elected to do so, of their entry into an alliance with an outside power such as the United States. This would have posed a major threat to the security of the remainder of the state, with the possibility of direct conflict between China and the United States extending beyond Laos and Vietnam to the heart of Burma. Such possibilities were not considered fanciful in 1962.

The federal issue was part of a general critique, widely shared within the army, of the nature of parliamentary democracy as it had been practised in Burma. Federalism and multi-party democracy were considered open to abuse by politicians representing landlords and capitalists and others seeking power and wealth for personal rather than public ends. This critique subsequently became not only the justification for the coup but also the justification for the changes in the nature of the state that followed from military rule.[5] It soon became clear as a result of this critique that the consequences of the coup for the state and society were far more significant than just the temporary replacement of one set of rulers by another. The weakness of the postcolonial state was attributed to parliamentary democracy and federalism, and therefore it seemed obvious that their abolition was necessary in order for the state to reassert itself over other institutions in civil society.

Though the Revolutionary Council did not initially phrase its seizure of power in the name of state reassertion, it did so twelve years later when formally passing power to the new legislative body, the *Pyithu Hluttaw* or People's Assembly, formed under the constitution inaugurated on March 2, 1974. In a detailed but unpublished report

4. See Nu's assessment of nationalization and the economy in his memoirs, *U Nu — Saturday's Son* (transl. by Law Yone, edited by Kyaw Win, New Haven: Yale University Press, 1975), pp. 215–20.
5. 'Political Report of the General Secretary', in Burma Socialist Programme Party Central Organizing Committee, *Party Seminar 1965* (Rangoon: Sarpay Beikman, 1966), pp. 28–33. See also Hpo Kyaw San, *Paliman Dimokayeisi Sannit hnit Myanma Naingngan* (Parliamentary Democracy and Burma) (Rangoon: San Pya, n.d.).

of its stewardship of the state, the Revolutionary Council wrote that after it 'took responsibility for the condition of the state (*naingngantaw*), it began a transitional revolution with the intention of establishing a socialist society of affluence and without human exploitation, with a strong governing power, and the long term independence for the state.'[6]

The achievement of state dominance after 1962 was a prolonged and dangerous task given the history of the previous twenty years. Institutional rivals were forced to accept the Revolutionary Council's terms for participation in a new political order or they were eliminated by law. Those institutions allowed to persist were made dependent upon the state, either through their personnel or their finances, and were therefore unable to organize opposition. The process of state reassertion was gradual, and in the end many compromises had to be made between the ideal of state autonomy and dominance and the political, economic and social conditions within which the state and its leading personnel functioned. Given the corporate experiences of the coup group prior to independence, a strategy of action avoiding foreign military or financial involvement seemed possible. A necessary measure was to ensure that no outside power had reason to intervene and capture the state immediately after the coup. Thus it is not surprising that the Revolutionary Council's first policy statement was a pledge to maintain the neutralist foreign policy of its predecessors.

In the two years between the coup and March 1964, by which time the bulk of the economy had been nationalized, the Revolutionary Council declared illegal all political opposition, took over the direct management of most educational and cultural organizations, and established the nucleus of a political party with ancillary mass organizations and its own ideology through which support for the state would be organized. The process required the demobilization of institutions which had rivalled the state for allegiance during the previous two decades and necessitated the creation of institutional substitutes tied directly to the state.

After organizing itself as a government of eight members and after issuing its announcement on foreign policy, on March 3 the Revolutionary Council eliminated the major organs established by the 1947

6. *Towhlanyei Kaungsi ei Hluthsaungchet Thamaing Akyinchut* (Concise History of the Actions of the Revolutionary Council) (Rangoon: Printing and Publishing Corporation, 2 March 1974), pp. *wa-ya*.

constitution, including the central legislature and the councils set up as the putative governments of the Kachin, Shan, Karen, and Kayah states and the Chin Special Division. (Administrative staffs were drafted in to replace the latter.[7]) Two days later, on March 5, all legislative, judicial and executive powers of state were placed in the hands of the Chairman of the Revolutionary Council. As both head of state and of government, Chairman Ne Win in theory possessed all state power and thus achieved a position of formal dominance within the state unprecedented since 1885. However, an attempt was made to suggest the collective nature of the Revolutionary Council government by substituting the designation 'Chairman' for 'Prime Minister'.

Revealing the Revolutionary Council's initial desire to gain the cooperation of other political groups in its attempts to recast the structures of the state, Council Chairman Ne Win met with the leaders of the civilian political parties on a number of occasions. Not surprisingly, the leadership of political groups which had been consistently denied state power during the previous fourteen years pledged their support for the Revolutionary Council, whereas the groups which had held power previously refused to cooperate for fear of losing their independence or because they believed that the military government would not last long. In meetings in April and May, the civilian party leaders refused to join with the Revolutionary Council in forming a single political party under its leadership.

In the initial months of the Revolutionary Council the state-centred and comparatively radical socialist economic policies subsequently instituted were little in evidence. Though the Revolutionary Council made it clear that one of the purposes of the coup was to put the economy back on the road to the socialist goals of the original AFPFL, within six days of the coup the Minister for Trade, the 'pragmatic' Brigadier Aung Gyi (then considered the second most influential member of the coup group), reversing the policy of the previous government, stated that any plans for the nationalization of import trade would be postponed for at least two years.[8] Not until August 1, when Imperial Chemical Industries

7. This discussion of the development of the Revolutionary Council government is based upon *Towhlanyei Kaungsi ei Hluthsaungchet Thamaing Akyinchut*; David I. Steinberg, 'Burma Under the Military: Towards a Chronology', *Contemporary Southeast Asia*, 4, 2 (Dec., 1981), pp. 244–85; 'Political Report of the General Secretary', in BSPP, *Party Seminar 1965*, and other publications listed in the bibliography.
8. *The Guardian*, IX, 4 (April 1962), p. 10.

was nationalized, was a major economic measure taken. Evidence of what was to come became clear in November when the government abolished the ten-year guarantee against the expropriation of foreign investments. More radical economic policies were not, however, introduced until after the resignation of Aung Gyi from the Revolutionary Council on February 8, 1963. The departure of Aung Gyi was probably necessary for the abrupt change in economic and political policy which followed.

But the change in economic policy in early 1963 lay in more than just a clash of wills between Aung Gyi's supporters and those of the chairman in the Revolutionary Council. During the preceding ten months the Revolutionary Council had sought, but from the perspective of its more ardently socialist members had not received, the cooperation of party leaders and national businessmen. Thus a majority of the government felt they would have to pursue their goals without the cooperation of other institutions and groups. A week after Aung Gyi's resignation the chairman announced thoroughgoing policies to nationalize both foreign and domestic trade as well as banking and manufacturing.

Earlier, however, the intention of the Revolutionary Council to intervene in aspects of society previously considered private was apparent. In a series of orders issued in March 1962 it was announced that horse racing would be banned in one year's time, that beauty contests and all government-sponsored music, song and dance competitions would be prohibited, and that gambling was to be banned in the Shan State.[9] The state assumed direct control of the universities on May 14 but divorced itself formally from the Buddhist faith on May 17 by dissolving the Buddha Sasana Council. In the next month the American Ford and Asia Foundations and the Fulbright programme as well as British and American language training schemes were closed and from then on only governments or international agencies (having been granted state approval) were permitted to train Burmese nationals.[10] In August, the state assumed control over all publishing by establishing a system of registered printers. By these moves, and others, such as an officially sponsored National Literary Conference in November, the state began to seal Burmese culture from outside influences and to focus public

9. *Ibid.*, IX, 4 (April 1962), p. 11; IX, 5 (May 1962). p. 8.
10. John F. Cady, *Post-War Southeast Asia* (Athens: Ohio University Press, 1974), p. 471; John H. Badgley, 'Burma: The Nexus of Socialism and Two Political Traditions', *Asian Survey*, III, 2 (Feb., 1963), p. 93.

attention on state-sanctioned cultural activities. At the same time, the state was distancing itself from social and religious issues which in its frame of reference were too politically threatening for the state to attempt to control, and which had, in the past, led to dissatisfaction among followers of different religious faiths.

The Revolutionary Council was aware of the utility of a state ideology around which the populace could focus its beliefs and loyalties, and which could be used as a means of mobilizing popular support for the state. The experiences of the military leadership during the anti-fascist resistance of the 1940s had convinced them of the need for a form of 'united front'-style organization to direct popular energies. A first step in the direction of shaping public opinion was taken on April 30 with the publication of the Revolutionary Council's policy statement, 'The Burmese Way to Socialism'.[11] To be useful for the state as a long-term doctrine, this statement had to be sufficiently vague not to tie the government to an explicit set of policies, but sufficiently emotive to appeal to public sentiment. Following the failure of the major civilian political party leaders to join them in forming a new national front, the Revolutionary Council launched its own party, the Burma Socialist Programme Party (BSPP), on July 4, thirty years to the day since the founding of the *Do Bama Asiayon*. Indeed, many of the Revolutionary Council's ideas and much of its style echoed the *Do Bama Asiayon's* prewar manifesto and evoked much the same response from established interests. At first the Party was composed only of members of the Revolutionary Council, although other politicians, especially of the left, became involved in its early organization.[12] A philosophical underpinning of the Party's ideology was issued the following January as the *System of Correlation of Man and His Environment*.[13]

The behaviour of the state after the coup baffled many observers both inside and outside Burma. Rather than the business-like military regime expected by many, the actions and words of the state's leading personnel

11. 'Myanma Hsoshelit Lansin' (Burma's Socialist Way), repr. as an app. to Myanma Hsoshelit Lansin Pati (Burma Socialist Programme Party), *Lu hnit Patwunkyindo ei Anya Manya Thabawtaya* (Law of the Interaction of Man and the Environment) (Rangoon: Printing and Publishing Corporation, 9th edn, 1973), pp. 81–96. An official translation entitled 'The Burmese Way to Socialism' is printed as an appendix to Burma Socialist Programme Party, *The System of Correlation of Man and His Environment* (Rangoon: BSPP, 1964), pp. 43–52.
12. Badgley, 'Burma: The Nexus', p. 94.
13. See fn. 11.

soon seemed bewildering. Its rhetoric owed much to leftist anti-imperialist thought current in Burma during the 1930s and 1940s which persisted in the critiques of the government of the 1950s as expressed by the legal left in the National United Front and by students and other left-wing intellectuals in Rangoon. But this rhetoric was now used to attack both the cautious Socialists and the radical Communists of the 1950s. The analysis of the past provided by the state's ideologies has been remarkably consistent since 1962. The following extract from the 1965 report of the BSPP General Secretary conveys the flavour of the ideology:

The national bourgeoisie, the class which had supplied in varying measures the political leadership in the nationalist movement for freedom from foreign rule, and political parties of the rightist or the leftist inclinations which operated under the influence of the bourgeoisie, made some efforts to reform the social life of the Union of Burma. Yet, those parties, rightist and leftist, born in the shadow of the feudal social system, nourished on the educational and spiritual values of the imperialists, wore the badge of their origins in all their activities. Their ideas, attitudes and policies were unwholesome with petit bourgeois sectarianism, narrowminded pragmatism, dogmatism, opportunism, fellow-travellerism, charlatanism, superficialism, bourgeois reformism, bureaucratic stylism, anarchistic stylism, 'leftist' infantile disorder, bourgeois militaristic style, and such evils and 'isms'.[14]

Difficult as it may seem, the Revolutionary Council clearly intended to avoid this near universal list of political errors through the ideology of the BSPP, which was described as a middle path between the social democracy of the bourgeois right and the Communism of the bourgeois left. The BSPP was to be the party of all the working people and therefore the Revolutionary Council and the post-coup state claimed a different class bias from its left- and right-wing predecessors. As made explicit in a document called the 'Specific Characteristics of the Burmese Way to Socialism', published on September 4, 1964,[15] the Revolutionary Council, in an attempt to defend itself from charges of being Communist and anti-religious in orientation, argued that the state had now become based not upon the narrow capitalist and landlord class which

---

14. BSPP, *Party Seminar 1965*, p. 29.
15. Pyihtaungsu Myanma Naingngan Towhlanyei Kaungsi (Union of Burma Revolutionary Council), *Myanma Hsoshelit Lansin Pati ei Witheitha Latkangamya* (Specific Characteristics of the Burma Socialist Programme Party) (Rangoon: Burma Socialist Programme Party, Party Affairs Central Committee, 4 Sept. 1964).

had primarily benefited from independence, nor that class's enemy, the Communist Party, but rather upon all the people.

The development of these ideological expressions stem from two characteristics of the coup group. First, the major figures of the period had been raised on the anti-imperialist and anti-capitalist rhetoric of the *Do Bama Asiayon* and of the Anti-Fascist Organization. During the war organizers from the Communist movement had worked among the Japanese-trained officer corps, instilling the rhetoric of Marxist-Leninist politics. Secondly, some former Communists and others of the left were among the first civilians to express support for the Revolutionary Council, and their skills with language and propaganda were thus used by the state. But unlike previous political movements in recent Burmese history the Revolutionary Council did not want to use the rhetoric of its ideology to mobilize one class against another in revolution or elections, but rather wanted to unite the entire nation by demonstrating that all classes had made their contribution to the national effort, but that, due to improper leadership, the revolution had gone astray.

The rhetoric of the Revolutionary Council belied its early appearance and behaviour. Though it said it was conducting a revolution, efforts were made to gain the cooperation of both previously legal and illegal political groups, and, initially, few political opponents were arrested.[16] In the first months after the coup life went on much as normal for most Burmese, and even when sweeping economic changes were introduced they tended to be implemented piecemeal. For example, though the press came under effective government control as early as August 1962, the Burmese-language papers *Hanthawaddy* and *Myanma Alin* were not nationalized until January 1969.

What most determined the style of the Revolutionary Council and has consequently become characteristic of the style of the state since 1962 is that a majority of its leading personnel have had their formative administrative and political experiences within the army. Thus, the army-style of command and planning has tended to become that of the state. Military analogies and examples most readily come to the minds of the senior leaders. Three years after the coup, for example, General Ne Win described his position as the leader of the Revolutionary Council in military terms: 'Like the commander of a military unit in disarray, I am faced with the problem of how to mobilise and regroup the people in order to set up an organisation that will serve the interests of the country

16. Badgley, 'Burma: The Nexus', p. 94.

in a spirit of unity.'[17] The leadership's working concept of a socialist economy was more like a system of military post exchanges than of a complex national organization of production and commerce. Again, a phrase from General Ne Win is suggestive: 'Internal trade is our real problem. I say trade only by convention. Internal distribution may be more appropriate for socialism.'[18] Military metaphors are common in state and party documents also. For example, in describing the first year of nation-wide monopoly paddy purchasing by the state, the Revolutionary Council's unpublished report to the first *Pyithu Hluttaw* noted that the local administrative committees 'supervised the whole process effectively in the form of a military operation'.[19]

Since 1962 the state has appeared to much of the rest of the world as isolated and *sui generis*. By the mid-1960s the economy was becoming less and less involved in world trade. Whereas in the 1950s the ratio of Burma's foreign trade (imports plus exports) to gross domestic product, a common indicator of an economy's external involvement, was 40 per cent, it fell to 26 per cent between 1960 and 1970, and to 13 per cent between 1970 and 1977, one of the lowest among developing economies.[20] There has been little change since. The state's radical economic autarky and general disengagement from the world, including in 1979 leaving the Non-Aligned Movement, has been exceptional. Its domestic economic policies — which appear to have been intended to reduce the economic level of the cities to that of the countryside rather than the reverse, which is the normal pattern in the rest of non-Communist Asia — have seemed perverse to observers who judge 'development' and well-being in terms of international hotels and 'GNP per capita in US dollar' terms. Indeed, some of their policies such as the 1964 edict which 'unified retail rice prices throughout the Union at the prices ruling in the Delta'[21] had to be abandoned because

17. 'Address of General Ne Win . . . at the Opening Session', BSPP, *Party Seminar 1965*, pp. 9–10.
18. *Address Delivered by General Ne Win at the Closing Session of the Fourth Party Seminar on 11th November 1969* (Rangoon: Sarpay Beikman, 1969), p. 6.
19. *Towhlanyei Kaungsi ei Hluthsaungchet Thamaing Akyinchut*, p. 289.
20. Stephen D. Krasner, *Structural Conflict: The Third World Against Global Liberalism* (Berkeley: University of California Press, 1985), p. 295.
21. H.V. Richter, 'Development and Equality in Burma' (unpubl. paper, Department of Economics, Research School of Pacific Studies, Australian National University, 1974, p. 32); Richter, 'The Union of Burma', in R.T. Shand (ed.), *Agricultural Development in Asia* (Canberra: Australian National University Press, 1969), p. 164.

of their economic impracticality. Why then, did the Revolutionary Council propose policies that seemed to fly in the face of 'common sense'?

Faced with what they perceived to be an obligation to strengthen and perpetuate the state, and having abandoned the option of turning to the outside world for material support, the Revolutionary Council had no option but to turn inwards and restructure the relationship of the state with the institutions of civil society. The postcolonial state stood, as it were, weak and suspended between the world economy, dominated by Western financial institutions, markets and states, and its own population. Rejecting the threats to security and independence that an outside alliance would have entailed, they turned to find means of gaining the cooperation and support of the largest sector of the population, the peasantry. Unlike the state-builders of Western Europe or North America, they sought not to please an entrepreneurial class of manufacturers or traders. No significant bourgeoisie existed in Burma. Rather, the only internal group powerful enough to bring down the state was the peasantry, and so this class's inherent and historical antipathy toward the state and its exactions had to be overcome.[22]

Territorial Reorganization

The trend since the Restored Toungoo dynasty toward greater uniformity and simplicity in the territorial organization of the state was resumed after 1962 following its partial reversal during the previous twenty years. The reification of 'race' or ethnicity, which had become part of the state's structure after 1948 with the creation of the Shan, Kachin, Kayah and Karen states and the Chin Special division, with additional Mon and Arakanese states promised after 1960, was modified so that while the cultural plurality of Burma was recognized, this was to have no bearing on the political structure of the state.

As the possible dissolution of the Union was perceived as justification for the 1962 coup, it is not surprising that the Revolutionary Council's first act after the disbandment of the legislature was the abolition of the councils of the four states and one special division and their replacement with administrative staffs under central control. On April 30, the separate Mon and Arakan ministries were dissolved, thus ending the pros-

---

22. See the stimulating remarks of Hans O. Schmitt, 'Decolonisation and Development in Burma', *Journal of Development Studies*, IV, 1 (Oct., 1967), pp. 103–5.

pect of semi-autonomous states for those regions. An additional complication in the structure of the state was terminated on February 1, 1964, when the special border districts which had been established during the civil war were abolished.[23] These had allowed the Prime Minister to directly govern areas along the border with East Pakistan (now Bangladesh) and China where insurgent activities were especially strong.

In its published accounts of its actions in the months following the coup, the Revolutionary Council did not discuss these actions or provide a full explanation for them. Rather, the re-organization of the territorial structure of the state was largely ignored while political means were used to try and persuade the population of the border areas that their cultural diversity and rights would be protected without the existence of nominally ethnic subordinate political organs. Though the ethnic states, special division and ministries before 1962 had not provided fundamental protection for any alleged unique political position, the ethnic claims they represented had become highly emotive. After 1962 the state's leading personnel sought means to de-politicize ethnicity. Ethnic identities, when politicized into non-negotiable demands for administrative and policy autonomy, are normally unresolvable by short-term political means, and every state attempts to translate such demands into lesser ones of a negotiable and non-personal nature. The effect of the Revolutionary Council's policies was to eliminate ethnicity as a constitutional issue and replace it with more tractable ones such as regional development and cultural diversity.

During 1963, two further attempts were made to terminate ethnic politics and the federal question by replacing them with other issues. At the annual Union Day celebrations held on February 12 General Ne Win outlined the Revolutionary Council's policies; these were quite simple and avoided any discussion of separate political institutions for ethnically defined categories. Rather, the basis of the policy would be equal rights and equal status for all minority group members within the state. In striving to make this principle a reality, economic equality would be given first priority. This, of course, was one aspect of the rationale behind the decision to equalize rice prices throughout the country in 1964, and there is significant evidence that the Revolutionary

---

23. *Towhlanyei Kaungsi ei Hluthsaungchet Thamaing Akyinchut*, pp. 8, 143, 159–60, 180.

Council made efforts to achieve its promise in subsequent years.[24] Equal access to health and educational facilities was also pledged. In order to ensure better medical treatment in remote areas, one of the first pieces of legislation promulgated by the Revolutionary Council was an amendment to the People's Military Service Law conscripting doctors into the armed forces in order to deploy them where most needed.[25] While promising equal treatment, the state reiterated its pledge to protect minority cultural practices as long as these did not run contrary to accepted health standards and other norms.[26]

In subsequent years, the state carried out other steps to unify the population around symbols and institutions of a non-divisible nature. In 1965 an Academy for the Development of National Groups was opened to train individuals from border areas to appreciate the diverse culture of the country while recognizing the need for the unity of the state. Graduates return to their home regions where they teach and often assume leadership positions in state and party organizations. Also, in keeping with the imposition of a uniform administrative pattern throughout the state's territories, legal codes previously applicable only to certain ethnic groups or areas were standardized. By the end of the 1960s, for the first time in history there had been achieved a basically common administrative and legal system for the entire state.

Another step the Revolutionary Council took in 1963 to end the divisive issue of ethnicity was to invite the leaders of insurgent groups to meet with it and attempt to negotiate a solution to their grievances. On July 11 not only ethnic insurgent leaders but leaders of the illegal Communist groups were invited to come to Rangoon for unconditional negotiations. This offer issued on April 1 was made only after a general amnesty for all prisoners other than rapists, murderers and certain politicians arrested at the time of the coup. Little success came from the negotiations, and barring agreement reached with one small Karen

24. John W. Henderson, *et al.*, *Area Handbook for Burma* (Washington, DC: United States Government Printing Office, 1971), p. 76.
25. *Towhlanyei Kaungsi ei Hluthsaungchet Thamaing Akyinchut*, p. 133.
26. See Myanma Hsoshelit Lansin Pati Baho Komiti Dana Chok (Burma Socialist Programme Party Central Committee Headquarters), *Taingyintha Lumyomya Ayei hnit Patthet ywei Towhlanyei Kaunsi ei Amyin hnit Khanyuchet* (Views and Considerations of The Revolutionary Council in Regard to National Groups) (Rangoon: Sapei Biman, 1963, 5th edn, 1982), such as, for example, the crushing of Palaung women's chests by the placing of brass rings around their necks.

group in March 1964, all the insurgent groups returned to insurrection within a few months.[27]

Given the historical memory of the state and the desire of the state's leading personnel to use known symbols to enhance its legitimacy, it was decided to maintain the existence of states named after ethnic groups — though in reality there is nothing linked to ethnic distinction in their organization and they are identical in structure and authority with the 'divisions'. Thus were seven states established named Kachin, Kayah, Karen, Chin, Mon, Rakhine (Arakan), and Shan along with seven divisions called Sagaing, Tenasserim, Pegu, Magwe, Mandalay, Irrawaddy and Rangoon. The administrative equality of the 'ethnic' states and of the divisions obscures the fact that 72 per cent of Burma's population live in the seven divisions; only the largest territorial state (Shan) has a higher population than the smallest division, Magwe. Both the importance of the border states to the security of the state and their 'feudal' historical legacies are recognized in the official Union Day celebrations. Every year the 1947 Panglong Agreement — whereby the British-recognized leaders of the frontier areas and the Shan States pledged their loyalty to the state by agreeing to join the Union — is commemorated along with the pledges of equality made by the Chairman of the Revolutionary Council on Union Day in 1963.[28]

The wording of the 1974 constitution ensured that there can be no mistake that the sub-states in the Union possess no political or administrative sovereignty or autonomy. Reiterating at many points that Burma is a country composed of many national groups (*taingyintha lumyo*), article 4 states explicity that 'state (*naingngantaw*) sovereignty must reside in the entire nation (*naingngan*)'.[29] The constitution is also explicit on the equality of all native born individuals, regardless of ethnicity. The only deviation from the principle of the irrelevance of ethnicity is made in reference to cultural practices. The constitution states in article 46 that the *Pyithu Hluttaw* 'will have the right to enact law if said

---

27. *Towhlanyei Kaungsi ei Hluthsaungchet Thamaing Akyinchut*, pp. 12–13, 144; BSPP, *Party Seminar 1965*, pp. 44–8; Pyithaungsu Myanma Naingngan Towhlanyei Kaungsi (Union of Burma Revolutionary Council), *Pyitwin Nyeingchanyei Hswenwei Pwe* (Internal Peace Discussions) (Rangoon: 1964).
28. See, for example, the speech of BSPP General Secretary Aye Ko to the 1984 Union Day rally in *The Working People's Daily*, 13 Feb. 1984, as well as the annual proclamations of the President on this occasion.
29. Translations are unofficial.

laws concern the culture (*wunkyeihmu*) of a national group only if more than half of the *Pyithu Hluttaw* members from the relevant state or division concur.' In the explanatory notes on the meaning of the constitution distributed before the constitutional referendum, the protection given to the states was made to appear somewhat broader by noting that in other matters such as name changes or boundary reformulations, decisions can only be made by the representatives of the affected states and divisions in the national legislature.[30]

The structure of the state is elaborated in Chapter III of the constitution, where it is noted that 'in organizing the state, the system used is central leadership and local management' (clause 28), or, as stated elsewhere in the constitution and numerous BSPP publications, the state is organized on the basis of 'socialist democracy', which means democratic centralism. The basic unit in rural society is the village; in urban areas it is the ward. Villages are grouped together to form village tracts and these, like the urban wards, are the primary unit of government and administration, maintaining the pattern established by the 1920s. Wards are organized into towns, and towns and village-tracts together form townships. Townships are in turn grouped into the fourteen states and divisions which together form the state's territorial organization (see Table 5.1.).

Changing Relations with State Authority

Unlike the representative principles that underlay the 1947 liberal democratic constitution, the Revolutionary Council attempted to develop forms of democractic socialism whereby the leadership of the state would establish direct relations with the population, especially the workers and the peasants. In order to achieve these goals the Revolutionary Council pledged to organize the working and peasant classes into a coalition to defend their rights and privileges.[31] Among the activities set up to achieve this was the holding of five peasants' 'seminars' between the end of 1962 and 1966 and several mass workers' 'seminars' in 1963 and 1966. These mass meetings provided a means by which the

30. *Pyi Htaungsu Hsoshelit Thammata Myanma Naingngan Phwetsinpun Akhyeikan Upadei hnit Pattaem thaw Asiyinhkansa.* (Report Concerning the Constitution of the Socialist Republic of the Union of Burma) (Rangoon: Printing and Publishing Corporation, 1973), pp. 55–6.
31. *Towhlanyei Kaungsi ei Hluthsaungchet Thamaing Akyinchut*, pp. 20–3.

Table 5.1. DATA ON THE TERRITORIAL ORGANIZATION OF THE STATE/DIVISION

State/Divison	Townships (1974)	Towns (1974)	Wards	Villages	Village tracts
Kachin	18	17	85	614	2,635
Kayah	6	6	27	79	625
Karen	7	7	33	377	2,096
Chin	9	9	29	376	1,358
Sagaing	38	38	165	1,816	6,281
Tenasserim	10	9	54	263	1,255
Pegu	28	32	233	1,391	6,504
Magwe	25	26	153	1,542	4,814
Mandalay	29	28	216	1,980	5,362
Mon	10	10	62	381	1,207
Rakhine	17	17	119	1,041	3,871
Rangoon	39	13	503	641	2,113
Shan	52	48	303	1,628	15,393
Irrawaddy	26	28	207	1,922	11,705
Total	314	288	2,189	13,751	65,319

State/Division	Area in sq. miles	Population (× 1,000)	% of Total	% Urban
Kachin	34,379	904	2.56	20.13
Kayah	4,529	168	0.48	24.67
Karen	11,730	1,058	3.00	10.44
Chin	13,906	369	1.05	14.72
Sagaing	36,534	3,856	10.92	13.72
Tenasserim	16,735	918	2.60	24.12
Pegu	15,214	3,800	10.76	19.46
Magwe	17,305	3,241	9.18	15.22
Mandalay	14,294	4,581	12.97	26.49
Mon	4,747	1,682	4.76	28.15
Rakhine	14,200	2,046	5.79	14.85
Rangoon	3,927	3,974	11.26	67.78
Shan	60,155	3,719	10.53	17.66
Irrawaddy	13,566	4,991	14.14	14.89
Total	261,228	35,314	100.00	23.95

[*Table continued on page 307*]

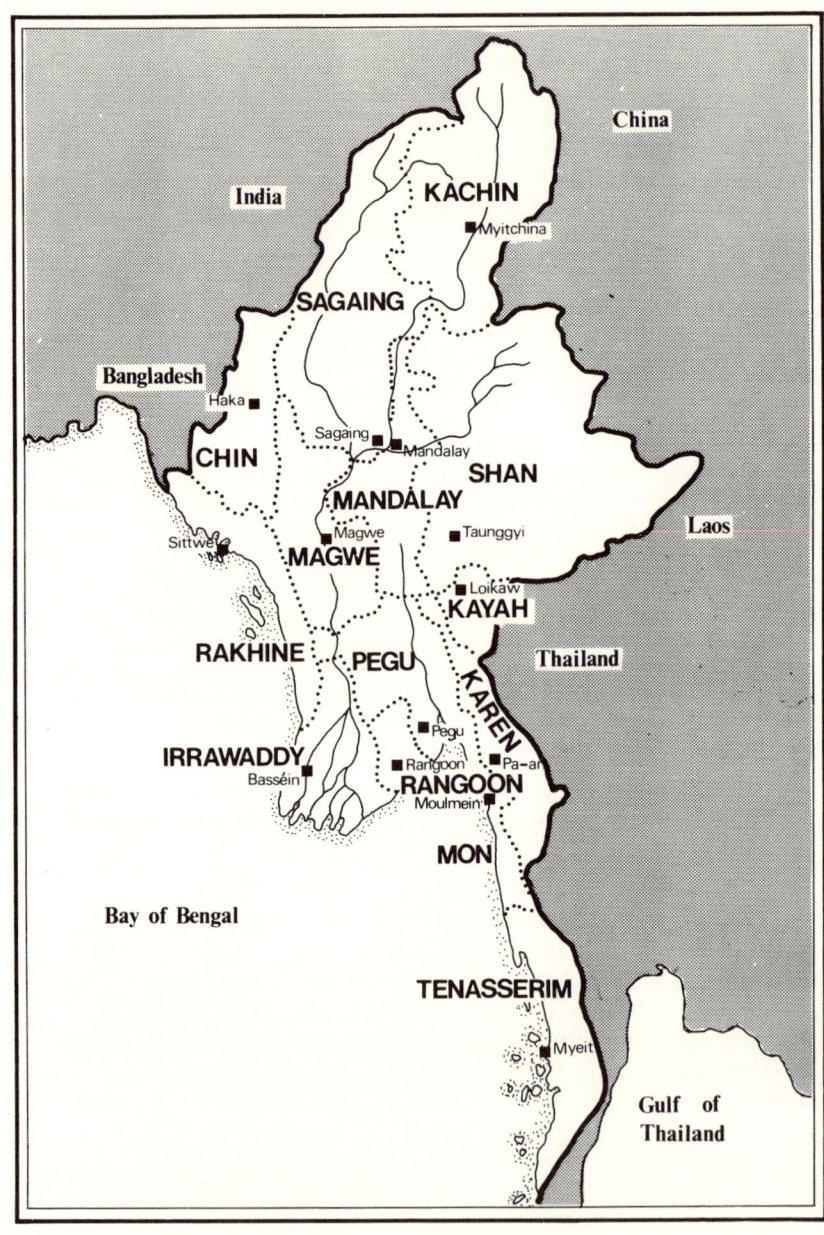

MAJOR ADMINISTRATIVE UNITS OF BURMA

Table 5.1. (continued)

State/Division	Population (1941)	Density per sq. mile (1973)	(1983)
Kachin	—	21	26
Kayah	—	28	37
Karen	—	74	90
Chin	—	23	27
Sagaing	46	85	106
Tenasserim	56	43	55
Pegu*	215	209	250
Magwe	69	152	187
Mandalay	153	296	320
Mon	—	277	354
Rakhine	74	121	144
Rangoon	—	812	1,012
Shan	—	53	62
Irrawaddy	198	306	368
Eastern areas	28	—	—

*Pegu included Rangoon town in 1941 census.

Sources: Nyi Nyi, *Myanama Naingngan Amyotha Mawkun (1975)* (Burma's National Record, 1975) (Rangoon: Pugan, 1978), pp. 125 and 139; *The Working People's Daily*, 18 Nov. 1983.

idea of the administration of mass organizations for the workers and peasants (formerly the Workers' Council and the Peasants' Council and now referred to as the Workers' Asiayon and the Peasants' Asiayon, to be undertaken under the auspices of the BSPP) could be presented. Though these mass and class bodies have primarily served the state as means of directing the political and economic activities of much of the population, the initial direct approach of the Chairman of the Revolutionary Council to the mass peasant and worker meetings in the first years after the coup proved very popular. Several hundred thousand individuals attended, and they created a sensation of participation by people who had rarely before been involved in matters of state.

Indicative of later, more formalized attempts by the leadership to change the people's image of the state was the laborious means by which the 1974 constitution was inaugurated. Using the argument that the 1947 constitution had been drafted by lawyers and conservative politicians without the participation of the people, and therefore had been incapable of achieving socialism and national unity, the leaders of the state developed a four-year process designed to give the perception of popular participation in the drafting, amending, and implementation of the new constitution. At the 1966 peasants' seminar in Rangoon the

Revolutionary Council reiterated its 1962 pledge that it was merely holding state power temporarily, and that power would be returned to its rightful possessors, the people, who would then govern through their own political party.[32] At the 1969 BSPP seminar, Revolutionary Council Chairman and Chairman of the BSPP Ne Win announced that a new constitution would be drafted in order to implement this pledge.

At the First Congress of the BSPP in mid-1971 guidelines for the drafting of the constitution were laid down and the constitution in its various drafts never deviated from these. Nonetheless, the State Constitution Drafting Commission appointed by the BSPP made various attempts to involve the public. The day after its formation, the Commission requested groups or individuals to submit suggestions. A month later a list of subjects was distributed to help elicit ideas from the public, and fifteen teams of Commission members toured the country soliciting ideas. During the final two and a half months of 1971 these teams met with over 100,000 people and received suggestions from 3,458 individuals as well as 1,883 letters sent directly to the Commission. A draft of the constitution was then discussed at a Commission meeting in February and the Commission used the advice it had received from the people to justify the establishment of a unitary state. After being discussed within the Central Committee of the Party, the draft constitution was published on April 30. Again, the fifteen Drafting Commission teams toured the country for two months, visiting every township. In their wake, 16,969 task groups were established at the local level to discuss the constitution and the Commission claimed that this process involved over 7 million people, or perhaps as much as 40 per cent of the population over fifteen years of age. These local discussions were followed by two more months touring by Commission teams in October and November. A further 2,000 letters were also sent to the Commission by individuals and groups.

A second draft of the constitution was then prepared and approved by the Party Central Committee in March 1973, and during May the fifteen teams toured the country again, meeting with large numbers of people. After the Commission agreed on various laws and by-laws necessary for the implementation of the constitution, as well as for the modalities of a

---

32. *Ibid.*, pp. 31–4; *The Guardian* (Rangoon), Jan. 1974, pp. 10–20, and Feb. 1974, pp. 14–15, repr. in Albert D. Moscotti, *Burma's Constitution and Elections of 1974* (Singapore: Institute of Southeast Asian Studies Research Notes and Discussions, no. 5, Sept., 1977), pp. 3–26.

national referendum to approve it, the fifteen teams made one final tour, again holding public meetings. At the Second Congress of the BSPP in October it was announced that the draft constitution would be passed on to the Revolutionary Council, which would then implement it when approved by national referendum. After a national census was conducted which gave the state its first complete accounting of national manpower since 1931 referendum and election commissions were established at various levels to compile voting lists.

The BSPP's local units and mass organizations were all involved in the referendum campaign and, according to the government, over 95 per cent of the 14,760,036 eligible voters cast ballots. Of these, 90.19 per cent voted in favour of the new constitution, but the populations in the border regions were less enthusiastic than were those more closely tied to the central state. The percentages in the states ranged from 66.40 per cent in the Shan State to 77.69 in the Karen State, while the redesignated Arakan State reported 86.09 and the Mon State, carved out of Tenasserim Division, 90.62 per cent for the new constitution.[33]

The state's managers after 1962 also tried to bring the state closer to the people and to make it seem a less awesome and distant institution by changing its nomenclature. Terms used under the civilian government were replaced with those considered more in keeping with a revolutionary government. Thus, the word for a minister used since the time of the monarchical state, *wun-gyi*, was replaced with *ta-wun-gan*, a rather perfunctory and matter-of-fact term. Even the royal suffix *taw* was deleted from *naingngan* in the state's formal title.[34] With the passage of time and, perhaps, with a slackening of the revolutionary spirit, such adjustments to nomenclature were abandoned, and the state and its officials once more took titles linking them to linguistic usages of 200 years ago.

'Bureaucracy', the word used in Burmese as in English to describe the corpus of state officials, had become anathema in nationalist thought in the 1930s. Just as it is only used perjoratively in the Soviet Union,[35] so too has it been used in Burma since before independence. One of the Revolutionary Council's allegations against their predecessors was that the politicians had been unable to take control of the state from the

---

33. *The Guardian* (Rangoon), 4 Jan., 1974, repr. in *ibid.*, p. 72.
34. Hla Pe, *Burma: Literature, Historiography, Scholarship, Language, Life and Buddhism* (Singapore: Institute of Southeast Asian Studies, 1985), p. 126.
35. Theodore H. Friedgut, *Political Participation in the USSR* (Princeton University Press, 1979), p. 38.

bureaucrats who had worked for the British. But Burma, like all modern states, functions at its core only through bureaucrats. The Revolutionary Council at the beginning of its tenure was quite aware of this, and strove to ensure that the civil servants who staffed the state were well treated and loyal. In keeping with its egalitarian sentiments, some distinctions previously made between higher and lower grades of employees were abolished, lower grade employees such as drivers and cooks received enlarged benefits and many temporary employees were made permanent.[36] With the passage of time and with the increasing poverty of the state, however, employees' salaries failed to keep pace with inflation.

Despite the Revolutionary Council's theoretical aversion to bureaucracy, though consonant with its effort to reassert the state, the civil service grew between 1962 and 1974 disproportionately to the increase in population. This is not surprising given the increasing number of functions the state assumed. However, despite the egalitarian impulse of the Council, increasing administrative costs prompted the state to turn once more to part-time employees. Though the total population of Burma grew by about 32 per cent between 1962 and 1974, the total number of government employees increased by 89.6 per cent, with full-time employees advancing by 69.3 per cent and part-time employees by 324.3 per cent. Table 5.2 shows the growth in departmental employment between the time of the military coup and the establishment of the new constitutional order.

Not unexpectedly, following nationalization those ministries whose primary responsibilities centred upon the economy experienced the greatest growth in full-time personnel. What is more surprising is the decline in the number of full-time employees in the Ministry of Home and Religious Affairs. The reduction of over 8 per cent was probably the consequence of the passing over of many of this ministry's former duties to other and often lower level state and party organizations. Changes in ministerial expenditure during the period of the Revolutionary Council reveal parallel trends.

Total expenditure growth (see Table 5.3) in current terms was 172.8 per cent during the period of the Revolutionary Council. The only areas of government expenditure to exceed that figure were those related to economic activities and information. Overall, the proportion of state

36. James F. Guyot, 'Bureaucratic Transformation in Burma', in Ralph Braibanti (ed.), *Asian Bureaucratic Systems Emergent from the British Imperial Tradition* (Durham, NC: Duke University Press, 1966), pp. 426–7.

Table 5.2. GROWTH IN FULL-TIME CENTRAL STATE EMPLOYMENT, 1962–1973.

	1962	1973	% change
POLITICAL FUNCTIONS			
Revolutionary Council Chairman	0	130	
Prime Minister	175	55	7.4
Central SAC	151	286	
Foreign Affairs	339	430	89.4
			26.8
Sub-Total	665	901	35.5
SOCIAL CONTROL FUNCTIONS			
Judicial Affairs	6,266	8,212	31.1
Home and Religious Affairs	91,542	84,006	–8.2
Information	2,553	11,554	352.6
Sub-Total	100,361	103,772	3.4
ADMINISTRATIVE AND SERVICE FUNCTIONS			
Planning and Finance	12,277	16,399	33.6
Labour	1,311	1,779	35.7
Health	15,411	29,485	29.3
Education	69,265	105,649	52.5
Culture	498	779	56.4
Social Services	445	1,004	125.6
Sub-Total	99,208	155,095	56.3
ECONOMIC FUNCTIONS			
Agriculture and Forests	33,592	67,630	101.3
Mining	27,599	41,595	50.7
Industry	31,120	78,765	153.1
Construction	6,471	8,068	22.8
Transportation	49,827	76,978	54.5
Trade	17,726	77,957	339.8
Cooperatives	1,732	12,768	637.2
Sub-Total	168,067	363,761	116.1
Total	368,301	623,529	69.3

Source: Author's calculations based on data in *Towhlanyei Kaungsi ei Hluthsaunchet Thamaing Akyinchut*.

Table 5.3. GROWTH IN TOTAL EXPENDITURE (CAPITAL AND CURRENT) OF CENTRAL MINISTRIES, 1961–73
(× 1,000 Kyat)

	1961–2	1972–3	% change
POLITICAL FUNCTIONS			
Revolutionary Council Chairman	0	5,161	
Prime Minister	3,531	2,305	111.4
Central SAC	0	20,905	
Foreign Affairs	13,757	20,288	47.5
Sub-Total	21,983	48,719	121.6
SOCIAL CONTROL FUNCTIONS			
Judicial Affairs	19,927	30,747	54.3
Home and Religious Affairs	221,068	278,258	25.9
Information	19,898	116,238	484.2
Sub-Total	260,893	425,243	63.0
ADMINISTRATIVE AND SERVICE FUNCTIONS			
Planning and Finance	71,045	144,480	103.4
Labour	9,036	10,711	18.5
Health	59,564	146,779	146.4
Education	141,504	353,804	150.0
Culture	2,104	6,053	187.7
Social Services	4,789	7,101	48.3
Sub-Total	277,291	538,927	94.4
ECONOMIC FUNCTIONS			
Agriculture and Forests	212,498	948,241	346.2
Mining	242,761	745,106	206.9
Industry	255,678	1,397,500	446.8
Construction	132,193	395,546	199.2
Transportation	304,602	617,842	102.8
Trade	1,171,989	2,713,226	131.5
Cooperatives	4,135	37,587	809.0
Sub-Total	2,323,848	6,855,048	195.0
Total	2,884,015	7,867,937	172.8

Source: Based on data in *Towhlanyei Kaungsi ei Hluthsaunchet Thamaing Akyinchut*.

expenditures devoted to political, 'social control' and other non-economic functions actually decreased. Unfortunately, comparable government data is not available for the changes in military expenditure, but estimates provided by the Stockholm International Peace Research Institute (SIPRI) show defence expenditure increasing by only 42.2 per cent, from 408 million Kt to 581 million Kt.[37] These patterns of employment and expenditure suggest that in terms of its relationship with the populace the agencies of the central state played an increasingly significant role between 1962 and 1974 as a proportionately larger proportion of the adult population came to depend directly upon it for their livelihood. Also, because of its increasing involvement in public information campaigns, coupled with the general suppression of non-state publications, the message the state wished to convey got across to a larger proportion of the population.

In terms of the internal management of the state, little at the central level changed formally between the time of the coup and March 15, 1972, when the colonial-style Secretariat was abolished and ministers were formally able to communicate directly with their subordinate government departments rather than through permanent secretaries. However, this change was largely cosmetic, since from 1962 most of the secretaries were military officers who worked under the direction of senior officers serving as ministers, and thus never had much possibility of frustrating the intentions of the cabinet. But at the same time as this reform was implemented, a significant change was brought about when the district level of local administration which had been introduced by the British, and which had become the linchpin of the initial rationalized structure of the state, was abolished. Administrative guidance and policy henceforth had only to pass from the centre to the townships through the states and divisions.[38]

Security and Administration Committees (SACs) The administrative changes which allowed for the abolition of the districts were only hinted at in May 1962, when the Home Ministry held a two-day conference to

---

37. *SIPRI Yearbook of World Armaments and Disarmament 1968/69* (Stockholm: Almqvist and Wiksell, 1969), Table 1A.13, p. 209 and *ibid.*, *1977*, Table 7A.18, p. 232.
38. *Towhlanyei Kaungsi ei Hluthsaungchet Thamaing Akyinchut*, pp. 8–9, 158; Jon A. Wiant, 'Loosening Up on the Tiger's Tail', *Asian Survey*, XIII, 2 (Feb., 1973), p. 181.

discuss the creation of a system of Security and Administration Committees (SACs) which came to serve as the main structure of the Revolutionary Council's control of subordinate administrative organizations.[39] A similar system had been used during the 1958–60 caretaker period and reinstalled in a modified form by the civilian government in 1961 when it proved effective in helping 'arrest the growing insecurity in the countryside'.[40]

The SAC system was organized from the centre downward through all the levels of administration to the village tract or ward. The Central SAC in Rangoon was directly responsible to the Revolutionary Council and was chaired by the Home Minister. The Committees, composed of local military commanders with police and civil administrative officers from the relevant level of administration, were chaired by soldiers at the divisional, state and also commonly at lower levels. The intention was to strengthen the state's administrative powers by increasing the power of the centre relative to the increasingly powerless district and other lower level executive officers. This was to be accomplished by improving the administrative coordination within a given region. In actual administrative routine, 'the role of the regional military commander as Chairman of the District SAC [was] probably less important in non-military activities' but had a crucial role in security matters.[41] The main functions of the SACs seemed to have been to check on local initiatives and to ensure that central directives were followed. Having army personnel in coordinating positions at all levels also gave the Revolutionary Council direct access to all subordinate administrative organs through two networks, the civil administrative hierarchy and the military chain of command.

During the first ten years of their existence the SACs had no non-official personnel among their members. However, in July and August 1972, at the time when the district level of administration was abolished, the SACs were instructed to add to their membership representatives from the relevant Party unit and Peasants' and Workers' Councils, with others appointed by the government.[42] In preparation for

39. *Party Seminar 1965*, p. 35; *Towhlanyei Kaungsi ei Hluthsaungchet Thamaing Akyinchut*, p. 8.
40. Josef Silverstein, *Burma: Military Rule and the Politics of Stagnation* (Ithaca: Cornell University Press, 1977), fn. 19, p. 93.
41. Jon A. Wiant, 'The Burmese Revolutionary Council: Military Government and Political Change' (seminar paper, Dept. of Government, Cornell University, 1971), p. 18.
42. *Towhlanyei Kaungsi ei Hluthsaungchet Thamaing Akyinchut*, p. 9; Wiant, 'Burmese Revolutionary Council', pp. 181–2; Silverstein, *Burma: Military Rule*, pp. 93–4.

turning the SACs into elected People's Councils as the core of the new socialist democratic state under the 1974 constitution, the SACs were given executive and judicial powers.

Organizing the State/Party and Mass/Class Organizations After its formation in mid-1962, the Burma Socialist Programme Party was developed as the main means for the mobilization of support for the state. The Party and its subsidiary organizations — initially the Peasants' and Workers' Councils, later the Peasants' and Workers' Asiayon, and followed by the Lansin Youth, the War Veterans' Organizations and groups for writers and artists — have all served the state as means of organizing the population into groups. This has also obviated the possibility of independent mobilizing organizations being formed which would create or express unacceptable or unattainable demands. In so doing, the BSPP system also serves to create participatory institutions of the type normally associated with the modern state. Members of such institutions tend to develop an attachment to the state and this encourages the individual to feel that along with his organization, he is playing a role in state management.

For the first decade of the BSPP's existence the Revolutionary Council was, in the words of the party constitution, 'the supreme authority of the Party during the transitional period of its construction'.[43] At the 1971 First Conference of the Party its status changed from that of a nucleus party to that of a mass party. Subsequently the Party was to lead the state, rather than the Revolutionary Council leading the Party. Between July 1962 and March 1964, it was not entirely clear what role the BSPP would play in the future. During the 1958–60 caretaker period the army had organized a National Solidarity Association with subordinate local councils as part of its psychological warfare campaign against both legal and illegal political parties, and in some ways the Party was a descendant of that organization. While the Party was described as part of the machinery needed to educate the people into the ways of a socialist democratic state and to organize the 'vanguard' of such a state so as to avoid the workers and peasants being misled by parties of the left or right, it was not until the March 1964 Law to Protect National Solidarity was promulgated that all other political parties were declared illegal.[44] Under the terms of this

43. 'The Constitution of the Burma Socialist Programme Party', section 2, printed as an app. to *System of Correlation of Man and His Environment*, p. 61.
44. *Towhlanyei Kaungsi ei Hluthsaungchet Thamaing Akyinchut*, p. 15: *Party Seminar 1965*, pp. 55–7.

law, all organizations, including religious bodies, were required to register and all political parties but the BSPP were to disband and turn their assets over to the state.

The pace of change in the relationship of the state with society accelerated at this time. Politically, BSPP units began to be organized in district centres as the Party began the process of its construction into a mass party. At the same time the first steps in the nationalization of internal trade were undertaken. With the March promulgation of the Law to Protect the Construction of the Socialist Economy, the state adopted wide powers of arrest and of seizure against crimes such as smuggling and blackmarketeering that were disrupting its economic policies. Then, on March 19, all trading and general merchants in Rangoon were nationalized and on April 9 trade in the rest of the country was nationalized. From then on, through a series of shops known as People's Stores, internal retail trade became the legal monopoly of the Ministry of Trade's Trade Corporation No. 1.[45]

The expansion of the Party was at first largely confined to individuals from organizations most trusted by the Revolutionary Council: the scrutiny of applicants served to create an aura of an élite and select organization. Until 1971 full membership was restricted to the members of the Revolutionary Council. On the first anniversary of the coup, the Party invited the application of 'candidate members'.[46] Nineteen months later the Party had received 681,906 applications for candidate membership,[47] many from individuals who had been excluded from positions in the old legal political parties. Members of previously powerful organizations usually refused to apply, believing that the BSPP would not last or would not be an avenue to influence. As shown in Table 5.4. most of the early applicants came from the armed forces and from nationalized industrial organizations in the towns and cities which were the easiest to organize. Peasants and others living in rural and remote areas, especially in the hill areas, found enrollment difficult — if they knew of the possibility at all. Despite the Party's intention of representing all of the population, peasants did not become a majority of members until the Fourth Party Conference in 1981.

Upon admission to the Party, individuals are given a membership card

---

45. *Towhlanyei Kaungsi ei Hluthsaungchet Thamaing Akyinchut*, pp. 40–41, 45; *Party Seminar 1965*, p. 67.
46. *Ibid*, p. 19.
47. *Party Seminar 1965*, p. 128.

Table 5.4. BSPP MEMBERSHIP FIGURES

Occupation	Full members	Candidate members	Total members	Party friends
1965				
Total	20	99,638	99,658	167,447
1966				
Armed forces	20	54,028	54,048	
Workers	0	91,999	91,999	
Peasants	0	15,383	15,383	
Police	0	2,975	2,975	
Others	0	21,662	21,662	
Total	20	185,947	185,947	185,967
1970		257,463		728,056
1971				
Armed forces			65,555	
Total			239,019	
1972				
Armed forces	42,359	63,537	107,896	
Workers	20,316	123,098	143,414	
Peasants	8,207	43,553	51,760	
Police	309	4,644	4,953	
Others	2,179	26,025	28,204	
Total	73,369	260,857	334,226	
31 March 1973				
Peasants	12,941	104,283	117,224	
Workers	76,883	185,448	262,331	
Others	6,877	80,994	87,871	
Total	96,701	445,449	542,150	
1 March 1977				
Total	171,153	517,426	688,579	819,511
31 Jan. 1981				
Armed forces	70,563	73,184	143,747	
Peasants			408,601	
Workers			242,532	
Total	425,789	1,075,113	1,500,902	981,859
31 Jan. 1985				
Armed forces	113,540	56,114		
Peasants			842,308	
Workers			478,616	
Total			2,230,000 +	1,200,000 +

Source: 1965: Burma Socialist Programme Party Central Organizing Committee, *Party Seminar, 1965* (Rangoon: Sarpay Beikman, 1966), p. 130; 1966 and 1972: Josef Silverstein, *Burma: Military Rule and the Politics of Stagnation* (Ithaca: Cornell University Press, 1977), Table 5, p. 103; 1970: *The Guardian*, Feb. 1971, p. 12; 1971: *Working People's Daily*, 1 July 1971, 31 March, 1973: *Myanma Hsoshelit Lanin Pati Ayeipaw Patia Nyilakhan 1973* (Special Conference of the Burma Socialist Programme Party, 1973 (Rangoon: Printing and Publishing Corporation, May 1973), p. 106; 1 March 1977 and 31 Jan. 1981: Burma Socialist Programme Party Central Committee Headquarters, *The Fourth Party Congress 1981* (Rangoon: Printing and Publishing Corporation, 1985), pp. 83–5; 31 Jan. 1985: *Working People's Daily*, 3 Aug. 1985.

and number. These indicate length of service, and the lower the number the greater the probability that an individual possessed influence in the early years of the Party's formation. Of the 260 individuals who were elected in 1981 to the Party Central Committee which guides the Party through its Central Executive Committee between quadrennial Party Conferences, 121 possessed party numbers below 1001000, and 44 below 1000200.[48] Over 75 per cent of Central Committee members had been in the Party as full or candidate members for eighteen or more years, and the longer the membership the greater the probability that an individual would hold high office in the state or the Party.[49]

48. Party numbers and other data concerning the membership of the 1981 Party Central Committee comes from short biographies of the members printed and distributed at the Party Conference. A photocopy has been made available to the author from a non-official source. Statements of a comparative nature about changing memberships in the leading committees of the Party must not be accepted as wholly accurate. They have been made on the basis of the analysis of lists of the names of members in Burmese and in English, and as Burmese do not have family names and several individuals can have the same name, perfection in analysis is impossible with the resources available. This following table gives the length of party membership of BSPP CC Members in 1981:

Years	Number	%
19	3	1.15
18	198	76.15
17	38	14.65
16	9	3.56
15	3	1.15
14	4	1.54
13	1	0.39
12	0	0.0
11	3	1.15
10	1	0.39

49. Serving in leading positions in the state in 1981 from among the lowest 200 numbers were:

U Ne Win, President (1000001)
U San Yu, Secretary of the Council of State (1000003)
U Thaung Kye, member of the Council of State (1000005)
U Myint Maung, Chairman of the Council of People's Attorneys (1000025)
U Ye Gaung, Minister for Agriculture and Forests (1000037)
U Maung Maung Kha, Prime Minister (1000042)
U Tha Kyaw, member of the Council of State (1000047)
Dr Maung Maung, member of the Council of State (10000060)
General Min Guang (1000086)

As the Party expanded, efforts were apparently made to increase its representative nature by recruiting more vigorously in the peripheral states and from groups not attached formally to the state. An ethnic breakdown of the total membership of the Party is not available, but of the 260 members of the Central Committee in 1981, 72 per cent identified themselves as Burman (*Myanma*) and the remaining 28 per cent said they came from minority ethnic communities. Of the Burman members, 83 per cent joined within the first thirteen months of the Party's existence, while only 64 per cent of the minority group members joined during the same period. In subsequent years, however, ethnic minority recruitment into the ranks of the Party élite increased beyond the Burman rate. Civilian recruits into the Central Committee were also greater among minority group members. Whereas 65 per cent of the Burman Central Committee members in 1981 were apparently retired or serving army officers and 35 per cent were civilians, these proportions are nearly reversed for minority representatives: 37 per cent and 63 per cent respectively. Minority group members, not surprisingly, are somewhat younger than the Burman members. While 41 per cent of the Burman members were more than fifty-five years old in 1981, only 26.5 per cent of the minority group members were. Nine per cent of the Burmans were under the age of 45 whereas this applied to 22 per cent of the minority group members. Burmans were a larger proportion of the 50–54 age category, 37 per cent as against 22 per cent for the minority group members, but minorities

---

U Kyaw Nyein, Minister of Education (1000128)
U Sein Lwin, Minister for Home and Religious Affairs (1000137)
U Than Tin, Minister for Mining (10000138)
U Tint Swe, Minister for Industry (10000139)
General *Thura* Kyaw Htin, Deputy Prime Minister and Minister for Defence (1000141)
U Zaw Win, secretary of the Council of State (1000142)
Thura U Saw Hpyu, Minister for Transport and Communications (1000147)
U Tun Tin, Deputy Prime Minister and Minister for Planning and Finance (1000159)
U Ba Thaw, member of the Council of State (1000165)
U Ban Ku, member of the Council of State (1000169).

The other 25 members of the Central Committee in 1981 with membership numbers below 200 were serving in leading positions in the Party organization and members of various state organization.

formed a larger proportion than Burmans of the 45–49 age category, 30 per cent to 12 per cent.[50]

With the passage of time and with the greater penetration of the Party into civil society the leadership has become more broadly-based not only in terms of ethnicity but also in terms of background. Whereas 75.5 per cent of Central Committee members in 1972 were from the armed forces,[51] 22 per cent were serving officers in 1981, though if retired officers are taken into account the proportion from the military still reached 70 per cent. Many senior Party leaders have followed the example of the Party Chairman and of twenty other officers who retired from the army in 1972 as the Revolutionary Council prepared to inaugurate the 1974 constitution. Of the 280 members of the Central Committee elected in 1985, 67, or 24 per cent, were currently serving in the army.

Indicative of the growing institutional maturity of the Party has been the nature of new persons added to the Central Committee as older members retire or die. Firm data is not available, but it would appear that of the 240 members who sat in the Central Committee selected in 1977, 193 were re-selected in 1981 but only 135 of the members in 1985 had been in place eight years earlier. This means that nearly half the members of the Central Committee in 1985 had been promoted in the previous four years.

Changes were also brought about in the membership of the senior committees of the Party between 1981 and 1985. Between meetings of

50. BSPP CENTRAL COMMITTEE MEMBERSHIP (1981) BY YEAR OF BIRTH, ETHNICITY AND MILITARY/CIVILIAN CAREER PATTERN

Year of birth	Army Burman serving		Army Burman retired		Army non-Burman serving		Army non-Burman retired		Civilian Burman		Civilian non-Burman		Total	
	No.	%	No.	%	No.	%	No.	%	No.	%	No.	%	No.	%
1911–19	0	0.0	4	1.5	0	0.0	1	0.4	0	0.0	0	0.0	5	1.9
1920–4	5	1.9	23	8.9	0	0.0	7	2.7	5	1.9	4	1.5	44	16.9
1925–9	24	9.3	49	18.9	6	2.3	12	4.6	10	3.9	1	0.4	102	39.9
1930–4	15	5.8	19	7.3	2	0.8	7	2.7	4	1.5	7	2.7	54	20.8
1935–40	4	1.5	1	0.4	0	0.0	2	0.8	17	6.5	20	7.7	44	16.9
1940+	1	0.8	0	0.0	0	0.0	0	0.0	6	2.3	4	1.5	11	4.2
Total	49	18.8	96	36.9	8	3.1	29	11.2	42	16.2	36	13.9	260	100.0

Non-Burmans included 10 Arakanese, 9 Mon, 1 Mon-Burman, 1 Mon-Shan, 3 Kayah, 12 Chin, 12 Karen, 1 Paku Karen, 6 Kachin, 1 Mayu, 1 Yawan, 8 Shan, 1 Dan, 1 Shan-Burman, 1 Gun-Shan, 1 Palaung, 3 Pa-O, 1 Wa, 1 Laha, and 1 Naga.

51. Wiant, 'Loosening Up on the Tiger's Tail', p. 180.

the Central Committee, the Central Executive Committee is the most powerful body; if the Party leads the state, the Central Executive Committee leads the Party. The most powerful individual in the country is the chairman of this Committee, as he is also the Chairman of the Party. Between 1962 and 1987, only one man has held this post, U Ne Win. The Central Executive Committee includes the General Secretary of the Party as well as the Joint General Secretary and, since 1985, a Vice-Chairman. The other members are all senior ministers and other high army and government officials. The Revolutionary Council itself was the initial Central Executive Committee, and its senior membership has been remarkably stable over a twenty-five-year period. Of the Committee's 23 members in 1977, 13 were re-elected in 1981, but only 9 of the 23 serving in 1977 continued after 1985. However, in the meantime the size of the Committee had been reduced from 23 to 17. Demonstrating more the changes that have been taking place in the Party is the composition of the Party Discipline Committee. Of the 19 members serving on it in 1977, 12 continued on after 1981 but only one member serving in 1977 was still sitting in 1985.

The building of the mass Party between 1962 and 1971 was conducted primarily under the auspices of army personnel. The first tier of the Party below the Revolutionary Council was composed of six Divisional Supervision Committees which corresponded with the six military regional commands. Below these were established 15 Sub-Divisional Committees which corresponded roughly with the states and divisions, with an organizing committee for the army. The basic level of Party organization was at the township level, thus bypassing the district administrative level of the state apparatus. The township Party units fell under the supervision of the Divisional Supervision Committee and of the Divisional Coordination Committee, placing effective supervision of township units just one level away from the highest central state authorities. Below the township Party units were formed village, ward and workplace groups and cells. Only at the township level and below was there room for any significant participation by civilians in the early formation of the Party.[52] This pattern has not significantly changed since the Party became a mass organization, though civilians have a larger role in the management of the regional committees which have replaced the Divisional Supervision Committee and its Sub-Divisional affiliates. In 1985, of the 112 members of the state and divisional Party regional

---

52. Wiant, 'Burmese Revolutionary Council', p. 10.

committees, 16 were serving officers. Of these, 9 were committee chairman or secretaries and doubtless other senior figures were retired military men.

Below the regional and township Party committees there are Party sections and cells. In 1981 the Party General Secretary reported that there were 17,940 Party sections and 113,409 Party cells. The number reported decreased in 1985 when the General Secretary revealed that there were 13,881 party sections and 111,002 Party cells. Not all of Burma's 314 townships had a party unit in 1985. In 1981, there were 281 Party units, but 27 townships had what are referred to as organizing committees. Between 1981 and 1985, 9 Party organizing committees became Party units after the holding of elections but 5 Party units were abolished and replaced by organizing committees. This left 26 organizing committees in existence while four townships had only one person attempting to form a Party unit.[53] Though there is no clear evidence to explain the absence of Party units in some townships, it is probable that the areas without basic Party units are on the periphery of the state where the authority of the central state is being most severely challenged by insurgents.

Despite the alleged relative equality of women in Burma's society[54] the Party's membership has remained dominated by men, though the proportion of female members has been increasing. Only 8 of the 280 members of the Party Central Committee in 1985 were women and there were none on the major central management and policy committees. In 1981, among the Party rank-and-file, women accounted for 15 per cent of members, and this had increased to around 17 per cent in 1985.[55]

While over 2.3 million people, or about 10 per cent of the population over the age of 15, were involved in fortnightly Party cell meetings and other Party activities by the mid-1980s, a much larger proportion of the population was organized into the Party's subsidiary organizations. As the Party General Secretary said in his 1981 political report to the Fourth Party Conference, 'in connection with the organization activities of the mass organizations, the Burma Socialist Programme Party is bringing together the dispersed forces under mass, class and

53. *The Working People's Daily*, 4 Aug. 1981; *Ibid.*, 3 Aug. 1985.
54. Mi Mi Khaing, *The World of Burmese Women* (Singapore: Times Book International, 1984), p. 1.
55. *The Working People's Daily*, 4 Aug. 1981; *Ibid.*, 3 Aug. 1985.

social organizations and creating conditions to enable the entire people to take part in socialist construction work.'[56]

The largest and most important of the mass/class bodies, the Peasants' Asiayon and the Workers' Asiayon, were first mooted by the Revolutionary Council in 1963 and 1964. When the Revolutionary Council issued a thirteen-point statement on workers' affairs on May 1 1963, it pledged to assist workers in the setting up of regional workplace-based organizations for the protection of their rights. At the 1964 Kabaung peasants' seminar the idea of a Peasants' Council was also raised and was approved by resolution at the 1965 Rangoon peasants' seminar.[57] However, progress in forming a central body to supervise these activities was slow, and not until April 1968 was a Central People's Workers' Council organized. The Central People's Peasants' Council had been set up in March of the previous year.[58] The two bodies were renamed Asiayon in 1977 when they held their first national conferences.

Though it is implied in the various documents that these organizations grew from a spontanious desire of the workers and peasants, the impetus behind their formation clearly came from the Revolutionary Council. They serve basically two purposes. One is as a medium for the transmission of the state's policies in the hope of generating popular support for them while obviating the problems that would arise from the organization of genuinely spontaneous and independent peasant and labour unions. The other is to provide a means by which the state can more effectively control productive labour. This was what the Party Chairman meant when discussing shortfalls in rice and other exports in his final address to the Fourth Party Seminar in November 1969. The problem lay in the inadequate organization of labour through the peasant and worker bodies. As a result, the state was 'not yet able to exactly forecast . . . production and exports. . . . In future, after the peasants' organisations have been systematically formed, we hope to be more specific' in forecasting production and thus meeting export contracts.[59] The socialist state, like a business concern, tends to view the population as part of its productive power.

When the third Workers' Asiayon conference was held in December

---

56. *Ibid*, 3 Aug., 1985.
57. *Party Seminar 1965*, pp. 57–9.
58. Sein Tin, *Myanma Akyaung hnit Kabama Akyaung* (Burma's Affairs and World Affairs) (Rangoon: Thidadimyaing, 1982), p. 32.
59. 'Address . . . by General Ne Win . . . Fourth Party Seminar', pp. 5–6.

1985, it was reported that 1,845,182 individuals were members, and that they were under the supervision of 273 Township Workers' Asiayon and twenty-four Township Workers' Organizing Committees.[60] Almost all employees of state and cooperatively-owned enterprises were members, but a large proportion of the workers in the private sector, except in 'stable' enterprises, were not. According to government estimates, in 1985 there were approximately 1,475,000 workers in the state-owned sectors appropriate for organization of Workers' Asiayons and another 3,727,000 in the cooperative and private sectors.[61] Thus, about 36 per cent of the potential members were involved in these organizations. As a significant proportion of those not organized would be involved in petty trade and small scale production activities, a large proportion of the easily organized working population was at least formally affiliated with the Asiayon.

The Peasants' Asiayon is a much larger body, but as its potential membership is scattered throughout the country's 13,700 villages, gaining the adherence of the peasantry is a much more daunting task. By November 1985, 272 Township Peasants' Asiayons had been organized along with seven Township Organizing Committees. Under these were 13,192 ward and village tract subordinate bodies; this suggests a reasonably complete coverage of the most important agricultural regions. In all, there were said to be 7,577,733 members. Only about 80,000 persons are involved in the state agricultural sector while the bulk of the labour force, 9,312,000 out of a total of 14,792,000, are in the private agricultural sector, with a few in cooperatives.[62] The official figures suggest that about 81 per cent of the peasant population is organized, however many of these memberships are probably only nominal. Nonetheless, by 1984–5 the organization was said to be self-sufficient in its expenditures (meaning that membership dues are sufficient to support the organization).[63]

Both the Workers' and Peasants' Asiayon are managed by Central Executive Committees elected at quadrennial conferences. All the senior

60. *The Working People's Daily*, 10 Dec. 1985.
61. In forestry, mining, processing and manufacturing, power, construction, transport and communications, social services, administration and trade; *Report to the Pyithu Hluttaw for 1985/86* (Rangoon: Ministry of Planning and Finance, 1985), Table 4, p. 23.
62. *Ibid.*
63. *The Working People's Daily*, 26 Nov. 1985.

leaders come from ranking state and party positions and their chairmen have always been senior ministers and/or members of the Council of State. Since 1981 the Minister for Labour has been the Chairman of the workers' organization and the Minister for Agriculture the Chairman of the peasants' organization. The initial memberships of the Central Executive Committees changed little until the 1980s, but only five or six of the thirty-five members of each committee had served more than eight years in 1985.

The Lansin Youth Organization by 1985 claimed 1,050,802 members over the age of eighteen of whom 211,954 were party members.[64] Formed in 1971, it had organized in 297 townships and at thirty-four educational institutions by 1985. Below it are various subordinate bodies designed to raise young people in the spirit of the Party. *Teza* Youth (named after the Japanese *nom de guerre* of Aung San) is for children aged six to ten, and *Hse Hsaung* (Forward) Youth is for youths aged 10–15. Lansin Youth accepts individuals aged 15–29.[65] All the organizations have over a million members. It is difficult to know to what extent they have affected the socialization process of the youth. They hold frequent meetings at the local level and hold annual meetings in Rangoon. The annual Lansin Youth conference, like many of the Party's activities, has a military character, and the youths are taught to parade as well as being introduced to the ideology of the Party. In rural areas one can also observe youths engaging in military drill with their local organization at the weekend: the movement is redolent of the Boy Scouts.[66]

The Party and its mass/class organizations serve to educate and guide their members, and through them the remainder of society, to understand and accept the policies and programmes of the central state managers. Their function is largely in the nature of ongoing political socialization and parallels the state's activities in the printed media and radio and television, attempting to get its message across while

64. *The Working People's Daily*, 3 Aug. 1985.
65. Sein Tin, *Myanma Akyaung hnit Kabama Akyaung*, p. 35.
66. Political Science as it is taught in Burma's universities also reflects the military imprint on the Party. In the third year final examination political science paper given at the Institutes of Economics, in Rangoon and Mandalay in 1984, eight questions were set. Of these, one asked the student to explain how the army played the leading role in the attainment and defence of national independence; others asked about the role of the masses in building economic systems, how capitalism creates fascism and world wars, and the nature of Burma's Second World War anti-fascist resistance.

preventing counter-messages being heard and understood. Such activities take up a good deal of the time of Party activists, but for many people these play only a marginal role in daily life. However the Party and its message cannot be ignored, for it is seen and heard in almost all places. Even remote villages and settlements miles from a township headquarters will have signboards proclaiming the presence of the village Party unit, the village branch of the Peasants' Asiayon and perhaps a Lansin Youth or other organization. Party publications, though far from saturating the society, tend to be widely available. The activities of state and Party officials dominate the news in radio broadcasts and in the newspapers, though the latter are difficult to find outside of the major towns. Various Party campaigns to aid the state by increasing production, by providing labour for building public buildings or by cleaning streets tend to be episodic and involve only a portion of the community (not all necessarily willing). The same is true of annual state ceremonies such as the trooping of a flag through each state which is then brought to Rangoon to mark Union Day every February.

Participation in State Management In order to gain the support of the population at more than a symbolic level, the Revolutionary Council developed a system of elections to administrative bodies at various levels which serve to engender a feeling of responsibility for the state and to involve some people in the management of affairs. The local government-elected bodies are the village and ward People's Councils, the township People's Councils, the State and Division People's Councils and, at the top of the state structure, the repository of state sovereignty on behalf of the people, the *Pyithu Hluttaw*. Direct popular participation in the *Pyithu Hluttaw* can only be achieved through the ritual of elections, though the obligation of members to report back to their constituents after each of its biannual sessions requires a public meeting to be held by *Pyithu Hluttaw* members, further linking the individuals who attend with the formal centre of the state.

In 1985 there was approximately one member of the *Pyithu Hluttaw* for about every 77,500 individuals in the country. Each township has at least one member in the *Pyithu Hluttaw*, and the constitution provides for additional members for townships with large populations and mandates that states or divisions with fewer than 1,000,000 residents or less than ten townships be given compensatory representation. Thus, in 1985, additional representation was provided for the Kayah, Karen and Chin

States and for Tenasserim Division. The states and divisions which were 'over-represented' in the *Pyithu Hluttaw* (in the sense that their proportion of total representation was larger than their proportion of the total population) were Rangoon, Mandalay, Kachin, Kayah, Chin, and Sagaing. The Kayah state was over-represented by a factor of over three and the Chin State by over two, but the difference for the other states and divisions was marginal. In Kayah, each of the state's 8 members represented 21,000 persons and in Chin each of the 21 members represented 28,400 persons.

Elections for the *Pyithu Hluttaw* take place every four years simultaneously with elections for the village, ward, township and state and divisional People's Councils. Only nationals of the country can be elected to these posts and, while it is not mandatory that a candidate be a member of the BSPP, in practice most of them are, as the single candidate put up for each position is previously selected by the relevant level Party unit and approved by the Central Executive Committee. At the voting booth the elector is faced with the choice either of accepting or rejecting the Party's nominee. There have been instances when the voters have turned down the official nominee and an immediate by-election has had to be called to fill the vacancy with someone who is acceptable to both the Party and to the local population.

The function of elections, especially to the *Pyithu Hluttaw*, is similar to that in the Soviet Union and other one-party socialist states. They 'are not presented as a possible redistribution of power, but as a affirmation of the existing power.' But the elections are more than just legitimizing rituals. 'The nominations, the campaigning, and the voting serve as an intensified period of recruitment into participation.' The socialization process is speeded during the campaigns as information is forced to circulate through the system.[67] Like the process of mass public discussion and the referendum that preceded the introduction of the 1974 constitution, or the intense public touring and public discussion by state officials before the passage of the 1983 Citizenship Law, elections are means of socializing individuals into the norms of the state, of legitimizing its activities and of communicating policy and other data to the public.

Since the new constitution was introduced, four elections have been held. The number of voters has grown from more than 14 million in 1974 to more than 19 million in 1985. The number of *Pyithu Hluttaw*

---

67. Friedgut, *Political Participation in the USSR*, p. 72.

representatives has increased from 450 to 489, while the number of persons elected to the state or divisional People's Councils has remained stable at 976. The number of township People's Council representatives has varied between about 21,600 and 22,850 at each poll, while the number elected to ward and village tract People's councils has steadily declined from 288,681 in 1974 to 166,763 in 1985.[68] Serving on these local bodies is often considered arduous and it may be increasingly difficult to persuade individuals to accept office. Perhaps the larger committees were found to be unwieldy and have been reduced in size for the sake of efficiency. The total of 15,940 ward and village tract People's Councils had an average of over ten members each in 1985.

It has been suggested that one function of elections in one-party socialist states is as a 'mobilization tool to bring into active participation sections of the population that might otherwise maintain traditional parochialism and political apathy'.[69] Without the findings of detailed research into the membership and backgrounds of members elected to the *Pyithu Hluttaw* and subordinate People's Councils, it is impossible to know the extent to which this has been true in Burma. It would seem that at the national level only a small proportion of individuals not otherwise previously involved in state activities have been brought into public life. Given the dominance of the military in the management of the state since 1962, it comes as no surprise that 40 per cent of the members of the *Pyithu Hluttaw* elected in 1977 were either serving or retired members of the armed forces. Of those from the military, a larger proportion represent central divisional constituencies and a larger proportion of the civilians came from the border states. This would suggest that the election to the *Pyithu Hluttaw*, like membership in the Party, serves as a means of involving individuals on the geographic periphery in the state's core activities. For example, all eight of the members from the Kayah State were civilians and had no known previous military career. Membership from the Karen State involved two serving officers, two retired officers, and nine civilians. Though there is no requirement that members of the *Pyithu Hluttaw* be residents or natives of the state or division from which they are elected, evidence on the basis of names suggests that most of the civilians elected from the border states come from one of the resident ethno-linguistic groups of the region. By

68. Sein Tin, *Myanma Akyaung hnit Kabama Akyaung*, p. 10; *The Working People's Daily*, 5 Oct. 1985.
69. Friedgut, *Political Participation in the USSR*, p. 91.

contrast, in 1977 Irrawaddy Division was represented by ten serving officers, fourteen retired officers and by twenty-four civilians, and Mandalay Division had twenty-nine civilians as against fourteen serving and eight retired officers.

One of the novel features of the 1974 constitution is that it requires all members of the *Pyithu Hluttaw* and other state-elected bodies to report back to constituents on their activities during the previous year. For the President, Prime Minister and other high-ranking state officials these meetings, widely reported in the press, are staid and formal affairs with only invited constituency representatives in attendance. Their set speeches do, however, serve as a report on the state of the economy and of the government and the problems that the leadership feels are most pressing. For less important individuals, including even cabinet ministers, the report-back meetings are described as being much more spontaneous and informal. Peasants come from miles around, and are known to have grilled a minister at some length as to why promises previously made have not been fulfilled. For members of the *Pyithu Hluttaw* without a great deal of influence within the government these must be uncomfortable occasions, and may be the reason why more embarrassing questions are being asked in the generally stage-managed meetings of the legislature.

Data for the nature of participation in the state and in divisional level People's Councils is more difficult to amass and analyse. The chairmanship and leading positions of these councils are often occupied by the regional Party chairman. There continues to be a great deal of overlap between state, military and Party personnel at this level, suggesting that control rather than participation is the primary purpose of this level of the state's structure. State and divisional People's Councils are responsible for passing on the directives of the central state to the subordinate structures and for coordinating the activities of the township Peoples's Councils and state-owned economic enterprises and agencies within their areas. Rather than policy-making bodies, they are essentially extensions of the administration of the central state.

It is at the township and village-tract and ward levels that the People's Councils become more genuinely participatory bodies. Though far from being institutions through which all people have equal access to influence or authority, they do provide a mechanism by which a large proportion of the state's activities which directly affect the lives of the people are conducted under the supervision of local residents. Antagonism against the system of village administration introduced by the British was often expressed during the colonial period, and after independence the government tried to modify that system to permit a greater degree of democracy in local government, but the attempt was generally considered a failure. In the view of the Party, in the central regions the old system destroyed the village community by means of its use of bureaucratic institutions and by the direct appointment of headmen by the state. In the peripheral states on the other hand, the British had maintained feudalism and kept the people there from participating in their own affairs, thus blocking their entry into the modern world.[70] One of the purposes of the SAC system was to prepare the way for the introduction of participatory government at the local level.

There are three functions of the local level People's Councils. One is to control the population: the mechanisms to do this were developed and elaborated during the SAC period. The second is organization, and here the People's Councils serve to assist the activities of the Party and of the mass/class organizations. The third is participation and the elective principle, with frequent meetings and campaigns serving as the main means of achieving this. The township and ward and village-tract People's Councils have no legislative powers and do not meet to deliberate policy. Rather, they are institutions intended to carry out the directives of the central state. This is one of the meanings of democratic socialism, a key principle of the constitution. Thus, among the organs of state power, the lower organs are to carry out 'the collective decisions and directives of the higher organs which in turn respect the views submitted by the lower organs'.[71] However, in carrying out the directives of the central state, the People's Councils are expected to adjust them as necessary to fit local conditions. While at the top and centre the structure of the state appears quite rigid and dogmatic, at the lowest levels local knowledge and sensitivities are intended to be used to obviate the more extreme and negative consequences of state policies.

The People's Councils choose the personnel from among their members to staff their Executive Committees (upon whom most of the work falls) and the People's Courts, as well as their Inspection and Affairs Committees. Few studies of the working of the People's Councils at the

70. Myanma Hsoshelit Lansin Pati, Pati Seyunyei Baho Kommiti Danachok (Burma Socialist Programme Party, Party Organization Central Committee Headquaters), *Myanma Hsoshelit Lansin Pati ei Pyei twinyei ya Ahmat 1* (Burma Socialist Programme Party's Internal Affairs Number 1) (Rangoon: Sapei Biman, 1966), p. 47.
71. Article 15 of the Constitution.

lowest levels have been made, though the author has experienced the operations of ward People's Councils in Rangoon, and one or two studies of conditions in villages have revealed aspects of their composition and activities. The Council's primarily devote their time to implementing plans provided by the Township People's Council. They, in turn, receive instructions from the State or Divisional People's Council — where the goals of the central state are divided into tasks and quotas to be achieved by each township. The village authorities then have to 'take part in the economic planning of the village, such as how many acres are to be brought under cultivation, how much paddy is to be sold, etc.'[72]

The goal of increasing the participation of individuals in the management of the state at the local level does not seem to have been fully achieved. Village People's Council leaders in one village studied came from the same families as the former headman and other village elders, and these tended to be the individuals 'who represent the "upper layer" of the village and who live in the "best" houses'. The same individuals also tend to dominate the leadership of other local branches of central organizations such as the BSPP, the Lansin Youth and the cooperative society.[73] In fact, despite the changes in the structure of the state introduced since 1962, by the mid-1970s many villages were still largely untouched by external changes. Though traditional village authorities such as monks and elders seem to be less influential than in the past, their place is not necessarily being taken by agents of the state. Outside influence is mediated through the same families as before because it seems that new social organizations with their own dynamics have not emerged in the villages studied.[74] This picture does not, however, seem to be universal. In villages in the dry zone where extensive but as yet unpublished surveys have been conducted on the effects of change on the delivery of health care, researchers have indicated a greater degree of state penetration. The author's observations in Rangoon and in central Burma would tend to confirm this latter view.

The way in which the state has delegated administrative responsibili-

72. Mya Than, 'A Burmese Village — Revisited', *The South East Asian Review*, II, 2 (Feb., 1978), pp. 13–14.
73. *Ibid.*, p. 14.
74. Khin Maung Kyi and Associates, 'Process of Communication in Modernisation of Rural Society: A Survey Report on Two Burmese Villages', *The Malayan Economic Review*, XVIII, no. 1 (April, 1973), pp. 58, 73.

ties to the village tracts and wards can be illustrated by the provisions of the 1975 Profit Tax Law. Under this legislation every ward or village-tract People's Council Executive Committee is obliged to form a committee of three members to prepare a list of persons in their area who are required to pay the tax, and to submit this list to the township People's Council Executive Committee. It then falls upon the township committee to organize a three-member assessment and collection committee which actually collects the tax under the supervision of the state or divisional People's Council Executive Committee. Appeals can be made, if the tax assessed is over Kt 500, to the above mentioned three-member committee and, from there, if the tax owed is more than Kt 10,000, to a central appeals body composed of three members of the *Pyithu Hluttaw* appointed by the Council of Ministers.

The activities of the township committee are aided by a Township Tax Officer who is responsible to the Ministry of Planning and Finance. He is required to advise the township committee as to who must pay tax from the list submitted by the village or ward committee. He also has the power to add names to the list of assessable individuals. His activities are supervised by state or divisional tax officers who advise the relevant appeals bodies. The Minister of Planning and Finance, with the approval of the cabinet, can overrule any assessment order given. The assessing body also has the power to impose fines for non-payment of taxes. The system is quite complex, and the legislation establishing it not only spells out the procedures to be followed, but concludes by reiterating the responsibility of the relevant level People's Councils to supervise the functioning of their respective assessment and collection committees, as well as to report what steps have been taken to the full People's Council. Not only do the state and divisional People's Councils have to follow these instructions, they must also report on their activities directly to the Minister for Planning and Finance.

The desire of the state to develop means of participation by local people in administration is clearly tempered by an equal desire to supervise affairs so as to ensure that decisions are not made which run contrary to central requirements. From time to time, leading state officials have expressed concern that some People's Councils have not been following directives but have developed too great a degree of local initiative. Like the previous district SACs, the current state and divisional People's Councils appear to be responsible for checking local initiative. Also, the *Pyithu Hluttaw* possesses the power to dismiss elected People's Councils for a variety of misdemeanours, including 'inefficient discharge of duties'. This gives the Home Minister the power of veto over all local government bodies.[75]

The concern of the central state manager with excessive local initiative is similar to that shown in the Soviet Union over what is known as 'localism'. There the authorities have developed a highly complex system of bureaucratic control which makes 'sense in terms of administrative functions only when viewed as an attempt to maintain centrally controlled administration together with a measure of local participation'.[76] The duplication of efforts at social control, planning and information that result at the local level from the existence not only of the People's Councils but also of the Party and its mass and class organizations provides a powerful set of cross-cutting controls upon the population while also permitting local administration to take place.

The Functions of the State

State Security and Public Order As a result of the Revolutionary Council's efforts at the development of non-coercive forms of social control, reliance upon force for the maintenance of the state in its core areas did not increase after 1962, despite the deteriorating economic condition of much of the population. In peripheral areas where separatist, Communist and smuggling forces developed in the late 1950s, the military has increased its control after initially losing ground and has brought the civilian institutions of the state in to dominate more territory. There has been little evidence of efforts to organize peasant rebellions, and despite the desire of the Communist Party and other insurgent groups to gain mass support among the majority of the population in the core areas of the state, they have all been unsuccessful.

This is not to argue, however, that there has been no significant armed opposition: distinct areas of discontent and protest exist in Burma's society twenty-five years after the military coup. Insurgency in peripheral areas still continues. The Communist Party, with an armed force estimated in 1985 to contain 12,000 regulars and 8,000 militiamen, controls an area along the border with China, but lost its foothold in the Pegu Yoma in central Burma in the mid-1970s as it faced increasing military opposition and declining peasant cooperation. The Karen

75. *Forward*, Nov., 1984.
76. Friedgut, *Political Participation in the USSR*, p. 39.

National Liberation Army, the armed force of the Karen National Union, had an estimated 4,000 troops in 1985 though its resources have been shrinking for several years due to greater army pressure against its strongholds along the border with Thailand. Various separatist and smuggling bands in the Shan State can field perhaps 10,000 anti-state forces and the Kachin Independence Army has an estimated 5,000 troops. Other small bands have no more than a few hundred troops each.[77]

As all of these groups exist on the periphery of the state and are unable to agree among themselves on a single course of action, they pose no major threat. But, of course, as long as they exist they contain the seeds of a challenge to the state's perpetuation, and therefore the state devotes a great deal of attention to trying to eliminate them. This is done not only by military means but also by arming loyal villagers and by extending the political and administrative system of the state into areas which have been recaptured by the army. The fact that 4 townships had only one party organizer in 1985 and 26 had organizing committees rather than fully functioning party units suggests that the state did not at that time have firm control of 30 of its 314 townships. As the average township has a population of 112,500 persons, this would suggest that about 3,487,500 persons, or slightly less than 10 per cent of the total population of Burma, was not under the state's hegemony. However, as the population density of the four peripheral states where insurgency has been most prevalent, Shan, Kachin, Kayah and Karen, is much lower than in the core divisions (see Table 5.1., p. 307), the proportion of the total population outside of state control was probably significantly less. The average population of the 83 townships of these states is 44,807, and if 30 of these are assumed to be under the partial control of anti-state forces, then 1,344,210 persons, or 3.81 per cent of the total population, were outside of the control of the state. This would seem to be a reasonable maximum estimate.

More immediately threatening to public order is the threat of unrest and protest in the cities. Here the activities of students and workers have been of particular concern. Given the tumultuous nature of Burma's urban politics in the 1930s and 1940s it is quite remarkable how free of political turmoil the cities have been in the years since 1962. However, there have been expressions of public discontent which have led to the

77. International Institute for Strategic Studies, *The Military Balance, 1985–86* (London, 1985), p. 122.

use of violence and to the threat of future violence against protesters. Students have been the most important group in this regard. Just four months after the 1962 coup, the army occupied Rangoon University and blew up the students' union building, killing at least sixteen and perhaps as many as 60–100 students protesting against the Revolutionary Council's moves to close independent political organizations within the student body.[78] In 1967 there were brief riots in Rangoon, ostensibly over the involvement of the government of China in exporting the Cultural Revolution to the Chinese community resident in Burma, but in large part because of the food shortages that then existed. In December 1969, student unrest at the university occurred again, forcing the government to remove at least 6,000 students from the campus during the Southeast Asian games.[79]

The greatest urban challenge to the state after 1962 came in 1974, when workers and students in Rangoon combined to protest against inflation and food shortages after changes in economic policy were introduced in 1973 which favoured the rural sector. The protests began with strikes in state-owned factories and workshops and soon spread to other towns. Violence occurred after the arrest of some strike leaders. At the same time, to avoid students becoming involved, schools and universities were closed. The two months of protests ended only with the use of force: at least 22 persons were killed and 73 wounded before order was restored on June 8th. Trouble erupted once more in December when students protested at the state's funeral arrangements for the former United Nations Secretary-General, U Thant. The students, joined by Buddhist monks, seized U Thant's corpse and took it to the site of the old students' union. Martial law was declared and the military recovered the body, though only after the students had attacked police stations and offices of the BSPP. Student sources say that over 100 of their number were killed in the demonstrations.[80] Students demonstrated again a year later when 500 marched from the university to the centre of the city. In a protest which in style was reminiscent of student demonstrations against the British more than fifty years earlier, the students camped at the Shwedagon Pagoda. But the indigenous government did not hesitate to

78. Badgley, 'Burma: The Nexus', p. 90
79. *New York Times*, 11 Dec. 1969.
80. Raja Segaran Arumugam, 'Burma: A Political and Economic Background', Institute of Southeast Asian Studies, *Southeast Asian Affairs 1975* (Singapore: Heinemann, 1976), pp. 42–3.

clear the pagoda and arrested 213 students.[81]

The military's response to these protests indicates its reliance upon minimal manpower and maximum firepower to demonstrate, as rapidly as possible, its determination to keep the unrest from spreading and to serve as a deterrent. However, the Party and mass and class organizations were also used to try to stem dissatisfaction. During the 1974 workers' strikes People's and Workers' Council officials were sent to negotiate with the workers, and the Lansin Youth workers at the university are constantly alert to signs of student discontent.

The armed forces since 1962 have grown in size and in expense, but not disproportionately to population growth or to the expansion of the economy and government expenditure generally. However, compared to other non-Communist states in Southeast Asia, the proportion of the population in the armed forces is relatively high. It stood at 6.8 per thousand in 1973 but declined to 5.9 per thousand in 1983, compared with 2.4 and 1.7 for these respective years in Indonesia and 5.8 and 4.9 in Thailand. Only Malaysia and Singapore had a higher ratio in 1983.[82] In 1985, it was estimated that Burma had 186,000 men and women in the armed forces, of whom 170,000 were in the army. Another 73,000 served in the People's Police Force and there were 35,000 members of the People's Militia.[83] This compares to an armed force of about 125,000 in 1968.[84]

The military is essentially an infantry force and possesses none of the technologically sophisticated equipment that many armies assume to be necessary for internal and external security. No significant amounts of foreign military assistance have been received since the termination of a United States aid agreement at the end of the 1960s. The total assistance offered over a period of more than 12 years was only US$85.5 million, and not all the credits available were used on time.[85] Consequently, it is a relatively inexpensive force per man. Expenditure for each soldier was only about US$1,111 per year in 1982 compared to a cost of US$6,575 per man per year for Thailand and US$10,498 for Indonesia. Annual

81. Raja Segaran Arumugam, 'Burma: Political Unrest and Economic Stagnation', in Institute of Southeast Asian Studies, *Southeast Asian Affairs 1976* (Singapore: Heinemann, 1977), p. 168.
82. United States Arms Control and Disarmament Agency, *World Military Expenditures and Arms Transfers 1985* (Washington, DC: Aug., 1985).
83. *The Military Balance 1985–86*, pp. 121–2.
84. *The Military Balance, 1968–69*, p. 47.
85. *New York Times*, 25 Aug. 1970; 18 Aug. 1971.

expenditure per sq. km. of territory is also lower than that of most other Asian armies, estimated at only US$295 per year in 1982 compared to US$2,980 for Thailand and US$1,481 for Indonesia. Personnel per sq. km. was also low at 265.5 men per sq. km. compared with 453.3 men per sq. km. in Thailand (though Indonesia had a lower ratio of 141.2 men).[86]

As a proportion of total government expenditure official defence spending has been declining fairly consistently since 1954, when at the end of the civil war it accounted for 40 per cent of total spending.[87] On average, during the years 1950/1 through 1954/5, defence accounted for 33.6 per cent of all government expenditure and fell to an average of 32 per cent between 1955/6 through 1960/61. One official foreign agency estimated that military expenditure in 1973 accounted for 33.4 per cent of the government budget; this fell to 25.5 per cent in 1977.[88] An analysis of the government's published budgets since 1982/3 shows that defence expenditure as a proportion of total government expenditure declined from 29.1 to a planned 20.7 per cent in 1986/7.[89] Of course, some military expenditure may be hidden in other departmental expenditures. For example, military officers posted to civilian duties are paid by their new departments. Burma imports a small amount of military equipment each year, only US$5 million in 1973, US$30 million in 1979 and US$20 million in 1983, compared to figures in the latter years for Thailand of US$110,350 and US$320 millions. However, as a proportion of total imports, these represent from 3.4 to 9.4 per cent of imports, while the Thai figure in these years did not exceed 5.3 per cent.[90] As a proportion of gross domestic product, military expenditure has been steadily declining from a high of 6.7 per cent to 6.3 per cent in 1962. By 1982, it was estimated to have fallen to 4.0 per cent, having reached a low of 3.9 per cent in 1975 and 1976.[91] In financial terms the army had

86. Calculations made from data provided in papers given at a conference in August, 1986, at the Institute for Southeast Asian Studies, Singapore, on defence expenditure and threat perception in Southeast Asia.
87. David I. Steinberg, *Burma's Road Toward Development: Growth and Ideology Under Military Rule* (Boulder, Colo.: Westview Press, 1981), p. 165.
88. *Ibid.*, p. 166.
89. Complete data is provided in the author's 'Defense Expenditure and Threat Perception in Burma', in Chin Kin Wah (ed.), *Defense Expenditure in Southeast Asia* (Singapore: Institute of Southeast Asian Studies, forthcoming).
90. *World Military Expenditures and Arms Transfers, 1985.*
91. Stockholm International Peace Research Institute, *World Armaments and Disarmaments 1976* (Stockholm: Almqvist and Wiksell, 1976), pp. 160–1; *ibid., 1977.*, p. 234; *ibid., 1984* (London: Taylor and Francis, 1985), pp. 280–4.

become by the mid-1980s less the centre of the state than it was under the civilian governments of the 1950s.

Courts and the Law Accepting the argument that the previous legal system had worked only to the advantage of 'the bourgeoisie, the landed gentry and the capitalists' and was distinctly prejudicial to the interests of the 'working people', the Revolutionary Council set about changing the judicial system and its relationship with the public. In the process, the courts lost what independence they had enjoyed under the civilian administration. On March 30, 1962, the two highest courts, the Supreme Court and the High Court, were abolished and replaced with a new Chief Court. A new procedure was also followed of establishing People's Courts (not normally composed of lawyers or judicial officers), when the Revolutionary Council thought necessary, for the trial of special criminal cases.[92] However, all existing laws continued to remain valid and the subordinate courts functioned as before.[93]

Not until August 7, 1972 were more radical changes made in the working of the court system. At the time of the abolition of the districts the role of district officers as judicial officers disappeared, and village-tract, ward, township and state or divisional Security and Administration Committees were given judicial powers. With the incorporation of local residents on the SACs, the latter were instructed to institute a system of People's Courts.[94] This system has continued under the present constitution.

The purpose of the People's Court system, as explained by the drafters of the constitution, was to replace the single judge system instituted by the British with a panel of judges chosen from the people. Emphasis in these courts was to be placed on 'reforming the moral habits of transgressors' and on educating people on the nature of the law as well as to defend life and property and to achieve justice. The new judicial system made it possible to abolish the former Justice Department and this was replaced by a Council of People's Justices chosen from among members of the *Pyithu Hluttaw* to supervise and administer the judicial system. The similarly chosen Council of People's Attorneys supervises the work of

92. Alan Gledhill, 'Burma', in John Gilissen (ed.), *Bibliographical Introduction to Legal History and Ethnology*, vol. E., no. 7. (Brussels: Editions de l'Institut de Sociologie, Université Libre de Bruxelles, 1970), p. 11.
93. *Party Seminar 1965*, pp. 33–4.
94. *Townhlanyei Kaungsi ei Hluthsaungchet Thamaing Akyinchut*, p. 192.

the state's law officers and prosecutors.⁹⁵ Ultimate appeal on the meaning of law and its correct implementation can be made to the fifteen-member Council of State, which is also appointed from members of the *Pyithu Hluttaw* and whose chairman is the state president.

The People's Court system is highly complex and, like the administrative system, combines features of participation with close supervision from the centre. However, the laws which have been passed since 1962 are relatively simple and easy to understand, though sometimes open to contrary interpretations. Drafting simplified law has been consciously pursued in order to make it understandable to non-lawyers. According to the leading lawyer involved in the drafting of the constitution and the new legal system, 'the people's judicial system is a system in accord with Burma's heritage and is modern'.⁹⁶ It combines the traditional practice of arbitration and the search for norms of justice with the use of rules of evidence and procedure taken from Western legal traditions. After the rotating judges chosen from the People's Council make their decision in a case, the enforcement of their judgement is carried out by full-time judicial officers (who also serve as advisors and guides to the judges in explaining the law and procedures of the court).

At the village and ward level, the working of the courts would appear to be in the hands of local individuals, often from quite humble positions in society. In Rangoon it is said that wealthy persons have had to face judgement from their own servants in minor trials. These courts have, according to critics familiar with the working of the previous judicial system, not placed much reliance on rules of evidence and procedure and have sometimes been highly informal. Others have suggested that their very informality and local personnel have made the courts seem accessible and no longer shrouded in mystery. However bribery of the panel of judges is said to take place, for, as in the past, individual judges were said to be open to financial persuasion.

In the township, state and divisional courts, closer adherence to procedure and a more formal atmosphere have apparently been maintained, though more than the usual amount of scepticism must be placed on this assessment of the courts as data on their working is very difficult to collect and analyse. Certainly in the *Pyithu Hluttaw* and in the press there

95. *Pyi Htaungsu Hsoshelit Thammata Myanma Naingngan Hpwetsinpun Akhyeihkan Upadei hnit Patthet thaw Adipape Shinlinhkyetmya*, pp. 63–7.
96. Maung Maung, *Taya Upadei Ahtweidwei Bahuthuta* (General Law Knowledge) (Rangoon: Win Maung U, 1975), p. 5.

has been an unusual amount of criticism of the courts, especially of their inability to produce justice with speed.[97] The courts have faced an increasing workload, and the appeals rate appears to be quite high. Each year the number of cases accepted for trial has increased and the number of cases kept pending for over a year has apparently also grown. The appeal courts at the regional level, composed of People's Judges who are also serving on other council committees with various duties to perform in the management of economic, political and social affairs, have apparently become overloaded.[98]

In particular, there had developed by 1984 a significant backlog of cases waiting for final appeal in the offices of the Council of State. As the members of this organization are all busy with other duties, including the presidency, prime ministership and ministerial and party posts, they have little time to settle cases. Similarly, as the Council of People's Justices members had many administrative tasks to perform, they had little time to sit as a court and decide appeals. One solution to this problem reached in 1985 was to expand the membership of the Council of People's Justices from 5 to 8. Another, and far more important, solution has been to exclude a number of the most important cases from the appeals procedure above the state and divisional level.

The right to use agricultural land is the most important legal issue that faces most of Burma's population. The tradition of the resort to the courts to settle land disputes goes back to before the British period, but during the colonial era it became very frequent. Under the 1974 constitution cases of disputed land usage are to be settled in the first instance at the level of the Township People's Council Executive Committee. Until March 1984, a Committee's decision could be appealed through the system to the Council of People's Justices, with resulting long delays in final decisions being reached. To solve this problem, the Law on the Duties and Rights of People's Councils at Different Levels and Executive Committees at Different Levels was amended by the *Pyithu Hluttaw* so that no appeals could be made from the decision of the relevant state or divisional People's Council.[99]

---

97. See, for example, *The Guardian* (Rangoon), 5 Oct. 1983 and 6 Oct. 1983; *The Working People's Daily*, 17 Sept. 1984.
98. See the summary of the report of the Council of People's Justices in *The Working People's Daily*, 11 March 1986. A similar account was provided in earlier years; see, for example, *The Guardian* (Rangoon), 5 Oct., 1983.
99. *The Working People's Daily*, 18 March 1984; 29 March 1984.

Economic and Financial The socialist economic policies of the state since 1962 have not significantly changed the structure of the economy or patterns of employment. However, the nationalization of external and internal trade and of large sectors of manufacturing, together with the introduction of quantitative physical planning as the basic mechanism of economic control, have had other significant consequences. First, and most immediately obvious, the nationalization of trade forced out of the economy most of the remaining Indian population as their enterprises were taken over by the various Trading Corporations. It is estimated that between 125,000 to 300,000 Indians and Pakistanis left the country in 1963, 1964 and 1965.[100] The egalitarian intentions of the state also worked to keep income and wealth disparities from becoming too great. Though adequate data on income distribution is difficult to find, a World Bank team estimated that income disparites in Burma in the mid-1970s were less than in neighbouring countries and that in urban areas the lowest 40 per cent of the population received 21 per cent of total income, in comparison to 15 per cent in India and 12 per cent in Malaysia.[101]

Moreover, the state's radical economic policies had two other significant consequences: one was to concentrate economic control and management in the hands of the state; the other was to decrease the involvement of Burma's economy in the world economy. Both these consequences are possible causes of Burma's relatively slow rate of economic development compared to many of its neighbours in Southeast Asia, and of the growing incentives for black market economic activity on the part of a significant proportion of the population. Nonetheless, the state's policies have also enhanced the control of the state over the population by making illegal and therefore potentially punishable a wide range of economic activities, thus limiting the development of private centres of wealth which could spawn independent political power.

Having elected to avoid the involvement of foreign multinational corporations and large-scale foreign aid, as well as avoiding significant foreign borrowing in the first decade after the 1962 coup, the state had to rely largely upon domestic sources of investment. Understandably,

---

100. John Badgley, 'Burma's Zealot Wungyis: Maoists or St. Simonists', *Asian Survey*, V, 1 (Jan., 1965), p. 55; Steinberg, 'Burma Under Military Rule', p. 260.
101. The World Bank, *Development in Burma: Issues and Prospects*, Report no. 1024-BA, July 27, 1976, South Asia Regional Office, p. 12.

given the state's goal of keeping prices low and of avoiding excess profits being made at the expense of consumers, as well as the state's inability to accumulate domestic savings through taxation, the rate of investment in the economy throughout the 1960s remained low and contributed to a slow rate of growth of the gross domestic product.[102] Details are provided in Table 5.5. By borrowing abroad, usually from multilateral sources and at concessionary rates, more funds for investment became available from the mid-1970s to the early 1980s before debt repayment became a concern. There followed a significant increase in growth as a

Table 5.5. GROSS DOMESTIC PRODUCT AND INVESTMENT AT CONSTANT 1969/70 PRICES, AND RATES OF GROWTH

	GDP (Kyat m.)	% change	Investment (Kyat m.)	% change
1961/2	7,798		806	
1965/6	8,715		912	
1966/7	8,355	-4.1	985	8.0
1967/8	9,200	10.1	1,015	3.0
1968/9	9,503	3.3	1,098	8.2
1969/70	9,976	5.0	1,153	5.0
1970/1	10,388	4.1	1,019	-11.6
1971/2	10,641	2.4	1,091	7.1
1972/3	10,538	-1.0	895	-18.0
1973/4	10,812	2.6	773	-13.6
1974/5	11,101	2.7	780	0.9
1975/6	11,562	4.2	808	3.6
1976/7	12,265	6.1	965	19.4
1977/8	12,996	6.0	1,430	48.2
1978/9	13,843	6.5	1,852	29.5
1979/80	14,562	5.2	2,206	19.1
1980/1	15,718	7.9	2,158	-2.2
1981/2	16,717	6.4	2,454	13.7
1982/3	17,654	5.6	2,787	13.6
1983/4	18,429	4.4	2,503	-10.3
1984/5	19,464*	5.6*	2,335*	-6.7*
1985/6	20,675*	6.2*	2,689*	15.2*

*Provisional figures

Source: *Report to the Pyithu Hluttaw on the Financial, Economic and Social Conditions of the Socialist Republic of the Union of Burma for 1977–8* (Rangoon: Ministry of Planning and Finance, 1977); *ibid., 1986–7* (1986).

102. *Ibid.*, pp. 39–40.

Table 5.6. ORIGINS OF GROSS DOMESTIC PRODUCT

	1961/2 % of total	1985/6 % of total
Agriculture	26.0	28.1
Livestock & fishing	5.6	6.8
Forestry	2.9	2.1
Mining	1.3	1.5
Manufacturing	10.5	10.5
Utilities	0.5	1.7
Construction	1.9	2.7
Transport & communications	6.1	5.9
Banking and finance	1.1	4.0
Wholesale & retail trade	29.3	20.6
Other services	14.8	16.1
GDP at factor cost	100.0	100.0

Source: Report to the Pyithu Hluttaw, 1986–7, pp. 46–7.

result of the state's borrowing as well as of other economic reforms, with real growth peaking in 1980/1 at 7.9 per cent.

Except for the late 1970s when the expansion of the economy was led by grain and other primary product exports, the state has generally assumed that investment in agriculture is to be left to the private sector, and the bulk of official investment funds have been chanelled into import substitution manufacturing, power production and transport and communications infrastructure. Following the nationalization of the 1960s and the fall-off of investment rates the state slowly began to encourage expansion of the private sector, including legislation to protect private investments in certain sectors, but the prevailing tax regime and other conditions under which entrepreneurs had to operate meant that there was little response to the state's appeals for private sector investment.[103]

As Table 5.6. shows in macro-terms, the economic structure of the country has changed little other than to increase the proportion of GDP derived from agriculture, including livestock and fishery, as well as from construction and power. Meanwhile trade has declined and manufacturing has remained constant. The decline in trade is paralleled by the fall in the import and export of goods and services as a proportion of total GDP. Legal imports represented 19 per cent of GDP in 1960 but had

103. See the comments of the BSPP General Secretary in his 1981 Political Report, *The Working People's Daily*, 3 Aug. 1981.

Table 5.7. DISTRIBUTION OF LABOUR FORCE, 1931 AND 1984/5

	1931%	1984/5%
Agriculture	66.4	63.5
Livestock & fishery	2.3	1.3
Forestry	0.9	1.2
Mining	0.6	0.6
Manufacturing	9.1	8.3
Power	n.a.	0.1
Construction	1.6	1.6
Transport & communications	3.5	3.3
Social services	3.9	2.1
Administration	0.8	3.9
Trade	9.0	9.8
Others	1.9	4.3
Total	100.0	100.0

Sources: Louis J. Walinsky, *Economic Development in Burma 1951–1960* (New York: Twentieth Century Fund, 1962), p. 33; *Report to the Pyithu Hluttaw, 1986–7*, p. 28.

declined to 2 per cent in 1981, and exports declined from 20 per cent to 9 per cent in the same period.[104] If it is accepted that illegal imports equal something between one-third and two-thirds of legal imports,[105] imports account for less than 3.5 per cent of GDP.

The structure of the labour force had, by the mid-1980s, changed remarkably little since the colonial period. Though the sources upon which the percentages provided in Table 5.7. are not consistent in their use of labour categories, the similarity of the two groups of figures is quite striking.

The proportion of the labour force in the state sector had reached only 10.6 per cent by 1985, and only in the relatively small construction, mining, forestry, power, social services and administration sectors did direct state employees outnumber those in the combined private and cooperative sectors. However, these figures belie the control the state has over the activities of the private sectors. After 1962, firms which were not nationalized were placed under strict supervision, and the state has maintained a tight rein over the allocation of foreign exchange for

104. The World Bank, *World Development Report 1984* (New York: Oxford University Press, 1984), p. 226.
105. As a World Bank team did in 1976; *Development in Burma: Issues and Prospects*, p. 8.

The Functions of the State

the import of capital equipment as well as of raw materials. Though there were still 39,239 private manufacturing establishments in 1985 (compared with 719 cooperatively owned and 1,763 state-owned concern), 34,596 of the private sector enterprises employed ten or fewer individuals. Only six private plants employed more than 100 workers while 446 state plants employed more than 100.[106] The small proportion involved in the state sector of the workforce, however, is responsible for producing over 39 per cent of all output and services as compared to 55.5 per cent for the private sector and 5.4 per cent for the cooperatives. In agriculture, 94.0 per cent of all production is in the private sector, with state farms producing only 0.5 per cent.[107]

Financing the State A commonly used indicator of a state's ability to control the economy and an indirect indicator of its strength *vis-à-vis* civil society is the proportion of total current revenue as a percentage of gross national product (GNP) or gross domestic product (GDP). Among the industrial market economies of the West, this percentage in GNP terms ran in 1982 from 18.4 per cent for Switzerland to 44.8 per cent for Belgium.[108] Such figures are of limited comparability, as they measure only central government revenue and ignore regional and local taxing authorities. As a general rule, however, low income countries tend to have centralized taxation systems and central government revenue accounts for nearly all taxation and governmental expenditure.

This is the case in Burma. By 1982, current state revenue from all sources as a proportion of GDP was 17.3 per cent, in comparison (in GNP terms) to Thailand's 14.4 per cent, Indonesia's 26.4 per cent, the Philippines' 11.7 per cent, and Tanzania's 19.6 per cent. The 1982 figure for Burma is nearly the same as that for 1958, when total government receipts were 17.1 per cent of GNP.[109] But in the case of Burma, the proportion must have fallen dramatically in the 1960s, for current revenue as a proportion of GDP was only 10.6 per cent in 1974 and 9.9 per cent in 1975. Subsequently, it has increased steadily to 17.7 per cent

---

106. *Report to the Pyithu Hluttaw, 1986/87* (Rangoon: Ministry of Planning and Finance, 1986), p. 176.
107. *Ibid.*, pp. 54–5.
108. *World Development Report 1984*, Table 27, pp. 270–1.
109. *Ibid.*, which gives the figure for Burma at 17.1 per cent; calculations for Burma made from the *Report to the Pyithu Hluttaw, 1985/86* for GDP at current prices and the International Monetary Fund's *Government Finance Statistics Yearbook 1985* for consolidated central government total revenue. Calculations for 1958 are based on data from Walinsky, *Economic Development in Burma*, p. 114 and p. 422.

in 1981 before declining marginally in 1982. The trend suggests that the Revolutionary Council's initial nationalization policies and administrative re-organization significantly hampered the state's ability to tax and raise revenue in other ways. However the reassertion of the state's capacities has returned these rates to something near a 'normal' ratio for comparable states.

Between 1974 and 1982, foreign grants (aid) as a proportion of total revenue averaged 5.1 per cent, varying (with no clear pattern) from 2 per cent in 1977 to 8.1 per cent in 1982. Import duties as a proportion of total state revenue in the nine years between 1974 and 1983 also changed little, averaging 15.3 per cent a year and ranging from 12.8 per cent in 1976 to 20.4 per cent in 1975. In comparison, customs revenue accounted for 24.7 per cent of receipts in 1958. Where the state has clearly strengthened its taxing ability is through what amounts to indirect taxation, while direct taxation as a proportion of receipts (but not in relationship to GDP growth) fell back toward the 1958 rate of 39.9 per cent. Total tax revenue, primarily composed of domestic taxes on goods and services, mainly as a sales tax, declined as a proportion of total revenue from 72.1 per cent in 1974 and a peak of 80.1 per cent in 1975 to a low of 56.0 per cent in 1981 and 56.8 per cent in 1982.[110] On the other hand, non-tax revenue entirely in the form of income from state-owned financial institutions and non-financial enterprises increased from 21.4 per cent in 1974 and a low of 13.3 per cent in 1975 to a peak of 40.2 per cent in 1981 and 35.1 per cent in 1982. Non-tax revenues in 1958 amounted to 35.7 per cent of the total. State-owned institutions and enterprises are the easiest for the state to tap, and the government's decision, taken at the First BSPP Congress in 1971, to limit subsidies to loss-making organizations and to require that they be run on a business basis has made them much more useful as a source of revenue. Or, put another way, running the socialist state on business principles has proved profitable.

To summarise, the capacity of the state to tax the economy directly has increased since 1974 regardless of the declining proportion of total revenue coming from this source. In every year since 1974, with the slight exceptions of 1978, 1980 and 1982, the rate of domestic tax

110. Calculated from IMF *Government Finance Statistics Yearbook 1985*; calculations from the official *Report to the Pyithu Hluttaw* for various years show a much more consistent pattern with tax revenues equalling around 60 per cent of total revenue and state economic enterprises providing 30 or less.

revenue increase has been greater than the growth of GDP in current terms.

Concentrating purely on the income of the central government reveals only part of the state's financial relations. Before 1971 the economy remained remarkably free from foreign capital inputs and in several years there were capital outflows as debt repayment exceeded new funds. It is estimated that between 1962 and 1972 Burma received on average only about US$28 million per year in foreign assistance; after 1972, aid and borrowing increased rapidly, and in 1979, for example, US$350 million was received.[111] As a consequence, debt rose rapidly and there developed problems of debt service in the mid-1980s. In 1970 Burma's long-term public and publicly guaranteed debt stood at only US$100.7 million. Eight years later this had increased by 759 per cent to US$864.4 million and by 1984 had grown another 157 per cent to US$2,311.2 million. By 1984 Burma's debt service ratio (gross external liabilities/gross national product [%]) had reached 36.3 per cent and was expected to increase for one or two years more before beginning to decline.[112] The problem of debt repayment was compounded by a fall in commodity prices, especially for rice, in the mid-1980s, and by the fact that since 1962 the economy had not diversified away from its reliance on primary product exports for its major foreign exchange earnings.

Because of the state's inability to change the structure of the economy, agriculture is still the principle source of livelihood for the bulk of the population and for the state. There remains a basic contradiction between the interests of the average peasant and the state: each claims a share of the produce of the country's fields and any increase in the share held by the state must be at the expense of the peasant, especially as the role of any putatively exploitative middleman has been removed by the government's nationalization policies. The peasantry makes its claim for the predominant share of the nation's agricultural surplus on the basis that if it were not for their labour, buffaloes, and tools used in the cultivation of the fields, there would be no annual crop. The state, on the other hand, claims that the land belongs to it, and that the farmer is merely using the land with its permission, and must therefore share the fruits of their mutual agricultural endeavour. Furthermore, the state

---

111. Research Institute for Peace and Security, *Asian Security 1980* (Tokyo, 1980), p. 160.
112. *World Debt Tables* (Washington, DC: International Monetary Fund, 1985), pp. 414–7.

claims that it has removed most of the insecurity of tenure and high cost of credit that plagued peasant farmers in the colonial and early post-colonial years, and therefore has eased the position of the peasant family. The state not only makes available inexpensive credit, but it buys the peasant's crop through an advanced purchase scheme, provides him with highly subsidized fertilizer, undertakes the cost of marketing the crop and provides an extensive planning system for determining what should be planted and in what quantities. Therefore the peasant has a moral obligation to fulfil his production and sales quotas.

The number of peasant families at the time of the coming to power of the Revolutionary Council was 2.78 million, but due to land redistribution, population growth and the resultant division of family farms when the original cultivator died, the number had grown to 4.35 million in 1974.[113] Since 1974, however, the number of farm families has begun to decline, and in 1982 there were 64,237 fewer farming households than eight years earlier. The 4.28 million farm families in 1982 farmed over 24.21 million acres. One of the state's key agricultural goals since 1962 has been the expansion of worked land, and there has been an increase in tilled acreage of almost 5 million acres since 1961.[114]

But because of farm population growth, there has been a significant reduction in the size of farms. In 1961/2, 84 per cent of farmers cultivated 10 or fewer acres; by 1982/3, 86 per cent of farmers cultivated 10 or fewer acres but 25 per cent cultivated 5 or fewer acres. There is a significant disparity in the size of holdings, as 2.7 per cent of farm families cultivate 15 per cent of land and 12 per cent of farm families till 29 per cent of all planted acreage with holdings between 10 and 20 acres.[115] While farms of over 20 acres are probably not wet rice farms but upland and dry-zone land able to support fewer individuals per acre, such a disparity does not result in significant income inequalities. However, if farmers possess more than 16 acres of wet rice land they probably have a greater income than their neighbours with fewer acres.

Since 1962, the state has implemented significant changes in its relationship with the peasant population which appear to have been intended to achieve incompatible goals. The first change was to ensure that the peasantry remained loyal and did not engage in rebellion or give support to the Communist Party and to other anti-government forces;

137. *World Development Report 1984*, Table 27, pp. 270–1.
114. *Report to the Pyithu Hluttaw 1984/85*, p. 46–7.
115. *Ibid., 1977/78*, p. 30; *ibid., 1985/86.*, p. 46.

the second was to increase the resources the state could extract from agriculture in order to finance the strengthening of the state both domestically and internationally by increasing its military and industrial capabilities. The efforts to implement these goals have led to compromises which have made it difficult, if not impossible, for the state to change agrarian relations; for when faced with a choice between antagonizing the peasant majority and increasing agricultural production, the state has normally chosen the former course. Also, as much of the lower level apparatus for organizing the peasantry including the village Party units and People's Councils are in the hands of those peasants who benefit most from the existing situation, the state has limited its ability to impose change against the interests of powerful local individuals.

This situation has come about as a result not only of the political and administrative structures introduced since 1962, but also because of the state's policies toward agrarian taxation, land control and rice purchasing. In keeping with the practice introduced by the government immediately after independence, land tax has not been resorted to as a major means of state revenue. Tax varies with the assessed quality of the land from 1.75 to 5 Kt per acre per year, a nominal sum.[116] The state exacts resources from the peasantry through the delivery system, whereby as the sole legal purchaser of crops it controls prices and keeps them artificially low.[117] In exchange for this, the state has attempted to guarantee the security of tenure for the cultivator and to keep his production costs low. The system provides the peasant with few incentives for investment, and until the state began making significant investments in agricultural technology in the mid-1970s, rice production stagnated. In the mid-1960s Burma ceased being one of the world's major rice-exporting nations, and even faced rice shortages in urban areas and in rural areas unable to provide for their own subsistence.[118]

---

116. Teruko Saito, 'Farm Household Economy under Paddy Delivery System in Contemporary Burma', *The Developing Economies*, XIX, 4 (Dec. 1981), p. 391.
117. The Revolutionary Council replaced the State Agricultural Marketing Board (SAMB) with the Union of Burma Agricultural Products Marketing Board (UBAM). The latter then became part of Trade Corporation No. 1 of the Ministry of Trade and has not become the Agriculture and Farm Produce Trade Corporation; *Ibid.*, fn. 11, p. 370.
118. The complications in assessing all of the problems involved in explaining this situation are set forth in H.V. Richter, *Burma's Rice Surpluses: Accounting for the Decline* (Canberra: Australian National University Development Studies Centre Working Paper), no. 3, 1976.

The basis of the agrarian system are the 1953 Land Nationalization Act and the Revolutionary Council's Tenancy Act of 1963. The Land Nationalization Act established the principle that land redistributed to peasants was not owned by them, but remained the property of the state as set forth in principle in the constitution. The state allowed them to cultivate the land with the authorization of the village Land Committee, and in most instances each year these committees recognized the right of existing peasant families to continue to work the same fields. This land could not be mortgaged, sold or rented, but only tilled by the approved peasant. However, by 1962 only 17 per cent of all land was held in this manner and the remaining 83 per cent was held in the name of private owners, either landlords or sitting farmers. The 1963 Tenancy Act was intended to change the condition of the remaining tenants and cultivating owners whose land had not been nationalized. Its provisions meant that landlords no longer had the right to determine who their tenants would be; this power fell to the village Land Committee. The payment of tenancy rents in kind was prohibited — thus giving the tenant control over his own produce, and allowing him to sell it at the most propitious time, or, when required, to sell it to the state — and an upper limit to tenancy rents was fixed. At the same time, a Peasants' Rights Protection Act was promulgated which made it impossible for creditors to seize the land and other assets of peasants or to seek their punishment for non-payment through the civil courts. In 1965 a further step was taken with an amendment to the tenancy act which made tenancy rents illegal. As a result, the selling, renting or collecting of farm rent was prohibited and the state, through the village Land Committees, became the sole arbiter of land use.[119] Initially, the determination of each peasant's obligatory annual crop was made by the local SAC as it estimated how to meet its quota as established by the central planners. After 1974 this responsibility was passed to the relevant People's Council.

Despite these measures to destroy the legal underpinnings of agricultural tenancy, the number of tenants in the country continued to increase up to 1970/71, the last year for which there are published figures. However, as a proportion of the total number of cultivators tenants had declined slightly from 43.9 per cent in 1961/2 to 41.8 per cent in 1970/1.[120] In non-paddy land, it seems that tenancy legislation

---

119. Saito, 'Farm Household Economy', pp. 368–9; John S. Ambler, 'Burma's Rice Economy under Military Rule: The Evolution of Socialist Agricultural Programs and Their Impact on Paddy Farmers' (unpubl. paper, Cornell University, Oct. 1983), p. 31.
120. Ambler, 'Burma's Rice Economy under Military Rule', p. 31.

only affected land control marginally, and the control of paddy land was far from complete. While the transfer of upland non-paddy land was conducted quite openly in the village studied by Saito in the mid-1970s, paddy land transfers were controlled, but only *ex post facto*. The Land Committee, and after 1976, the People's Council, had 'almost been reduced to a land registry office'.[121] What the legislation did was to drive tenancy underground and to make it extremely unlikely that paddy fields could be rented on more than a temporary basis[122] and on more flexible terms than in the past — though with kinship arrangements perhaps playing a large role.[123] Complaints about irregularities in the management of land by the Land Committees and People's Councils had been a recurrent theme appearing in the government press in 1969 and 1970 and alluded to in the discussions in the *Pyithu Hluttaw* subsequently.[124]

After the nationalization of internal and external trade in rice and other major products, a paddy procurement scheme was implemented. 'It is a system which controls the distribution of farm products by means of price controls on paddy and other major farm products and it also encompasses the compulsory delivery of farm products by farmers to the government.'[125] As Saito argues in her study of one village in southern Burma, it is the combination of the land tenure system and the paddy procurement system that provides the means by which the state controls the economic life of the peasantry. As the state has never been able to implement complete land reform, it is only the paddy procurement scheme which keeps a form of free trade in land and a return to something like the agrarian conditions of the pre-1962 period from re-emerging. The land tenure system and the paddy procurement system 'seem to originate in the same idea of controlling distribution relations of farm rent between the state and the producers'.[126]

Under the procurement system each cultivator is obliged to deliver a quota of paddy, as much as a third of the crop, to a paddy purchase centre at the end of the harvest. The size of the peasant's quota is calculated on the basis of a national average yield per acre and on the number of acres cultivated. A massive annual effort by officials of the relevant state

121. Saito, 'Farm Household Economy', p. 394.
122. *Ibid.*, p. 391.
123. Ambler, 'Burma's Rice Economy', p. 34.
124. Henderson *et al.*, *Area Handbook for Burma*, p. 67; see, for example, *The Guardian* 5 Oct. 1983.
125. Saito, 'Farm Household Economy', p. 368.
126. *Ibid.*, p. 368.

ministries, the Party, the Peasants' Asiayon and the military is involved in making this system work. Peasants are encouraged, cajoled or perhaps threatened into meeting their quotas. Failure to meet quotas can lead to loss of the right of access to land and to limitations on state-provided credit. The reason why the peasants do not wish to sell to the state, of course, is because there still exists a free market for rice in which a higher price can be obtained.[127] In some cases, farmers may have taken out illegal loans with a moneylender and are obliged to repay in paddy at or near the official procurement price.[128] The state attempts to control this by making the movement of paddy from one area to another illegal without the permission of the local township People's Council (except in certain rice deficient areas).

'The basic idea underlying the delivery system', according to Saito, 'seems to be that the state will absorb the differential rents into its own hands.' Thus, there is 'no room for private rent so long as the delivery system . . . absorb[s] nearly all of the marketable surplus of paddy.'[129] In fact, the system apparently does this for farmers with fewer than 16 acres of land, and some are actually forced to buy paddy on the open market to meet their quota obligations and have food and seed left for themselves. However, for farmers with 16 or more acres of land, there is a surplus left over which can be sold at the free market price; the income of these families is significantly greater than those of their neighbours.[130] Thus, having access to land is the key to wealth in the village, and land is controlled by the local People's Council. Membership of the Council, despite the extra burdens it imposes on individuals, also serves as a means of protecting and enhancing the value of members' property.

Despite the inefficiencies and iniquities of the present agrarian system, there is little incentive for the state to alter it. There are two possible avenues of change. One is to introduce large-scale cooperatization or, more radically, to collectivize agriculture, but this would probably provoke widespread peasant resistance. The other is to return to the conditions of the free sale of land and farm produce. This would be politically undesirable, since it would raise the spectres of large-scale peasant insecurity, of even greater income disparities in the countryside, and of a loss of control over the peasantry by the state. The paddy procurement

127. Ibid., pp. 370–1.
128. World Bank, *Agricultural Sector Review*, vol. 1, p. 20.
129. Saito, 'Farm Household Economy', p. 395.
130. Ibid., pp. 395–6.

system not only allows the state to gain direct access to agricultural surpluses, but also ensures that a free market in land does not re-emerge on a large scale and thus restore capitalist agriculture. There is thus a political as well as an economic incentive in keeping paddy procurement prices low. If the margin of profitability of agricultural investment were to increase to near free market prices, the land control system would collapse under the pressure of wealthier farmers increasing their holdings or moneylenders reclaiming land for debts.[131]

However, the state has sought to increase production through the provision of new technology, the appointment of village agricultural managers and through the establishment of producers' cooperatives. The cooperative movement remains weak and has not been accepted by the bulk of the peasantry. Although over 1,000 agricultural producers' cooperatives with over 90,000 members had been established up to 1979/80, according to the General Secretary of the BSPP, in 1981, 'these societies were not in a position to function in accord with the aims of the agricultural producers' cooperatives' as defined by the state.[132] The situation has not changed since. In the agricultural sector, as in much of the rest of the economy, the state has developed power 'sufficient to inhibit initiative, but insufficient to impel developments on the planned lines.'[133] Under the present system, 'those persons in positions of influence in the local communities have benefited most',[134] and any attempt to consolidate smallholdings either 'privately or collectively, will create social tensions in the agrarian system that may even shake the very foundations of the existing social structure.'[135] Only powerful and autonomous states are willing to take such a risk.

External Relations As the state's personnel turned their attention to its reassertion on the basis of autarkic policies, international political activities and attempts to involve the country in general international issues declined relative to their importance in the 1950s. This was made

131. As implied by Saito, *ibid.*, p. 395.
132. *The Working People's Daily*, 4 Aug. 1981.
133. Richter, 'Development and Equality in Burma', p. 35.
134. Harvey Demaine, 'Current Problems of Agricultural Development Planning in Burma', in Institute of Southeast Asian Studies, *Southeast Asian Affairs 1979* (Singapore: Heinemann, 1979), p. 102.
135. Khin Maung Kyi, 'Problems of Agricultural Policy in Some Trade Dependent Small Countries: A Comparative Study of Burma and Thailand', *Kajian Ekonomi Malaysia*, XVI, nos. 1 and 2 (June/Dec. 1979), p. 350.

possible by the Revolutionary Council continuing its predecessor's policy of neutrality and non-alignment and by extending its military implications to economic, cultural and educational policy as well. There has been little deviation from that policy since 1974, although during certain periods particular aspects of international issues have been emphasized more than others. Special attention has been given to relations with the state's immediate neighbours, and conscious efforts have been made to ensure that disputes with these states could not be used to allow outside powers to interfere in domestic politics. When such events occurred, however, as in 1967 when the Chinese Cultural Revolution led to anti-Ne Win demonstrations in Rangoon and to increased Chinese Communist support for the Kachin Independence Army and the Burma Communist Party,[136] or when the influx of Muslim refugees from Bangladesh threatened to lead to a border war in 1979, the state has stood firmly by the five principles of peaceful coexistence including non-interference in the internal affairs of another state and has implicitly appealed to the United Nations and its member states for support.[137] The only major foreign policy document Burma has released since 1962 came in 1968, when it sought to demonstrate its international probity in the face of China's provocations.[138] On matters of international conflict such as the question of the Vietnamese invasion of Kampuchea in 1979, the government has urged that all states follow these same principles.

The Revolutionary Council strove to ensure that conflicts between neighbouring states did not expand so as to involve Burma. Burma was active in both the 1962 Geneva Conference on the neutralization of Laos and the 1962 Colombo Conference of African and Asian nations which discussed the Chinese-Indian border conflict of that year.[139] Subse-

---

136. The most complete account is the declassified United States Central Intelligence Agency Directorate of Intelligence Report, 'Peking and the Burmese Communists: The Perils and Profits of Insurgency' (RSS no. 0052/71, July, 1971; declassified Dec. 5, 1980).
137. See Albert D. Moscotti, 'Current Burmese and Southeast Asian Affairs', in Institute of Southeast Asian Studies, *Southeast Asian Affairs 1978* (Singapore: Heinemann, 1979), pp. 83–94; and Robert H. Taylor, 'Burma's Foreign Relations Since the Third Indochina Conflict', in *ibid.*, *1983* (Aldershot: Gower Publishing, 1983), pp. 102–12.
138. Burma Socialist Programme Party, Central Organising Committee, *Foreign Policy of the Revolutionary Government of the Union of Burma* (Rangoon: Sarpay Beikman for the BSPP, 1968).
139. *Party Seminar 1965*, p. 43.

quently, Burma was less active in such multilateral diplomacy and tended to eschew opportunities to involve itself in other conflicts. However, the government did offer to make available facilities for a negotiated settlement of the Vietnam war in the mid-1960s and for the Kampuchean question in 1980, although to no avail.

The state's radically autarkic economic policies and its nationalization of foreign-owned enterprises placed strains on its relations with India and Britain, but did not lead to serious conflict. The nations of Eastern Europe and the Soviet Union initially looked upon developments in Burma with some favour and believed that Burma had partly joined the socialist camp.[140] Despite the fact that there was some greater openness shown to the socialist bloc in terms of the receipt of advisors and the despatch of Burmese students to Eastern Europe and the Soviet Union, the state was careful to balance this with ties to other countries. The United States military aid agreement, for example, was not ended until 1970, and Burma continued to receive significant amounts of Japanese assistance in the form of war reparations throughout the 1960s as well as aid from West Germany, other European countries, and China both before and after the Cultural Revolution.

Despite Burma's less obvious involvement in international politics since 1962 the country has received a variety of official visitors including heads of state and government, and some of the state's leading personnel have travelled widely. During the 12 years between the coup and the inauguration of the 1974 constitution, heads of state or government visited Burma from Rumania (1962), China (1963, 1964, 1965, 1966), North Korea (1964), India (1965, 1969), Thailand (1966), Japan (1967), West Germany (1967), Nepal (1970), Mauritius (1971, 1972), the Soviet Union (1971), Hungary (1972), Malaysia (1972), Indonesia (1972) and Zaire (1973); and the Chairman of the Revolutionary Council visited Sri Lanka (1962, 1966), Thailand (1962, 1966, 1973), India (1965, 1970), Pakistan (1965, 1966, 1969), China (1965, 1971), the Soviet Union (1965), Czechoslovakia (1966), Rumania (1966), the United States (1966), Japan (1966, 1970, 1973), Nepal (1966), Singapore (1968),

---

140. *Pravda* noted that Burma was pursuing the 'correct path' to socialism in January, 1965 (Steinberg, 'Burma Under the Military', p. 259), but subsequent Soviet analytical writings on Burma express greater scepticism and noted the 'reactionary' nature of the ideology of the BSPP. See Rostislav Ulyanovsky, *National Liberation*, 'The New Burma' with P.P. Anikeyev (Moscow: Progress Publishers, 1978), pp. 265–304.

Malaysia (1968, 1973), Philippines (1970), Hungary (1972) and Indonesia (1973).[141] A similar pattern has been maintained since, revealing a conscious effort to balance visits between opposing states, especially India and China.

As Burma's armed forces do not possess the ability to project military power any appreciable distance beyond the state's borders, it poses no threat to any of its neighbours. Only if Burma became a base for the operation of a more powerful state, such as the United States or the Soviet Union, would India or China see Burma as threatening. For this reason, and because of the absence of any desire to have larger states affecting either domestic politics and society or foreign policy direction, neutrality is a convenient policy for the state. Burma's withdrawal from the Non-Aligned Movement in 1979 because of the aggressively interventionist programme advocated by some of its more vocal members as well as their own actual alignment, reiterated the state's determination not to become embroiled in external affairs which do not directly and immediately affect the security of Burma. Since then, trade and aid relations have been the dominant concerns of the state in the international sphere.

Legitimacy and the State

The Revolutionary Council chose to maintain only part of the legacy of the previous state managers in its search for legitimacy. While maintaining the slogans and promises of egalitarian socialism and the creation of an affluent society along welfare state lines, it eschewed the use of religion as a basis for legitimacy. Rather, it argued that U Nu's use of religion had not only created greater dissatisfaction with the state by raising fears in the minds of non-Buddhists, but had also encouraged the politicization of the monkhood and thus diverted it from its religious duties. Furthermore, the state had increasingly ignored its obligations to create a socialist society because of its concentration upon religion and upon the abandonment of the secular goals of the pre-independence nationalist movement. The state's leading personnel saw the utility of a state ideology in the form of the ideology of the ruling party as a means of creating a potentially non-divisive set of ideals and concepts around which state-society relations could be rebuilt.

141. *Towhlanyei Kaungsi ei Hluthsaungchet Thamaing Akyinchut*, pp. 218–23.

Among the first actions of the Revolutionary Council was the order to cease state support for Buddhism. The directors of government joint venture firms were immediately ordered to halt payments for the reconstruction of the Mahazedi pagoda in Pegu.[142] In May the Buddha Sasana Council was dissolved.[143] Two years later, at the same time as the dissolution of political parties other than the BSPP, all Buddhist and other religious organizations were ordered to register with their local SAC and to refrain henceforth from political activities, but in May the order had to be rescinded after a monk immolated himself in protest.[144] The state attempted again in 1965 to bring the *sangha* under its control, but failed to do so because of continuing factionalism in the *sangha* and because of opposition to demands that monks had to be registered and had to carry documents. The opposition led to the arrest in April of ninety-two monks for political and economic activities, and forced the Revolutionary Council to defend itself repeatedly against charges that it was anti-religious and therefore no different from the Communist Party.[145] The Revolutionary Council, for its part, viewed the protests by the monks as the consequence of their acting in collusion with illegal political parties.[146]

During this period the Revolutionary Council was also implementing restrictions on foreign missionaries and nationalizing religious schools and hospitals usually run by Christian orders. It maintained, however, that the right to freedom of religion was preserved, and justified its actions in the name of economic policy and the need to develop an egalitarian educational system. Missionaries of long-standing in the country were allowed to continue to function as before, and while contacts with outside religious bodies became increasingly difficult, this was the result of the general closing of foreign contacts with indigenous institutions, and not of religious discrimination.

The large-scale involvement of Buddhist monks in overt political activity did not occur after 1965 until the 1974 demonstration over the burial of U Thant. However, state managers were always concerned about the possibility of the development of opposition to the state through the monkhood — to which individuals could retreat and gain

142. Donald Eugene Smith, *Religion and Politics in Burma* (Princeton University Press, 1965), p. 170.
143. Steinberg, 'Burma Under the Military', p. 250.
144. Badgley, 'Burma's Zealot Wungyis', p. 57.
145. Silverstein, 'Burma: Ne Win's Revolution', p. 101; Maung Maung, *Burma and General Ne Win* (New York: Asia Publishing House), p. ix.
146. *Party Seminar 1965*, pp. 62–3.

immunity from the state's laws. The monkhood existed in a sort of legal limbo in relationship to the state, and the presence within it of many factions made it a loose organization, highly penetrable by individuals with a variety of intentions. Having dissolved the politicized self-governing institutions through which Nu had unsuccessfully tried to control the monkhood, for fifteen years after 1965 the state was unwilling to assault directly the independence of the monkhood.

Then, in May 1980, the relationship between the state and the *sangha* was fundamentally altered. The details of how this change was implemented have not become available, but at that time there was held in Rangoon the First Congregation of the Sangha of All Orders for the Purification, Perpetuation and Propagation of Sasana. This meeting adopted a constitution and other rules for the removal of individuals who did not, in the terms of the organization which was controlled by senior monks cooperative with the state, fulfil the requirements of proper monks. The meeting had been carefully prepared in advance by the Ministry of Home and Religious Affairs. The constitution adopted is essentially identical in structure to that of the state. Committees of leading monks are organized from the village-tract and ward level upwards to a state central working committee which manages the sects in its area and which, through its executive committee, ensures that monks behave according to the *Vinaya*, the Buddhist code of behaviour.[147] Failure to do so results in the relevant executive committee of the monkhood reporting violations to the township People's Council, which is empowered to take action against an individual or entire monastery found to be misbehaving.[148]

From the perspective of the state, the successful conclusion of the 1980 meeting of the *sangha* and of a second congregational meeting in mid-1985 are indicative of greater control by the state over the Buddhist monkhood than for many years previously. The purpose of the organization of the *sangha* body was clearly to strengthen the authority of the

---

147. Thathanatow Thanshin Tetanpyanpwayei Gaingpaungsu Thaya Asiaweipwekyi Hpyitmyaukyei Thaya wanhsaukhpwet, *Pyihtaungsu Hsoshelit Thammata Myanma Naingngantow Thaya Ahpweasin Akhyeihkansinmyin (Mukyan)*. (Rangoon: Kaba Ei Thathanayei Usi Dana Press), 1980.
148. Law on Solution of Cases and Conflicts in Accordance with the Rules of the Order (Pyithu Hluttaw Law no. 3, 1980), *The Working People's Daily* 4 July 1980. See also Aung Kin, 'Burma in 1980'.

state over the monkhood; one of the goals of the state throughout Burma's history.[149]

Having denied the use of religion as a legitimizing ideology for the state, the state's managers chose to follow a secular socialist argument which stresses the state's obligation to create prosperity for the population. Yet the impecunious condition of the state has made this goal elusive. The stagnant economic conditions of the 1960s made it especially difficult to obtain capital for investment in human resources. Nonetheless, in macro terms, between 1962 and 1980 significant advances were made in the development of educational, health and other services designed to raise living standards. Burma's population has increased from approximately 22.7 million in 1962 to 35.3 million in 1983, a rise of 55.5 per cent, and it has grown at an estimated average of over 2 per cent per year for more than twenty years, though it was believed that the average would fall to 1.99 per cent in 1985/6.[150]

Education has received a significant amount of state expenditure, equal to 15 per cent of total government budgeted expenditure in the first half of the 1980s. Between 1962 and 1985 the number of primary, middle and secondary school teachers nearly tripled, and the number of vocational teachers and university teachers nearly quadrupled. These increases, however, have barely kept pace with the growth in student numbers as the proportion of students from each relevant age category attending school has risen. By 1981, an estimated 81 per cent of all those of primary school age were attending school, while 20 per cent of those of secondary school age and 4 per cent of tertiary age were doing so (this compares with 56 per cent, 10 per cent and 1 per cent respectively in 1960). The government's efforts have resulted in an increase in literacy from 57 per cent in 1963 to 81 per cent in 1985.[151]

Increases in health care have also been significant. Expenditure on health has remained at less than 10 per cent of government expenditure since 1962. Life expectancy for men has increased from 45 in 1964 to 61 in 1983, and for women from 48 to 65.[152] Since 1960, the infant mortality rate has dropped by more than one-third to 96 per 1,000 live births and the child death rate has been halved to 12 per 1,000 live births. The

---

149. E. Michael Mendelson, *Sangha and State in Burma* (edited by John P. Ferguson; Ithaca: Cornell University Press, 1975), p. 118.
150. *Report to the Pyithu Hluttaw, 1986/1987* (Rangoon: Ministry of Planning and Finance, 1986, in Burmese), p. 25.
151. *The Working People's Daily*, 7 Aug. 1985.
152 *Ibid.*

provision of doctors has risen from one for every 15,560 people in 1950, to one for every 4,660 people in 1980, and the number of nurses has grown from one for every 8,520 people to one for every 4,750 people.[153]

However, it is not possible to know to what extent the population credits the state with these improvements. School classes are still very large and equipment, if available, is poor. Hospitals, like schools, are not completely free, and individuals seek to use private medicine and educational facilities where possible. The state thus devotes a good deal of attention to trying to limit the activities of private schools and of doctors, who, working privately, can earn large incomes. Particularly for the urban population (23 per cent or more), the promise of improvements may seem hollow. While unemployment and underemployment rates are not available, they are thought to be high, even among the better-educated. Expenditure on social welfare measures remains miniscule. The state has, to a certain extent, been able through its mass organizations to lower costs for itself by using 'volunteer' labour for certain projects such as sanitation and the construction of schools and other public buildings. How far these activities are actually voluntary is difficult to gauge, but where such activities are seen to be of direct benefit to residents, such as the construction of a village school or of a water tank in a dry zone, they do seem to give their help willingly. Whatever the situation in the case of a given individual, the ability of the state's organizations to induce such free labour on the part of the population demonstrates a degree of control over their lives which a weaker state could not generate.

The ideology of the state as developed by the Revolutionary Council and promulgated through the organizations and publications of the state and Party is sufficiently vague and general to appeal to a large proportion of the population without tying the state to specific policies other than general goals such as socialism and affluence. The ideology is grounded in Buddhist epistemology but gains its analytical language from Marxism and, to a certain extent, its political ideas from Leninism. The ideology combines classical Buddhist notions of the origin and purpose of the state with twentieth-century notions of political organization and state practice. It thus serves as a rationale for the socialist state without providing a justification for the creation of social and economic demands upon it. Thus, just as the ideological justifications of other states explain

---

153. *World Development Report 1984*, pp. 264, 266.

both the need for obedience and sacrifice, so the ideology of the BSPP serves to control and to mobilize its believers in the interests of the state and to obviate the desire to seek an alternative ideology.

The state ideology was not perceived by its formulators as a set of firmly held and immutable principles. Rather, it serves as a basis and viewpoint from which Party and government policies and programmes are to be analysed and implemented in the light of experience. It is intended to provide a perceptual lens for its followers which will allow them to see conditions as they are from the position of the state; the ideology itself can be altered with changing circumstances.[154] At the heart of the ideology lies the concept of correlation. Dialectic, interaction, correlation and cause and effect are seen as essentially the same phenomenon, and all these terms in various forms are key philosophical concepts in Theravada Buddhism.[155] When it is realized that in the ideology of the BSPP 'correlation' means several different ideas in European philosophical traditions, the remainder of the Party's doctrines and the philosophy that underlies them as delineated in the *System of Correlation of Man and His Environment* and derivative Party publications becomes comprehensible and internally consistent.

The ideology begins by making certain assumptions about the nature of man and of nature derived from Buddhist thought. Man, like all matter, is mutable, and within man there coexists in correlation a mind and a body. It is man's mind that distinguishes him from other animals and makes his social existence possible. It is man's social existence which gives rise to politics and ultimately to the state, because man 'is an egocentric animal' who 'instinctively seeks freedom in which to live and act'; but, secondly, man 'is also an altruistic social animal' who lives in a society which 'is but an institution of human beings organized by them under their codes of law and behaviour'. Through society man strives to achieve both his personal and social needs of mind and body, and thus there is a correlation between his needs and the needs of society. Man's egotistical and altruistic characteristics have to be balanced.

The theory is nearly identical to that used in the time of the kings to justify the functions of the state, but its contemporary purpose is in keeping with modern political expectations. Rather than existing to

154. *System of Correlation of Man and His Environment*, p. 38.
155. See Shwe Zan Aung and Rhys Davids, *Compendium of Philosophy* (a translation from Pali of *Abhidhammattha-Sangaha*, translated by Shwe Zan Aung, revised and edited by Mrs. Rhys Davids) (London: Pali Text Society, 1910), Part VIII, Compendium of Relations, especially Section 7, The System of Correlation.

create order to allow for man's religious salvation or achievement of *nirvana*, the state now must establish order so as to mobilize man's resources for the economic and cultural advancement of the society upon which he is dependent. But in bending to the requirements of the larger society and the state which guides it, man's egotism, 'his instinctive spirit of freedom incites him to rise and shake off his fetters and clear his path of obstacles'.[156] Thus there exists in the relationship between man and society another 'correlated relationship' or 'dialectic' which is potentially antagonistic.

Within society there exists a dialectic or correlation between the material life and the spiritual life. The spiritual life, caused by man's thinking, interacts with society's need for material progress and is thus the engine of history. In the historical process, certain classes and social groups arise from time to time and these create social antagonism and conflicts between progressive and non-progressive forces. As the currently dominant institution in human society, the state exists, by implication, to regulate this conflict.

The role of the Party as the leading institution of the state arises from the historical role of the working people. Since man is selfish and only enters into society for selfish purposes — for he cannot live alone and fulfil either his spiritual or material needs — social constraints which check man's nature must exist to keep 'within bounds' man's 'self-aggrandizement and desire for freedom'. Society is capable of doing this to a certain extent through institutions such as marriage. It is at this point, however, that the ideology implicity justifies the role of socialism as an economic system to control man's egotism: the basis of his greed, for it states that, 'Our socialist economy shall be based on the dialectical unity of the individual and social interests of the citizens of the Union of Burma. Our socialist system is a system which will achieve a harmony between the individual and the social interests of the people.'[157] Socialism is seen as the means to regulate man's natural acquisitiveness, which if allowed full reign would not be to either his own or to society's long-term advantage. It is at this point that the case for the justification and legitimization of the modern authoritarian state begins to emerge.

In both Buddhist thought and the ideology of the Party there is nothing inevitable about human progress as assumed in Marxism and most other Western ideologies. Rather, because of man's nature, either

---

156. *System of Correlation*, pp. 6–7. All quotations are from the official translation.
157. *Ibid.*, p. 25.

human improvement or degeneration is possible. In order to ensure that it is progress or good which takes place, society needs a guide. In historical Burmese thought the king provided the basis of good by preserving order in society to allow Buddhism to flourish. Under the BSPP, the Party and the state provide good by creating a cadre of superior people to lead society by a 'reorientation of views' to eradicate 'fraudulent practices, profit motive, easy living, parasitism, shirking and selfishness.'[158] Eradication of these evils, however, is a difficult goal to achieve and in reality the Party is willing merely to regulate and limit the consequences of man's inherent greed.

The ideology condemns both capitalism and communism on moral grounds. Both are erroneously based upon materialism. Capitalism seeks the solution to man's problems through his greed, operationalized as the profit motive, while communism tends to over-restrict man's egotism and kills his creative powers, perhaps achieving a spurious equity but not achieving spiritual happiness. Through the practise of socialist democracy in the Party and the state, the extreme errors of capitalism and Communism are avoided because:

Socialist democracy includes the unity of *the will and initiative* of the individual man and group on the one hand and the *centralized guidance* of the society on the other. In a society which aspires for progress two features are necessary, viz., centralism resting with the State and the freedom of initiative resting with individuals or the majority.

Without centralism society will tend towards anarchism. Again without freedom of initiative of individuals society becomes mechanical and its progress is retarded.[159]

The Party has now replaced the king in ensuring that the correct balance between order and initiative is maintained.

The function of the ideology, like Buddhist teachings, is essentially moral and hortatory. The Party and its cadres, who are trained in a manner of withdrawal from society like both Buddhist monks and modern soldiers, exist to ensure that the purpose of the state is successfully carried out by moral men and women who are able to provide the remainder of society with proper leadership. As the *Party Member's Handbook* states:

Only if there is an organization and leadership for all the working people which

158. *Ibid.*, pp. 18–19.
159. *Ibid.*, p. 31.

leads to the economic advantage of man, which is able to judge each man as a man, which is able to have just relations of man with man, which does not have great greed [*lawba*], hatred [*dawtha*] or conceit [*mana*], which is of good mind, will the socialist economic system be successful.

Socialist ideology is an important matter to be able correctly to lead the people. Socialist ideology is an important matter for not retreating [i.e., turning back, corrupting — *mahpauk mapyan*].

Man is able to retreat (be corrupted). Therefore it is necessary to establish a socialist democratic living relations society which is able to analyze and control constantly the misconduct which causes retreat by humans.[160]

Throughout the ideology there is a clear perception of the need for order to be created and to be maintained by the state. Only in this way can greed be suppressed and equity achieved. The ideology does not posit the eventual creation of a classless or conflict-free society; the nature of man would not allow for this. Rather, the goal of the Party is to create a balanced society which is able to understand and control the dialectic of extremes between anarchy and repression.

The plausibility of the ideology stems not only from its philosophical basis in classical Burmese Buddhist thought, but also from the recent history of Burma which provides it with meaning. Burma has experienced capitalism and colonialism, depression and poverty and rebellion and anarchy during the lifetime of the generation that came to power after independence. Personal experience has convinced many Burmese that balance is required and that authority needs to exist to create social harmony.

Politics under the Socialist State

The consequences of the reassertion of the state for the practise of politics have been significant. Largely hidden are the arguments about the nature and future of the state that dominated politics in the 1930s and 1950s. The press reports nothing of the daily life of the leaders of the state other than their public appearances. The rumour and innuendo that were once the heart of so much of Rangoon's politics — when ministers were made or broken on the basis of votes bought or cajoled in the

160. Myanma Hsoshelit Lansin Pati Baho Komitti Danachok (Burma Socialist Programme Party Central Committee Headquarters), *Myanama Hsoshelit Lansin Patiwinmya Letswe* (Burma Socialist Programme Party Member's Handbook) (Rangoon: Burma Socialist Programme Party, 1978, repr. 1980), pp. 19-20.

House of Representatives — cannot be found in print. Also missing are the local bosses who wielded influence through their henchmen over local electorates and upon whom central politicians depended for support. Other political types have largely disappeared also, including student politicians assiduously labouring to bring down the government through street demonstrations, and union or party organizers ready to start new bodies in order to apply political pressure or to foment a 'genuine' revolution. Gone also is the political rhetoric which promises the voters all that they desire at little personal cost.

In the place of these political types Burma has become, viewed from the capital, dull and tedious: an annual cycle of public meetings, guidance offered, and calls for unity and sacrifice interladen with reams of statistics. But underneath there is a current of rumour and plot. The press reports the endless series of meetings to coordinate plans and to give awards attended by state and party officials from various levels of the administration. The tea shops, meanwhile, provide explanations of what is 'really' going on which often have the makings of a fine political novel, but which rarely approximate developments. Rather, significant political events, including the arrest and replacement of leading state personnel and announcements of significant changes in government policy, are largely unpredicted and often take observers by surprise.

On closer analysis, there appear to be three different kinds of politics present under the socialist state. There is, first, the politics of the central Party and of state organizations, including the Party Central Committee, the State Council and cabinet, and that which surrounds the Party Chairman. Involved here are questions of state policy in terms of the direction of economic affairs, the control of personnel and the question of political succession to the top leadership. The second level of politics concerns the institutions and personnel which provide the means by which central state policy is relayed to the populace. Here, at the level of state and divisional People's Councils and Party units regional military commands, administrators in the judicial service and other central ministries which service and guide regional and local administrations and the managers of state-owned factories, there exists a form of administrative politics which attempts to satisfy the requirements of the centre by encouraging, cajoling, ordering, demanding or threatening subordinates in their respective political and administrative organizations to fulfil production targets while maintaining political order. At the township and village level, but perhaps somewhat less at the urban ward level, a third kind of politics is practised. There, state officials come directly into contact with the population and are faced with the task of balancing the demands of the centre, as relayed to them through regional intermediaries, against the unwillingness of the population to abandon their time, produce or labour to the state.

Politics at the top or central level has about it something of the aura of court politics. One man, Party Chairman Ne Win, has so long dominated the state that he has developed a degree of loyalty and respect from his associates that no other political figure has achieved. He is the only member of the political leadership who has taken a leading role in the state's life from 1942 to the present. Involved in the displacement of the state in 1942 as one of the Thirty Comrades, Ne Win has worked for the state ever since as an officer in forces dominated by the Japanese and by the British, as the chief of the armed forces from 1948 through the civil war and KMT intrusion, as deputy prime minister when the Socialists and others abandoned power between 1948 and 1950, and as prime minister between 1958 and 1960, when the army intervened to 'clean up the mess' the civilian politicians had made of the first ten years of independence. As Chairman of the Revolutionary Council from 1962 to 1974, President of the state from 1974 to 1981 and as Chairman of the Burma Socialist Programme Party since its inception, Ne Win has achieved the status of a founding father of modern Burma, equal only to the assassinated Aung San, to whom Ne Win is linked by the comradeship of arms.

During the initial years of the Revolutionary Council Ne Win's position was rather that of *primus inter pares*. The council had the potential of becoming just another military junta living off the state in blatant corruption. In 1964 a Revolutionary Council member was given a life sentence for benefiting financially from the order demonetizing large denomination *kyat* notes.[161] Such action, taken early and publicly to punish an obvious misuse of public responsibility, has kept the state largely free of the corruption scandals that would have cost the Revolutionary Council public prestige.

Unlike in many other states which have created a socialist one-party state in the political lifetime of one leader, there has been no obvious and conscious plan to create a cult of personality around Ne Win. He was a

---

161. Silverstein, 'Burma: Ne Win's Revolution Reconsidered', p. 100.

most unlikely charismatic figure, and compared with the public persona of Aung San and Nu before him seems self-effacing. He affects no public poses and launches no crusades; his is the political style of gradual and cautious organization. Nonetheless, a kind of charisma has grown around Ne Win; not so much a personal charisma, more a reflected charisma derived from his position in the state. Ne Win's personal power comes from the charisma of office, though it must be acknowledged that in the 1950s his position within the armed forces was developed through his personal relations with hundreds of men, most of whom remain personally loyal to him today.[162]

Ne Win's treatment of his politically historical 'equals' in Burmese politics since the 1940s illustrates how his particular charisma developed. After the 1962 coup, he not only held negotiations with the leaders of the legal political parties in Rangoon, but summoned to the capital leaders of the illegal groups, including the different Communist factions and the separatists. When these talks failed to result in a solution satisfactory to both the Revolutionary Council and the opposition groups, the leaders of the illegal parties were permitted to return to their base areas and to resume armed conflict with the government. Many of the leaders of the formerly legal parties were arrested and placed under detention. Two or three years later they were released, and following the disorder that occurred during the food shortages of 1967–8 and the adoption of a hostile stance toward Burma by China during the Cultural Revolution, Ne Win invited them to discuss with him and the Revolutionary Council the nature and future of the state. For six months, thirty-three leading figures in the politics of the 1950s, including former Prime Minister Nu and former Deputy Prime Ministers Ba Swe and Kyaw Nyein, met under state auspices and prepared a majority report which essentially called for the abandonment of the direction the Revolutionary Council had been taking the state for the past seven years, and for the restoration of the pre-coup political system. These demands were unacceptable to the Revolutionary Council and the discussions were terminated.[163]

162. On kinds of charisma and their relationship with society, see the useful discussion by William H. Swatos, Jr., 'Revolution and Charisma in a Rationalized World: Max Weber Revisited and Extended', in Ronald M. Glassman and Vatro Murvar (eds), *Max Weber's Political Sociology: A Pessimistic Vision of a Rationalized World* (Westport, Conn.: Greenwood Press, 1984), pp. 203–5.
163. *Pyihtaungsu Myanma Naingnan Towhlanyei Kaungsi tho Tinthwin thaw Pyihtaungsu Myanma Naingngan Pyin twin Nyinyatyei Akyanpei Ahpwei ei Asiyinhkansa* (Union

Nu then left Burma and along with other political leaders of the 1940s and 1950s began to plan to oust the Revolutionary Council by leading a resistance organization from Thailand. The government-controlled press in Burma reported these activities for a few days in October 1970 much as they were presented in the world press at the time.[164] Nu's call for rebellion evoked little response from the public eight years after his ouster, and despite his personal charisma in the 1950s he now posed no political threat to the Revolutionary Council. The publicity that the Revolutionary Council press gave to the rebels was a way of demonstrating their impotence when confronted with the new state structures.

The final act to demonstrate Ne Win's power over his rivals of the 1960s came in 1980 when the state offered an amnesty for all political offenders, including insurgents (who had to surrender to state authorities within ninety days). At the same time, the state gave remissions to other convicted criminals. The amnesty was announced by the Council of State 'as a token of joyously honouring the successful conclusion of the First Congregation of the Sangha of All Orders for the Purification, Perpetuation and Propagation of the Sasana and thereby to promote unity and peace'.[165] The same day the Council of State, over the signature of its Chairman, Ne Win, announced an order instituting a title known as the '*Naing-Ngant Gon-Yi*' to honour persons who had served the state. Together with legislation passed later in the year providing for pensions for almost all the leading figures in Burmese politics and administration since the Hsaya San rebellion, the state declared that, regardless of their political opposition, the state that Ne Win headed was willing to take them back and to look after them in their last years.[166]

While a few of the then active Communist and separatist insurgents accepted the amnesty, the majority did not. However, large numbers of people who had joined Nu in his 1970 effort to overthrow Ne Win returned to Burma, as did the former Prime Minister himself. On August 11, 1980, Ne Win gave a lunch for the leading recipients of his

---

of Burma Internal Unity Conference's Report Which Was Submitted to the Union of Burma Revolutionary Council) (n.p. [Rangoon]: n.d. [1969]).
164. Wiant, 'Burmese Revolutionary Council', pp. 27–8; *The New York Times*, 19 Oct. 1970; 27 Nov. 1970.
165. *The Working People's Daily*, 28 May 1980.
166. Details are provided in Aung Kin, 'Burma in 1980: Pouring Balm on Sore Spots', in Institute of Southeast Asian Studies, *Southeast Asian Affairs 1981* (Singapore: Institute of Southeast Asian Studies, 1982), pp. 106–10.

benevolence. In the film and photographs of the event released to the public and widely distributed throughout the country the Party Chairman was seated in a slightly raised chair surrounded by his previous opponents. Not only were all of the leading legal political figures of the 1950s seated on his right, along with former senior army officers from the 1950s who had opposed him, but the major dialectician and theorist of Burmese radical thought, the former Communist leader, Thakin Soe, sat on his left. It was as if all of the major mobilizers of mass action against the state between 1942 and 1980 had come to recognize the reassertion of the state and to acknowledge its legitimacy.

The general recognition of the *de facto* legitimacy of the present state structure and of Ne Win's supremacy within it has, in recent years, made more conspicuous another form of political activity at the centre. Access to and being trusted by the Party Chairman are the only ways of ensuring objectives are achieved, and his approval of a project is the key to its successful implementation. The central political position in the state is now that of Party Chairman. Rivalries within the army and the Party have posed the greatest political challenges to Ne Win and those closest to him. While in the mid-1960s anti-party organization within the party took place in the form of alleged Communist cells within the military (as occurred in the 1940s), during the 1970s more formidable challenges emerged.

Following the worker and student protests of 1974 and 1975, the Minister of Defence and Chief of Staff of the Armed Forces, General Tin U, was forced to resign from his posts, which were then divided between two men, the Prime Minister, U Sein Lwin, and the Deputy Chief of Staff, General Kyaw Htin. Tin U left office, it was rumoured at the time, because of the corrupt activities of his wife, a common allegation in Rangoon about most leading figure's wives. It was also rumoured that there had developed a split within the armed forces between a pro-Tin U faction of field commanders who had been facing the brunt of fighting against the insurgents, and the officers who had taken a leading part in the development of the Party and the state in Rangoon. Then, on July 21, 1976, seven military officers were arrested and tried for allegedly plotting to assassinate Ne Win and other top leaders, including Party General Secretary and State Council Secretary, U San Yu, and the chief of the National Intelligence Bureau, Colonel Tin U.[167] By the time the seven officers came to trial in September, General Tin U, who some had seen as a likely successor to Ne Win, was charged

---

167. *The New York Times*, 21 July 1976.

with knowledge of the assassination plot and placed on trial with a total of fourteen officers. He was found guilty and sent to prison.

Less than a year later another plot to assassinate Ne Win and the cabinet was alleged, and two former officials of the BSPP were arrested and tried. As the main defendants were described as a Karen and an Arakanese, the motive for their action was rumoured to be disagreement with the Party over the rights of ethnic groups. In September 1977, two ministers who had been appointed in the previous March were dismissed and arrested, while more than 50 other top officials were removed from office in what was described as a 'purge' of the BSPP. This followed the second BSPP Congress, at which Ne Win was rumoured to have come second or third in the balloting for position (the implication being that Secretary General San Yu was more popular with the party rank-and-file than was the Chairman). The dominant rumour at that time explaining the removal of leading figures from the political scene was that they disagreed with the partial liberalization of economic policy represented by the legislation passed in the *Pyithu Hluttaw* in August to guarantee private investments from nationalization. Those dismissed were said to be leading members of the party's alleged 'pro-Soviet' faction to which San Yu was thought to belong.[168] Others explained the political conflict of the period in terms of the army reasserting its position *vis-à-vis* the Party within the state's guiding institutions.[169]

After this flurry of removals, there ensued a six-year period of remarkable calm at the centre of the state. The routine of meetings and speeches ground on, highlighted only by the departure of Ne Win as President and his replacement by San Yu, who, at the same time, gave up the apparently more influential position of General Secretary of the Party. Then, in June 1983, retired Brigadier General (formerly Colonel) Tin U, at that time serving as General Secretary of the Party, formerly the Director-General of the National Intelligence Bureau, who had risen in power when his namesake was arrested in 1976, was dismissed from office along with the Home Minister, Colonel Bo Ni. Tin U had also been rumoured to be Ne Win's heir-apparent, rather than San Yu, who had held that distinction between 1977 and 1981. Tin U was tried and convicted on charges of misappropriating public funds, and Bo Ni was convicted of abetting corruption on the part of his wife and son and of

---

168. *Far Eastern Economic Review*, 7 Oct. 1977.
169. *The Burma Committee Information Quarterly*, vol. 3, no. 4 (Fall, 1977); this was an anti-government publication issued from Montreal, Canada, by Burmese exiles.

illegally using state property.[170] With Tin U out of the way, San Yu once again became the likely heir to Ne Win and was made Vice-Chairman of the Party at its 1985 Conference. At the same time many leading officials appointed by Tin U during his tenure as the Director of the National Intelligence Bureau were removed, and legislation was passed placing intelligence operations under a committee controlled by the Prime Minister and the Ministers for Defence and Foreign Affairs.[171]

This litany of leading personnel shifts and the commonly accepted explanations for them reveal no pattern and little consistency, other than to suggest that at the top of the state there exist strong rivalries which centre upon the control of the Party apparatus and the position of the Party Chairman. These manoeuvreings have their echo in the politics of the Soviet Politburo or the Chinese Central Communist Party's Committee, for they take place within the confines of the structures of a socialist one-party state. The important point that these episodes illustrate is that capturing the top posts in the Party had become the route to political power. None of the leading rivals for office have indicated that they wished to see the state system replaced; they wished to control it.

The most ambitious participants in the middle level of politics, be they regional military commanders, party officers or technicians and managers, realize that the route to power is through impressing their superiors at the centre with their abilities to produce the goods and services required by the state's plans. These individuals are constantly trying to extract more from the peasants and workers who live and work in the areas they are responsible for. Like the institutions to which they are responsible, the political actors at this intermediate level are all part of the state machinery, and wish to use it to further their own power and that of the state they serve and depend upon.

It is at the village and township level that politics becomes much more complex, for it is here that individuals can identify and try to act upon sets of interests which are not only personal, but potentially and often actually contrary to the interests of the state. The responsibility given to township and village tract or urban ward party or mass and class organizations by the state is one of convincing people at the local level that it is in their interest to support the state voluntarily. Here, as in comparable

---

170. Details in Tin Maung Maung Than, 'Burma in 1983: From Recovery to Growth?', in Institute of Southeast Asian Studies, *Southeast Asian Affairs 1984* (Singapore: Institute of Southeast Asian Studies, 1984), pp.116–8.
171. *The Working People's Daily*, 13 Oct. 1983.

political systems, it is the state's intention to draw people into participation in administration which 'may serve as an informational mechanism, may aid in legitimizing the regime in the citizen's eyes and may be used to augment an inadequate administrative apparatus in distributional and supervisory activities in society'.[172] However, it is difficult to know to what extent the state has been able to legitimize itself in the eyes of the bulk of the population and thus ensure its dominance and perpetuation. Personal observation and the research of others suggest that the language of the state is almost universally accepted and that its symbols and ceremonies are widely followed.[173] The all-encompassing ideology of the Party appears to be reflected in public and private discourse and, at least at the verbal level, its message is accepted. People seem also to have developed the capacity (that exists in all societies to varying degrees) to recognize and accept with resignation the gap that exists between the ideals and goals of the state and the actual behaviour of its institutions and personnel. Most people have contact with the Party and the People's Councils in their daily life, and the local agents of the state who live in the community are recognized and used as intermediaries with the authorities at the middle and top levels of the state. For better or worse, the state is accepted as inevitable and dominates other institutions.

---

172. Friedgut, *Political Participation in the USSR*, p. 29.
173. Supported by the research of Khin Maung Kyi, 'Indians in Burma: Problems of an Alien Subculture in a Highly Integrating Society', in K. Sandhu and S. Mani (eds), *Indians in Southeast Asia* (Singapore: Heinemann, forthcoming).

BIBLIOGRAPHY

Note: References to Burma Office files (BOF) and India Office files (IOF) are located in the India Office Archives and Library, London. Numbers given are the original file numbers. The press of Burma, the United States and Great Britain have been cited but not listed here.

BOOKS AND MONOGRAPHS IN ENGLISH

Adas, Michael, *The Burma Delta: Economic Development and Social Change on an Asian Rice Frontier, 1852–1941*. Madison: University of Wisconsin Press, 1974.

Anderson, Benedict, *Imagined Communities: Reflections on the Origin and Spread of Nationalism*. London: Verso, 1983.

Andrew, E.J.L., *Indian Labour in Rangoon*. London: Oxford University Press, 1933.

Aung San, *Burma's Challenge 1946*. South Okkalapa: Tathetta Sapei, 1974.

Aung-Thwin, Michael, *Pagan: The Origins of Modern Burma*. Honolulu: University of Hawaii Press, 1985.

Ba Maw, *Breakthrough in Burma: Memoirs of a Revolution*. New Haven: Yale University Press, 1968.

Becka, Jan, *The National Liberation Movement in Burma during the Japanese Occupation Period (1941–1945)*. Prague: Oriental Institute, Dissertationes Orientales, vol. 42, 1983.

Bendix, Reinhard, *Max Weber: An Intellectual Portrait*. Garden City, NY: Doubleday, 1960.

Butwell, Richard, *U Nu of Burma*. Stanford University Press, 2nd imp., 1969.

Cady, John F., *A History of Modern Burma*. Ithaca and London: Cornell University Press, 1958, supplement, 1960.

——, *Post-War Southeast Asia: Independence Problems*. Athens, Ohio: Ohio University Press, 1974.

——, *Contacts with Burma, 1935–1949: A Personal Account*. Athens, Ohio: Ohio University Center for International Studies, 1983.

Callis, Helmut G., *Foreign Capital in Southeast Asia*. New York: International Secretariat, Institute of Pacific Relations, 1942.

Chakravarti, N.R., *The Indian Minority in Burma: The Rise and Decline of an Immigrant Community*. London: Oxford University Press for the Institute of Race Relations, London, 1971.

Cocks, S.W., *Burma Under British Rule*. Bombay: K. and J. Cooper, 2nd edn, n.d.

Colbert, Evelyn, *Southeast Asia in International Politics 1941–1956*. Ithaca: Cornell University Press, 1977.

Crosthwaite, Charles, *The Pacification of Burma*. First published 1912, repr. London: Frank Cass, 1968.
Donnison, F.S.V., *Public Administration in Burma: A Study of Development During the British Connexion*. London: Royal Institute of International Affairs, 1953.
——, *Burma*. New York: Praeger; London: Benn, 1970.
Foucar, E.C.V., *I Lived in Burma*. London: Dennis Dobson, 1956.
Friedgut, Theodore H., *Political Participation in the USSR*. Princeton University Press, 1979.
Furnivall, J.S., *Colonial Policy and Practice: A Comparative Study of Burma and Netherlands India*. Cambridge University Press, 1948; New York University Press, 1956.
Glass, Leslie, *The Changing of Kings: Memories of Burma, 1934–1949*. London: Peter Owen, 1985.
Golay, Frank H., Ralph Anspach, M. Ruth Pfanner, and Eliezer B. Ayal, *Underdevelopment and Economic Nationalism in Southeast Asia*. Ithaca: Cornell University Press, 1969.
Grantham, S.G., *Studies in the History of Tharrawaddy*. Cambridge University Press (for private circulation), 1920.
Hall, D.G.E., *A History of South East Asia*. London: Macmillan, 3rd edn, 1968.
Harvey, G.E., *History of Burma*. London: Frank Cass, 1967 (orig. publ. 1925).
——, *British Rule in Burma 1824–1942*. London: Faber and Faber, 1946.
Henderson, John W., et al., *Area Handbook for Burma*. Washington, DC: United States Government Printing Office, 1971.
Herbert, Patricia, *The Hsaya San Rebellion (1930–1932) Reappraised*. Melbourne: Monash University Centre of Southeast Asian Studies Working Paper No. 27, 1982.
Hla Pe, *Burma: Literature, Historiography, Scholarship, Language, Life and Buddhism*. Singapore: Institute of Southeast Asian Studies, 1985.
International Institute for Strategic Studies, *The Military Balance 1985–86*, London: 1985.
International Monetary Fund, *World Debt Tables*. Washington, DC: International Monetary Fund, 1985.
——, *Government Finance Statistics Yearbook 1985*, Washington, DC: International Monetary Fund, 1985.
Khin Maung Kyi and Tin Tin, *Administrative Patterns in Historical Burma*. Singapore: Institute of Southeast Asian Studies Southeast Asian Perspectives no. 1, 1973.
Krasner, Stephen D., *Structural Conflict: The Third World Against Global Liberalism*. Berkeley: University of California Press, 1985.
Lieberman, Victor B., *Burmese Administrative Cycles: Anarchy and Conquest. c. 1580–1760*. Princeton University Press, 1984.
Lu Pe Win, *History of the 1920 University Boycott*. (Rangoon?): The author, for

Bibliography 375

the Organization for the Celebration of the Golden Jubilee of the National Day, Nov., 1970.

Mahajani, Usha, *The Role of the Indian Minorities in Burma and Malaya*. Bombay: Vora, 1960.

Marr, David G., *Vietnamese Anti-Colonialism, 1885–1925*. Berkeley: University of California Press, 1971.

Maung Maung, *Burma's Constitution*. The Hague: Martinus Nijhoff, 2nd edn, 1961.

——, *Burma and General Ne Win*. New York: Asia Publishing House, 1969.

Maung Maung, *From Sangha to Laity, Nationalist Movements of Burma, 1920–1940*. Australian National University Monographs on South Asia no. 4, New Delhi: Manohar, 1980.

Mendelson, E. Michael., *Sangha and State in Burma, A Study of Monastic Sectarianism and Leadership*, edited by John P. Ferguson. Ithaca: Cornell University Press, 1975.

Milne, Patricia M., trans., *Selected Short Stories of Thein Pe Myint*. Ithaca: Cornell University Southeast Asia Program Data Paper no. 91, June, 1973.

Mi Mi Khaing, *The World of Burmese Women*. Singapore: Times International, 1985.

Montgomery, John D., *The Politics of Foreign Aid: American Experience in Southeast Asia*. New York: Praeger, 1962.

Moscotti, Albert D., *British Policy and the Nationalist Movement in Burma 1917–1937*. Honolulu: Asian Studies at Hawaii, no. 11, University of Hawaii Press, 1974.

——, *Burma's Constitution and the Elections of 1974*. Singapore: Institute of Southeast Asian Studies Research Notes and Discussions no. 5, Sept., 1977.

Mya Sein, *Administration in Burma: Sir Charles Crosthwaite and the Consolidation of Burma*. Rangoon: Zabu Meitswa Pitaka Press, 1938; repr. Kuala Lumpur: Oxford University Press, 1973.

Ni Ni Myint, *Burma's Struggle Against British Imperialism (1885–1895)*. Rangoon: The Universities Press, 1983.

North, Douglas C., and Robert Paul Thomas, *The Rise of the Western World. A New Economic History*. Cambridge University Press, 1973.

Nu, U Nu — *Saturday's Son*. Trans. by Law Yone, edited by Kyaw Win. New Haven: Yale University Press, 1975.

Pearn, B.R., *History of Rangoon*. Rangoon: A.B.M. Press, 1939.

People's Literature Committee, *Who's Who in Burma, 1961*. Rangoon: Sarpay Beikman, 1962.

Pollack, Oliver B., *Empires in Collision: Anglo-Burmese Relations in the Mid-Nineteenth Century*. Westport, Conn.: Greenwood Press, 1979.

Purcell, Victor, *The Chinese in Southeast Asia*. London: Oxford University Press, 2nd edn, 1966.

Rao, A. Narayan, *Indian Labour in Burma*. Madras: Keshari Press, 1944.

Research Institute for Peace and Security, *Asian Security 1980*. Tokyo: 1980.
Richards, C.J., *Burma Retrospect and Other Essays*. Winchester, England: Herbert Curnow Ltd., the Cathedral Press, 1951.
Richter, H.V., *Burma's Rice Surpluses: Accounting for the Decline*. Canberra: Development Studies Centre, Australian National University, 1976.
Robinson, M., and L.A. Shaw, *The Coins and Banknotes of Burma*. Manchester: The authors, 1980.
Saimong Mangrai, *The Shan States and the British Annexation*. Ithaca: Cornell University Southeast Asia Program Data Paper no. 57, 1965.
Scott, James C., *The Moral Economy of the Peasant: Rebellion and Subsistence in Southeast Asia*. New Haven: Yale University Press, 1976.
Scott, J. George, and J.P. Hardiman, *Gazetteer of Upper Burma and the Shan States*. Rangoon: Government Printing and Stationery, 1900.
Sen, N.C., *A Peep into Burma Politics (1917–1941)*. Allahabad: Kitabistan, 1945.
Sein Win, *The Split Story*. Rangoon: Guardian Press, 1959.
Shein, *Burma's Transport and Foreign Trade (1885–1914)*. Rangoon: Dept of Economics, University of Rangoon, 1964.
Shwe Zan Aung and Rhys Davids, *Compendium of Philosophy*. London: Pali Text Society, 1910.
Silverstein, Josef, *Burma: Military Rule and the Politics of Stagnation*. Ithaca: Cornell University Press, 1977.
Singh, Ganga, *Burma Parliamentary Companion*. Rangoon: British Burma Press, 1940.
Smith, Donald Eugene, *Religion and Politics in Burma*. Princeton University Press, 1965.
Spiro, Melford E., *Buddhism and Society: A Great Tradition and Its Burmese Vicissitudes*. New York: Harper and Row, 1972.
Steinberg, David I., *Burma's Road Toward Development: Growth and Ideology Under Military Rule*. Boulder, Colo.: Westview Press, 1981.
Stockholm International Peace Research Institute, *SIPRI Yearbook of World Armaments and Disarmament, 1968/69*. Stockholm: Almqvist and Wiksell, 1969.
——, *SIPRI Yearbook of World Armaments and Disarmament, 1976*. Stockholm: Almqvist and Wiksell, 1977.
——, *SIPRI Yearbook of World Armaments and Disarmament, 1984*. London: Taylor and Francis, 1985.
Tambiah, S.J., *World Conqueror and World Renouncer: A Study of Buddhism and Polity in Thailand Against a Historical Background*. Cambridge University Press, 1976.
Taylor, Robert H., *Foreign and Domestic Consequences of the KMT Intervention in Burma*. Ithaca: Cornell University Southeast Asia Program Data Paper no. 93, 1973.

——, *An Undeveloped State: The Study of Modern Burma's Politics*. Melbourne: Monash University Centre of Southeast Asian Studies Working Paper no. 28, 1983.
——, *Marxism and Resistance in Burma, 1942–1945: Thein Pe Myint's 'Wartime Traveller'*. Athens, Ohio: Ohio University Press, 1984.
Thiha, *The Chindits and the Stars*. London: Regency Press, 1971.
Tinker, Hugh, *Foundations of Local Self-Government in India, Pakistan and Burma*. Bombay: Lalvani, 1967.
Trager, Frank N., *Building a Welfare State in Burma, 1948–1956*. New York: Institute of Pacific Relations, 1958.
——, *Burma: From Kingdom to Independence*. London: Pall Mall Press, 1966.
——, and William J. Koenig. (eds), *Burmese Sit-tans 1764–1826: Records of Rural Life and Administration*. Tucson: University of Arizona Press for the Association for Asian Studies, 1979.
Tun Wai, *Burma's Currency and Credit*. Bombay: Orient Longmans (revised edn), 1962.
Ulyanovsky, Rostislav, *National Liberation*. Moscow: Progress Publishers, 1978.
United States Arms Control and Disarmament Agency, *World Military Expenditures and Arms Transfers 1985*. Washington, DC: 1985.
Walinsky, Louis J., *Economic Development in Burma, 1951–1960*. New York: Twentieth Century Fund, 1962.
Weber, Max, *Economy and Society*. Edited by Guenther Roth and Claus Wittich. New York: Bedminster Press, 1968, vols. I–III.
World Bank, *World Development Report 1984*. Oxford University Press, 1984.

ARTICLES IN ENGLISH

Adas, Michael, 'Immigrant Asians and the Economic Impact of European Imperialism: The Role of South Indian Chettiars in British Burma', *Journal of Asian Studies*, XXXIII, 3 (May, 1974), pp. 385–401.
——, 'From Avoidance to Confrontation: Peasant Protest in Precolonial and Colonial Southeast Asia', *Comparative Studies in Society and History*, 23, 2 (April, 1981), pp. 217–47.
Anderson, Benedict R. O'G., 'Old State, New Society: Indonesia's New Order in Comparative Historical Perspective', *Journal of Asian Studies*, XLII, 3 (May, 1983), pp. 477–96.
Arumugam, Raja Segaran, 'Burma: A Political and Economic Background', in Institute of Southeast Asian Studies, *Southeast Asian Affairs 1975*. Singapore: FEP International, 1976, pp. 41–8.
——, 'Burma: Political Unrest and Economic Stagnation', in Institute of Southeast Asian Studies, *Southeast Asian Affairs 1976*. Singapore: FEP International, 1977, pp. 167–75.

ASMI, 'The State of Arakan', *The Guardian* (Rangoon) 1/10 (Aug., 1954), pp. 28–9; 1/11 (Sept., 1954), pp. 21–3.
Aung Kin, 'Burma in 1980: Pouring Balm on Sore Spots', in Institute of Southeast Asian Studies, *Southeast Asian Affairs 1981*. Singapore: Heinemann, 1982, pp. 103–25.
Aung-Thwin, Michael, 'Kingship, the *Sangha*, and Society in Pagan', in Kenneth R. Hall and John K. Whitmore (eds), *Explorations in Early Southeast Asian History: The Origins of Southeast Asian Statecraft*. Ann Arbor: Michigan Papers on South and Southeast Asia no. 11, 1976, pp. 205–56.
——, 'The Role of *Sasana* Reform in Burmese History: Economic Dimensions of a Religious Purification', *Journal of Asian Studies*, XXXVIII, 4 (Aug., 1979), pp. 671–88.
——, 'Jampudipa: Classical Burma's Camelot', in John P. Ferguson (ed.), 'Essays on Burma', *Contributions to Asian Studies*, vol. 16, Leiden: E.J. Brill, 1981, pp. 38–61.
——, 'Divinity, Spirit, and Human: Conceptions of Classical Burmese Kingship', in Lorraine Gesick (ed.), *Centers, Symbols, and Hierarchies: Essays on the Classical State of Southeast Asia*. New Haven: Yale University Southeast Asian Studies Series no. 26, 1983, pp. 45–86.
Aye Hlaing, 'Observations on Some Patterns of Economic Development', *Burma Research Society Fiftieth Anniversary Publications no. 1*. Rangoon: Burma Research Society, 1961, pp. 9–16.
Badgley, John H., 'Burma: The Nexus of Socialism and Two Political Traditions', *Asian Survey*, III, 2 (Feb., 1963), pp. 89–95.
——, 'Burma's Zealot Wungyis: Maoists or St. Simonists', *Asian Survey*, V, 1 (Jan., 1965), pp. 55–62.
Baldwin, J.W., 'The Karens in Burma', *Journal of the Royal Central Asian Society*, XXXVI (1949), pp. 102–13.
Demaine, Harvey, 'Current Problems of Agricultural Development Planning in Burma', in Institute of Southeast Asian Studies, *Southeast Asian Affairs 1979*. Singapore: Heinemann, 1979, pp. 95–103.
Everton, John, 'The Ne Win Regime in Burma', *Asia*, 2 (Autumn, 1964), pp. 1–17.
Finer, Samuel E., 'State and Nation-Building in Europe: The Role of the Military', in Charles Tilly (ed.), *The Formation of National States in Europe*. Princeton University Press, 1975, pp. 84–163.
Furnivall, J.S., 'The Fashioning of Leviathan', *The Journal of the Burma Research Society*, XXIX, 3 (1939), pp. 1–138.
——, 'South Asia in the World Today', in Phillips Talbot (ed.), *South Asia in the World Today*. University of Chicago Press, 1950, pp. 3–24.
Gledhill, Alan, 'Burma', in John Gilissen (ed.), *Bibliographical Introduction to Legal History and Ethnology*, vol. E, no. 7. Brussels: Éditions de l'Institut de Sociologie, Université Libre de Bruxelles, 1970.

Guyot, James F., 'Bureaucratic Transformation in Burma', in Ralph Braibanti (ed.), *Asian Bureaucratic Systems Emergent from the British Imperial Tradition*. Durham, NC: Duke University Press, 1966, pp. 354–443.

Heine-Geldern, Robert, 'Conceptions of State and Kingship in Southeast Asia', *The Far Eastern Quarterly*, 2 (Nov., 1942), pp. 15–30.

Hla Aung, 'The Effect of Anglo-Indian Legislation on Burmese Customary Law', in David C. Buxbaum (ed.), *Family Law and Customary Law in Asia: A Contemporary Legal Perspective*. The Hague: Martinus Nijhoff, 1968, pp. 67–88.

Khin Maung Kyi, et al., 'Process of Communication in Modernisation of Rural Society: A Survey Report on Two Burmese Villages', *The Malayan Economic Review*, XVIII, no. 1 (April 1973), pp. 55–73.

Khin Maung Kyi, 'Problems of Agricultural Policy in Some Trade Dependent Small Countries: A Comparative Study of Burma and Thailand', *Kajian Ekonomi Malaysia*. XVI, nos. 1 and 2 (June/Dec. 1979), pp. 344–52.

——, 'Modernization of Burmese Agriculture: Problems and Prospects', in Institute of Southeast Asian Studies, *Southeast Asian Affairs 1982*. Singapore: Institute of Southeast Asian Studies, 1983, pp. 115–31.

——, 'Indians in Burma: Problems of an Alien Subculture in a Highly Integrating Society', in K. Sandhu and S. Mani (eds), *Indians in Southeast Asia*. Singapore: Heinemann (Asia), forthcoming.

King, Winston L., 'Contemporary Burmese Buddhism', in Heinrich Dumoulin (ed.), *Buddhism in the Modern World*. London: Collier-Macmillan, 1976, pp. 81–98.

Lieberman, Victor B., 'The Political Significance of Religious Wealth in Burmese History: Some Further Thoughts', *Journal of Asian Studies*, XXXIX, 4 (Aug., 1980), pp. 753–69.

——, 'Provincial Reforms in Taung-ngu Burma', *Bulletin of the School of Oriental and African Studies*, XLIII, 3 (1980), pp. 548–69.

Linter, Bertil, 'The Shans and the Shan State of Burma', *Contemporary Southeast Asia*, vol. 5, no. 4 (March 1984), pp. 401–50.

Lissak, Moshe, 'The Class Structure of Burma: Continuity and Change', *Journal of Southeast Asian Studies*, 1, 1 (March 1970), pp. 60–73.

——, 'Social Change, Mobilization and Exchange of Services between the Military Establishment and the Civil Society: The Burmese Case', *Economic Development and Cultural Change*, XIII, 1, pp. 1–19.

Mills, J.A., 'Burmese Peasant Response to British Provincial Rule 1852–1885', in D.B. Miller (ed.), *Peasants and Politics*. Melbourne: Edward Arnold (Australia), 1978, pp. 77–104.

Moscotti, Albert D., 'Current Burmese and Southeast Asian Relations', in *Southeast Asian Affairs 1978*. Singapore: FEP International, 1979, pp. 83–94.

Mya Maung, 'Socialism and Economic Development of Burma', *Asian Survey*, IV, 12 (Dec. 1964), pp. 1182–90.

Mya Than, 'A Burmese Village — Revisited', *The South East Asian Review*, II, 2 (Feb., 1978), pp. 1–15.

Perlin, Frank, 'State Formation Reconsidered', *Modern Asian Studies*, 19, 3 (July, 1985), pp. 415–80.

Pfanner, David E., 'A Semisubsistence Village Economy in Lower Burma', in Clifton R. Wharton, Jr. (ed.), *Subsistence Agriculture and Economic Development*. Chicago: Aldine, 1969, pp. 47–60.

Richter, H.V., 'The Union of Burma', in R.T. Shand (ed.), *Agricultural Development in Asia*. Canberra: Australian National University Press, 1969, pp. 141–80.

——, 'The Impact of Socialism on Economic Activity in Burma', in T. Scarlett Epstein and David H. Penny (eds), *Opportunity and Response, Case Studies in Economic Development* (London: C. Hurst, 1972), pp. 216–39.

Rueschemeyer, Dietrich, and Peter B. Evans, 'The State and Economic Transformation: Toward an Analysis of the Conditions Underlying Effective Intervention', in Peter B. Evans, Dietrich Rueschemeyer and Theda Skocpol (eds), *Bringing the State Back In*. Cambridge University Press, 1985, pp. 44–77.

Saito, Teruko, 'Farm Household Economy under Paddy Delivery System in Contemporary Burma', *The Developing Economies*, XIX, 4 (Dec., 1981), pp. 367–97.

Sarkisyanz, E., 'Buddhist Backgrounds of Burmese Socialism', in Bardwell L. Smith (ed.), *Religion and Legitimation of Power in Thailand, Laos and Burma*. Chambersburg, Pennsylvania: Anima, 1978.

Schmitt, Hans O., 'Decolonisation and Development in Burma', *Journal of Development Studies*, IV, 1 (Oct., 1967), pp. 97–108.

Shein, Myint Myint Thant and Tin Tin Sein, ' "Provincial Contract System" of British Indian Empire, in Relation to Burma — A Case of Fiscal Exploitation', *Journal of the Burma Research Society*, LII, Part II (Dec., 1969), pp. 1–26.

Silverstein, Josef, 'Burma: Ne Win's Revolution Reconsidered', *Asian Survey*, VI, 2 (Feb., 1966), pp. 95–104.

Skocpol, Theda, 'Bringing the State Back In: Strategies of Analysis in Current Research', in Peter B. Evans, Dietrich Rueschemeyer and Theda Skocpol (eds), *Bringing the State Back In*. Cambridge University Press, 1985, pp. 3–43.

Stein, Burton, 'State Formation and Economy Reconsidered', *Modern Asian Studies*, 19, 3 (July, 1985), pp. 387–414.

Steinberg, David I., 'Burma Under the Military: Towards a Chronology', *Contemporary Southeast Asia*, 3, 3 (Dec. 1981), pp. 244–85.

Sutton, Walter D., 'U Aung San of Burma', *The South Atlantic Quarterly*, vol. XLVII, 1 (Jan., 1948), pp. 1–16.
Swatos, William H., Jr., 'Revolution and Charisma in a Rationalized World: Weber Revisited and Extended', in Ronald M. Glassman and Vatro Murvar (eds), *Max Weber's Political Sociology: A Pessimistic Vision of a Rationalized World*. Westport, Conn. and London: Greenwood Press, 1984, pp. 201–16.
Taylor, Robert H., 'Politics in Late Colonial Burma: The Case of U Saw', *Modern Asian Studies*, 10, 2 (April, 1976), pp. 161–94.
——, 'Burma in the Anti-Fascist War', in Alfred W. McCoy (ed.), *Southeast Asia under Japanese Occupation*. New Haven: Yale University Southeast Asian Studies no. 22, 1980, pp. 159–90.
——, 'Perceptions of Ethnicity in the Politics of Burma', *Southeast Asian Journal of Social Science*, 10, 1 (1982), pp. 7–22.
——, 'Burma's Foreign Relations since the Third Indochina Conflict', in Institute of Southeast Asian Studies, *Southeast Asian Affairs 1983*. Aldershot: Gower, 1983, pp. 102–14.
——, 'Burma', in Zakaria Ahmad and Harold Crouch (eds), *Military-Civilian Relations in South-East Asia*. Singapore: Oxford University Press, 1985, pp. 13–49.
——, 'Burma', in Haruhiro Fukui (ed.), *Political Parties of Asia and the Pacific*. Westport, Conn.: Greenwood Press, 1985, vol. I, pp. 99–154.
——, 'The Burmese Concepts of Revolution', in Mark Hobart and Robert H. Taylor (eds), *Context Meaning and Power in Southeast Asia*. Ithaca: Cornell University Southeast Asia Program, 1986, pp. 79–92.
Tilly, Charles, 'Reflections on the History of European State-Making', in Charles Tilly (ed.), *The Formation of National States in Western Europe*. Princeton University Press, 1975, pp. 3–83.
Tin Maung Maung Than, 'Burma in 1983: From Recovery to Growth?', in Institute of Southeast Asian Studies, *Southeast Asian Affairs 1984*. Singapore: Institute of Southeast Asian Studies, 1984, pp. 89–122.
Turton, Andrew, 'Limits of Ideological Domination and the Formation of Social Consciousness', in Andrew Turton and Shigeharu Tanabe (eds), *History and Peasant Consciousness in South East Asia*. Osaka: Senri Ethnological Studies no. 13, National Museum of Ethnology, 1984, pp. 19–74.
Wiant, Jon A., 'Burma: Loosening Up on the Tiger's Tail', *Asian Survey*, XIII, 2 (Feb., 1973), pp. 179–86.
——, 'Insurgency in the Shan State', in Lim Joo-Jock and S. Vani (eds), *Armed Separatism in Southeast Asia*. Singapore: Issues in Southeast Asian Security, Institute of Southeast Asian Studies, 1984, pp. 81–110.

OFFICIAL PUBLICATIONS IN ENGLISH

Address Delivered by General Ne Win at the Closing Session of the Fourth Party Seminar on 11th November 1969, Rangoon: Sarpay Beikman, 1969.

British Burma Political Department, *Report on the Administration of Hill Tracts, Northern Arakan, 1870–71*. Rangoon: Secretariat Press, 1872.

Burma, 1, 1. Rangoon: Foreign Affairs Association, Sept., 1944.

Burma Handbook, Simla: Government of India Press, 1944.

Burma Socialist Programme Party, *The System of the Correlation of Man and His Environment*. Rangoon: Burma Socialist Programme Party, 1963.

——, Party Central Organizing Committee, *Party Seminar 1965*. Rangoon: Sarpay Beikman, 1966.

——, *Foreign Policy of the Revolutionary Government of the Union of Burma*. Rangoon: Sarpay Beikman, 1968.

——, Central Committee Headquarters. *The Fourth Party Congress 1981*. Rangoon: Printing and Publishing Corporation, 1985.

Census of Burma, 1931, Volume XI of the *Census of India, 1931*. Rangoon: Government Printing and Stationery, 1933.

Correspondence for the Years 1825–26 to 1842–43 in the Office of the Commissioner Tenasserim Division, Rangoon: Government Printing and Stationery, 1929.

Economic Survey of Burma 1958, Rangoon: Government Printing and Stationery, 1958.

Final Report of the Administration Reorganization Committee, 1951, Rangoon: Government Printing and Stationery, 1951.

Fiscal Enquiry Committee Report, Second Report, Rangoon: Government Printing and Stationery, 1938.

Report of the Education Reconstruction Committee, Rangoon: Government Printing and Stationery, 1947.

Report of the Indian Statutory Commission, Cmd. 3568. London: H.M.S.O. 1930.

Report on Indian Immigration, Rangoon: Government Printing and Stationery, 1941.

Report of the Land and Agriculture Committee, Rangoon: Government Printing and Stationery, 1939.

Report on the Progress of Arakan Under British Rule from 1826 to 1875, Rangoon: Government Press, 1876.

Report to the Pyithu Hluttaw on the Financial, Economic and Social Conditions of the Socialist Republic of the Union of Burma for 1977–78, Rangoon: Ministry of Planning and Finance, 1977.

Report to the Pyithu Hluttaw on the Financial, Economic and Social Conditions of the Socialist Republic of the Union of Burma, 1985–86, Rangoon: Ministry of Planning and Finance, 1985.

Riot Inquiry Committee, *Interim Report*. Rangoon: Government Printing and Stationery, 1938.

Selected Correspondence of Letters Issued from and Received in the Office of the Commissioner Tenasserim Division from the Years 1825–26 to 1842–43, Rangoon: Government Printing and Stationery, 1928.
Shan States Manual, Rangoon: Government Printing and Stationery, 1933.
A Study of the Social and Economic History of Burma (The British Period), Rangoon: Economic and Social Board, Office of the Prime Minister, roneoed, 1957, Parts I–V.
Two-Year Plan of Economic Development for Burma, Rangoon: Government Printing and Stationery, 1948.

UNPUBLISHED SOURCES IN ENGLISH

Abu Talib bin Ahmad, 'Collaboration, 1941–1945: An Aspect of the Japanese Occupation of Burma', Ph.D. diss., Monash University, 1984.
Ambler, John S., 'Burma's Rice Economy under Military Rule: The Evolution of Socialist Agricultural Programmes and Their Impact on Paddy Farmers', Cornell University, Oct., 1983.
Ba Thann Win, 'Administration of Shan States from the Panglong Conference to the Cessation of the Powers of the Saophas 1947–1959', MA thesis, Rangoon Arts and Sciences University, n.d.
Cady, John F., 'The Character and Program of the Communist Party in Burma', Rangoon: American Consulate General, 26 March 1946.
Central Intelligence Agency, Directorate of Intelligence, 'Peking and the Burmese Communists: The Perils and Profits of Insurgency', July 1971 (declassified 1980).
Guyot, Dorothy Hess, 'The Political Impact of the Japanese Occupation of Burma', Ph.D. diss., Yale University, 1966.
Khin Maung Kyi, 'Patterns of Accommodation to Bureaucratic Authority in a Transitional Culture (A Sociological Analysis of Burmese Bureaucrats with Respect to Their Orientations Toward Authority)', Ph.D. diss., Cornell University, 1966.
Khin Mya, 'The Impact of Traditional Culture and Environmental Forces on the Development of the Kachins, a Sub-Cultural Group of Burma', Ph.D. diss., University of Maryland, 1961.
Koenig, William J., 'The Early Kon-baung Polity, 1752–1819: A Study of Politics, Adminstration and Social Organization in Burma', Ph.D. diss., University of London, 1978.
Kozicki, R.J., 'India and Burma, 1937–1957: A Study in International Relations', Ph.D. diss., University of Pennsylvania, 1959.
Lieberman, Victor B., 'Continuity and Change in Burmese History: Some Preliminary Observations', subsequently published as 'Reinterpreting Burmese History', *Comparative Studies in Society and History*, 29, 1(January, 1987), pp. 162–94.

Maung Maung, 'Nationalist Movements in Burma, 1920–1940: Changing Patterns of Leadership: From Sangha to Laity', MA thesis, Australian National University, 1976.

Richter, H.V., 'Development and Equality in Burma'. Canberra: Department of Economics, Research School of Pacific Studies, Australian National University, 1974.

Taylor, Robert H., 'The Relationship Between Burmese Social Classes and British-Indian Policy on the Behaviour of the Burmese Political Elite, 1937–1942', Ph.D. diss., Cornell University, 1974.

Than Aung, Moses, 'A General Study in the Economic Development of Burma with Special Reference to Economic Planning (1948–1958)', MA thesis, Rangoon Arts and Sciences University, 1973.

Wiant, Jon W., 'The Burmese Revolutionary Council: Military Government and Political Change', seminar paper, Department of Government, Cornell University, 1971.

World Bank, South Asia Regional Office, *Development in Burma: Issues and Prospects*, report no. 1024–BA, 27 July 1976.

———, South Asia Projects Department, Agriculture Division, *Burma: Agricultural Sector Review*, vol. I: 'The Main Report', 30 Aug. 1977.

———, South Asia Regional Office, 'Burma: Country Economic Memorandum', report no. 1700–BA, 19 Oct. 1977.

BOOKS AND MONOGRAPHS IN BURMESE

Hpa Hsa Pa La — Konmyunit Apyanahlan Peisa (AFPFL — Communist Correspondence). Rangoon: Pyithu Ana Punhnat Taik, 1947.

Hpo Kyaw San, *Paliman Dimokayeisi Sannit hnit Myanma Naingngan* (Parliamentary Democracy and Burma State). (Rangoon: San Pya, n. d.).

Lei Maung, *Myanman Naingnganyei Thamaing* (History of Burma's Politics). Rangoon: Sapei Biman, 1974, 2 vols.

Maung Maung, *Taya Ubadei Ahtweidwei Bahuthuta* (General Legal Knowledge). Rangoon: Win Maung U, 1975.

Nyi Nyi, *Myanma Naingngan Amyotha Mawkun (1975)* (Burma's National Record [1975]). Rangoon: Pagan, 1978.

Saw, *Gyapan Lan Nyunt* (Japan Points the Way). Rangoon: Thuriya, 1936.

Sein Myin, *Hnit 200 Myanma Naingngan Thamaing Abidan* (Dictionary of 200 Years of Burma History). Rangoon: Sapei Yatana, 1969.

Sein Tin (ed.), *Myanma Akyaung hnit Kabama Akyaung* (Burma Affairs and World Affairs) (Rangoon: 1982).

Than Htun, *Pyithu Sit Pyithu Ana* (People's War, People's Power). Rangoon: publisher unnamed.

Thein Pe Myint, *Ashei ka Neiwun Htwetthe Bama* (As sure as the sun rises in the east). (Rangoon: Myat Sapei, n.d.), 2 vols.

Tin Htun Aung, *Myanma Naingnganyei hnit Thakin Ba Thaung* (Burma's Politics and Thakin Ba Thaung). Rangoon: Sapeu Sapei Hpyanchiyei, 1980.

ARTICLES IN BURMESE

Aung Hsan, 'Naingnganyei Amyomyo' (Kinds of Politics), *Dagun Maggazin*, no. 234 (Feb. 1940), pp. 61–70; no. 236 (April 1940), pp. 17–26.

Ono Toru, 'Konbaung hkit Kyeitow Ywa Ngweihkyei Sanit' (The village money lending system of the Konbaung era). *Myawati*, March 1976, pp. 37–42.

OFFICIAL PUBLICATIONS IN BURMESE

Myanma Hsoshelit Lansin Pati Baho Kommiti Danachok (Burma Socialist Programme Party Central Committee Headquarters), *Myanma Hsoshelit Lansin Pati Pati Winmya Letswe* (Burma Socialist Programme Party Party Members' Handbook). Rangoon: Burma Socialist Programme Party, 1978, repr. 1982.

Myanma Hsoshelit Lansin Pati, Pati Seyunyei Baho Kowmiti Danachok (Burma Socialist Programme Party, Party Organization Central Committee Headquarters), *Myanma Hsoshelit Lansin Pati ei Pyei twinyei ya Ahmat 1* (Burma Socialist Programme Party's Internal Affairs no. 1). Rangoon: Sapei Biman, 1966.

——, *Myanma Hsoshelit Lansin Pati Pwesepun Achekhan Sinmyin* (Constitution of the Burma Socialist Programme Party). Rangoon: 1983.

Myanma Hsoshelit Lansin Pati (Burma Socialist Programme Party), *Lu hnit Patwunkyindo ei Anya Manya Thabawtaya* (The System of the Correlation of Man and His Environment). Rangoon: Jan. 1964.

Pyihtaungsu Myanma Naingngan Towhlanyei Kaungsi (Union of Burma Revolutionary Council). *Myanma Hsoshelit Lansin Pati ei Witheitha Latkangamya* (Specific Characteristics of the Burma Socialist Programme Party). Rangoon: Burma Socialist Programme Party Party Affairs Central Committee, 4 Sept. 1964.

Pyi Htaungsu Hsoshelit Thammata Myanma Naingngan Hpwetsinpun Ahkyeihkan Upadei (Constitution of the Socialist Republic of the Union of Burma). Rangoon: Burma Socialist Programme Party, Printing and Publishing Corporation, 1973.

Pyihtaungsu Myanma Naingnan Towhlanyei Kaungsi tho Tinthwin thaw Pyihtaungsu Myanma Naingnan Pyi twin Nyinyatyei Akyanpei Apwei ei Asiyinhkansa (Union of Burma Internal Unity Conference's Report Which Was Submitted to the Union of Burma Revolutionary Council). Rangoon, 1969.

Pyi Htaungsu Hsoshelit Thammata Myanma Naingngan Hpwetsinpun Akhyeihkan Upadei hnit Patthet thaw Adipape Shinlinhkyetmay. (Explanatory Points

Regarding the Constitution of the Socialist Republic of the Union of Burma). Rangoon: Burma Socialist Programme Party, Printing and Publishing Corporation, Sept., 1973.

Pyi Htaungsu Hsoshelit Thammata Myanama Naingngan Hpwetsinpun Akhyeihkan Upadei hnit Patthem thaw Asiyinhkansa. (Report Concerning the Constitution of the Socialist Republic of the Union of Burma). Rangoon: Burma Socialist Programme Party, Printing and Publishing Corporation, 1973.

Thathanatow Thanshin Tetanpyanpwayei Gaingpaungsu Thaya Asiaweipwekyi Hpyitmyaukyei Thaya Wanhsaukhpwet (Sangha Executive Body for the Purification, Perpetuation and Propagation of the Sasana Making the Union of Sects Meeting to Purify the Sangha). *Pyihtaungsu Hsoshelit Thammata Myanma Naingngantow Thaya Ahpweasin Akhyeihkansinmyin (Mukyan)* (Organization Rules of the Socialist Republic of the Union of Burma State Sangha Body [Draft]). Rangoon: Kaba Ei Thathanayei Usi Dana Press, 1980.

Towhlanyei Kaungsi ei Hluthsaungchet Thamaing Akyinchut (Concise History of the Actions of the Revolutionary Council), Rangoon: Printing and Publishing Corporation, 2 March 1974.

1986–87 Hkunit atwet Pyi Htaungsu Hsoshelit Thammata Myanma Naingngantaw Bankayei, Sipwayei, Luhmuyei Ahkyei Anei hnit pathetthe Pyithu Hluttaw tho Asiyinhkansa (Report to the Pyithu Hluttaw on the Financial, Economic and Social Conditions of the Socialist Republic of the Union of Burma 1986–87). Rangoon: Simankein hnit Bankayei Wunkyi Dana, 1986.

UNPUBLISHED WORKS IN BURMESE

San San Myin, 'Hpa Hsa Pa La Hkit Myanma Naingnganyei Thamaing 1948–1958' (Political History of Burma in the AFPFL Era, 1948–1958). MA thesis, Rangoon Arts and Sciences University, 1979.

INDEX

Academy for the Development of National Groups, 302
Adas, Michael, 15, 16, 109, 137n, 143n
AFO, 234, 244, 287, 298
AFPFL, 217, 226–8, 229–30, 232, 234–6, 238, 240–8, 251, 255, 265–8, 274–6, 278, 283–4, 287, 294
Agriculturalists' Debt Relief Act (1947), 275
ahkin-wun (revenue officer), 34
ahmu-dan (crown service men), 32–34, 42–3, 46–7, 63, 80, 115
Alaungpaya (r. 1752–60), 18–19, 61
All Burma Peasants' Organisation, ABPO, 245
All Burma Students' Union (ABSU), 205–9
All Burma Youth League, 207, 209
Anarchical Revolutionary Crimes Act (1919), 196
Anderson, Benedict R. O'G., 3, 4n
Anglo-Burmese Wars: First, 62, 74, 153, 155; Second, 63–4, 153, 155, 156; Third, 116
Anti-Boycott Act, 196
Anti-Fascist Organisation, *see* AFO
Anti-Fascist People's Freedom League, *see* AFPFL
Anti-Separation Leagues, 171, 186
appanage system, 27–9, 36, 43–5, 88 174
Arakanese, 155, 290, 370
army, *see* precolonial state; military, precolonial; Burma Army
athi (free service men), 32–3, 35, 41, 46–7, 61–3, 80
atwin-wun (interior ministers), 30
Aung Gyaw, Maung, 208
Aung Gyi, Col., 248, 294–5
Aung San-Attlee Agreement, 226, 231, 261
Aung San, Gen., Thakin, U, 207–9, 211, 215, 225, 232–5, 237, 239–40, 245, 261, 287, 325, 366
Aung-Thwin, Michael, 17n, 25n, 51n, 52n, 58n
Australia, 262
Avan interregnum, 20, 22, 24, 35, 50

Bagyidaw, 28
Ba Hein, Thakin, 208
Baho administration, 223
Ba Maw, Dr, 170, 172, 183, 200, 203, 208, 223–5, 239, 250, 253–4, 261, 280, 283–4
Bangladesh, 301, 354
Ba Pe, U, 171–2, 177–8, 183, 185–6, 197
Baptists, American, 87, 155
Ba Swe, U, 246–8, 287, 289, 367
Ba Thaung, Thakin, 209
Ba Tin, U, 173
bayin (provincial governors), 23, 27
BCP, 229–30, 234, 241, 246, *see also* Communist Party
BDA, 232
BIA, 221–3, 232–3, 236, 244, 265
black market: under Mindon, 64; under postcolonial state, 316, 341
BNA, 232–6, 242
Bo, 266–9
Bodawpaya, 28
bodhissatta (emergent Buddha), 58
Bo Ni, Col., 370
boycott idea, 179, 184, 187, 246–7; *see also* elections, *wunthanu athin*
bribery, 89, 339; *see also* corruption
British East India Company, 63, 69
British-Indian empire, 19, 62–4, 69, 76, 217, 219, 221
British Military Administration, 235, 251, 257, 265, 274, 278
'Browderism', 239
bu athin 194, 196–7, 240
Buddha Sasana Council, 245, 288, 295, 357

387

Buddhism: and Marxism, 287–8, 360–3; and nationalism, 10, 150–1, 162, 176–7, 180–5; and the state, 8, 14–15, 52, 54–60, 287–90, 291, 295, 356–9; *see also* monarchical system, legitimacy

Buddhist monkhood, *see sangha*

bureaucracy: collapse of in the 1940s, 265–6; growth of in the 1960s, 309–11

Burma: history of, 1, 71; colonialism and, 73–7; pacification of, 81; political parties in, 174–88; postcolonial state, 217–18; *see also* colonial state

Burma Army, 229, 231–4, 243, 248, 336–7, 356; *see also* BDA, BIA, BNA, People's Army

Burma Communist Party, 229, 354; *see also* BCP, Communist Party, CP(B)

Burma Defence Army, *see* BDA

Burma Economic Development Corporation, 257

Burma Frontier Service, 96

Burma Immigration (Emergency Provisions) Act (1947), 271

Burma Independence Army, *see* BIA

Burma National Army, *see* BNA

Burmans, 101, 155, 157

'Burma proper', 79

Burma Reforms Committee, 121

Burma Socialist Programme Party (BSPP): 296–7, 304, 307–9, 315–6, 331, 353, 365–6, 370; Central Committee membership, 318–21; 1st Congress, 308, 315, 346; 2nd Congress, 309, 370; 4th Congress, 317, 322; functions of, 325–7; ideology, 297, 356–7, 360–4; membership, 316–23; *Party Members' Handbook*, 363–4; women in, 322

Burma Workers' and Peasants' Party, 245

Burmese Chamber of Commerce, 172

'Burmese Way to Socialism', 296

Butler, Sir Harcourt, 118

bye-daik (Privy Council), 30–1

cakkavatti (aspect of kingship; universal monarch), 57

Cambodia *see* Kampuchea

capital accumulation, 257–8, 263, 341–2

'caretaker government', 217, 243, 248, 267, 277, 281, 291, 315

cellular organization of society, 25–6, 46

census records, 36, 309

Chakravarti, N.R., 136n, 137n

Chamber of Commerce, 117

Chelmsford, Lord, 119

Chettiars, 142–5, 170, 194, 201–2, 277, 278

Chief Commissioner, 74, 81, 103–4, 118

Chief Court, 105

Chin, 22, 88, 92, 100, 160, 226, 236, 286, 294, 300, 303, 326, 327

China, 79, 92, 99, 154, 262–4, 276, 292, 301, 335

Chinese, 76, 100, 108, 154, 199n; *see also* class structure

Chinese Communist Party, 210, 354

Chinese Communist Revolution, 232, 354–5, 367

Chinese Nationalists, *see* KMT

Chit Hlaing, U, 169–72, 178–9, 183, 186

circle boards, 86, 184, 194

Citizenship Law (1983), 327

civil police, 101, 250–1; *see also* People's Police Force

civil service, 265, 282–3, 309–10

civil war, 217, 228, 251, 366

class structure: analysis of colonial, 124–47; changes in (1942–62), 270–83; and ethnicity, 126–9; and plural society, 124–5; workers and peasants, 145–7; *see also* middle class

Cocks, S.W., 119n

colonial state: centralization of 68; compared to European state, 76–7; evolution of, 66–79; expenditures of, 112; finance of, 88–91; functions of, 98–115; judicial system of, 102–6; legitimacy of, 115–23, 152; military power of, 99–101, 198–9; nature of, 67–79; politics of, 148–52; rationalization of authority relations in, 82–8; relationship with society, 66–8, 79;

revolts against; security and order, 99–102; territorial organization of, 79–82; threats to, 99–101; *see also* rebellions, Hsaya San rebellion
Commissioner, 80–81
Commonwealth, British, 119, 263
Communist Party, 212, 220–2, 234–6, 268, 275–6, 284–5, 287–8, 297–8, 302, 333, 348, 367–9, *see also* BCP, CP(B)
Congregation of the Sangha of All Orders, 358, 368
constitution: **1947**, 227–8, 287, 290, 292, 304, 307; **1974**; 292, 303–4, 307–9, 327–8
Cooperative Credit Department, 111
corruption, 84, 366
corvée, 37, 43–4, 88
CP(B), 229, 239, 241, *see also* Communist Party
Craddock, Sir Reginald, 120, 178
crime rates, 102, 105, 250–1
Criminal Law Amendment Act (1922), 196
Criminal Procedure Code, 196
Criminal Tribes Act (1924), 196

dacoity, 33, 45, 102, 222, 236, 250–1
Dawson's Bank, 143
debt, 346–7
Defence Services' Institute (DSI), 257
demobilization, 293
departmental agencies, 32–3
dependent provinces, zone of, 22, 32, 79
Deputy Commissioner, 80–1
dhamma (law), 56–7
dhammakatika (Buddhist monks who toured villages organizing peasants in the 1920s), 182, 196
dhammaraja (aspect of kingship; lord of the law), 56–7
Disposal of Tenancies Act (1948), 275
Do Bama Asiayon: 200, 206–16, 237–8; manifesto of, 211–14, 296, 298
Dominion status, 119
Donnison, Vernon, 113n
Dutt, Palme, 215

dyarchy, 74, 96, 111, 121–3, 171–2, 175

East Asia Youth League, 240
Ecclesiastical Courts Act (1949), 288
economy: 38–40, compared to Europe, 38, 42–3; colonial, 68, 106–10, 125, 190–5, European interests in, 131–3; Indian role in, 131–45; postcolonial (1962–87), 220, 272–83, 340–53; planning, 253–4; precolonial, *see also* class structure, GDP
education and ethnicity, 114–15
education system: colonial, 112–15, 125; current, 359–60
elections: *1920*, 179; *1922*, 184; *1925*, 186; *1928*, 184; *1932*, 122, *1936*, 186, 203; *1947*, 246–7; *1951*, 247; *1956*, 247; *1960*, 248; *1973–4*, 308–9; *post-1974*, 327–8
élite-mass gap theory, 188–9
ethnic homogenization, 7, 24–5, 150
ethnicity: and the colonial state, 116–18; and income, in the 1930s, 131, 135–6; and legitimacy, 289–94, 300–4; *see also* class structure
excluded areas, *see* frontier areas
external relations, 260–4, 292, 299, 353–6

Federated Shan States, 227; *see also* Shan State Federation
1st Kachin Rifles, 236
First World War, 10, 75–6, 92, 100, 233
Force 136, 239
4th Burma Rifles, 236
France, 99, 116
Freedom Bloc, 203
Free State League, 186
French Indochina, 79
frontier areas, 79–80, 87–8, 105, 156–60, 226–8, 233, 284–7, 301
Frontier Areas Administration, 268
Frontier Force, 101
Furnivall, J.S., 14n, 72n, 77n, 78, 141n, 276

Gandhi M.K., 179
gaung (subordinate to headman during colonial period who served as a police officer), 84
GCBA, 164, 169–71, 178–86, 193–6, 198, 199, 210
GCSS, 120, 182–5, 193
GDP, 253, 256, 260, 343, 345–6; *see also* economy
General Council of Burmese Associations, *see* GCBA
General Council of Sangha Sammeggi, *see* GCSS
Geneva Conference (1962), 354
gentry (hereditary headmen), 8, 14–15, 35–6, 39, 43, 159–60; *see also thugyi*
Government of Burma Act (1935), 123, 212, 225, 228
Government of India Act (1919), 119
Governor (British), 74, 81, 118
Governor-General of India, 74
Governor's executive committee, 240
governors, provincial, 8
Greater East Asia Co-Prosperity Sphere, 273, 284
gross domestic product, *see* GDP

Habitual Offenders Restriction Act (1919), 196
Haji, S.N., 170
headman, *see thu-gyi*
health provision, 359
High Court, 338
hill areas, *see* frontier areas
Hla Aung, 40n
Hlaing-Pu-Gyaw, GCBA, 185–6, 196
Hla Pe, Thakin, 216
hluttaw (Council of Ministers), 30–3; 48, 53–4
Home Rule Party, 186
House of Representatives, 208, 365
Hsaya San, Hsaya San rebellion, *see* San, Hsaya
Hse Hsaung Youth, 325
Hsinyeitha Party, 171, 231

independence: from Britain, 217–8; Japanese grant of, 225, 283–4

India, 262, 355
Indian Civil Service (ICS), 67
Indian Communist Party, 239
Indian immigration: 77, 107, 126–7, 145–7; and emigration, 271, *see also* class structure; ethnicity
Indian National Congress, 179, 210, 230, 272
Indian Ocean trade, 17, 45–6
indirect rule, 92, *see also* frontier areas; Shan states
Indonesia, 5, 336, 345
Irrawaddy Flotilla Company, 110, 257
Irwin, Lord, 119

Japan: 99, 172, 173, 182, 209–10, 260–1; empire of, 217; Imperial Army, 232; invasion by, 218, 221, 233, 260–1, 271; war reparations, 255, 263, 355
Judicial Commissioner, 104–5
Judicial system: socialist, 338–40; colonial, precolonial, *see* colonial state, or precolonial state, judicial system
Judson College, 115, 180

Kachin, 22, 25, 88, 92, 100, 160, 226, 236, 286, 294, 300, 327, 334
Kachin Duwa, 243
Kachin Independence Army, 333, 354
Kachin National Congress, 244
Kampuchea, 354–5
Kandy agreement, 235
Karen, 22, 80, 87, 92, 100–2, 155, 157, 222, 229, 231–3, 284–7, 294, 300, 302, 303, 326, 328, 334, 370
Karen Central Organization (KCO), 243
Karen National Association, 155
Karen National Defence Organization (KNDO), 242, 268
Karen National Liberation Army, 333–4
Karen National Union (KNU), 229, 236–7, 243, 247, 334
Karenni, 22, 270, 284, 286, *see also* Kayah
Karenni Sawbwas, 227, 286, 287
Karen Rifles, 236

karma, 59–60
Kayah, 92, 291–2, 300, 303, 326–8, 334
Kayah Sawbwas, 270, 291
Kempetei, 250
Kengtung, 226
Koenig, William, 40
Khin Maung, C.P., 196
Khin Maung Kyi, 40, 44
kingship, *see* monarchical system
kin-wun (customs), 43–4
KMT, 236–7, 248, 263, 268
Kodaw Hmaing, Thakin, 209
Ko Min Ko Chin, 210, 211
Konbaung dynasty (1752–1885), 8, 13, 17–19, 22, 27–8, 30, 34, 38, 42–3, 47–8, 55, 60–2, 109, 150, 158, 159, 218
Korea, 173, 245
Korean War, 245, 256, 262–3
Kyan Aung, U, 167–8, 184, 191, 264
Kyaw Htin, Gen., 369
Kyaw Min, U, 266
Kyaw Nyein, U, 245, 246, 367
Kyaw Sein, Thakin, 214
Kyaw Zaw, Brig., 248
kyedangyi (a subordinate to village headman responsible for taxation), 84, 101

labour force: structure of in colonial period, 129–32; current, 344–5
Labour government, British, 230
Labour Party, British, 210, 245
Land and Agriculture Committee (1938–1940), 140
Land committees, 246, 350–1
Landlords' Association, 202
Land Nationalization Act: (1948), 276 (1954), 277, 350
land ownership, colonial period, 138–45
Land Records Department, 192
land reform, 275–7
land usufruct: precolonial system of, 40–2; post-1962 system, 348–53; *see also* land ownership
Lansin Youth Organization, 315, 325–6, 331, 336

Laos, 99, 291, 292
Law to Protect the Construction of the Socialist Economy, 316
Law to Protect National Solidarity, 315
Left Book Club, 215
legal profession and ethnicity, 138–9, 164
Legislative Council (1897–1936), 74, 117, 184–6, 197
Let Ya-Freeman agreement, 261
liberalism, 66, 219, 285–6
Lieberman, Victor B., 17n, 18n, 22, 29, 37n, 45n, 59n, 60
Lieutenant-Governor, 74

Maha Bama, 231, 243
Mahasmmat, 55
Maingy, A.D., 41n, 72n, 78, 83, 89, 108, 116, 156
maistry, 146–7
Malaya, 108, 154
Malays, 87
Malaysia, 5, 336, 341
Manchuria, 173
Mandalay Intermediate College, 114
Manu, Code of, 53
Marxism, 163, 208–9, 211, 214–5; *see also* socialism
Maung Gyi, Sir J.A., 198
Maung Gyi, Thakin, 166
Maung Maung, Brig., U, 193n, 195, 247
Maung Nge, U, 167
middle class: evolution of, 124, 134–42; political élite, 162–74; and postcolonial state, 279–83; *see also* political parties, colonial period
military: precolonial, 32–4, 47–9, 63; colonial *see* colonial state, military; postcolonial, *see* Burma Army
military coup, 1962, 217; consequences of, 291–300
Military Police, 101, 196, 200; *see also* punitive police, Union Military Police
Mills, J.A., 117n
Mindon, Min (King) (r. 1853–73), 16, 19, 23n, 28–30, 39, 46, 63–5, 94, 107, 289

Min Gaung, Bo, 248
mobilization movements, and the state, 8, 11, 189, 195, 219–20, 229
Mon, 24, 155, 157, 290, 291, 300, 303
monarchical system: classical ideas of, 2; functions of, 46–7, 71–2; justifications for, 54–60; king's interests in, 36; king's relations with subordinates, 25–9, 33; nationalist symbol of, 203, 228; political nature of, 60–5; relationship with society, 11, 196; rivalry within, 26–30, 31; theory and reality, 19–20
moneylending: colonial, 109, 142–5; postcolonial, 278–9, 352–3; precolonial, 40; see also Chettiars, middle class
Mongols, 17
Montagu, Edwin, 119
Mountbatten, Admiral, 235, 261
municipal governments, 117
Mya, Henzada U, 173
myei-daing (assistant to *thu-gyi* with special responsibilities for property and taxation), 35
Myinzaing, prince, 158
myo, 35
Myochit (Patriots) Party, 173, 187, 200
myo-ok (British-appointed township officer), 81, 84, 197
myo-sa, 26–7; see also appanage system
myo-thu-gyi, 36, 39; see also gentry, *thugyi*
myo-wun, 22–3, 27, 34–5, 44

Nagani Book Club, 208
naingngan (taw) (state), 1–3, 303, 309
National Intelligence Bureau, 369–71
nationalism, 10, 96–7, 116, 118, 149–51, 162, 285; see also Buddhism
National Literary Conference, 295
National Party, 185, 197
National Solidarity Association, 243, 267, 315
National United Front (NUF), 247, 297
nats, 55–6, 58, 289
Naw Seng, 268

Ne Win, Lt. Col., Gen., Chairman, 236, 237, 248, 252, 269, 291, 294, 299, 301, 308, 321, 354, 366–71
New Order Plan, 225, 253
Non-Aligned Movement, 299, 356
nuclear zones, nucleus, 20, 22, 32, 79
Nu, Thakin, U, 207, 208, 217, 220, 244–5, 248–9, 261–2, 270, 287–90, 291, 292, 358, 367–8
Nyaungyan Min (r. 1587–1606), 19

Ohn, U, 207
Ohn Pe, U, 166, 167
Ottama, U, 120, 178–9, 182–3, 195

Pagan, kingdom of (c. 849–1287), 2, 7–8, 13, 16, 17, 20–2, 24, 35, 52, 55, 71, 150
Pagan Min, 64
pahtamabyan examination, 29–30
Pakistan, 262
Panglong Agreement, 286, 303
Patriotic Alliance, 243
patron-client relations, 7, 15, 25–7, 35, 45–6, 80, 83–4, 86, 88, 153, 189
peasantry and politics, 151, 161–2, 186–202, 272–9; see also class structure
Peasants' Asiayon, 315, 323–6, 340, 352
Peasants' Councils, 304, 314, 326–33, 350, 352, 365
Peasants' Rights Protection Act, 350
peasants' seminars, 304, 307, 323
peasants' unions, 240, 242
People's Army, 234–5; see also Burma Army
People's Courts, 330, 338–9
People's Economic and Cultural Development Organization, 243
People's Military Service Law, 302
People's Militia, 336
People's Party, 172, 185
People's Police Force, 336
People's Revolution Party, see Socialist Party
People's Volunteer Organization, see PVO
Perlin, Frank, 4

Index 393

plural society, 77–9, 82, 190
Po Lun, U, 166
political bosses, see Bo
political élite, colonial, 149–51; see also political parties
political leaders: local, colonial, 164–9; gentry, see thu-gyi; postcolonial, see Bo; precolonial, see gentry, thu-gyi
political parties: colonial, 163–5, 174–88; postcolonial, 219–20, 229–31; see also Burma Socialist Programme Party
political *pongyi* (monks), 120, 182–3, 194–5
pongyi kyaung, 112–13
Pongyi's GCBA, 186, 195
population of Burma: precolonial, 13n; growth, colonial, 154; postcolonial, 348, 359
postcolonial state: **(1942–62)** economic role of, 253–60; economic and social change under, 270–83; expenditures of, 261, 255; functions of, 249–64; law and order in, 250–3; legitimacy of, 219–21, 283–90 nature of, 219; reorganization of, 222–8; rise of rivals to, 252–8; role of army in, 252; and society, 217–9 —— **(1962–87)**, changing authority relations, 304–33, compared to Europe, 300; economic policies of, 294–5, 315–6, 341–53; expenditure of, 311–12, 336–7, 359–60; functions of, 333–56; legitimacy of, 356–64; nature of, 291–2; participation in, 326–33; politics under, 364–72; relation with society, 299–300
precolonial state: agencies of, 46–54; authority relations in, 25–37; bureaucratic tendencies within, 28–9; causes of change within, 13, 39–40; centralization of, 23–4; compared to colonial state, 148–52; compared to European state, 18, 27, 31–2; judicial system, 36, 52–4; and legitimacy, 47, 54, 55, military, 48–9; religious institutions, 50, 52; competition within, 14–19; evolution of, 13–19; financing of, 37–49;

military in, 32–4, 47–9, 63; patrimonial nature, 15; politics under, 60–5; and religious institutions, 50–2; territorial organization of, 20–25; threats to, 20, 22–23; tributary relations of, 22–5, 37; see also monarchical system
Profit Tax Law (1975), 331
public employment, 281–3, 310–11, 313; see also bureaucracy
public services, ethnic composition of, 111–12, 137–9
punitive police, 101, 250
Pu, Shwegyin U, 171–2
Pu, Tharrawaddy U, 178, 186
PVO, 235–6, 242, 245, 247, 266
Pyinmana agricultural institute, 114
Pyithu Hluttaw (People's Assembly), 292, 299, 303–4, 326–9, 332, 338–40, 351, 370

Rangoon College and University, 114–15, 171, 179, 203, 335
Rangoon University Students' Union, 207
Raschid, M.A., 276
Rauf, Dr M.A., 276
rebellions and revolts: against the colonial state, 99, 100–1, 115, 116, 117, 153–162; against postcolonial state, 333–5; against precolonial state, 24, 27, 47, 115, 153; see also civil war, San, Hsya
Recorder of Rangoon, 104–5
Red Flags, see CP(B)
Restored Toungoo Dynasty, see Toungoo Dynasty, Restored
Revolutionary Council, 291–304, 307–10, 313–6, 320, 321, 323, 326, 333, 338, 346, 348–9, 354, 356–7, 360, 366–7
Richards, C.J., 167
Rowlatt Act (1919), 196
Rural Self-Government Act (1921), 194

Saito, Teruko, 351–2
sangha (Buddhist monkhood), 8, 14–15

30, 38, 41, 50–2, 56, 65, 181–2, 220, 290, 357, 358
San, Hsaya, rebellion of (1930–32), 100, 170–1, 173, 191, 195, 198–9, 203
San Yu, U, 369, 370
Saw, U, 170–4, 187, 200, 203, 219, 260, 261
Second World War, 92, 97–8, 100, 217, 218, 286
Security and Administration Committees (SACs), 313–5, 330, 332, 338, 350
Sein Lwin, U, 369
Sein Win, Pegu U, 173
separation from India question, 121–3, 171, 186; *see also* elections, 1936
Separation League, 186
Sessions Courts, 105
Sgaw Karen, 155
Shan *sawbwas*, 23, 25, 34, 37, 92–8, 226–7, 229, 243, 268–70, 291
Shan State Federation, 96–7
Shan State Manual, 95
Shan State Military Co-ordination Committee, 269
Shan State People's Freedom League, 244
Shan states, 91–8, 100, 160, 226, 237, 248, 285, 292–3, 300, 303, 333–4
Siam: 79, 99, 153; monarchy compared to Burma, 19
sibwayei athin (economy organization), 194
Silverstein, Josef, 268
Sima Duwa, 243
Simon, Sir John, 121, 122
sit-ke (military officers assigned by the monarchical court to supervise local administrations), 34
Sixth Great Buddhist Council, 288
slavery, 33, 41, 45–7
Social Democratic Party, 269
socialism, 118, 187, 210, 214, 218–9, 291–2; *see also* Marxism
socialist democracy, 304, 332–3, 363
Socialist Party, 220–1, 231, 237, 242, 244–7, 278, 288, 289, 297, 366
social mobility, 14, 41, 68–9, 222–3
Society for the Propagation of Buddhism, 288

Soe, Thakin, 208, 214, 234–5, 237–9, 241, 284, 369
Soe Thein, U, 183, 186, 195
Soviet Union, 238, 262, 263, 327, 355, 356
'Specific Characteristics of the Burmese Way to Socialism', 297
State Agricultural Bank (SAB), 278
State Agricultural Marketing Board (SAMB), 257, 281
state: analytical problem of, 3–12; dominance strategies, 12; early modern, 13; institutions of, 9–10; name of, 1–2; nomenclature, 309; personnel of, 3, 66–7, 149, 217–8; purpose of, 67–8; reorganization of, 218–9; resource base of, 7, 19; and society, 1, 4–6; *see also* colonial state, postcolonial state, precolonial state
St. Paul's English High School, 170, 172
Strachey, John, 215
student strike (1920), 120, 179–80, 184, 202, 207
students and youth, 163
student unions, 204–5
Superintendents, 105
Supreme Council of United Hill Peoples, 226
Supreme Court, 252, 338
student unions, 204–5
Superintendents, 105
Supreme Council of United Hill Peoples, 226
Supreme Court, 252, 338
Suzuki, Col., 232
'Sweat Army', 273
swidden agriculture, 37, 46–7
System of Correlation of Man and His Environment, 296, 361

Tai, 17, 37, 43, 46
taik (township in the colonial period), 35; *see also* township
Taiwan, 237
taxation system: colonial, 89–91, 96, 191, 192, 196–7; postcolonial **(1942–62)**, 220, 255, 273–8;

—— (1962–87), 341–343, 345–346, 349; precolonial, 38–40, 43–6; 64–5
Tenancy Act: (1939), 214 (1963), 350
Tenancy Standard Rent Act (1947), 275
territorial agencies, 32–3
Teza Youth, 325
Thailand, 5, 226, 237, 333, 336, 337, 345, 368; *see also* Siam
Thakin movement, *see Do Bama Asiayon*
thammata, 1–2, 55
Thant, U, 357
Than Tun, Thakin, 238–41, 244, 261
thathameda tax, 23, 41, 94, 185, 191–2, 220
thathanabaing, 51, 159
Thein Maung, Dr, 172, 174, 178
Thein Maung, Thakin, 209
Thein Pe, Thakin, 244
Thibaw Min (r. 1873–85), 1, 28, 53, 65, 81, 99, 157–8, 216, 221
Thi Han, U, 207
'Thirty Comrades', 232, 366
thu-gyi (headman), 35–6, 39, 42, 54, 80–5, 89, 92, 101, 156, 161, 167, 191, 194–5; *see also* gentry, *myo-thu-gyi*
Thuriya (The Sun), 172–3
Thwin, Sir U, 166
Tilly, Charles, 6n, 9n
Tin, Thakin, 246
Tin Tin, 40–1n, 44n
Tin Tut, 181n
Tin U, Col., Brig. Gen., 369, 370–1
Tin U, Gen., 369
Toe Lon, U, 167
Toungoo Dynasty: First, 48, 51; Restored, 1, 8, 13–19, 20, 22–31, 34–8, 42, 45–53, 60–2, 107, 300
township, 14, 80–2; *see also myo* and *taik*
Trade Union Congress — Burma (TUC-B), 244, 246, 279
Trager, Frank N., 40
Tun Aung Kyaw, U, 178
Tun Ok, Thakin, 210, 215, 223, 261
Twenty-One Party, 185
Two Year Plan, 285

Union Day, 301, 303, 326
Union Military Police, 246
Union Party, 248, 291
United GCBA, 185, 186
United Hill People's Congress, 244
United Nations, 245, 262, 354
United States of America: 227, 237, 248, 269, 292, 356; aid from, 245, 262, 263, 336, 355
University Act, 207
urban classes, 279–83
urban communal rioting, 197–201
urban politics after 1962, 334–5

vagabondage, 33, 45
Vietnam: 5, 116, 161, 237, 292, 354, 355; South, 291
village (*ywa*) authorities, 14
Village Act (1887), 81, 194, 196, 202
Vinaya, 182, 289, 358
volunteer corps, 204–206

War Veterans' Organization, 315
White Band PVOs, *see* PVO
White Flags, *see* BCP
Who's Who in Burma, 1961, 165–6, 215
Wisara, U, 183
Workers' Asiayon, 307, 315, 323–5
Workers' Council, 304, 314, 336
workers' seminars, 304
World Bank, 341n
wun-gyi (chief minister), 31, 196, 309
wunthanu athin, 182–3, 185, 192–9, 210, 240, 247
Wunthanu Rethkita, 196
Wuntho *Sawbwa*, 160

yazawut, 56
Young Men's Buddhist Association (YMBA), 162, 163, 171, 172, 177, 178, 179
Youth Improvement Society, 207
youth movements, 204–7
Yunnan, 25, 268
Yunnanese, 100
ywa-thu-gyi, see thu-gyi
YWBA, 178–9

Zau Lawn Duwa, 243
Zerbadi (Indo-Burmese Muslims) 201